Photographing the
NUDE

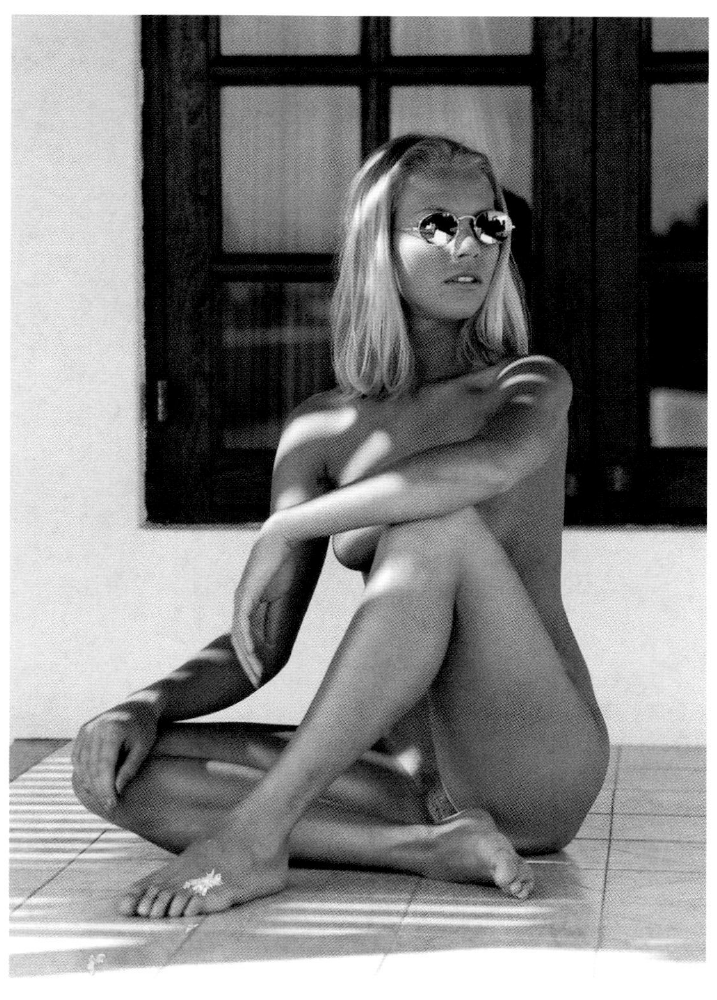

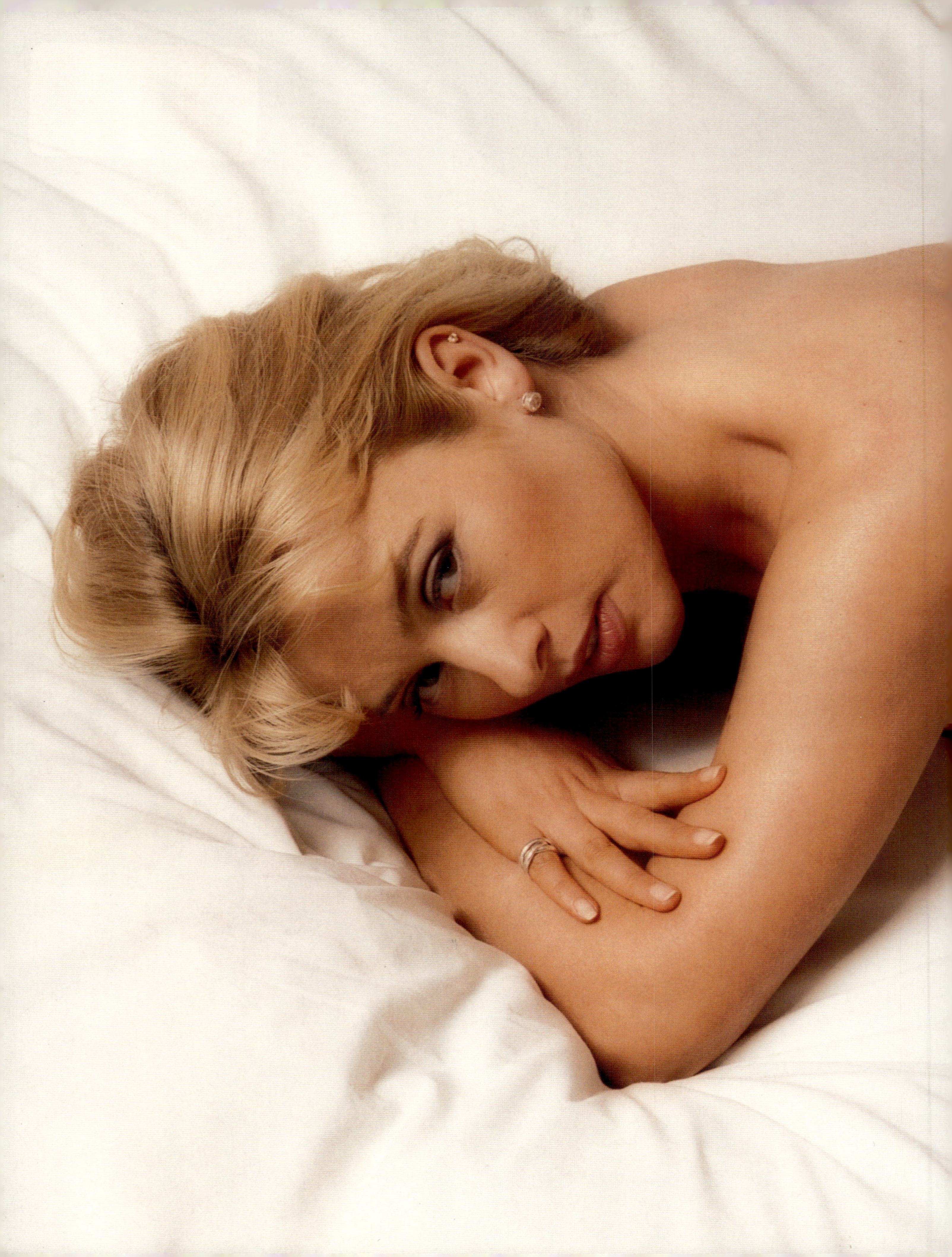

Photographing the
NUDE

MIKE CRAWLEY

David & Charles

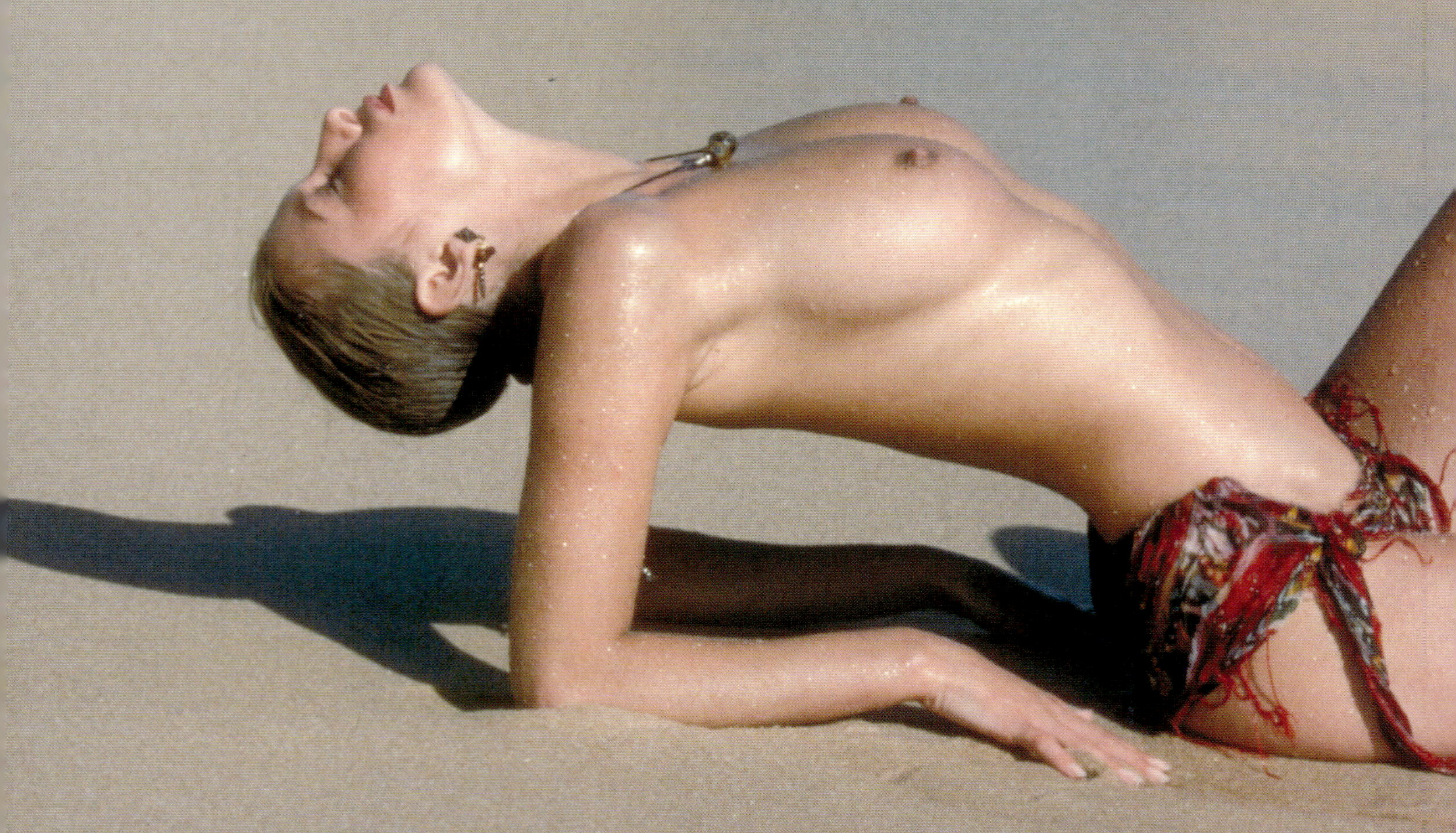

A DAVID & CHARLES BOOK

Commissioning editor Sarah Hoggett • **Art editor** Sue Cleave • **Senior editor** Freya Dangerfield • **Production director** Roger Lane

First published in the UK in 2002

Copyright text and photographs © Mike Crawley 2002

Mike Crawley has asserted his right to be identified as author of this work in accordance with the Copyright, Designs and Patents Act, 1988.

All rights reserved. No part of this publication may be reproduced, stored in a retrieval system, or transmitted, in any form or by any means, electronic or mechanical, by photocopying, recording or otherwise, without prior permission in writing from the publisher.

A catalogue record for this book is available from the British Library.

ISBN 0 7153 1302 9 (hardback)
ISBN 0 7153 1455 6 (paperback)

Printed in Great Britain by Butler and Tanner Ltd for **David & Charles**   Brunel House   Newton Abbot   Devon

Contents

Introduction

RIGHT: **Body painting.** Using textures can be highly effective. Metallic paint used on the model gives her the look of a golden statue. (MINOLTA 8000i; 100mm LENS; 1/125 sec at f/8; KODACHROME 64.)

BELOW: **Toning.** This can add another dimension to black-and-white nude images. (BRONICA ETRSi; 150mm LENS; 1/125 sec at f/11; ILFORD FP4 PLUS.)

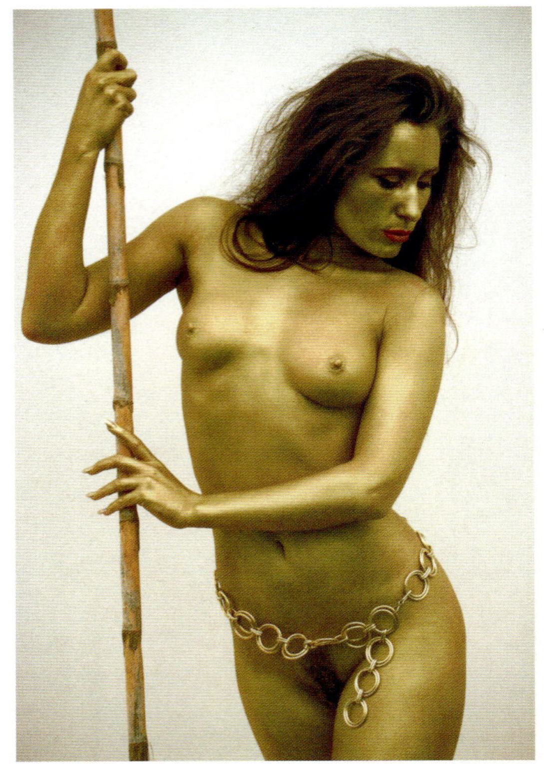

Photographing the Nude was conceived as a book driven by imagery rather than technicalities. The fine art or glamour photographer – whether novice, experienced or professional – will be able to find images in this book that inspire and feed the imagination. A plethora of helpful hints and tips on the art of nude photography is also provided, which the practising nude photographer will want to refer to time and time again. It will soon become apparent that the main prerequisite for success in this branch of photography is

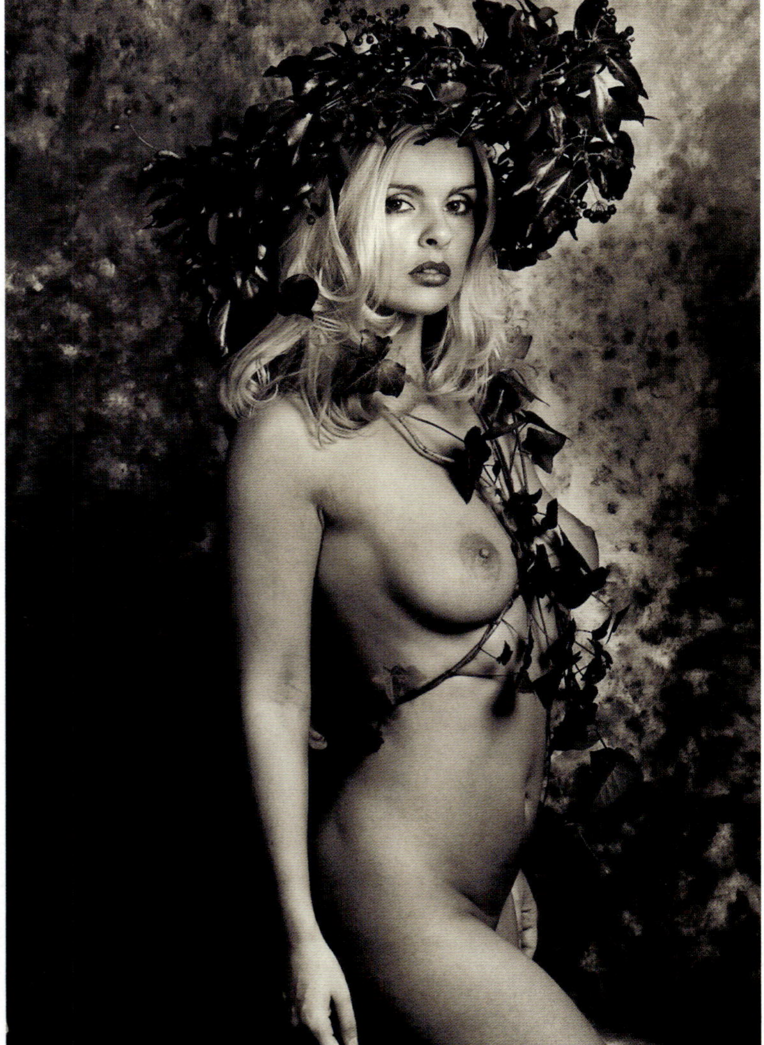

a sense of design, composition and imagination – an eye for an artistic photograph is far more important than the hardware used.

The seven chapters are broken down into easily digested sections of information, beginning with equipment. Next is advice on how to go about finding and working with nude models. The third chapter is dedicated to lighting and metering and discusses how to work with a variety of lighting situations using daylight and electronic flash. Following this is a chapter on arranging poses, which contains tips on improving images by subtle positioning of the body. The fifth chapter is the core of the book, where many different styles of nude photography are explored, amply illustrated by a wealth of creative images. For the darkroom enthusiast and fine-art printer, the sixth chapter is invaluable, as it gives information on how to create images rather than just taking them. The final chapter is an introduction to the use of digital manipulation, and digitizing the nude.

OPPOSITE: **Figure study.** Images like this depend on effective lighting and strong composition for the best results. (BRONICA ETRSi; 150mm LENS; 1/125 sec at f/11; KODAK PORTRA 160NC.)

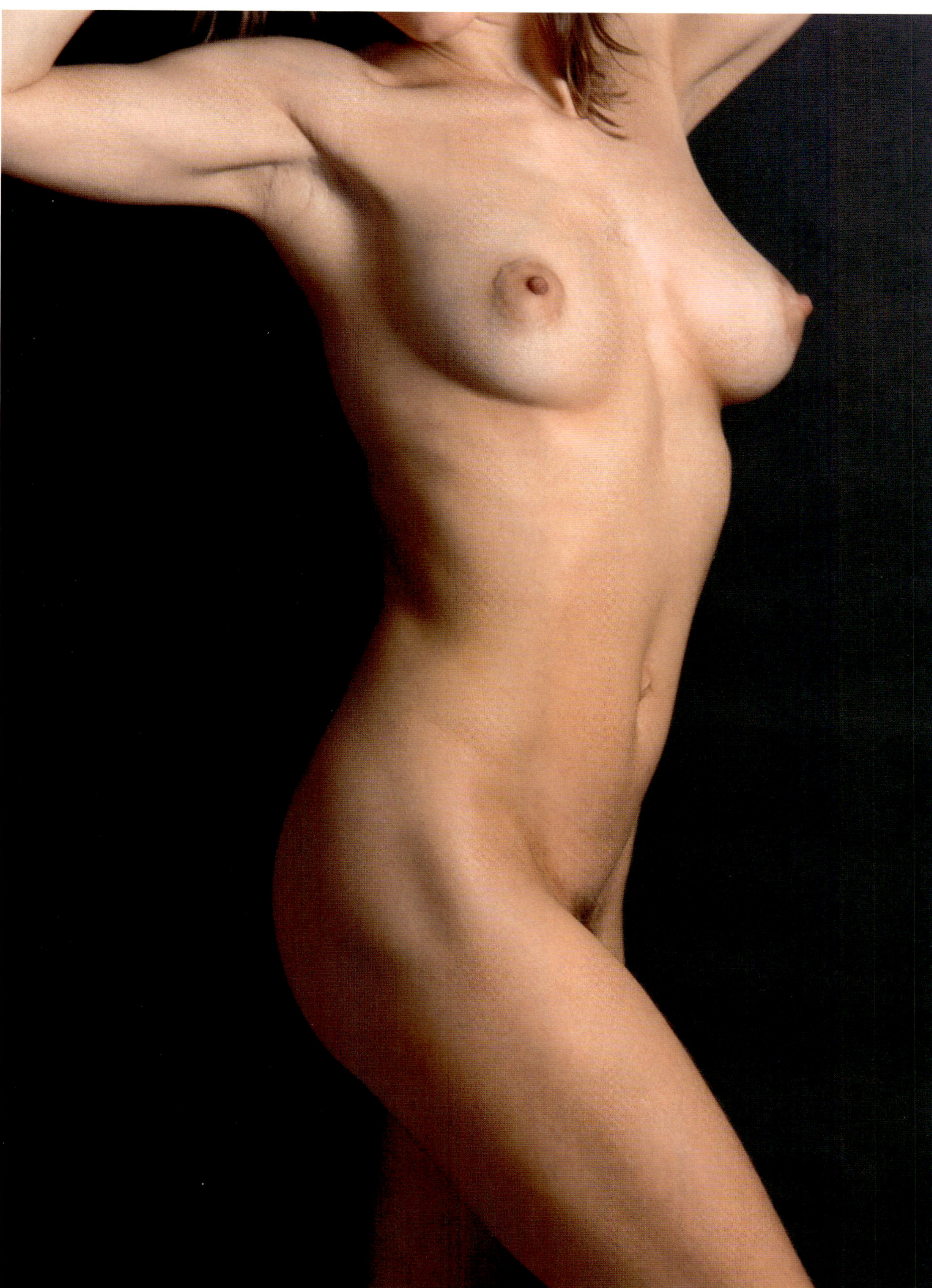

To quote an old saying: it is not the camera that takes the image but the person behind it. In other words, it doesn't matter how much money is spent on photographic equipment. If you don't know how to use it – or appreciate what constitutes a good picture – then the likelihood of taking good pictures is not that great. It is better to spend time developing a sense of 'seeing the image' rather than continually updating to the latest camera equipment. Having said that, good equipment in the hands of a competent photographer and the use of the right tools for the job will certainly increase the chances of better-quality images, so buy the best you can afford at the outset.

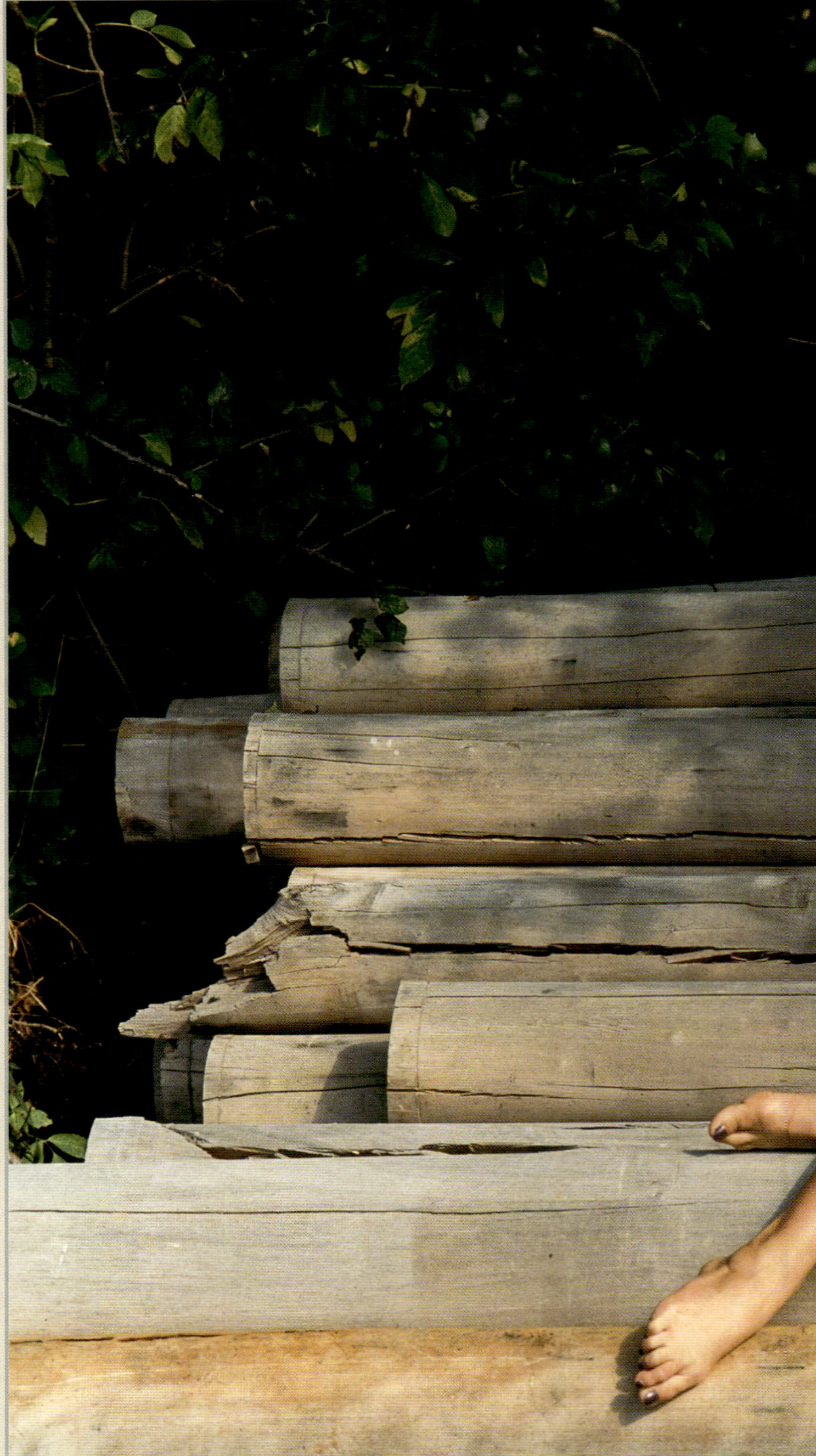

RIGHT: **Rustic backdrop.** A pile of logs in the French countryside makes a rustic foil for this nude study. The camera used to take this picture is at least 12 years old, but is rugged and reliable and so familiar to me that I hardly have to think twice about its operation, leaving me more time to concentrate on taking the picture. (BRONICA ETRSi; 75mm LENS; 1/125 sec at f/8; KODAK PORTRA 160NC.)

Equipment

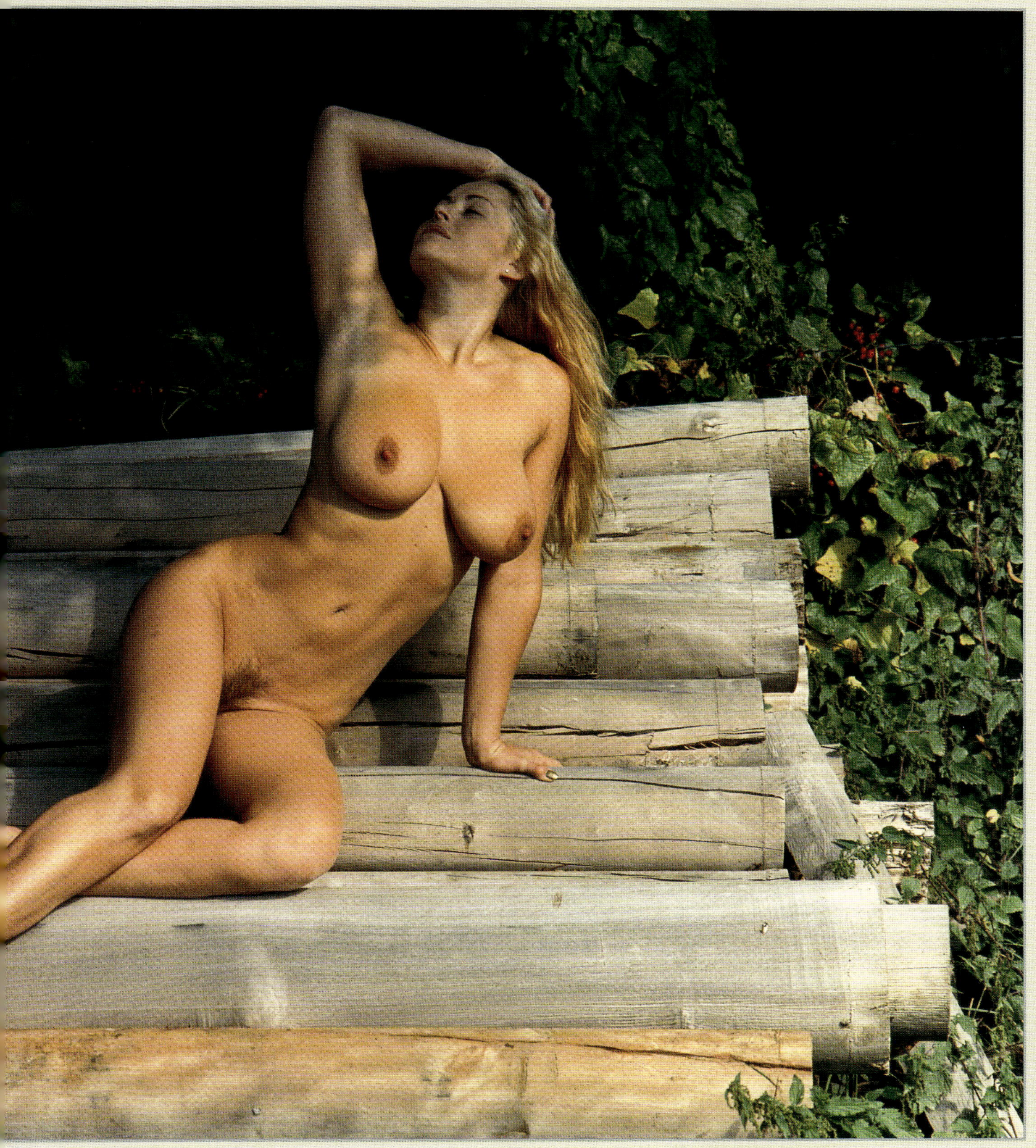

Camera formats

OPPOSITE: **Interiors.** Interior location photographs, such as this study captured under studio lighting conditions in a French chateau, are ideally suited to the medium format, where the camera can be mounted on a tripod.
(BRONICA ETRSi; 150mm LENS; 1/125 sec at f/11; KODAK PORTRA 160NC.)

BELOW: **Exotic locations.** 35mm equipment is often the best choice when working in exotic locations, where portability and weight become important factors. This photograph of a model on a desert sand dune was one instance where the advantages of medium format were outweighed by the lighter SLR equipment.
(MINOLTA 8000i; 70–210mm ZOOM LENS; 1/250 sec at f/8; KODAK GOLD 100.)

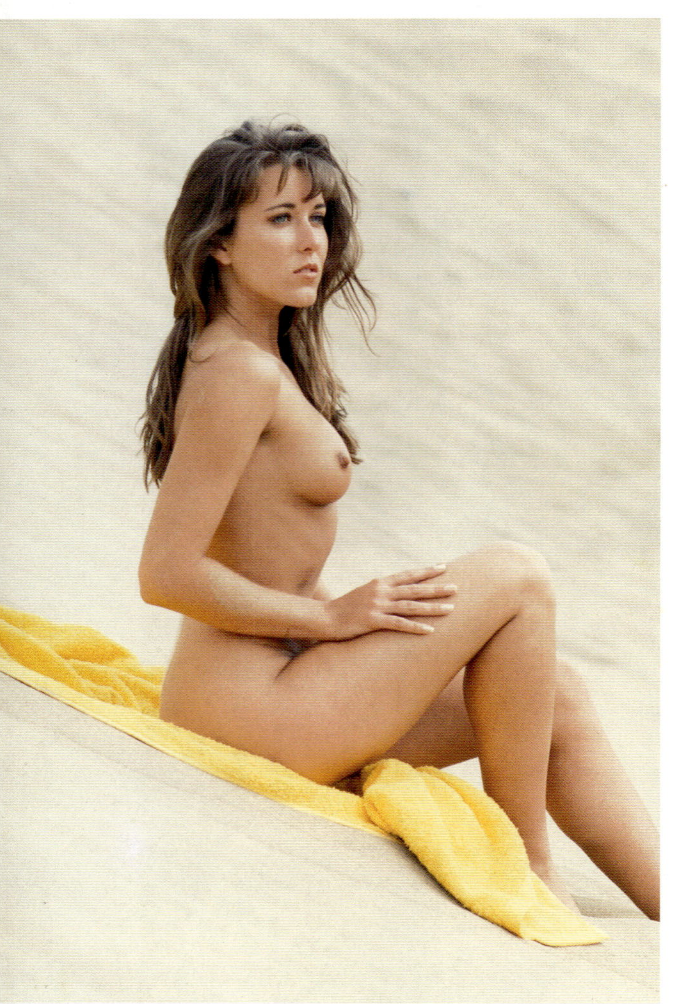

A camera is the one essential piece of equipment required for nude photography, but which is the best choice? The main format options are 35mm, medium format and digital. Each has its own advantages and disadvantages to be considered before purchasing.

35mm Many features of modern 35mm single lens reflex (SLR) cameras – weight, size and inbuilt technology such as autofocus, film auto-advance, and the like – can outweigh the heaviness and, sometimes, basic technology found in medium format (MF) cameras. Also, system costs are usually much lower. SLR cameras use a smaller negative size than MF cameras, but the quality of film is now so good that excellent results can be obtained at very high enlargements, and, for most purposes, size is not a problem. The 35mm format is ideal for location work, especially when coupled with zoom lenses.

medium format The main advantage that MF cameras have over 35mm SLR cameras is the bigger film size and the increase in image quality that this provides. Medium format is therefore worth considering if high-quality exhibition work is anticipated. Most of these cameras have interchangeable lenses and film backs that can be removed part way through a film, which is advantageous. The increased size and weight of this format makes the cameras less easy to handle than 35mm, but they are very good for studio use.

digital Cameras that have all the advantages of conventional SLR and MF cameras are now available with digital backs. The main drawback is the high initial cost of the best high-resolution backs. Offset against this is the elimination of the need to buy and process film. Image storage in the studio is not a problem as pictures can be almost instantaneously downloaded to a PC, but on location this may not be so easy.

CAMERAS IN THE STUDIO

To use a camera in the studio with flash lighting, it is essential that the camera should have some means of firing the lights. A built-in PC socket for connecting the sync cable to the flash lighting units, or an independent socket that can be attached to the camera via a hot-shoe connection, is an ideal choice. If neither of these options is available on your camera system then a small flash unit attached to the camera can be used to trip slave units on the flash equipment. It is also worth carrying a spare sync cable, as these often stop working for no apparent reason.

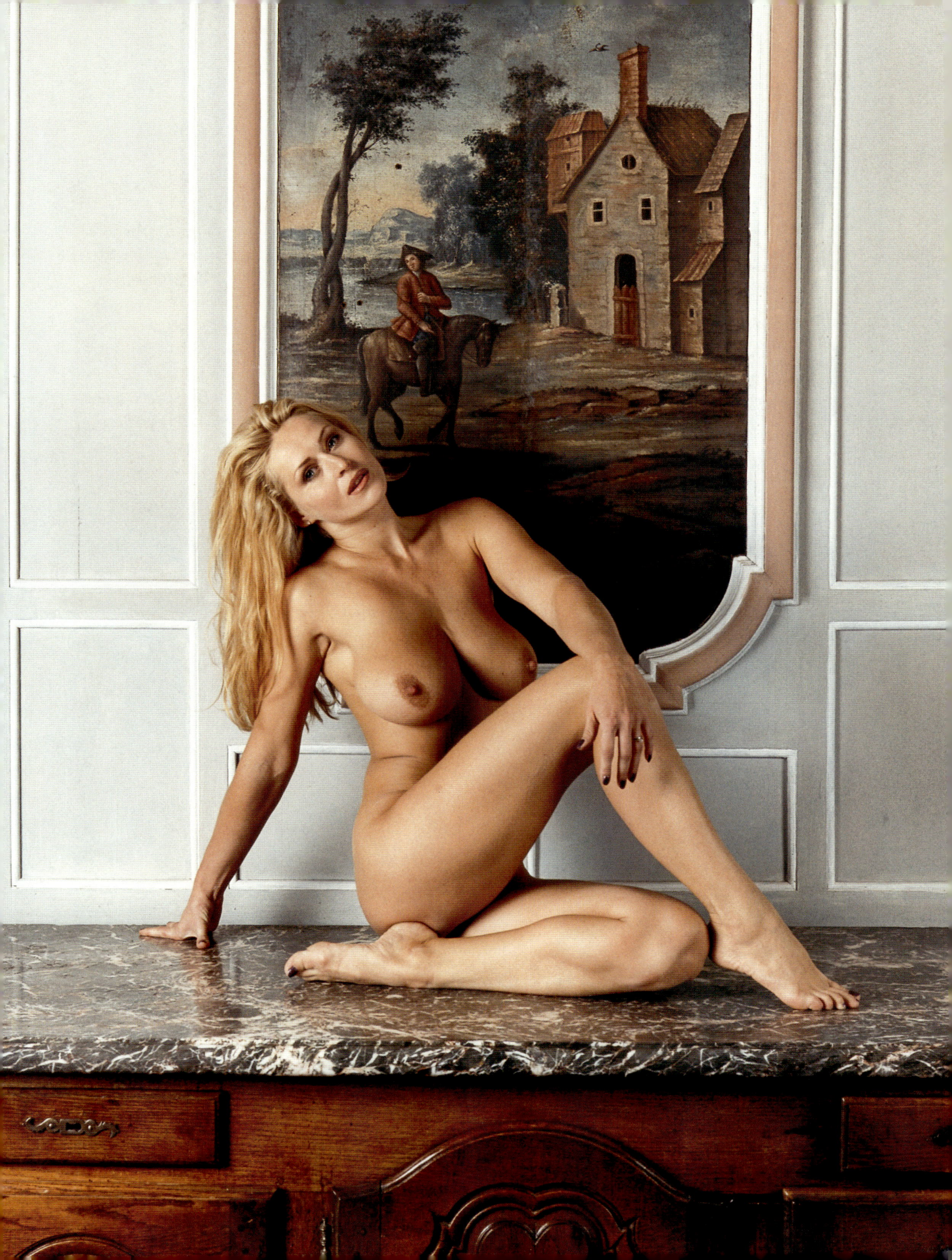

Lenses

The type of lenses that are best suited for photographing the nude are usually found in the middle of the focal-length range, from wide-angle through standard to portrait and medium telephoto lenses.

choice of lens

Extreme optics such as fish-eye and long-range telephoto lenses have limited application, but macro lenses can be useful where there is a need to get close to the subject. An extensive range of fixed-focal-length lenses and variable-focal-length (zoom) lenses are available for both 35mm SLR cameras and MF cameras. For 35mm cameras, a selection of lenses covering the range from 28mm to 300mm will deal with most situations, as will MF camera lenses that range from 40mm to 250mm. For those on a tight budget, a standard lens and a medium telephoto lens is a good starting

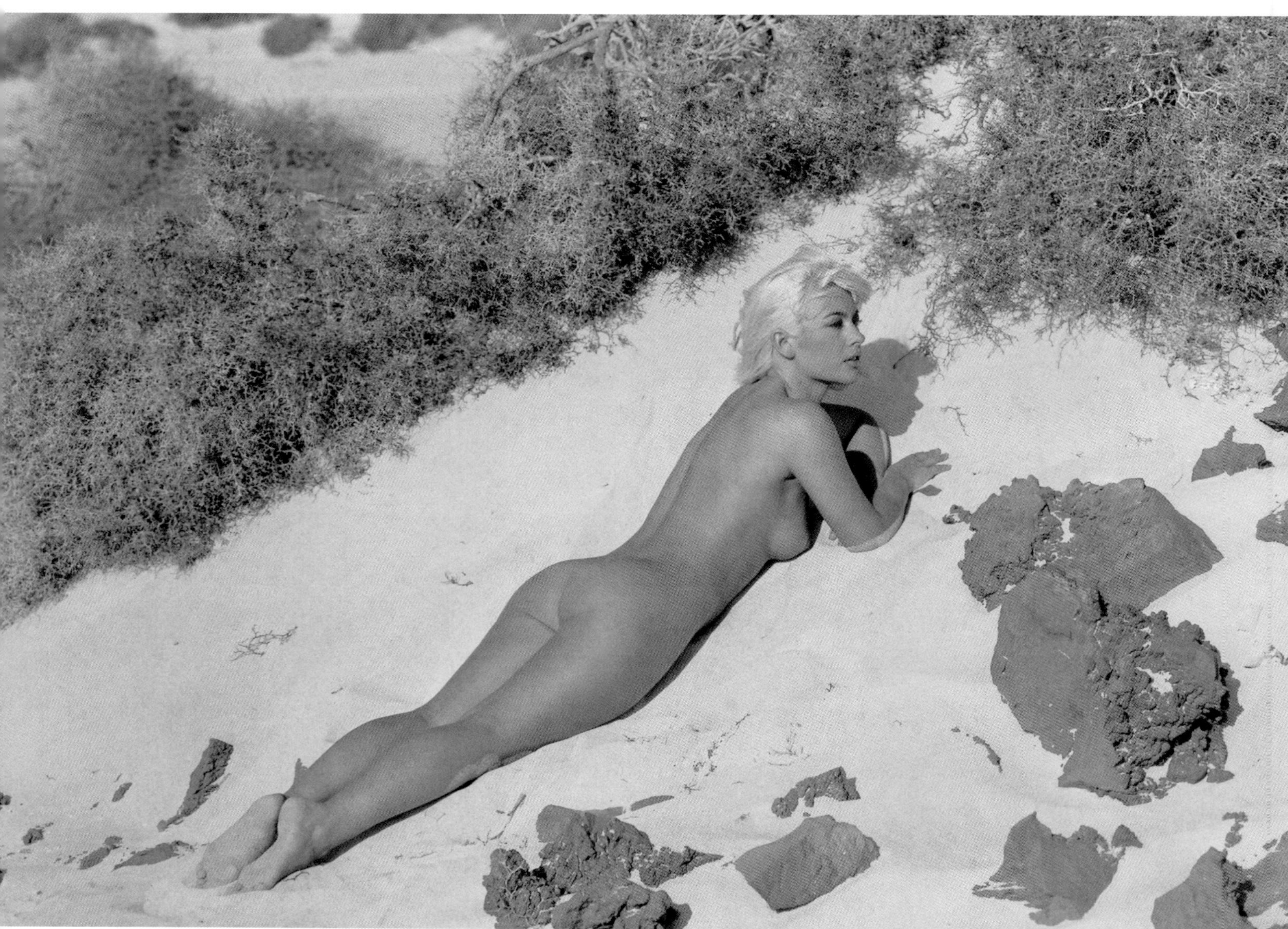

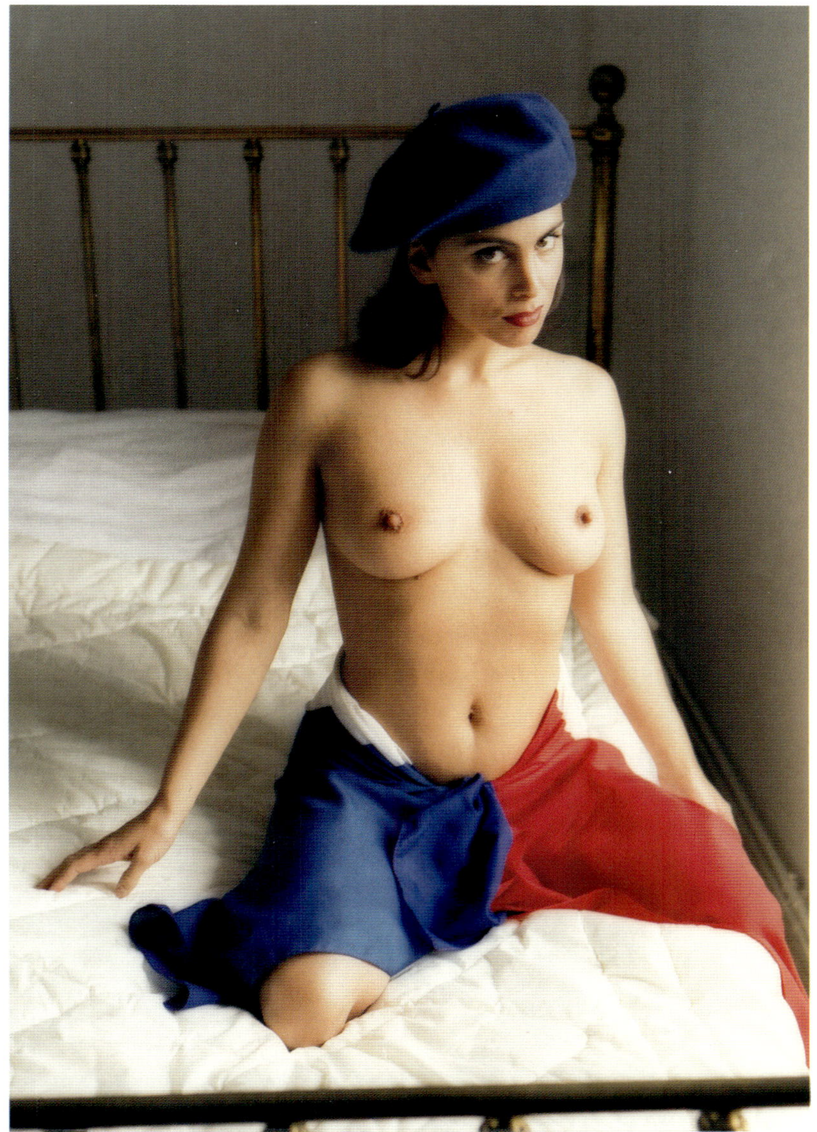

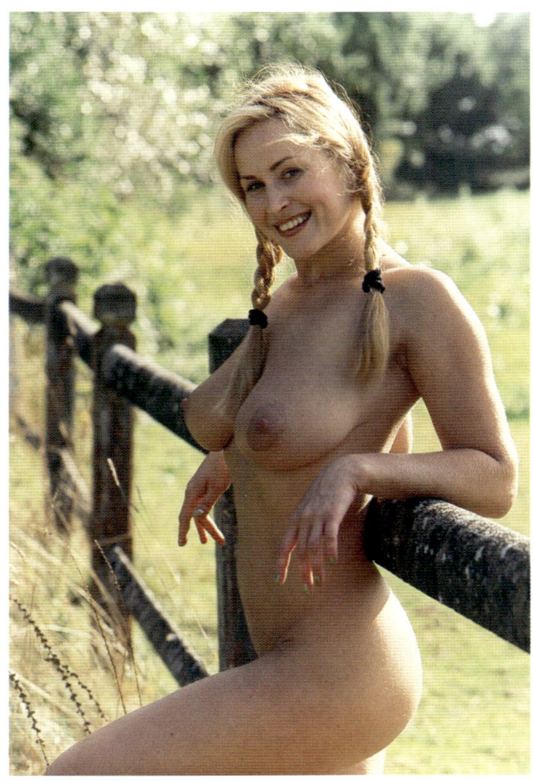

ABOVE: **Long lens.** A medium telephoto lens and a large lens aperture were used in this shot to diffuse the background and make the model the focus of attention. (BRONICA ETRSi; 150mm LENS; 1/250 sec at f/4; KODAK PORTRA 160NC.)

LEFT: **Standard lens.** In the confined space of this bedroom location, an MF camera with a standard 75mm lens was the equipment of choice. (BRONICA ETRSi; 75mm LENS; 1/60 sec at f/8; KODAK GPX.)

point. For 35mm SLR cameras, this would be a 50mm lens and a 90 or 100mm lens, and for MF cameras a 75 or 80mm lens and a 150mm lens. A medium-range fixed-focal-length telephoto is the most useful lens for figure work, as this can accommodate close-up to full-length shots and can also double as a portrait lens. Zoom lenses that span a range of focal lengths are particularly useful for location and candid work and are better when travelling or when space is at a premium. Two 35mm zoom lenses can cover the whole range of focal lengths required – a 28–70mm and a 70–300mm lens would fit the bill. Lower resolving power has been a problem with zoom lenses in the past, but modern designs, particularly apochromatic (APO) zoom lenses, compete well with fixed-focal-length lenses for quality.

speed Another factor to consider is lens speed, which is a reference to the maximum lens aperture. For instance, a standard f/1.4 lens is said to be faster than a lens with a maximum aperture of f/2. The faster the lens, the greater the exposure latitude it permits, which is useful in low-light conditions. Fixed-focal-length lenses tend to have higher speeds than zooms and fast lenses are more expensive than slow lenses. Fast lenses are useful for the technique of throwing a background out of focus and isolating the subject, as they have less depth of field at maximum aperture.

Lighting equipment

OPPOSITE: **Shadow effect.** To create the shadow of the Venetian blind on the model and background, a light fitted with a dish reflector was placed as far from the subject as the studio would allow. A Venetian blind was then placed between the light and close to the model but out of shot. This created a near pinpoint light source and a shadow similar to that produced by natural daylight. A second light was used as a fill light from the model's right to lift the key.
(BRONICA ETRSi; 150mm LENS; 1/125 sec at f/4; ILFORD FP4.)

ABOVE: **Remote sensing.** A small flashgun with a remote sensor was placed behind the model while a large soft box was used to light the front of the subject and trigger the flash unit.
(MINOLTA 8000i; 100mm LENS; 1/125 sec at f/11; KODAK VERICOLOR.)

RIGHT: **Using soft boxes.** Two soft boxes were used to light and photograph this reclining nude.
(BRONICA ETRSi; 75mm LENS; 1/125 sec at f/11; KODAK PORTRA 160NC.)

There are many occasions when daylight illumination is insufficient and an artificial light source will be needed to supplement or replace it. There are several options that can be used, including tungsten lighting units, portable and studio flashlights, and supplementary flashguns.

flashguns

When just a little supplementary light is required, an on-camera flashgun can be sufficient. Less sophisticated SLR cameras have built-in flash units, which emit an indiscriminate burst of light. Flashguns attached to a camera via the hot shoe, or side mounted, are more flexible and allow the head to be moved so light bounces off walls, ceilings and reflectors. The power output of this type of flashgun can also be adjusted, with sophisticated models having sensors that allow automatic through-the-lens (TTL) exposure. Light bounced off a reflective surface will give a more even and softer light with less obvious shadows. It will also prevent the phenomenon called 'red eye', which is caused by light being reflected off the back of the retina.

studio lighting

Where supplementary lighting is inadequate, larger studio flash units will be required that allow complete control of the lighting. These units come in many types, sizes and power outputs. Popular heads used in studios and also available as portable lighting kits are called mono-blocks. They consist of a mains-powered flash unit, a modelling light and accessories for connecting attachments to the front of the unit. Power level is usually controlled from the heads with this type of unit, while less expensive units that do not have built-in power controls can be controlled from a separate power pack. Useful attachments for studio lighting are soft boxes, umbrellas, barn doors, honeycombs, snoots and gels, which all alter the way the light is delivered to the subject. All types of electronic flash lighting are compatible with daylight.

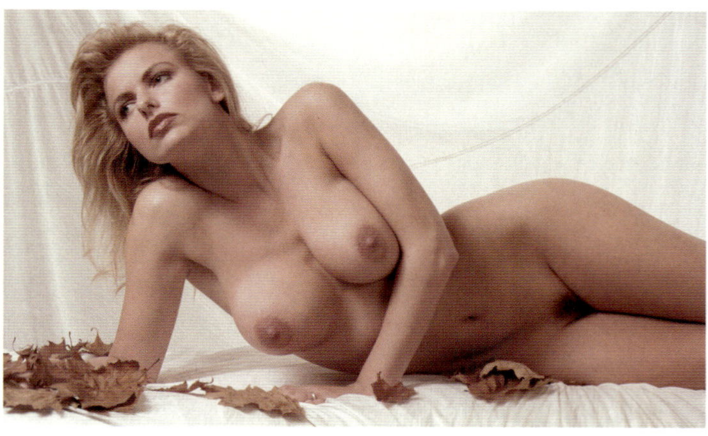

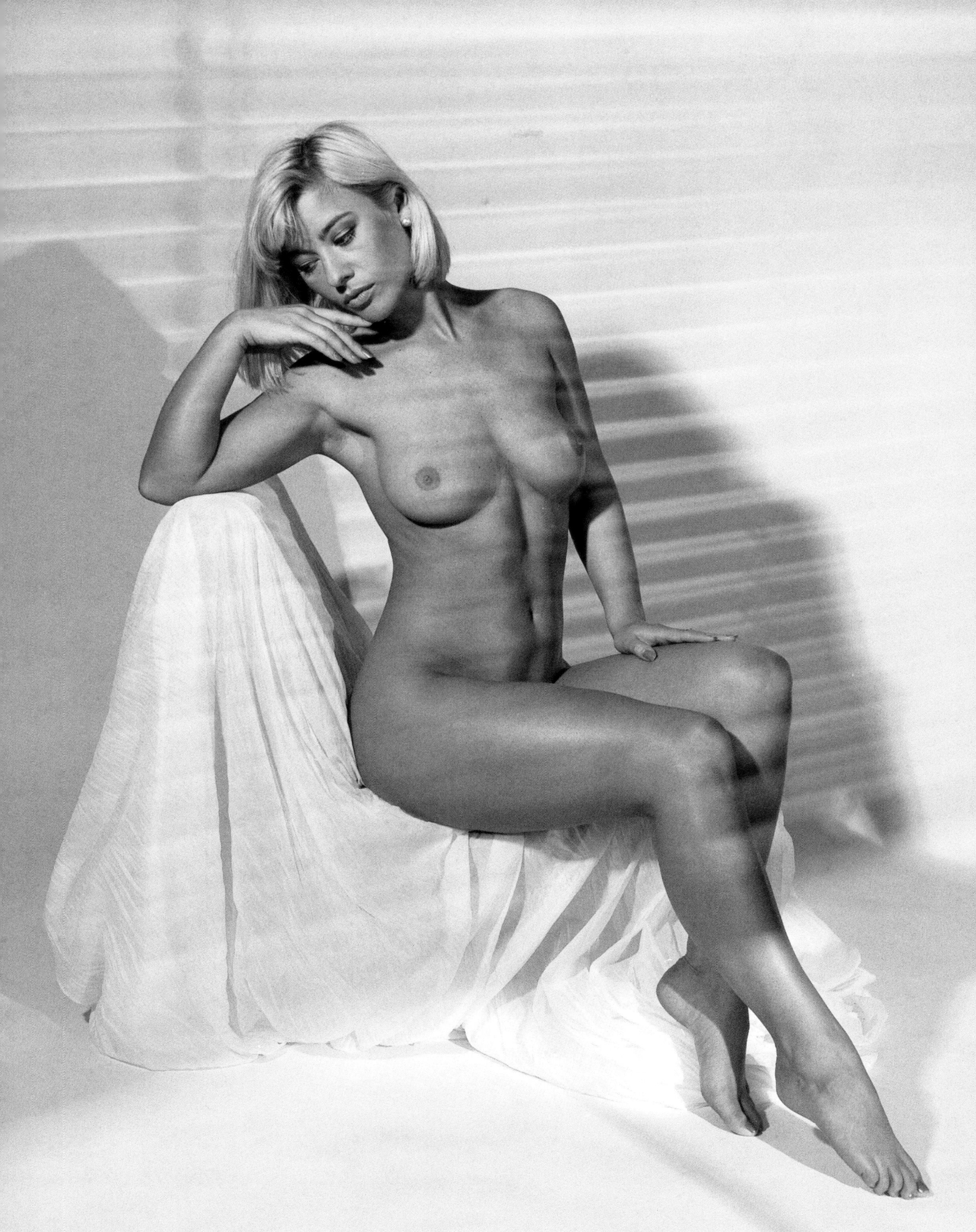

Accessories

BELOW: **Reflected sun.** Late-afternoon sunlight bounced off a large gold reflector gave this model's body a warm, vibrant glow. (BRONICA ETRSi; 150mm LENS; 1/250 sec at f/11; KODAK PORTRA 160NC.)

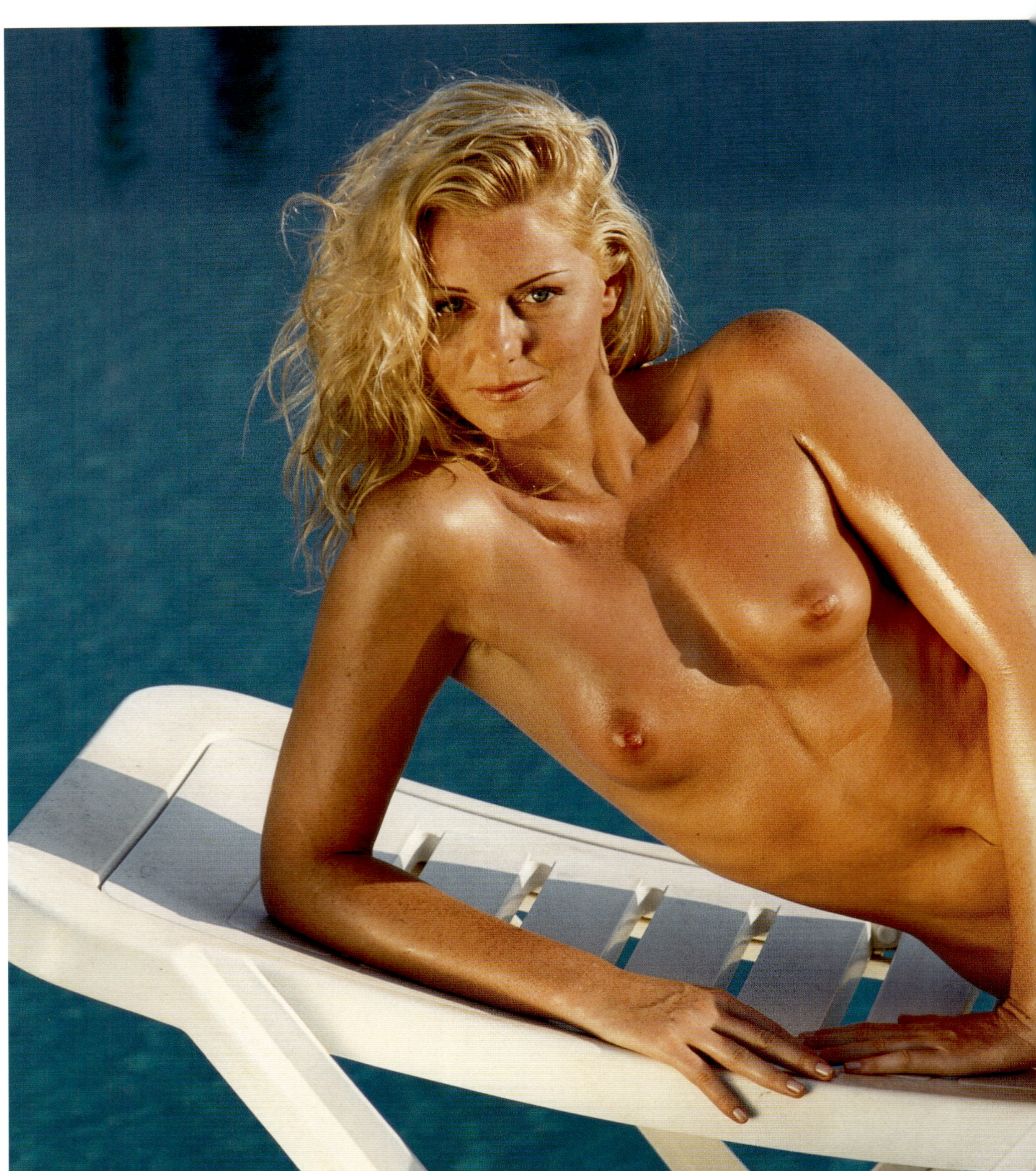

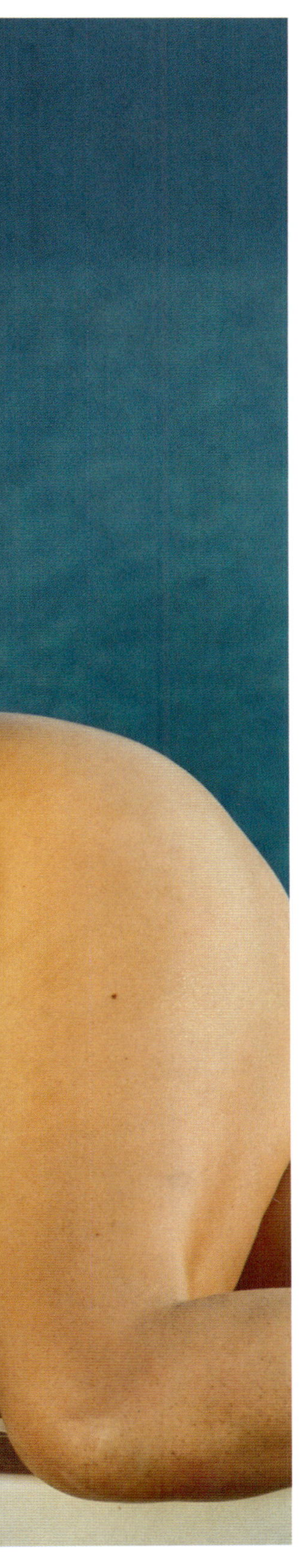

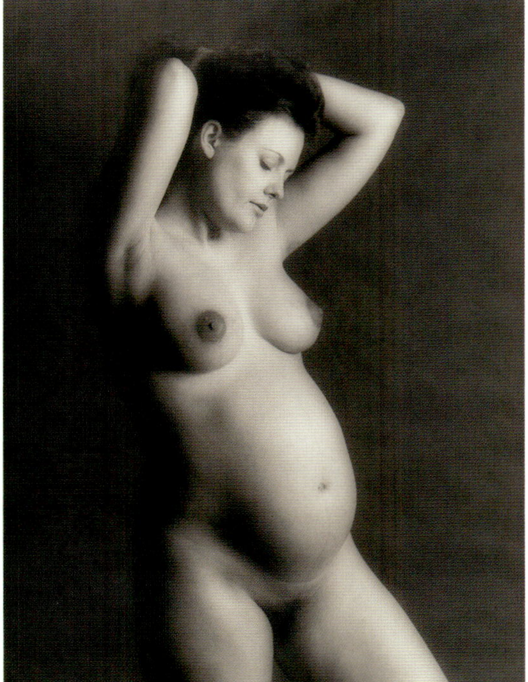

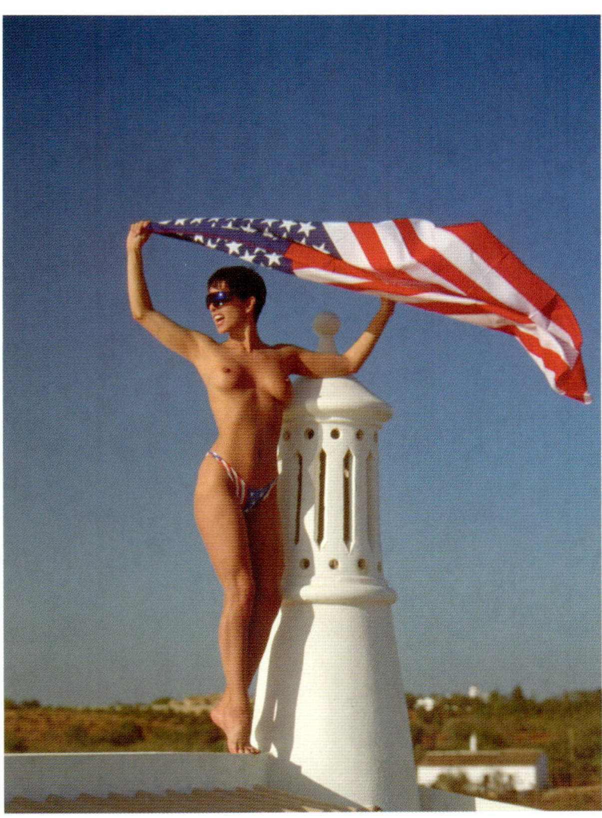

LEFT: **Black filter.** A black 'stocking' filter was used over the lens to create a soft art image of this young mother-to-be. (BRONICA ETRSi; 75mm LENS; 1/125 sec at f/11; ILFORD FP4 PLUS.)

ABOVE: **Polarizing filter.** To enhance the colour saturation in the flag and darken the blue sky, a polarizing filter was used. (MINOLTA 8000i; 75–300mm ZOOM LENS; 1/125 sec at f/8; KODACHROME 64.)

For studio and location work in particular, a speed grip is an indispensable accessory for MF cameras as it gives freedom of mobility – essential when working interactively with a model. A sturdy tripod and cable release can help, though I prefer not to use one unless absolutely necessary.

A Polaroid back for MF cameras is useful for checking the film exposure and set details – especially where lighting conditions may be difficult – and a portable flashgun is useful on location for providing fill flash, should this be necessary to complete the lighting set-up.

filters

When photographing the nude, the most appropriate lens filters to keep in the camera case are a selection of soft-focus and warm-up filters, though it is also worth carrying polarizing and colour correction filters and coloured filters for black-and-white and infrared photography (see pages 112–5). A homemade soft-focus filter made from 18-denier nylon stockings and a cardboard 6 x 6 slide mount is a personal favourite. A filter holder is required for this type of filter. An efficient lens hood is also essential when working outdoors to prevent light flare. Lens-cleaning equipment, including a blower brush, compressed air and lens-cleaning tissue are useful when working in dusty locations. A good-quality film-changing bag is also something worth considering, especially if infrared film is going to be used frequently.

Light reflectors are great accessories for both indoor and outdoor work. A selection of white, silver and gold examples is recommended. Other miscellaneous essentials are pins, safety pins, needle and thread, clamps, cramps, butterfly clips, pegs, gaffer tape and assorted pieces of string. It is surprising how often these little extras will be pressed into service when pursuing the perfect composition.

Backgrounds and props

There are three essential ingredients in a successful nude picture: the model and the pose are the major contributors that set the scene; the lighting is another, which sets the mood; the third, which is often underrated, is the background against which all this happens.

background This is important in determining the overall feel of the image, as even a plain paper backdrop will have an effect on the viewer. For instance, a nude photographed against a white backdrop will appear very different from an identical pose against a black backdrop.

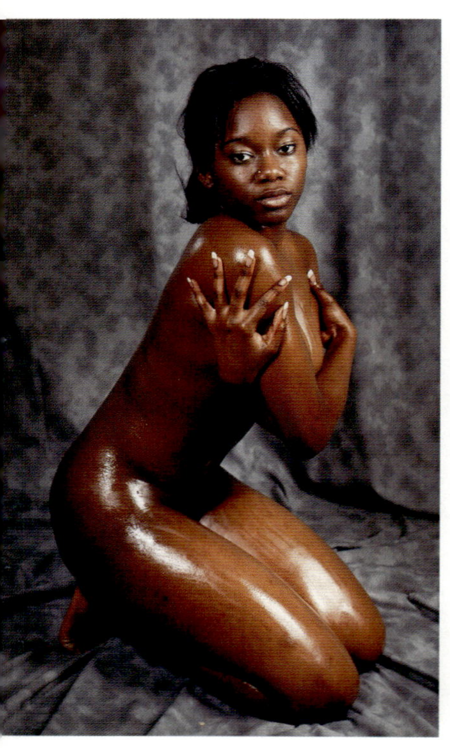

BELOW LEFT: **Cloth backdrop.** Cloth backgrounds, such as this grey mottled material, are readily available in many colours and patterns and make a versatile addition to the photographic armoury. They are particularly suited to the photographer working at home with limited space.
(BRONICA ETRSi; 75mm LENS; 1/125 sec at f/11; KODAK PORTRA 160NC.)

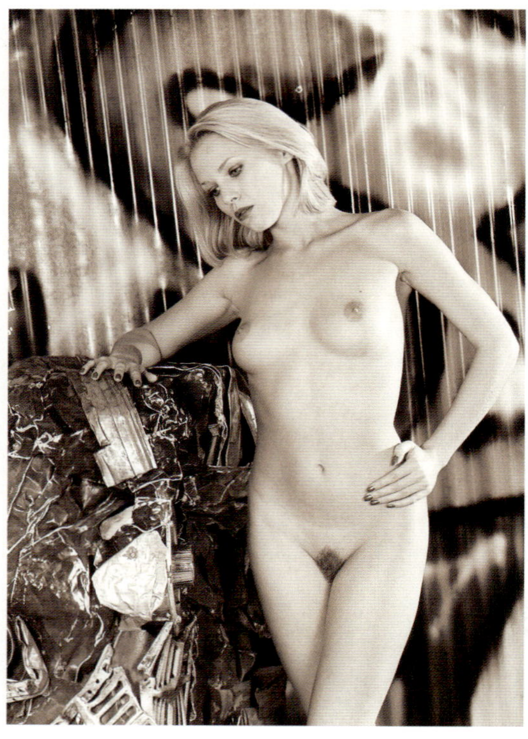

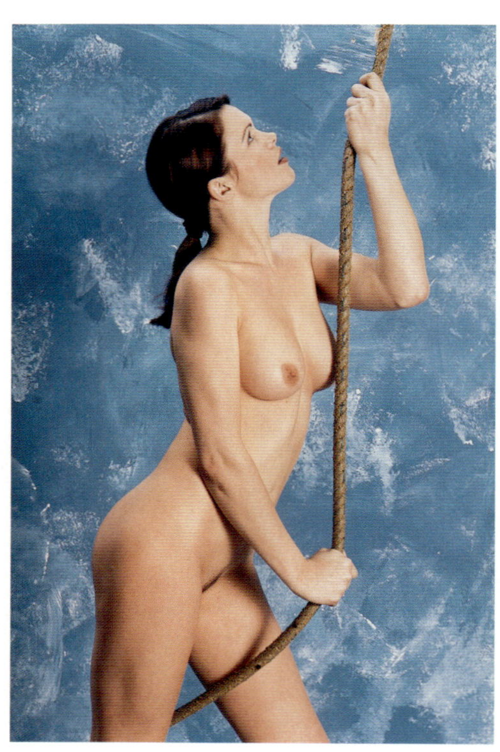

ABOVE CENTRE: **Iron backdrop.** In this image, a piece of corrugated iron painted with a spray can and a crushed car serves as an interesting backdrop to the nude figure.
(BRONICA ETRSi; 150mm LENS; 1/125 sec at f/16; ILFORD FP4 PLUS.)

ABOVE RIGHT: **Wall painting.** A brightly painted wall, like the one shown in this shot, makes a dynamic studio background.
(BRONICA ETRSi; 150mm LENS; 1/125 sec at f/11; KODAK GPX.)

In some cases, the background will play an apparently minor role; in others, it may be the dominant part of the picture and act as a prop that is an important feature of the composition. Either way, attention should be paid to the detail and steps taken to ensure that the background is uncluttered. Do some 'gardening' if necessary to tidy up and remove unnecessary items that detract from the main image. This is particularly important when using backgrounds such as house interiors and outdoor locations. For studio work, a selection of coloured paper rolls, including white and black, is a good investment, and various plain and patterned material backgrounds are readily available. Silk parachutes are fairly cheap and may be used plain or tie-dyed in various ways.

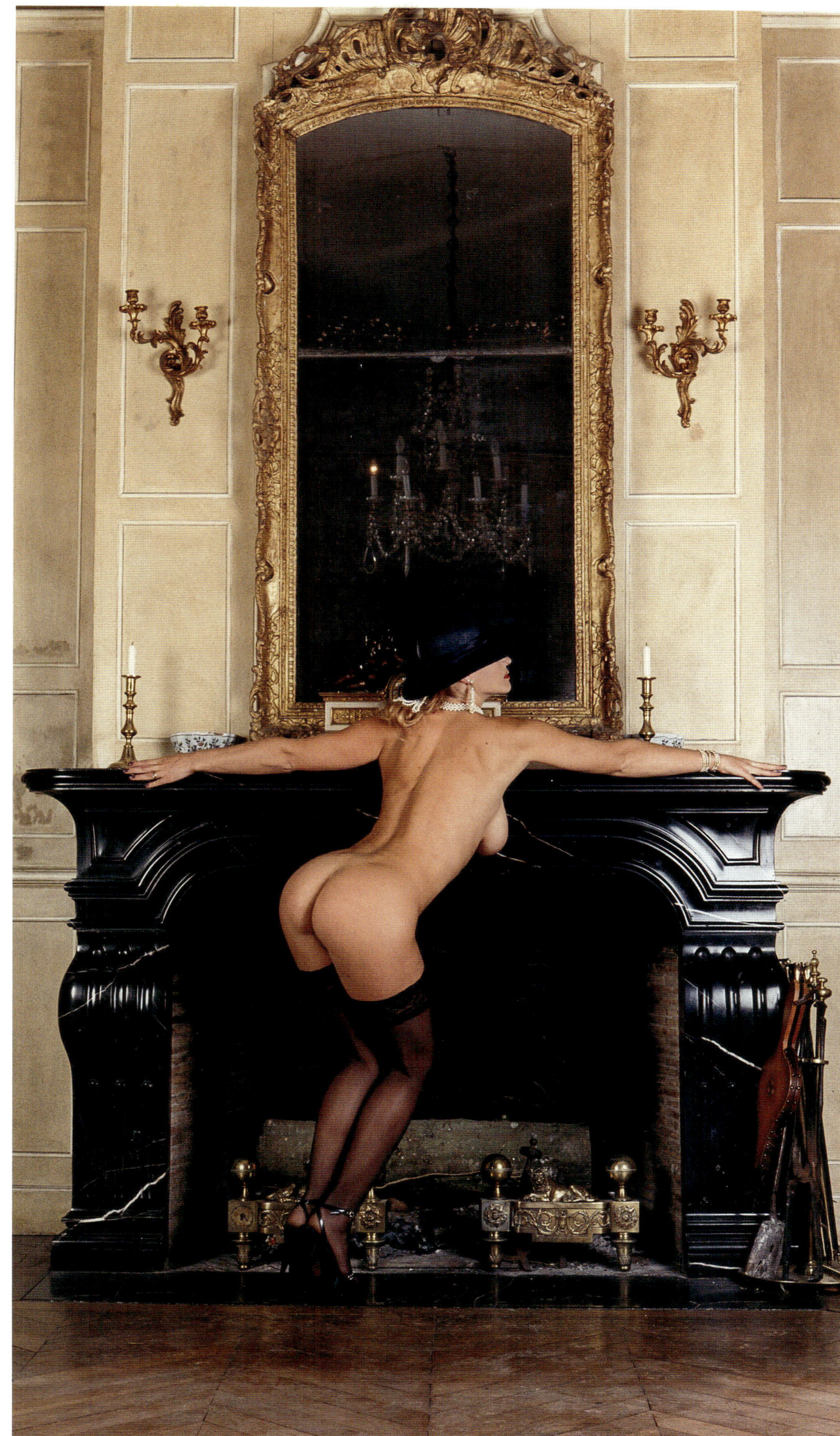

RIGHT: **Background prop.**
This magnificent fireplace
with its ornamental mirror
not only makes a grand
background for a nude
study, but also acts as an
impressive prop for the
model to interact with.
(BRONICA ETRSi; 150mm LENS;
1/125 sec at f/11; KODAK
PORTRA 160NC.)

Film

RIGHT: **Saturated colour.** The image shown here was taken in strong natural light on a sunny day using colour transparency film. This copes well with high-contrast lighting conditions, giving bright, highly saturated colours. (MINOLTA 8000i; 100mm LENS; 1/250 sec at f/11; KODACHROME 64.)

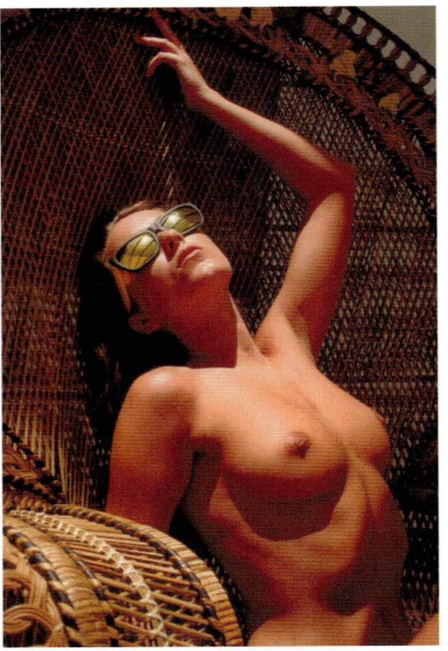

The many different brands of photographic films that are available can be placed in four major categories: reversal films, black-and-white negative films, colour negative films, and specialist films. Film speeds range from around ISO 25 to ISO 1000. Fast films are grainier than slow films. Film for MF cameras comes in the 120-roll format, whereas 35mm and advanced photo system (APS) cameras use cassettes.

reversal films

Reversal films, also known as transparency or slide films, give a positive image designed for projection. The image is a first derivative and therefore less prone to degradation by copy processes. This quality is favoured by many commercial image-buyers – a serious consideration if you intend to sell your work. However, to get that perfect image, everything has to be right at the time of exposure. The lighting has to be spot on and the exposure correct to the nearest 1/2 stop. Everything in the final image must be there when the image is captured.

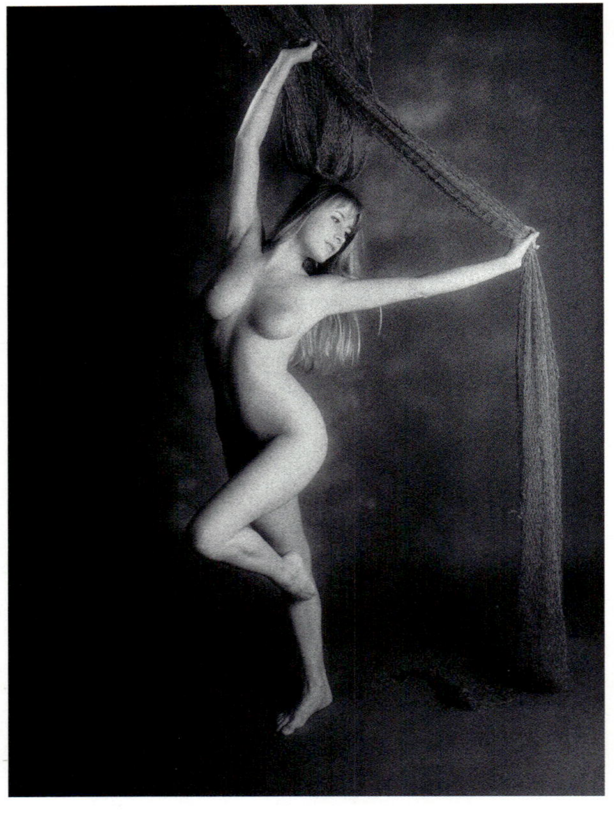

ABOVE: **Infrared filtration.** Infrared film can give very beautiful and delicate images. In this studio study, an orange filter was used over the lens. The exposure was increased by one stop to allow for the filter. (MINOLTA 8000i; 100mm LENS; 1/125 sec at f/8; KODAK HIGH SPEED INFRARED (HIE) RATED AT ISO 400.)

OPPOSITE: **Low-contrast conditions.** Colour negative film gives excellent reproduction characteristics under many lighting conditions and is particularly good in low-contrast situations, such as this nude study taken in natural light on a slightly overcast day. (BRONICA ETRSi; 75mm LENS; 1/125 sec at f/8; KODAK PORTRA 160VC.)

negative films

These are print films designed to produce printed images. They have greater exposure latitude than reversal films and are more forgiving when it comes to processing. This is true of both colour and black-and-white films. An acceptable print can be made from a negative that has been underexposed by two stops or overexposed by three stops, and many exposure errors can be corrected at the printing stage. These media are ideal for 'creating' images in the darkroom, and the exhibition photographer or fine-art printer who wants to produce large prints would naturally gravitate towards working with negative films.

specialist films

Those of interest to the nude photographer include tungsten films, which are balanced for redder tungsten light, and infrared films. The latter are sensitized to infrared radiation of various wavelengths as well as visible light, and record a certain amount of the heat radiating from, or reflecting from, an object. Because light meters do not register infrared radiation, an accurate ISO/ASA rating cannot be given for these films. Some cameras use an infrared device for measuring the DX coding on film and infrared film cannot be used in these. There is more information on this subject on pages 112–5.

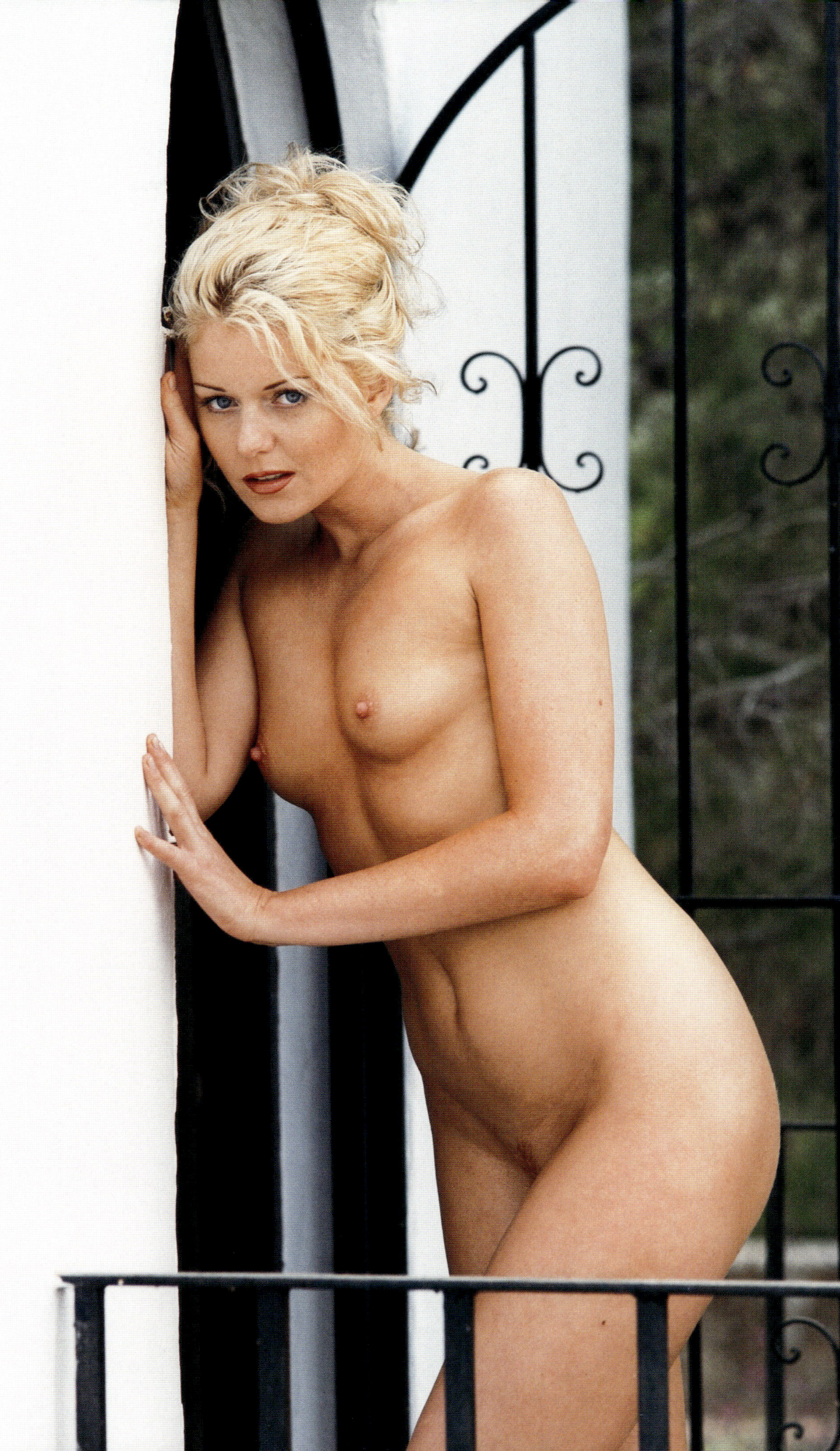

How does a photographer enter into the world of nude and glamour photography? Where do you start and how do you do it? These are just two of the questions I am frequently asked about my photography. The most difficult problem for the novice nude photographer is finding someone willing to be photographed in the nude, so the chapter starts with this subject and continues to the next stages of deciding where and how to photograph the model. This process, called 'setting up the shoot', is a prelude to meeting the model and photographing her at the chosen location. All the stages of this creative process are described in this chapter, with useful tips on what to do… and what *not* to do.

RIGHT: **Natural settings.** Take advantage of natural settings when they present themselves. When I was walking across these dunes, looking for suitable locations, the dead branches lying in the sand suggested a natural frame for the model. (BRONICA ETRSi; 75mm LENS; 1/125 sec at f/11; KODAK PORTRA 160NC.)

Getting started

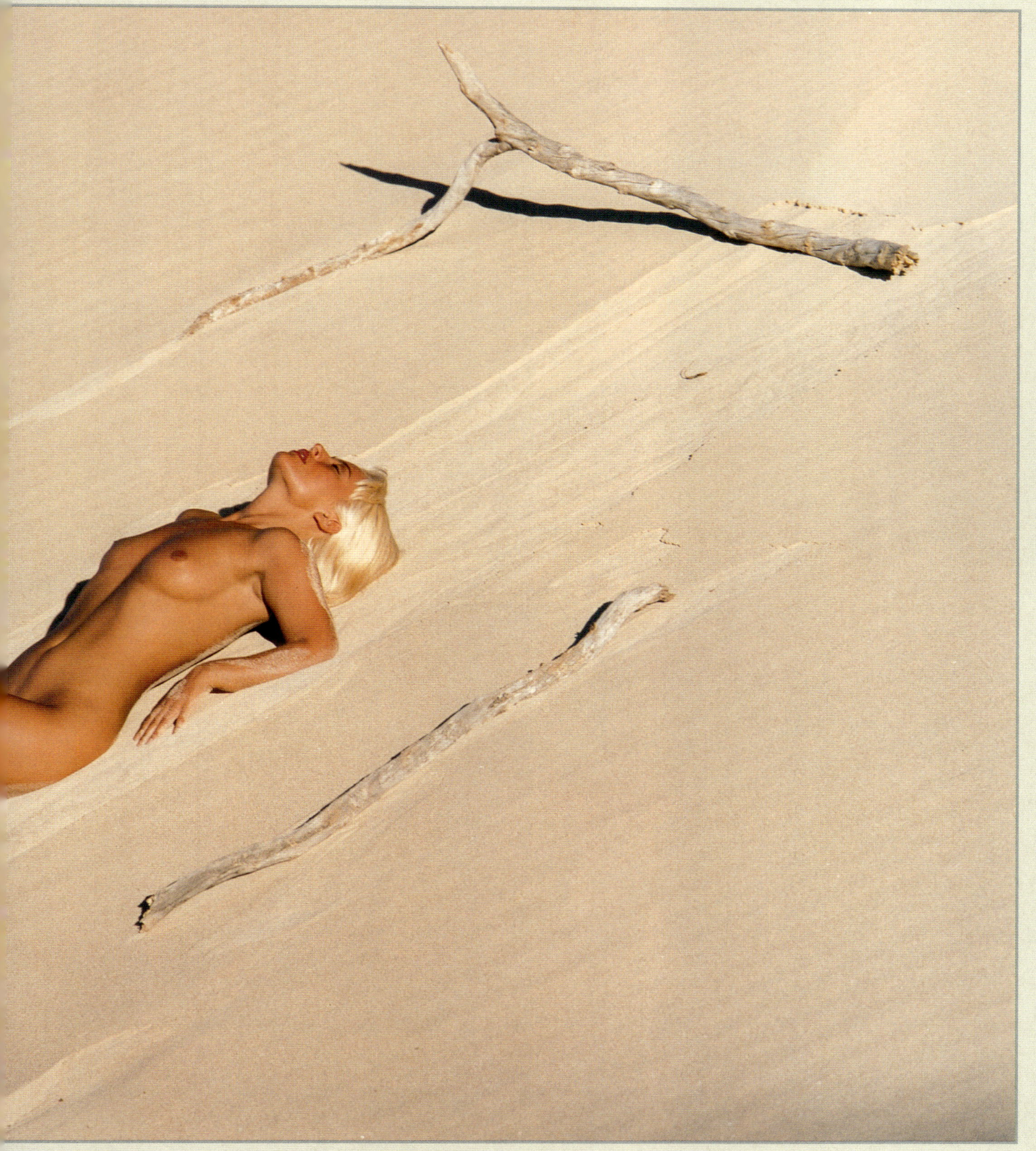

Finding models

Perhaps the most difficult task for the novice photographer wishing to try nude photography is finding a model who will be willing to work with you. The first consideration – before even thinking about finding a model – should be your credibility as a photographer. If you want someone to remove their clothing for you and commit their image to film, they will want to be sure that you are at least a competent photographer. A small portfolio of your images will go a long way to convincing potential models that you are serious about your ambitions, but only use your very best photographs. If you have no images to show and no previous experience of photographing people, then it is advisable to start with portraiture and fashion pictures. Once you have gained some experience of working with a model in front of your camera, you can then move on to nude photography.

amateur models The term amateur is not meant to be in any sense derogatory – many amateur models are as proficient as professionals. The only distinction being made here is that amateurs do not model for a living. Many nude photographers have started by photographing close friends and relatives, such as a girlfriend or spouse, or made contact through a friend who knew someone who had an interest in modelling. Camera clubs often run practical photographic sessions, and this is an excellent opportunity for the novice to meet a model and become familiar with studio lighting and etiquette. Chance meetings can pay dividends, so be prepared by having a few printed cards giving your name, address and telephone number to pass to potential models. I have made many successful contacts this way at weddings, social gatherings, and even in shopping malls.

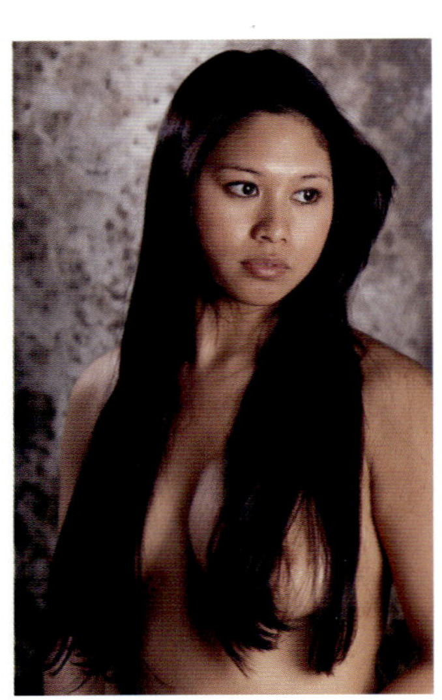

ABOVE: **First-time model.** An introduction to a friend's niece, who had never modelled before, resulted in this candid image. (BRONICA ETRSi; 150mm LENS; 1/125 sec at f/11; KODAK PORTRA.)

RIGHT: **Professional confidence.** This professional model radiates confidence, which may be lacking in a less experienced model or an amateur who is only just starting out. (MINOLTA 7000i; 100mm LENS; 1/125 sec at f/8; KODAK GPX160.)

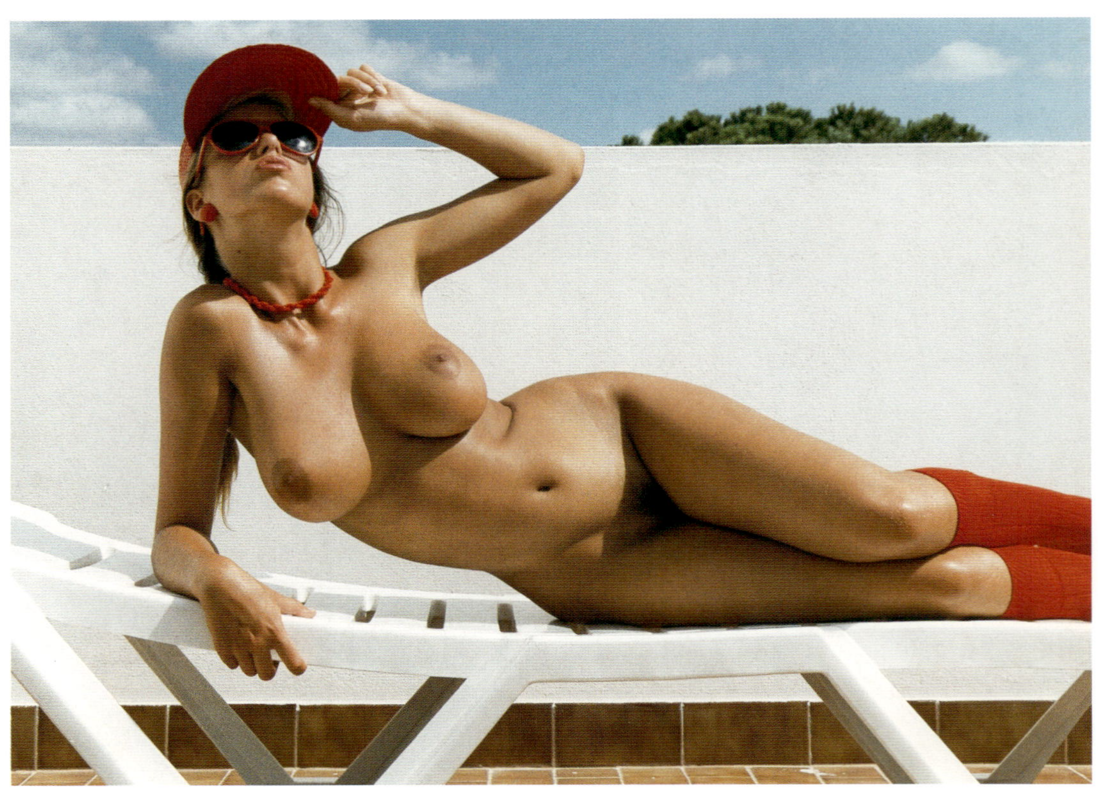

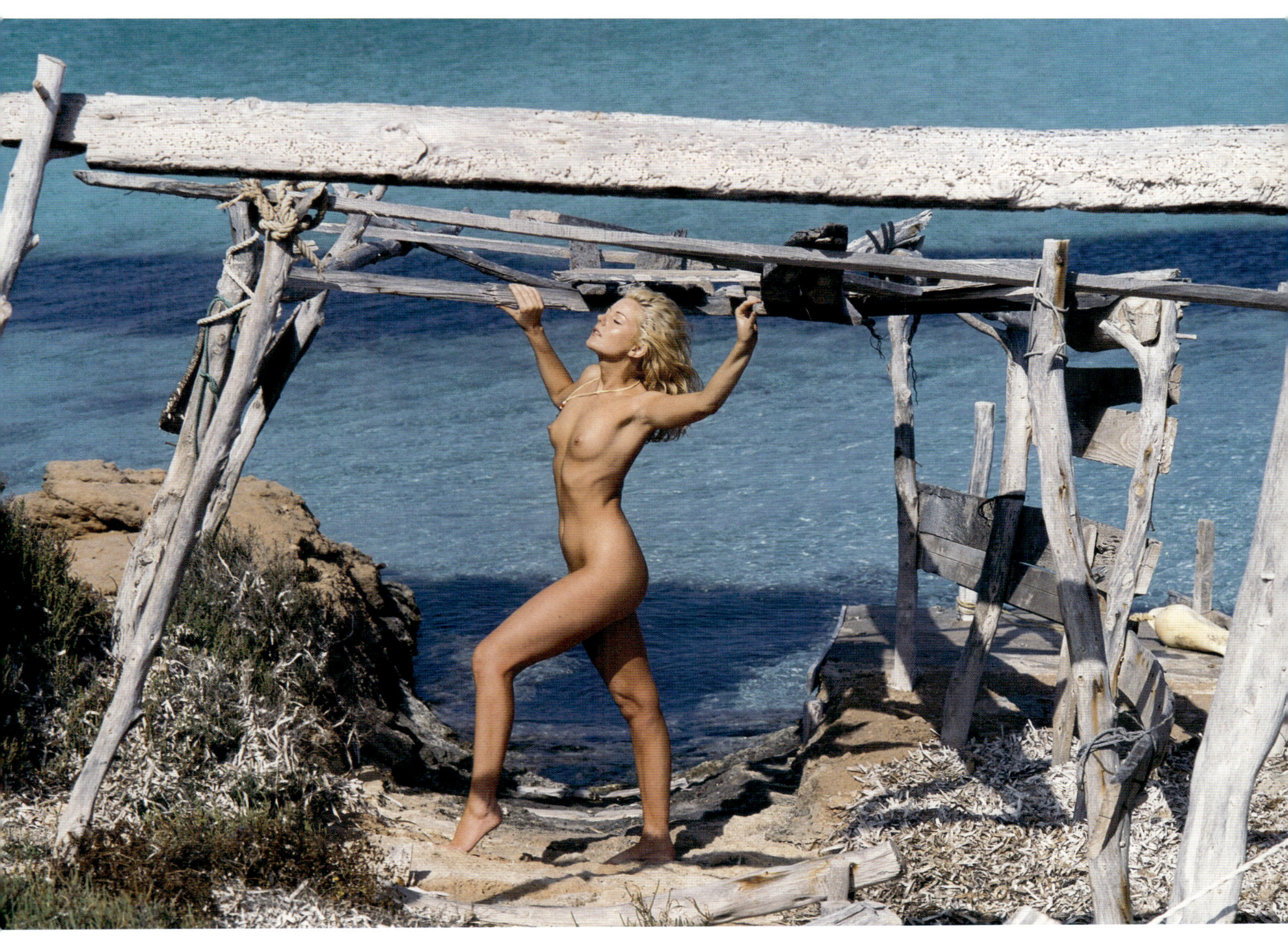

professional models

Finding professional models to work with is relatively easy – if potentially expensive – and there are several options available, depending on your budget. Photographic magazines often run advertisements for individual models, amateur studios, and photographic workshops or seminars that provide relatively inexpensive access to nude models. Most studios have a list of models who can be hired at an hourly rate, and this can provide a good opportunity for both novice and experienced photographers to work solo or with friends to reduce costs. Model agencies tend to cater for the professional photographer, and their models are often too costly for the amateur. Once established as a photographer of some merit, word of mouth becomes an important factor in finding new models to work with.

THE INTERNET

The Internet is a rich source of both amateur and professional models, and is becoming increasingly important in this respect. Setting up a website is relatively easy and inexpensive, and many amateur and professional models have their own sites where photographers can view pictures and ascertain modelling rates. There are also specialist sites that allow both models and photographers to register their details and portfolios so that they can contact each other. For the dedicated photographer, a website containing examples of work and a request for models to respond may result in the fomation of successful contacts.

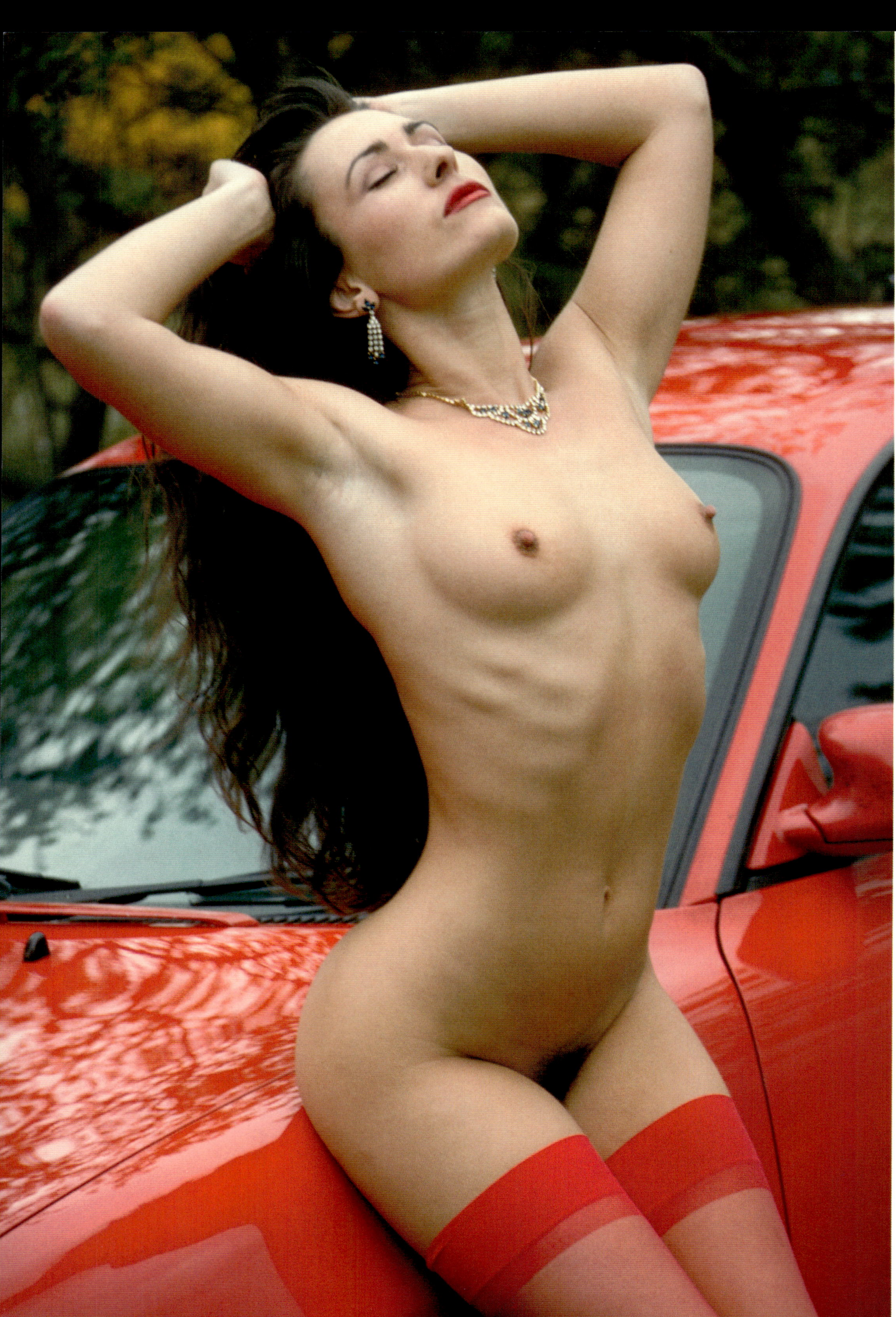

Finding locations

OPPOSITE: **Outdoor setting.** A secluded garden and a familiar prop were used to make this nude study. (MINOLTA 8000i; 75–300mm ZOOM LENS; 1/125 sec at f/16; KODAK EKTACHROME 100.)

For the novice photographer on a tight budget, finding locations for the first shoot with a model may be difficult. One option is to use your own house, a friend's house, or the model's house as a setting. A room with a large window or a conservatory is ideal for daylight photography and does not rely on elaborate lighting equipment – reflectors may

semi-permanent studio. Background supports and a basic set of studio lights are relatively inexpensive and a good investment if you intend to try this. Secluded gardens may also be used for daylight photography.

Another option is hiring a photographic studio, which should have a wide range of electronic lighting, props and other ancillary

RIGHT: **Library setting.** The library location suggested this particular pose, where the model is using the books to interact with the setting. (BRONICA ETRSi; 75mm LENS; 1/125 sec at f/11; KODAK PORTRA 160NC.)

FAR RIGHT: **Subtle colours.** The simplicity of this Victorian bathroom and the subtlety of the colours allows all the attention to be placed on the model. (BRONICA ETRSi; 75mm LENS; 1/125 sec at f/8; KODAK PORTRA 160NC.)

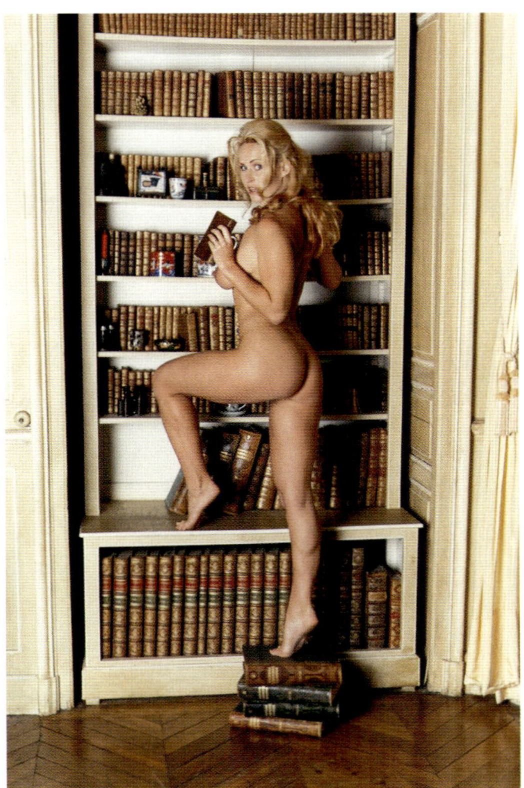

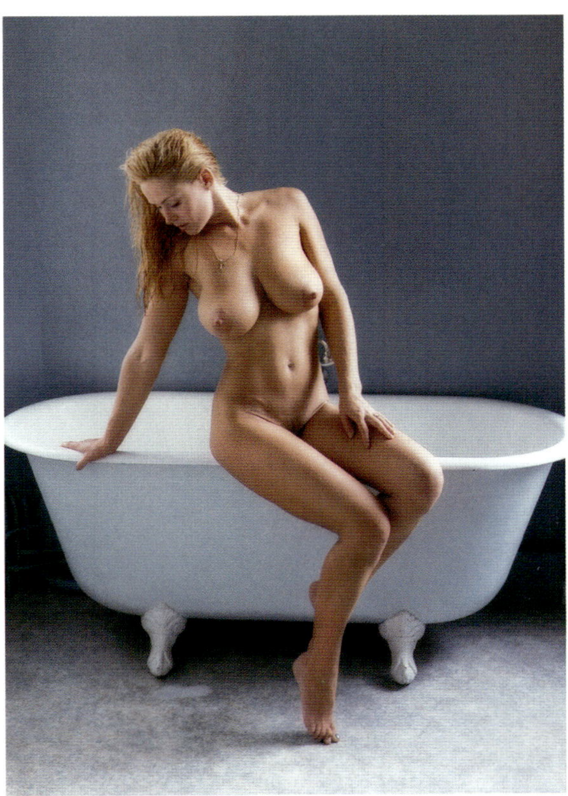

be all that is required in this situation. The domestic setting of a room may be satisfactory as it is. Otherwise some rearrangement of the furniture may be necessary to make it as uncluttered as possible. Rooms that have a special feature – such as a polished wooden floor, a Victorian bath or a library – should be fully exploited. A spare room can be converted into a makeshift home studio using paper rolls or material for the background, whereas a large room or a garage may be suitable as a

equipment. The variety of equipment is usually commensurate with the hire costs, and in some cases more exotic pieces of equipment, such as focusing spots and wind or smoke machines, are supplied at an additional charge. Most studios will allow you to take your own model, or let you hire one from the studio's books. Look in your favourite photographic magazine for studio listings and, if possible, visit the studio to check out space, equipment, and props before making a booking.

Setting up the shoot

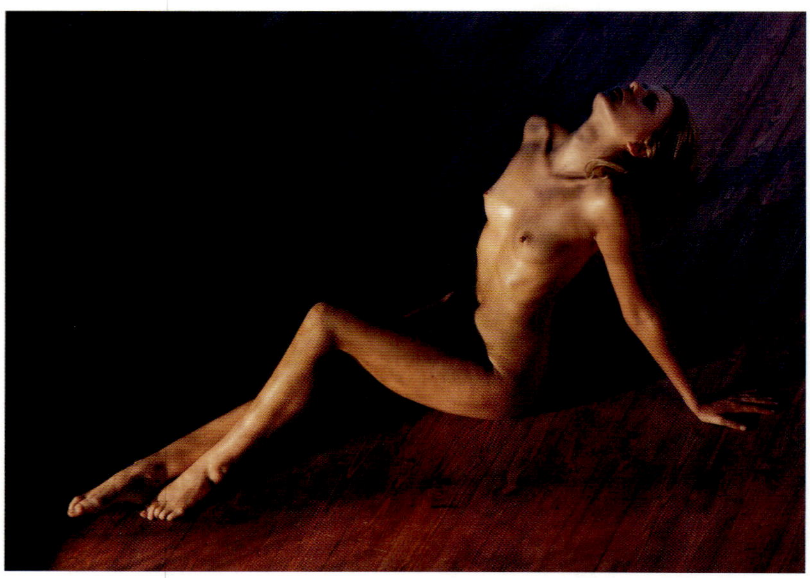

OPPOSITE: **The gel effect.** In this shot, the model was lit with two lights. The main light was used with an orange gel to warm the skin tone, and the smoke was lit by light passing through the holes in the wheel. A blue gel was used on this light source to add colour contrast. Hire of special equipment, such as a smoke machine, should be arranged well in advance of the shoot. (MINOLTA 8000i; 70–300mm LENS; 1/125 sec at f/8; KODAK VERICOLOR 160.)

RIGHT: **Predetermined poses.** Poses such as this can be discussed before a shoot, perhaps by reference to images taken on previous occasions, books or magazine cuttings. (BRONICA ETRSi; 75mm LENS; 1/125 sec at f/11; KODAK PORTRA 160NC.)

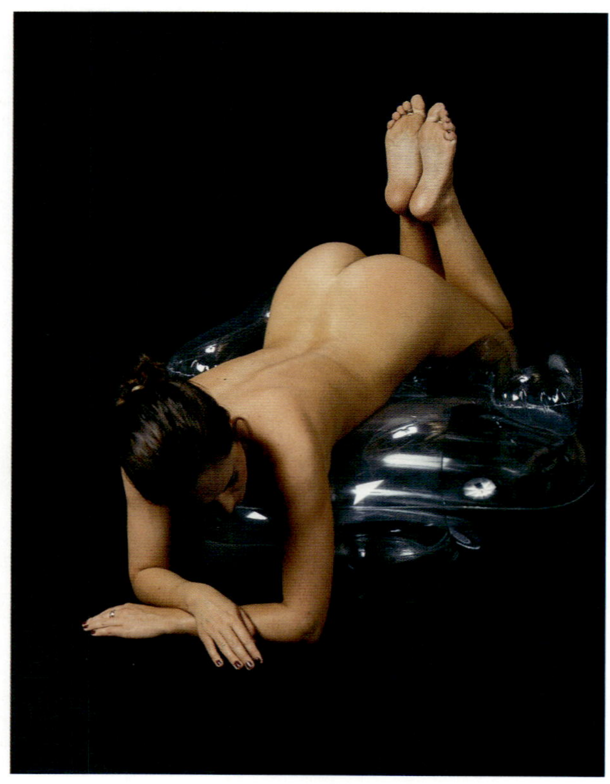

ABOVE: **Studio facilities.** Most studios have a selection of props that the photographer can exploit, such as this transparent inflatable chair. They may even supply a list in advance to provide imaginative ideas for poses. (MINOLTA 8000i; 75–300mm LENS; 1/125 sec at f/8; KODAK VERICOLOR 160.)

A model has been found and a location has been decided upon. It is an excellent start, but where do you go from there?

preplanning If the model is someone you know, discuss details of the forthcoming shoot at leisure. Ideally, this should be done before the shoot and topics such as the date, time, place and duration of the shoot, fees (if applicable), model release, pictures to be supplied, and so on can be discussed along with ideas for proposed pictures.

This is an opportunity to show your previous work to the model. If she has a portfolio too, then it will be possible for you to see how she looks in print. The model may have her own ideas for pictures. Encourage this – a good shoot is a cooperative event between photographer and model and will benefit greatly from any synergy. If you want the model to supply particular items of clothing for the shoot, this is the time to ask. You should also discuss make-up. Unless you can afford the services of a make-up artist, you will be reliant on the model doing her own.

Ask your model not to wear tight clothing before she comes to the shoot – it marks the skin. Often, an initial meeting is not possible and, as these arrangements must be dealt with by telephone, email, or via a third party such as the booking agency or studio manager. Discuss special arrangements for lighting, ancillary equipment, props and backdrops with the proprietor when booking a studio and, if planning to photograph outdoors, always have a back-up indoor location in case of bad weather. Check your camera equipment, making sure that you have more than enough film and some spare batteries.

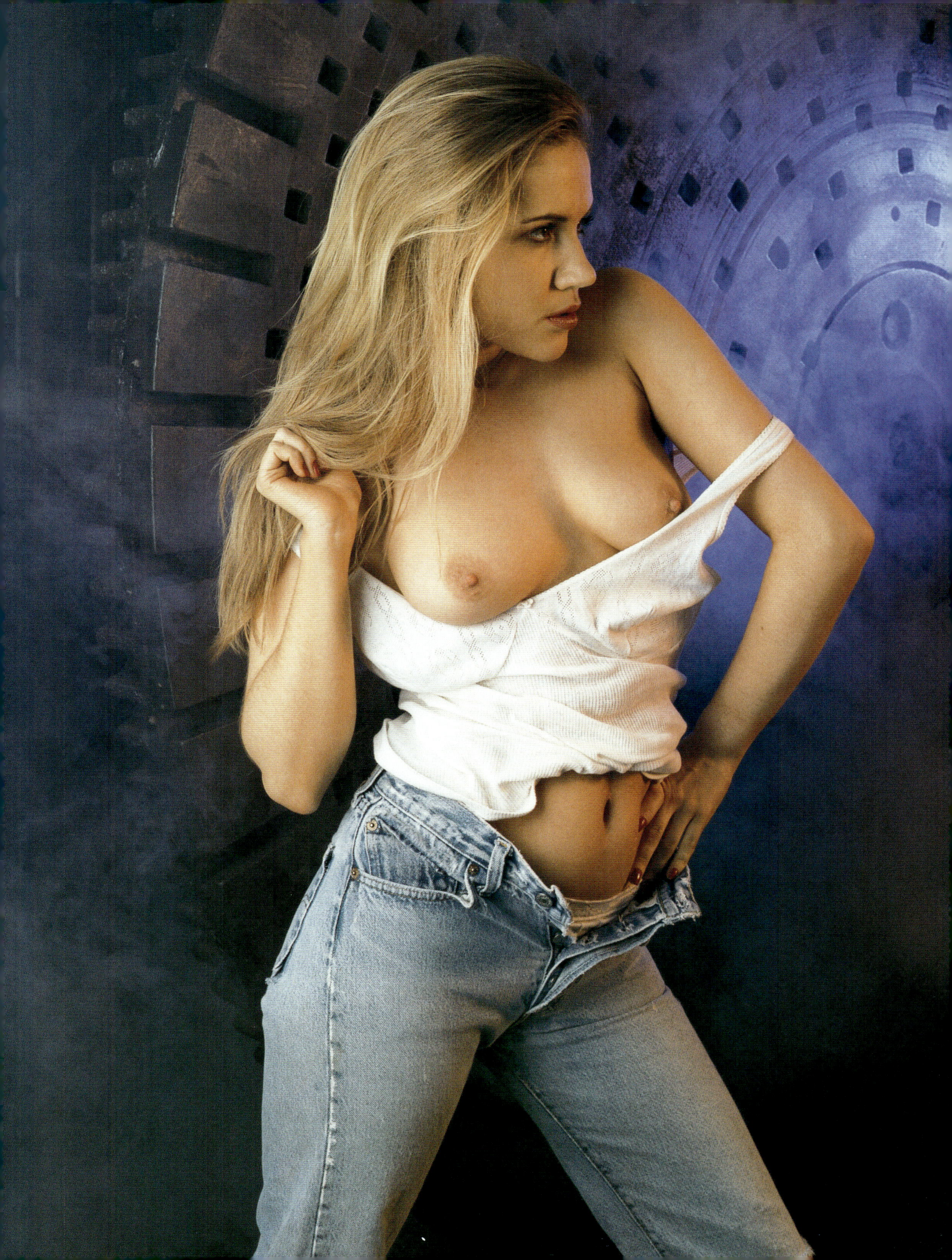

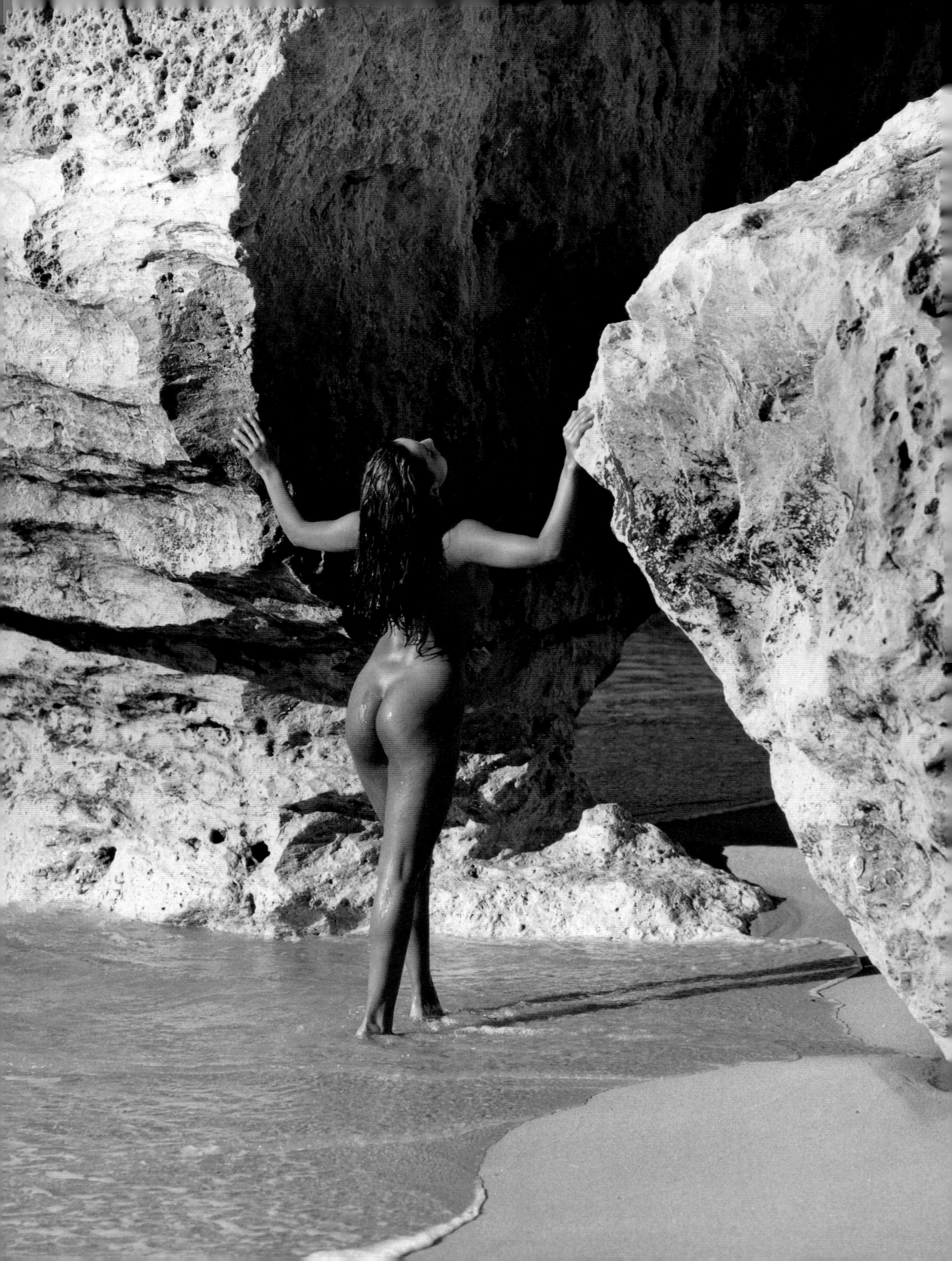

Meeting the model

The day of the shoot has arrived and you are about to meet the person you are going to photograph. This can be an anxious time for the first-time model – and indeed the novice photographer – especially if this is the first time that model and photographer have met, which is likely to be the case if the model was booked through a studio or agency. The first few minutes of contact can be very important, and it is essential that the photographer shows a positive and confident attitude towards the model. A new model will understandably be a little nervous, especially if she hasn't modelled in the nude before, so the photographer's first job is to make her feel comfortable and relaxed in his or her presence.

know your model
Whether the meeting is at a studio, at your home, or elsewhere, greet the model and take a few minutes to put her at her ease. Comment on her hair, clothes, make-up, how nice she looks, and so on; enthusiastic praise does not go amiss as long as it is genuine. If you haven't done so on a previous occasion, discuss the project you have in mind and what you expect of the model.

Depending on the circumstances, this may be a good time to look briefly at portfolios and get to know your model a little better. This may be appropriate at your own home, say, but if you are using a studio this will rapidly eat into your allocated time, which will be a costly waste.

Make sure that the model is shown where she can change her clothes and either put on make-up, or adjust it if already applied. Ask her to put on a loose-fitting robe or dressing gown as soon as possible so that any marks on the skin from clothing will have a chance to dissipate before the shoot. It is useful to bring a robe for this purpose in case the model hasn't got one with her.

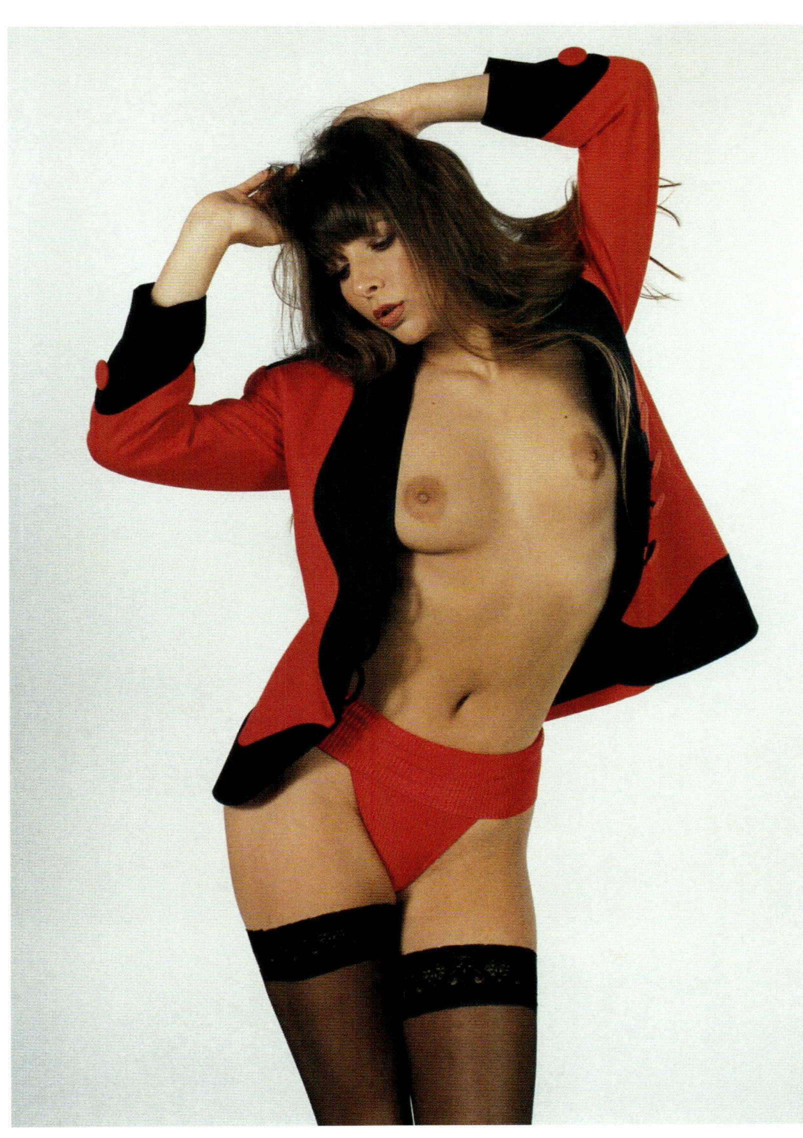

The shoot

Amateur models who have little or no experience of modelling may be shy and awkward, so be sympathetic to their feelings.

natural results It is most important that your model is relaxed and at ease to obtain natural results. Be courteous and polite at all times, but also positive in your attitude, giving clear instructions on the poses required. Explain what you want your model to do as concisely as possible. Show her a picture or demonstrate the pose yourself if you have trouble explaining it effectively. Don't be afraid to allow the model some freedom to try out her own ideas. Do not touch the model unless absolutely necessary, but if you need to adjust

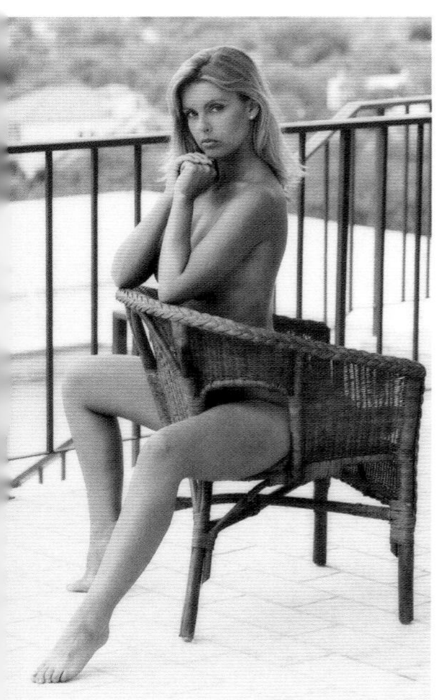

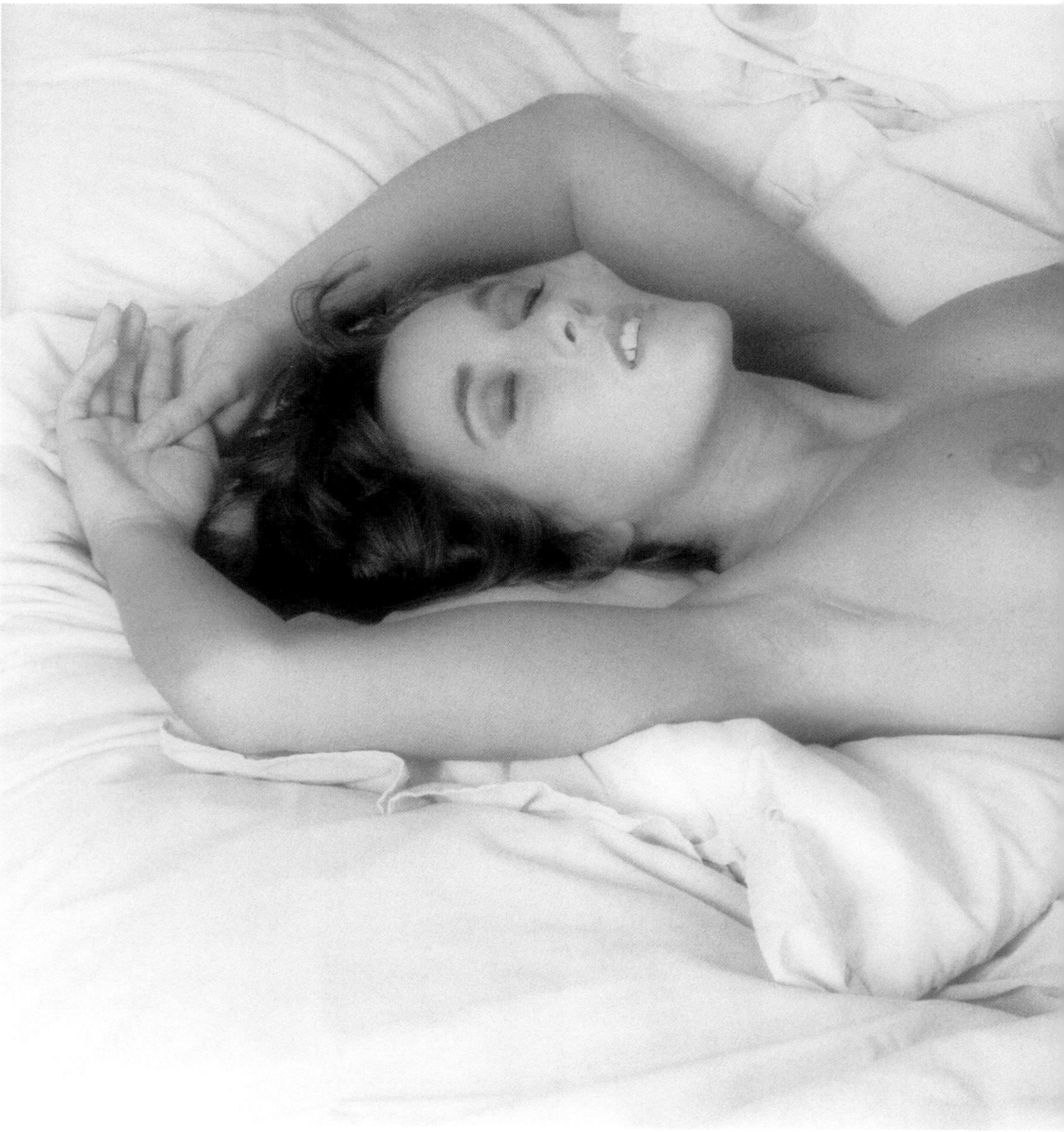

ABOVE: **The chosen look.** Explain to the model the type of pose and look you want. In this case, a relaxed but sophisticated look was the requirement. (BRONICA ETRSi; 150mm LENS; 1/125 sec at f/5.6; SEPIA TONED; ILFORD FP4 PLUS.)

RIGHT: **Free interpretation.** In this image, the model was allowed freedom to interpret the pose, given the general brief that a feeling of sensuality was wanted. (MINOLTA 8000i; 50mm LENS; 1/125 sec at f/5.6; ILFORD FP4 PLUS.)

a garment or the model's hair, then explain your intentions before you do it. Keep the conversation going throughout the shoot and make sure the model knows what you are doing and why you are doing it. If you need to adjust the lights, for instance, explain that you are changing the lighting ratio to change the mood – or whatever the reason happens to be.

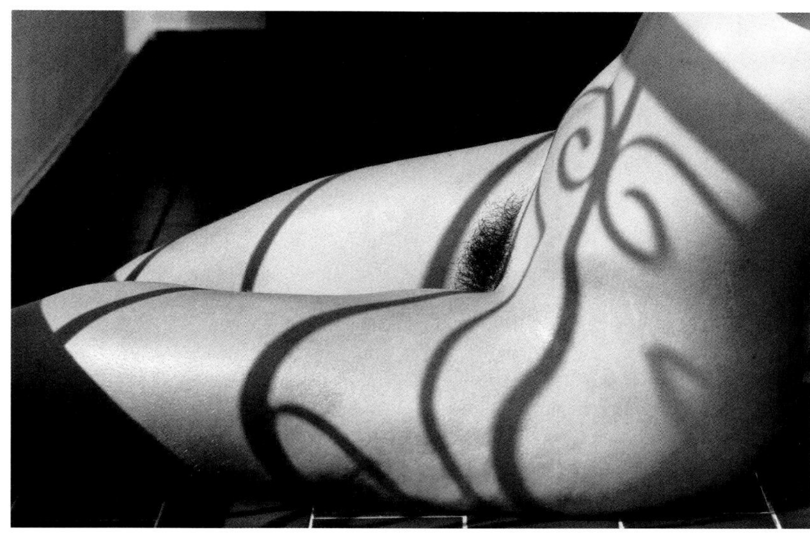

ABOVE: **Intimate shots.** When photographing details of the body, it is particularly important to explain to the model exactly what you are planning to do, or your intentions may be misinterpreted.
(BRONICA ETRSi; 150mm LENS; 1/60 sec at f/5.6; ILFORD FP4 PLUS.)

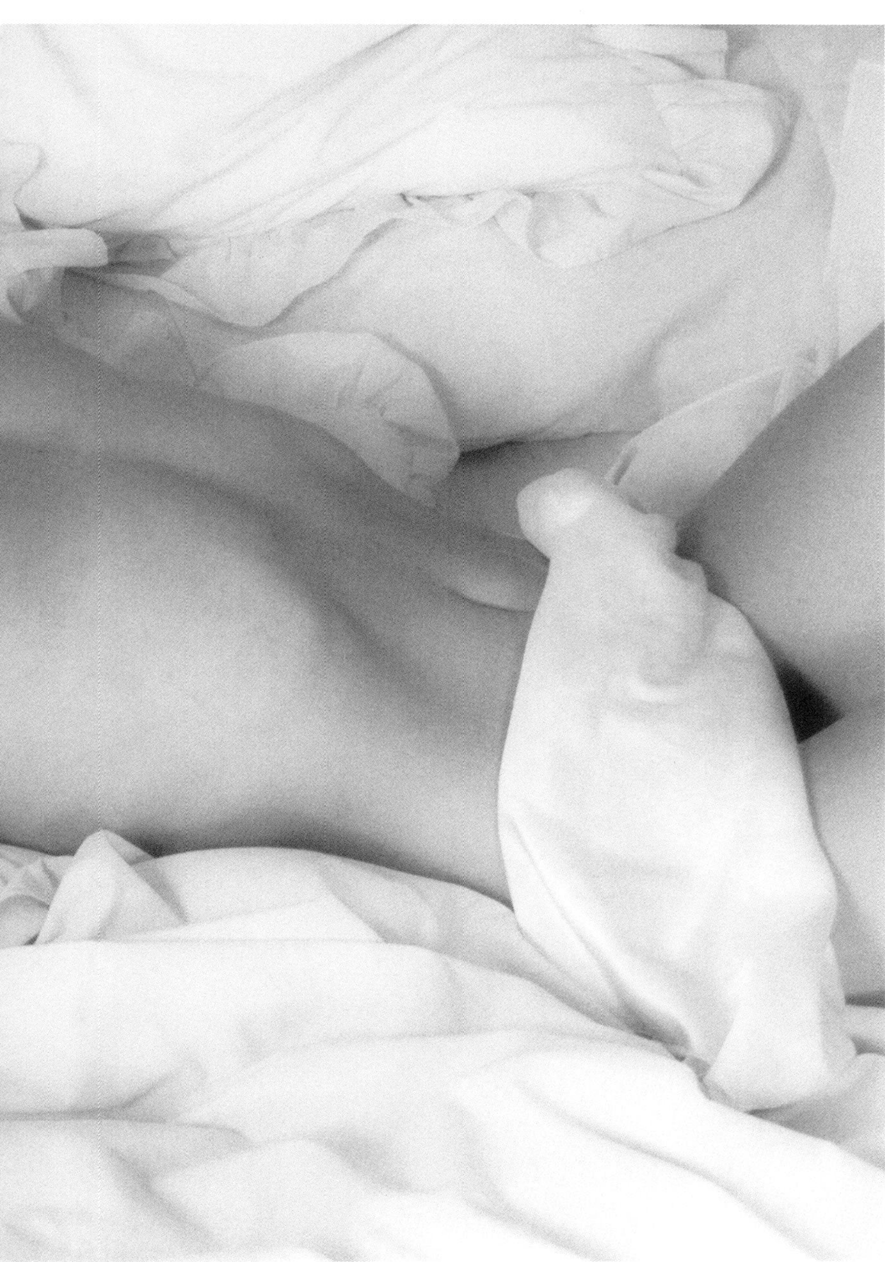

Give praise and encouragement all the time and tell her if a particular pose looks good.

Have short breaks from time to time and provide some cool refreshments – it can get quite warm in front of flashlights. It is a good idea to have some background music playing in the studio. An appropriate sound for the mood of the image being created will often help the shoot go more smoothly, especially if you let the model choose the music. After the shoot, praise the model and tell her how well the shoot went. Don't forget to pay her (if she requires payment in cash) and if you have promised to provide prints or contact sheets, then make sure you send them. Should you ever intend to sell your pictures, ask the model to sign a consent form called a model release, to avoid potential problems later on (see Appendix, page 156).

Successful photography depends on the effective interaction of light, subject and the surrounding environment to form an interesting image that can be captured by the photographer. Many factors – including the colour of light, intensity of light, the direction from which the light is coming, and the relative contrast of light to dark areas – combine to make a myriad of lighting scenarios that can affect the composition of an image. This chapter illustrates a few of the many possible lighting situations that can be deployed by the nude photographer in outdoor locations and the studio to achieve a range of interesting and creative images. It also demonstrates how light can be metered imaginatively to produce optimum creative results.

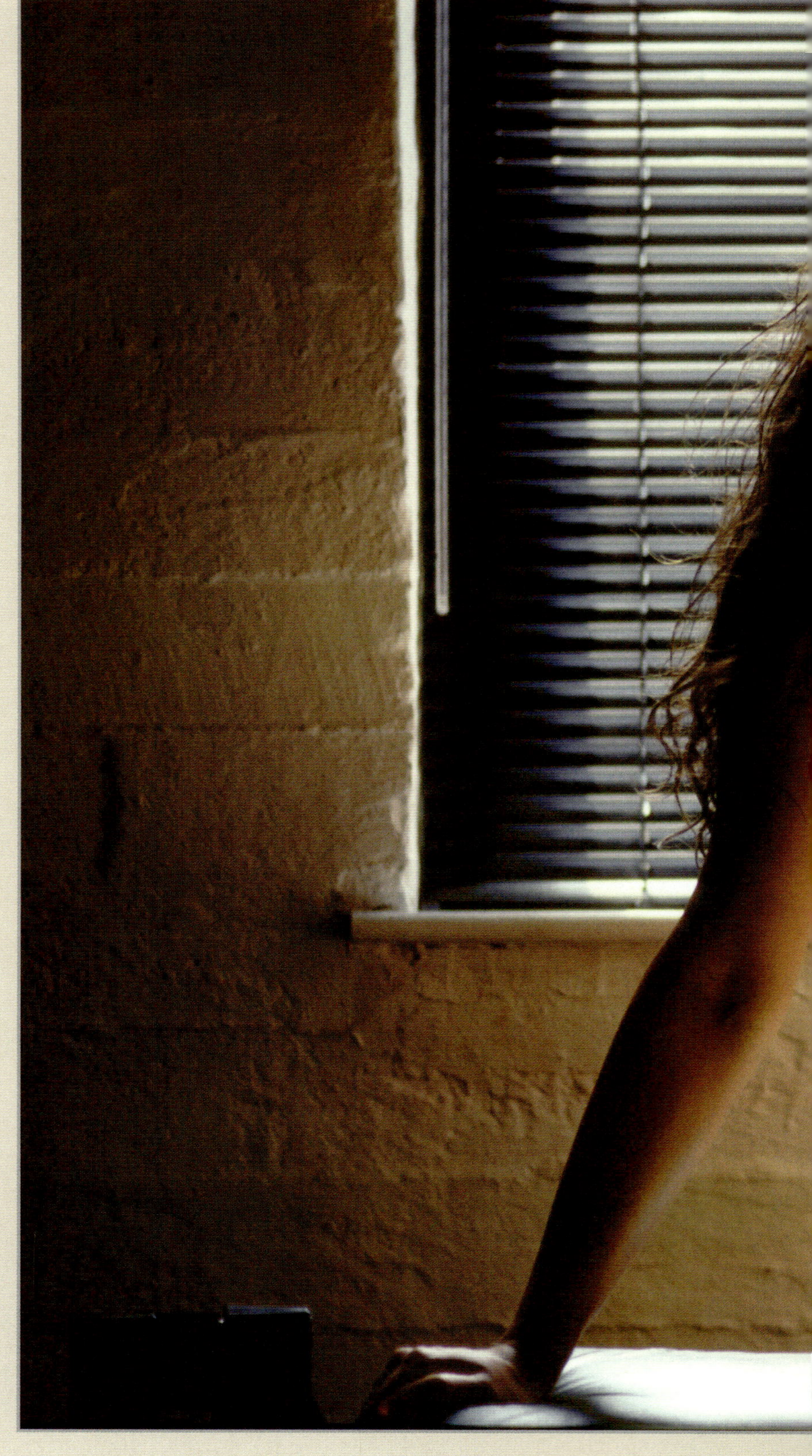

RIGHT: **Light and shadow.** Daylight behind a Venetian blind, from an overhead skylight, and bounced with a gold reflector, combine to make a powerful image with interesting and creative lighting.
(MINOLTA 8000i; 50mm LENS; 1/60 sec at f/11; KODACHROME 64.)

Lighting & metering

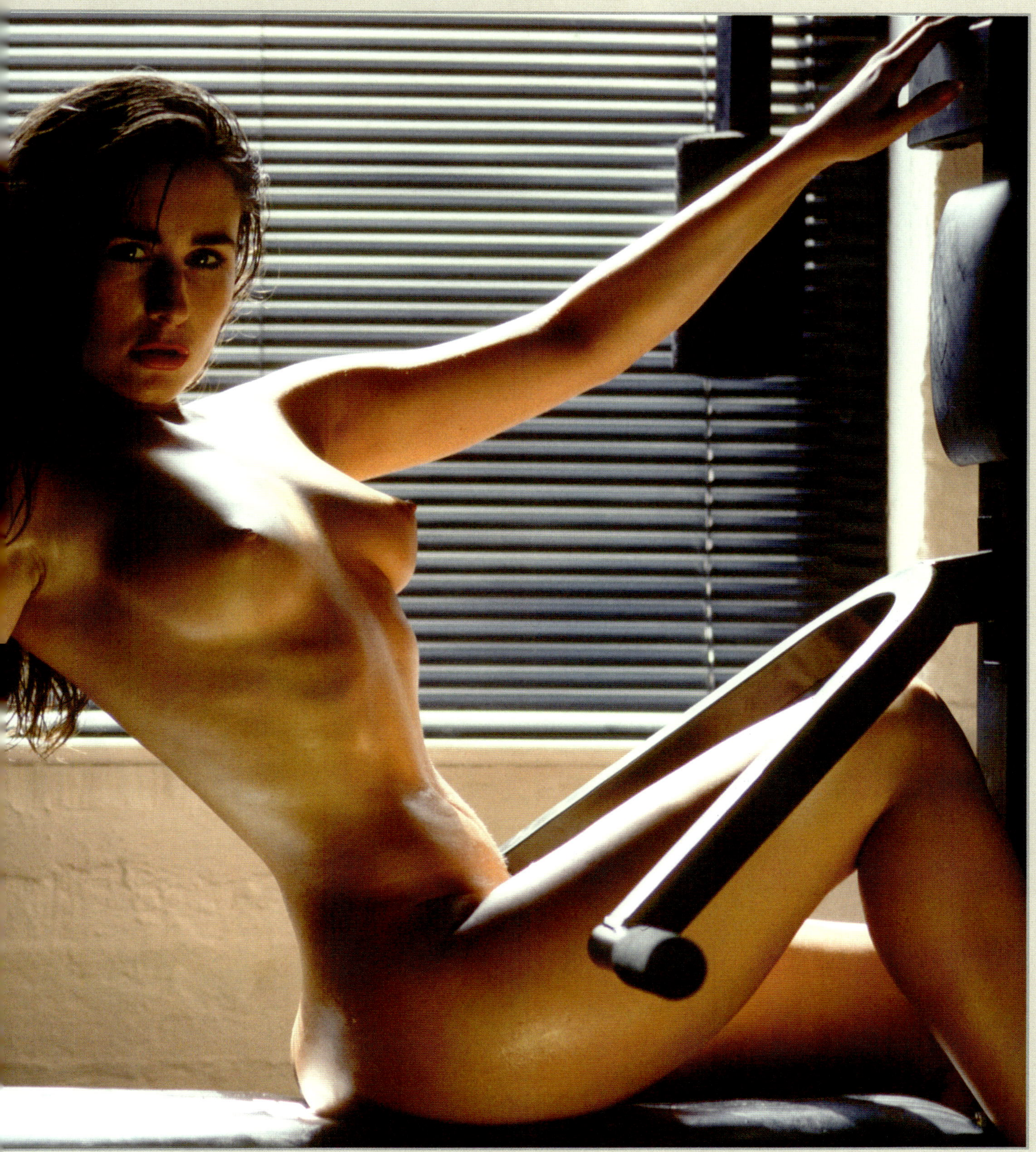

Metering methods

ABOVE: **Highlights and shadows.** In this moody image, the film was exposed for the model's face and upper torso, giving full detail in the highlights and mid-tones while deliberately losing some detail in the shadows. (BRONICA ETRSi; 150mm LENS; 1/125 sec at f/8; KODAK PORTRA 160VC.)

Modern single lens reflex (SLR) cameras have built-in incident light meters that can be used to estimate the light falling on a scene. The simplest cameras have average metering where the light entering the lens is averaged to grey and an appropriate combination of aperture and speed indicated to give an exposure that is correct for this measurement. More sophisticated cameras have more accurate options, such as automatic centre-weighted metering and matrix metering. If there is a lot of white (eg, where the model is against a white wall or contre-jour lighting) or a lot of black in a scene, this can over- or underbias the grey point and consequently lead to under- or overexposure of the subject. Spot metering, which meters from a small area of the scene, is useful in overcoming problems in these situations.

hand-held light meters

Portable light meters are useful as they can measure both incident light (the light falling on a subject) and reflected light (the light reflecting from a subject). In difficult lighting situations, it may be preferable to measure the light falling on the model. To take an incident-light reading, place the diffusion dome over the sensor and point the meter from the subject to the camera position. Hand-held spot meters are the most precise, with measuring angles as small as one degree, allowing accurate reflected readings from different parts of the scene.

flash meters

In the studio, a flash meter is an indispensable accessory. It is very similar to a hand-held light meter, being able to measure both incident and reflected light. Flash meters have a PC socket that allows the meter to be connected directly to a flash unit via a sync cable for remote triggering of the studio lights. In practice, the most common method of metering in the studio is by taking incident-light readings from each of the lights. Occasionally, it is useful to take reflected light readings from a light background.

PERMITTED EXPOSURE LATITUDE

In some situations, the range of brightness values of a scene can be extremely high and beyond the exposure latitude of the film (the range of tones that the film can record), so a judgment has to be made. Exposing for the mid-tones will result in diminished shadow and highlight detail; exposing for the shadows will result in loss of highlight detail; and exposing for highlights will result in loss of shadow detail. None is wrong – it is just a matter of personal preference. As a rule of thumb, when using negative materials, it is often preferable to expose for the shadows and let highlights look after themselves. For transparency materials, expose for highlights and let the shadows take care of themselves.

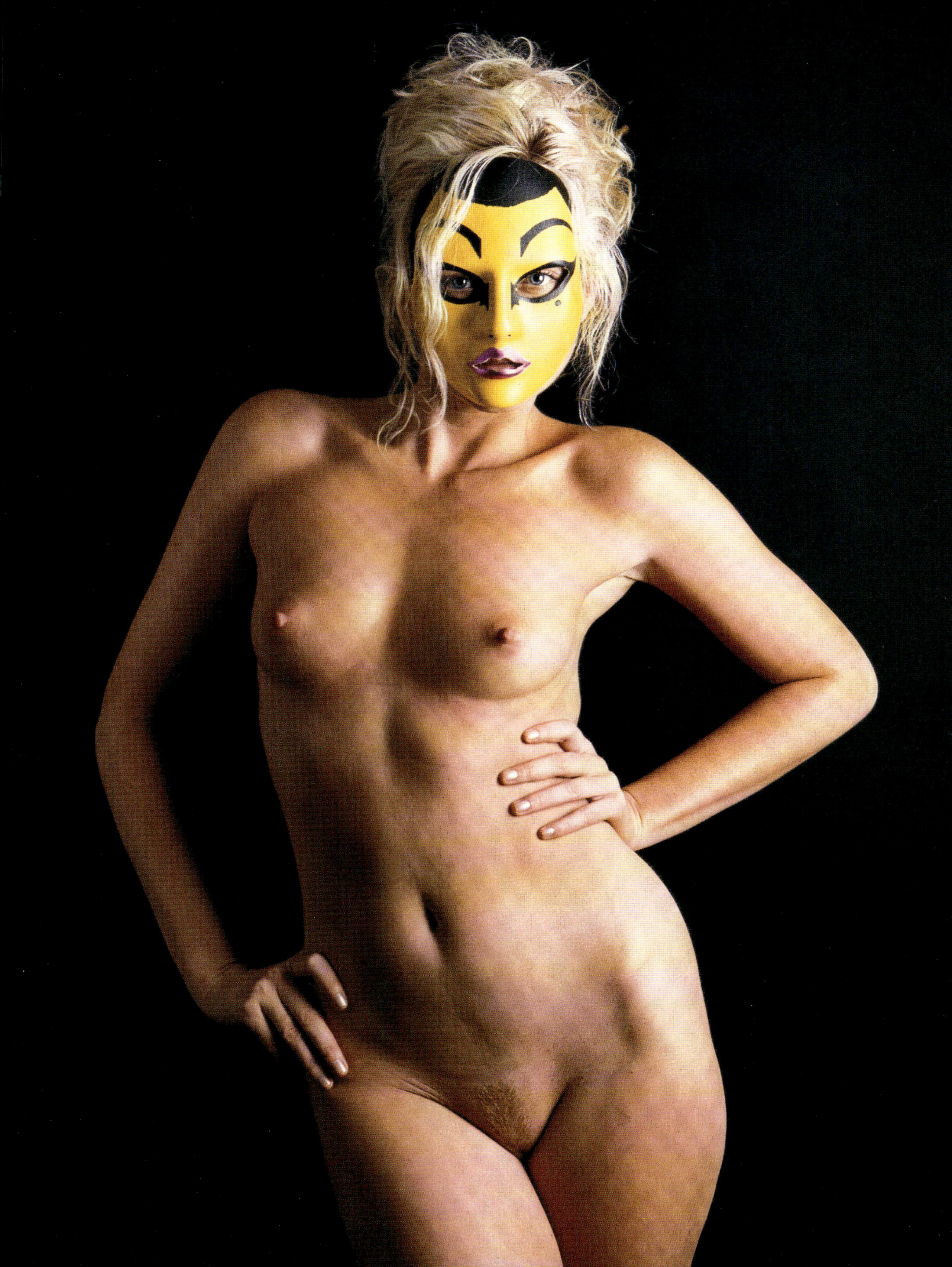

Metering for skin tones

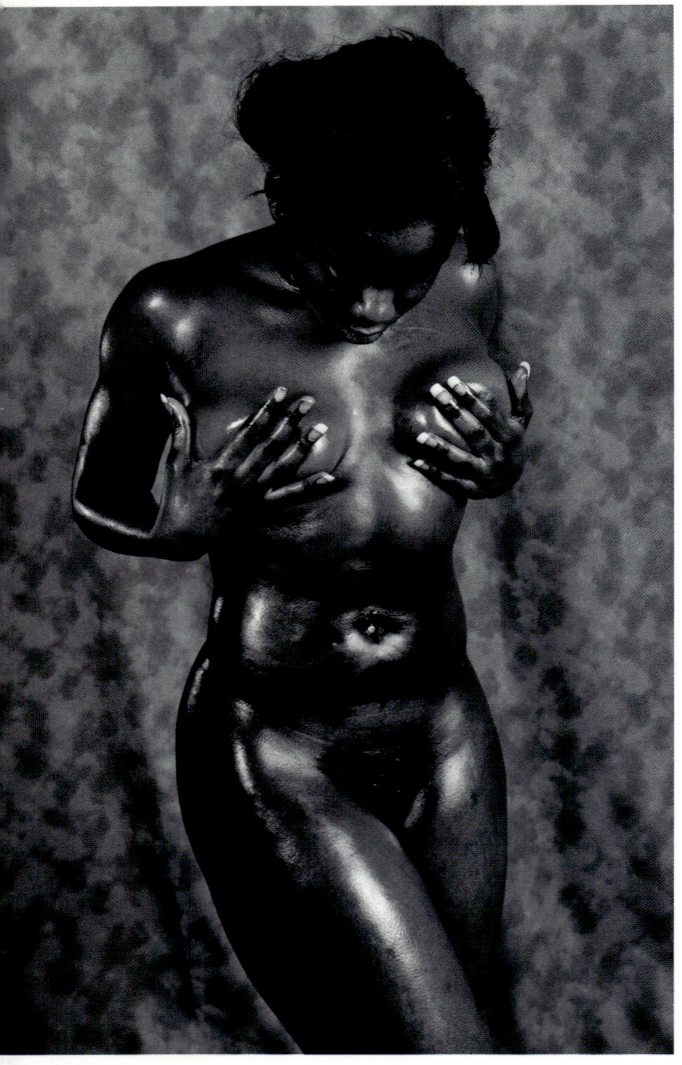

OPPOSITE: **Accentuating pale skin.** White or very pale skin reflects a lot of light. Here, the luminosity of pale skin has been accentuated by using a silver reflector just below the model to direct light into her face.
(BRONICA ETRSi; 150mm LENS; 1/125 sec at f/8; KODAK VPS160.)

ABOVE: **Enhancing reflections.** Dark skin reflects less light than paler skin. The addition of a light covering of body oil adds eye-catching reflections and helps to increase contrast.
(BRONICA ETRSi; 150mm LENS; 1/125 sec at f/11; ILFORD FP4.)

When photographing the nude, the major part of the image is usually the model. The colour, tone and brightness of the skin is therefore relatively important when deciding on the exposure that should be given to the film. This is particularly important when using transparency film, which requires the exposure to be accurate to within 1/2 a stop, but less important with negative materials, which have wider latitude and can also be compensated for at the printing stage.

in the studio
Meter readings in the studio are usually taken as incident light measurements, (ie, the light falling on the model is measured) and no account is taken of the reflectivity of the subject. If the model has a medium-toned skin, such as an olive, light-brown or lightly tanned skin, then no special exposure adjustments are necessary to give the correct rendition. Black or dark-coloured skin does not reflect as much light as white or light-coloured skin, so may be underexposed. When using transparency film, try increasing the exposure by 1/2 a stop. For example, if the nominal aperture is f/11, use f/9.6. For models with white or very pale-coloured skin, it may be preferable to decrease the exposure by 1/2 a stop to prevent loss of highlight detail.

on location
In an outdoor location, the usual method of metering is reflective through-the-lens (TTL) metering (ie, light reflecting from the model is measured), which automatically compensates for any differences in skin colour and tone. The main problems arise when there is a large contrast difference between the model's skin and the background. For instance, photographing a black model on a white-sand beach in full sunlight would cause the model to be underexposed if relying on average TTL metering. Similarly, positioning a very pale-skinned model against a black background would cause the model to be overexposed. In these situations, a compromise has to be made and spot metering on the model is the most satisfactory solution in most cases.

MAKING THE MOST OF SKIN TYPES

The application of body oil or cream can improve the appearance of black and dark-coloured skin. This adds specular reflections to the skin and increases the contrast ratio between highlight and shadow areas. It is particularly effective in a monochrome image. For white and light-coloured skins where the rendition of skin texture is important, exposure for highlights and use of lighting that gives good modelling emphasizes the body shape. If the desired emphasis is more on accentuating the paleness of the skin, expose for mid-tones or shadows and use a flatter type of lighting such as high key or ring flash.

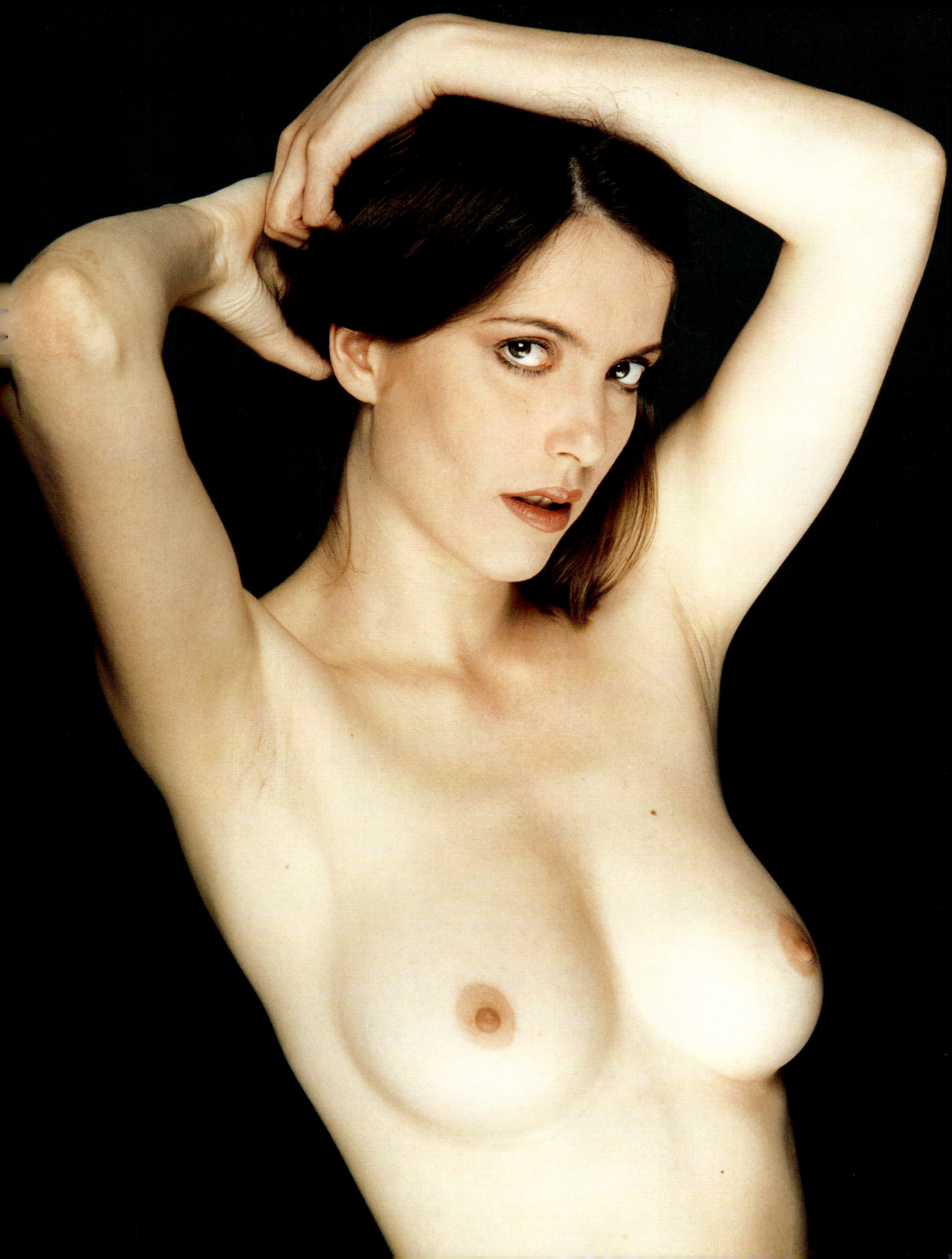

Colours of daylight

The quality (or colour) of daylight can vary considerably according to the time of day, prevailing weather conditions, time of year and latitude. With some forethought, however, most kinds of lighting conditions can be exploited to take pleasing photographs.

taking the temperature Colour temperature describes the colour of light and is measured in degrees Kelvin. A warm or reddish light has a low colour temperature, and a cold or bluish light has a high colour temperature. Colour film is usually balanced for white light with a colour temperature of 5,500 degrees Kelvin, the kind of light that would be expected on a

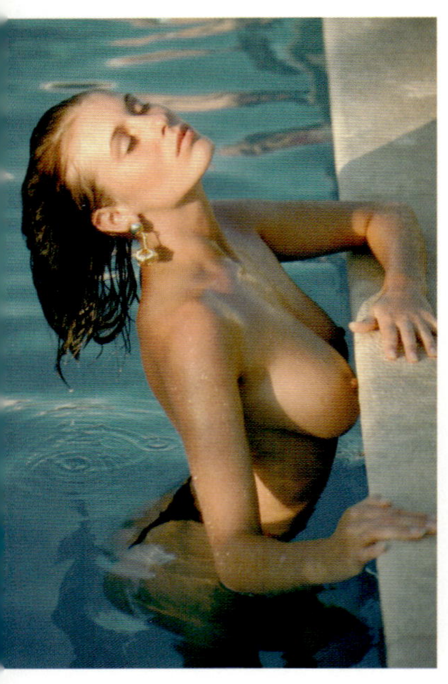

ABOVE: **Evening light.** Late evenings sometimes afford the best light of all. About an hour or so before the sun sets, everything can be bathed in a wonderful soft golden light that is ideal for the nude and glamour photographer. (MINOLTA 8000i; 75–300mm ZOOM LENS; 1/125 sec at f/5.6; KODACHROME 64.)

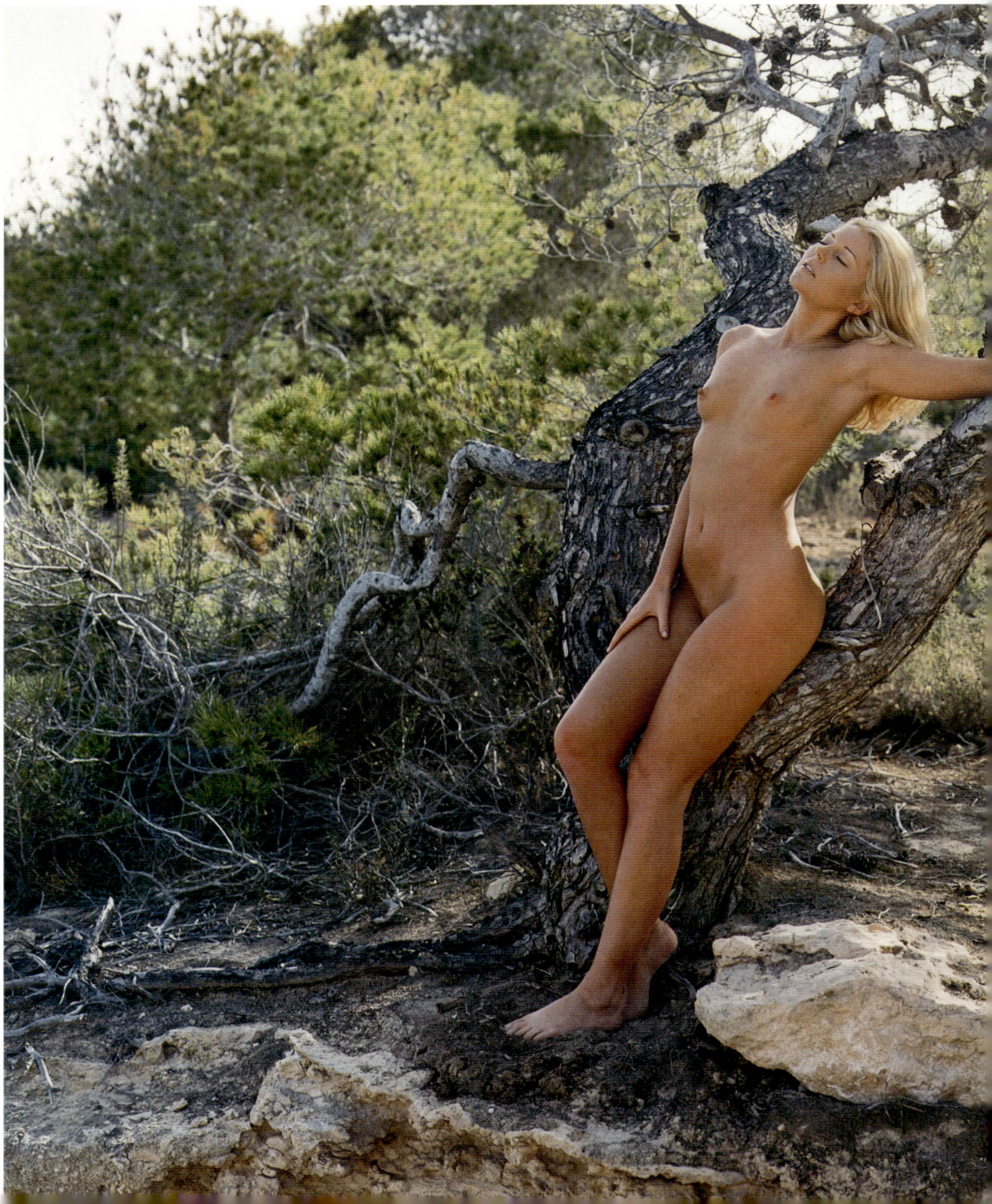

summer's day at midday. Studio flash is close to this standard. After the sun has risen, early morning offers the possibility of a warm or delicate silvery light (around 4,000–5,000 degrees Kelvin), which can give pleasing results, though these conditions may quickly disappear. Midday sun usually gives light with a colour temperature close to 5,500 degrees Kelvin, but harsh shadows limit the types of image that can be shot unless methods such as fill-in flash or reflector boards are used. On location, this is a time to relax and wait until later in the day, or a time to try shadow shots (see pages 86–7). Late afternoon on warm summer or autumn days is a favourite time for photography, when the sun is low and the light is a rich golden colour (3,500 degrees Kelvin or lower). Cold, hazy and overcast days will invariably give colder light (6,000–10,000 degrees Kelvin) and necessitate the use of a warm-up filter. At altitude or when shooting snow, additional UV filtration is advisable.

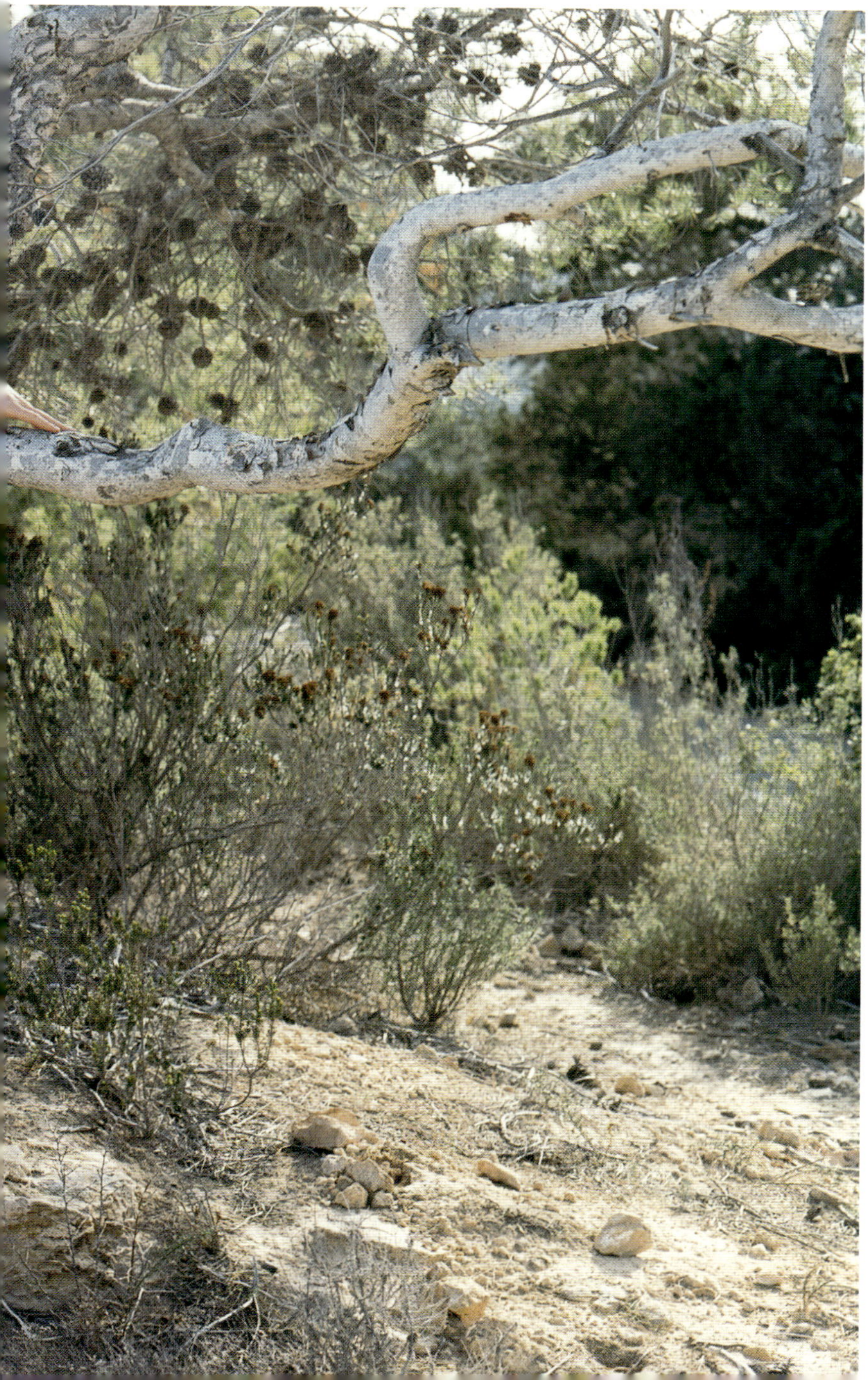

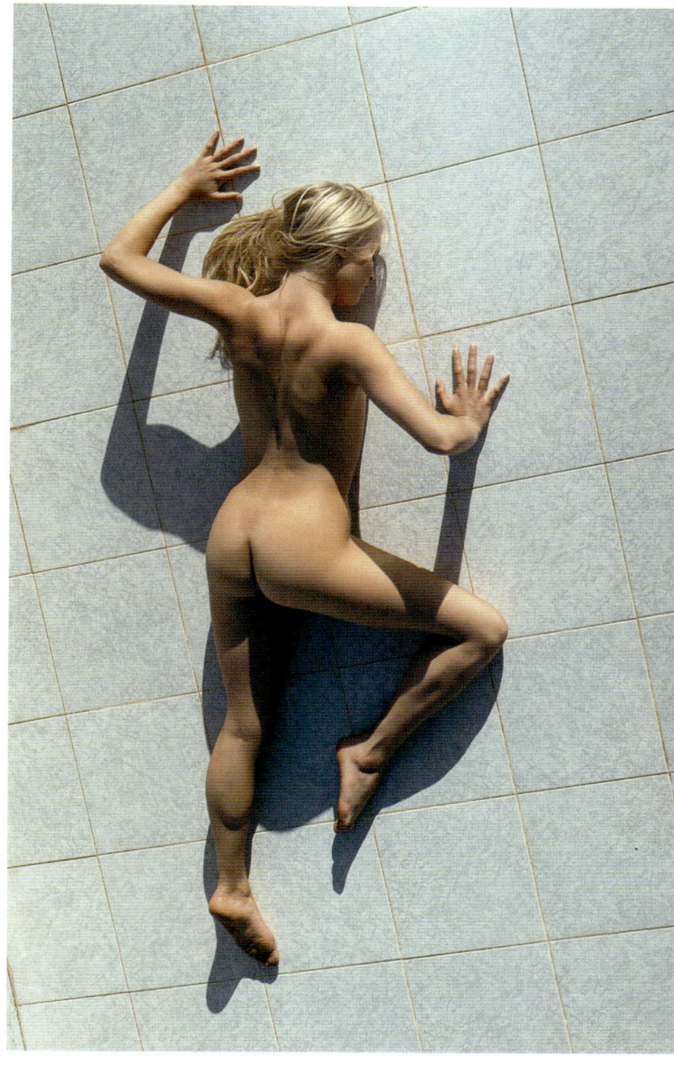

ABOVE: **Midday shadows.** Shooting at midday, when the sun is high in the sky, can cause many problems with hard shadows. Here, the harsh light and contrast is exploited to create a striking image that utilizes the model's shadow. (BRONICA ETRSi; 150mm LENS; 1/250 sec at f/8; KODAK PORTRA 160NC.)

LEFT: **Morning light.** Early morning light can impart a cool, airy feel to a scene. In this image, the sun is rising behind the model and cloud cover is light. Contrast is not too high, giving good detail in all parts of the image. (BRONICA ETRSi; 150mm LENS; 1/125 sec at f/11; KODAK PORTRA 160NC.)

Quality and direction of light

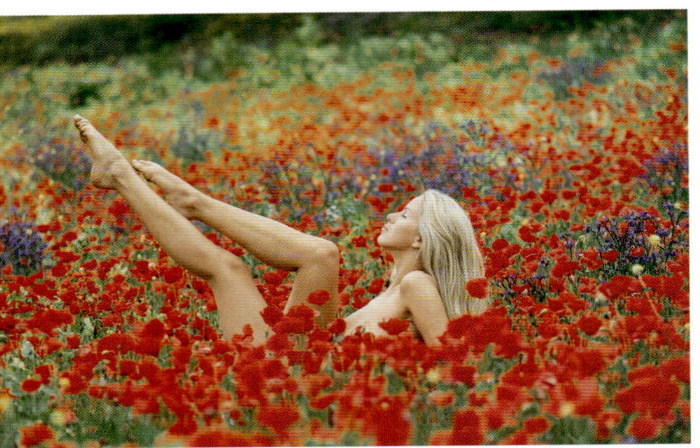

ABOVE: **Low-contrast lighting.** A bright day with cloud cover was used to provide soft, low-contrast lighting conditions ideal for this romantic image.
(BRONICA ETRSi; 150mm LENS; 1/125 sec at f/8; KODAK PORTRA 160VC.)

BELOW: **Dappled light.** Diffuse lighting conditions were essential to create the atmospheric character of this delightful composition.
(BRONICA ETRSi; 150mm LENS; 1/60 sec at f/5.6; KODAK PORTRA 160NC.)

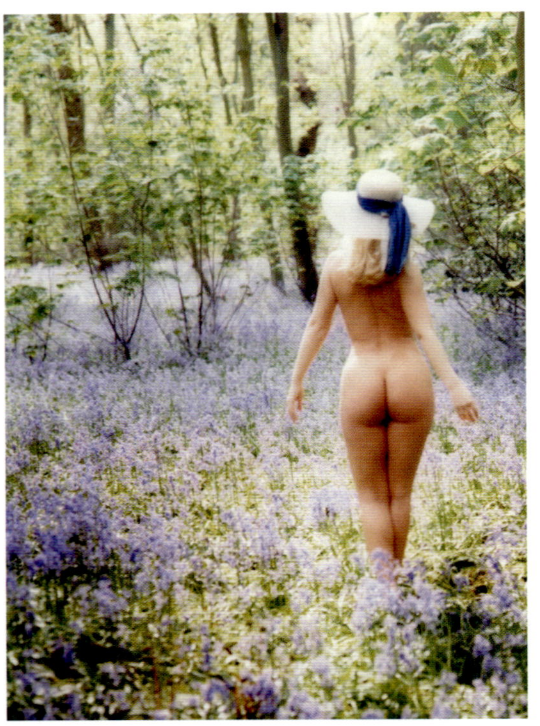

With outdoor locations, the quality of light and type of lighting conditions can have an enormous impact on the photographic results. Overcast days often lead to dull pictures, and bright sunny days to high-contrast images fit only for the waste bin. Quality of light is difficult to describe in words, but is best summed up as a favourable combination of all the contributing factors such as colour, intensity, direction and ambience. With experience, photographers learn to recognize and exploit good light quality when they see it. Lighting conditions are a little easier to understand, but both are important.

soft light Perhaps the easiest lighting conditions to cope with are bright days with 70–100 per cent light cloud cover. Sunlight is reflected inside the clouds and the resultant light is soft and even. This type of light is reminiscent of that delivered by a large softbox and will give similar results. Soft light levels are usually quite adequate for good exposure and the contrast is relatively low, leading to the creation of images with good highlight and shadow detail.

diffuse light Diffuse light is similar to soft light, but is a more local effect. The sunlight may be bright and strong, but is intercepted in some way that causes the light to be reflected and consequently softened. A good example is the type of light that may be encountered in woodland, especially in spring, where new leaves have the effect of moderating the amount of light available. Light coming through a window and reflecting off white walls is another type of diffused light that the photographer can use to advantage.

high-contrast light Deep shadows (especially around the eyes and under the nose and chin) and burnt-out highlights often coincide with high-contrast lighting conditions, such as those found at midday. When the sun is bright, the model is prone to squint, so have your model face away from the sun and use fill-in flash or reflectors to counteract shadows, or move your model into a light but shadier area.

back light Sunlight behind a model can result in a beautiful rim-lit effect if used with care. Position the model at an angle so that the sun is not directly behind the subject and pointing towards the lens. Shield the lens from flare by using a lens hood or by shooting from a position where the camera is not in direct sunlight. Spot metering from the model will ensure correct exposure.

COPING WITH CONTRE-JOUR LIGHTING

One of the most difficult outdoor lighting conditions that the photographer has to contend with is contre-jour, or direct backlighting. When the sun is directly behind the model, the contrast ratio of the light falling on the camera is very high and an average light-meter reading will result in underexposure of the model with the consequence that a silhouette image is obtained. There are two ways to overcome this problem. Taking a light reading from an average-lit area of the model's body with a spot meter (many cameras have a spot meter option) will ensure that the model is exposed correctly, though the background will be highly overexposed. Counterbalancing the backlight with fill-in flash or by using a reflector or mirror to bounce light onto the front of the model will usually result in a good overall exposure. Use a good lens hood to prevent flare.

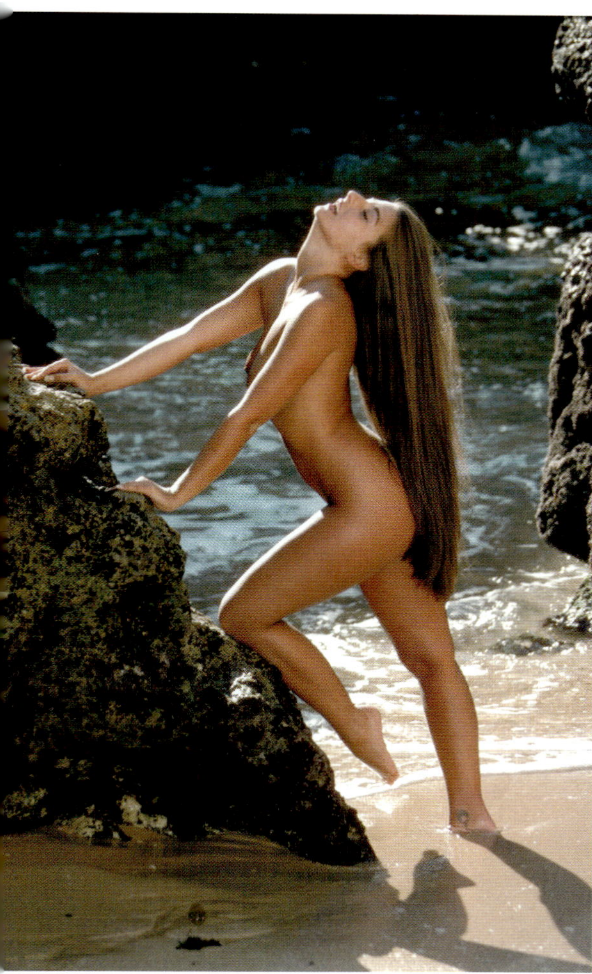

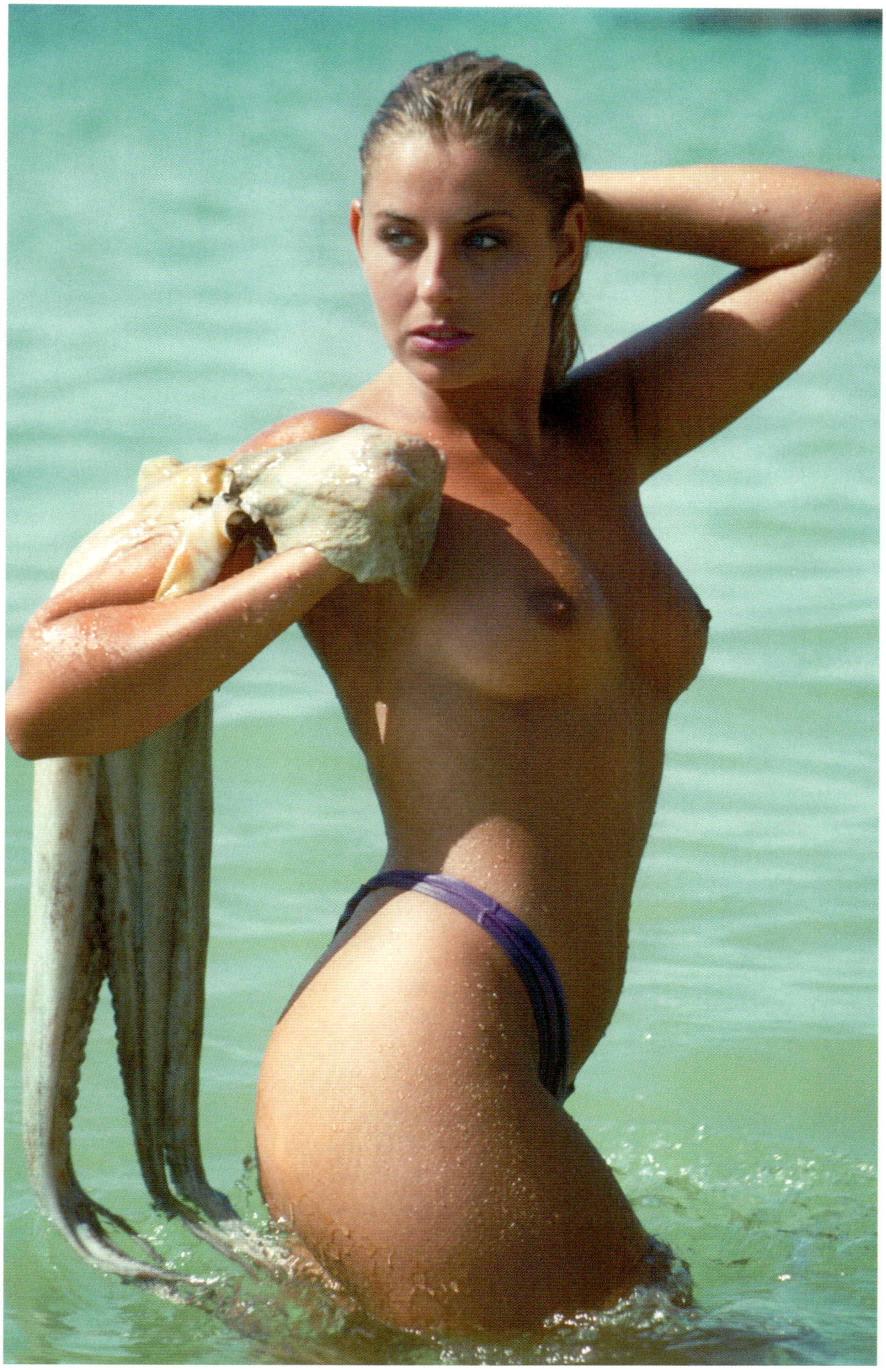

ABOVE: **Striking contrasts.** For backlit shots, take a light-meter reading from an average-lit area of the model to prevent underexposure. This image was spot metered from the model's left side. Alternatively, use fill-in flash or a reflector to add light to the front. (MINOLTA 8000i; 100mm LENS; 1/125 sec at f/11; KODACHROME 64.)

RIGHT: **Contrasty light.** A cloudless sky and strong mid-morning sunlight was essential to this high-contrast image with bright highlights and deep shadows. When using transparency film, bracket the exposure by 1/2 a stop to ensure a well-exposed result or use fill-in flash to eliminate shadows. (MINOLTA 8000i; 75–300mm ZOOM LENS; 1/250 sec at f/11; KODAK EKTACHROME 100.)

Natural window light

OPPOSITE: **Patterned light.** Golden, early- morning light coming through a leaded-light window created this moody image. Exposure was based on the highlights, throwing the background into deep shadow. (BRONICA ETRSi; 75mm LENS; 1/60 sec at f/8; KODAK PORTRA 160VC.)

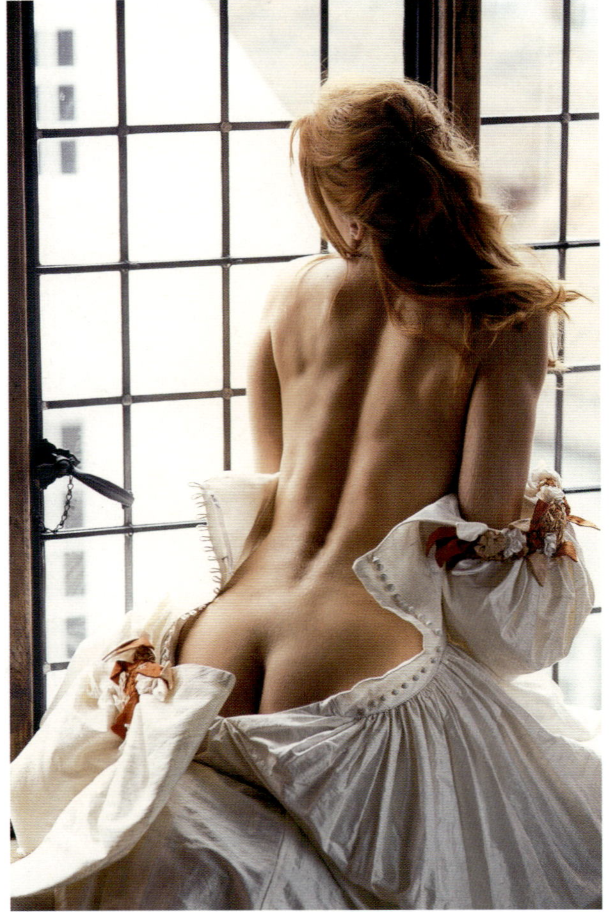

ABOVE: **Balanced light.** The set-up for this shot is shown in the diagram at right. To prevent the model from becoming a silhouette, inside light was added to balance outside light (f/8). A softbox, set at f/5.6, was positioned to the right of the model and used as a fill light. A reflector was placed behind the model to throw light back from both the flash and the window. (BRONICA ETRSi; 150mm LENS; 1/125 sec at f/8; KODAK PORTRA 160VC.)

Windows provide an excellent setting in which to frame a model. However, care must be taken when setting up a photograph in this situation. Silhouettes are often obtained because contrast is usually higher than it first appears. The closer the model is to the window, the greater this effect will be. Reducing contrast is the best way to overcome this problem. Covering the window with translucent paper or a fine-mesh material can help reduce the outside light, while the use of reflectors to bounce back the daylight can increase the internal light source. This may, in turn, be supplemented by flash, preferably bounced to give a more natural look. Including the window in the photograph is the most difficult scenario, as the photographer has to allow for the intensity of exterior light as well as interior light. In such situations, it is best to balance the outside light intensity with that inside by using flash.

subtle imagery Light coming into a room early in the morning or late in the afternoon will enter at a low angle and can be used to create subtle images with varied shadows and patterns. Leaded lights, net curtains (see page 87) and Venetian blinds are excellent for pattern images. Windows will receive differing light at certain times of the day, so study where the light falls and where it travels to with time before attempting the shot with your model. Light in these situations does not stay in one position for very long, so you have to work quickly to get results. Beware of reflections that may ruin the image where window glass is in the picture. When using flash, be particularly careful that umbrella reflectors from the flash units are not in shot. Their reflection may not seem very obvious at first glance, but if present they will stand out distinctly in the image when the units are fired.

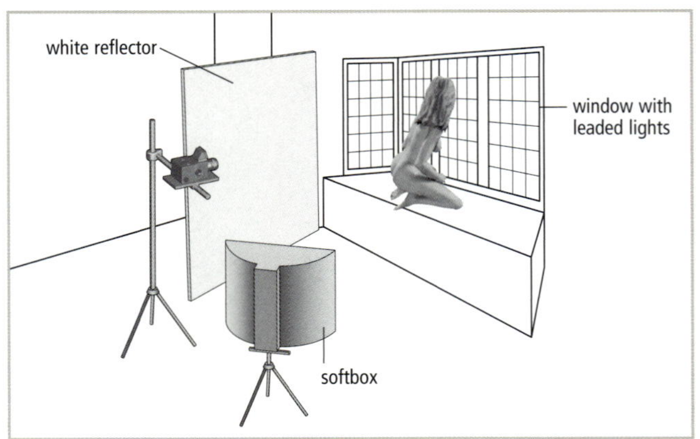

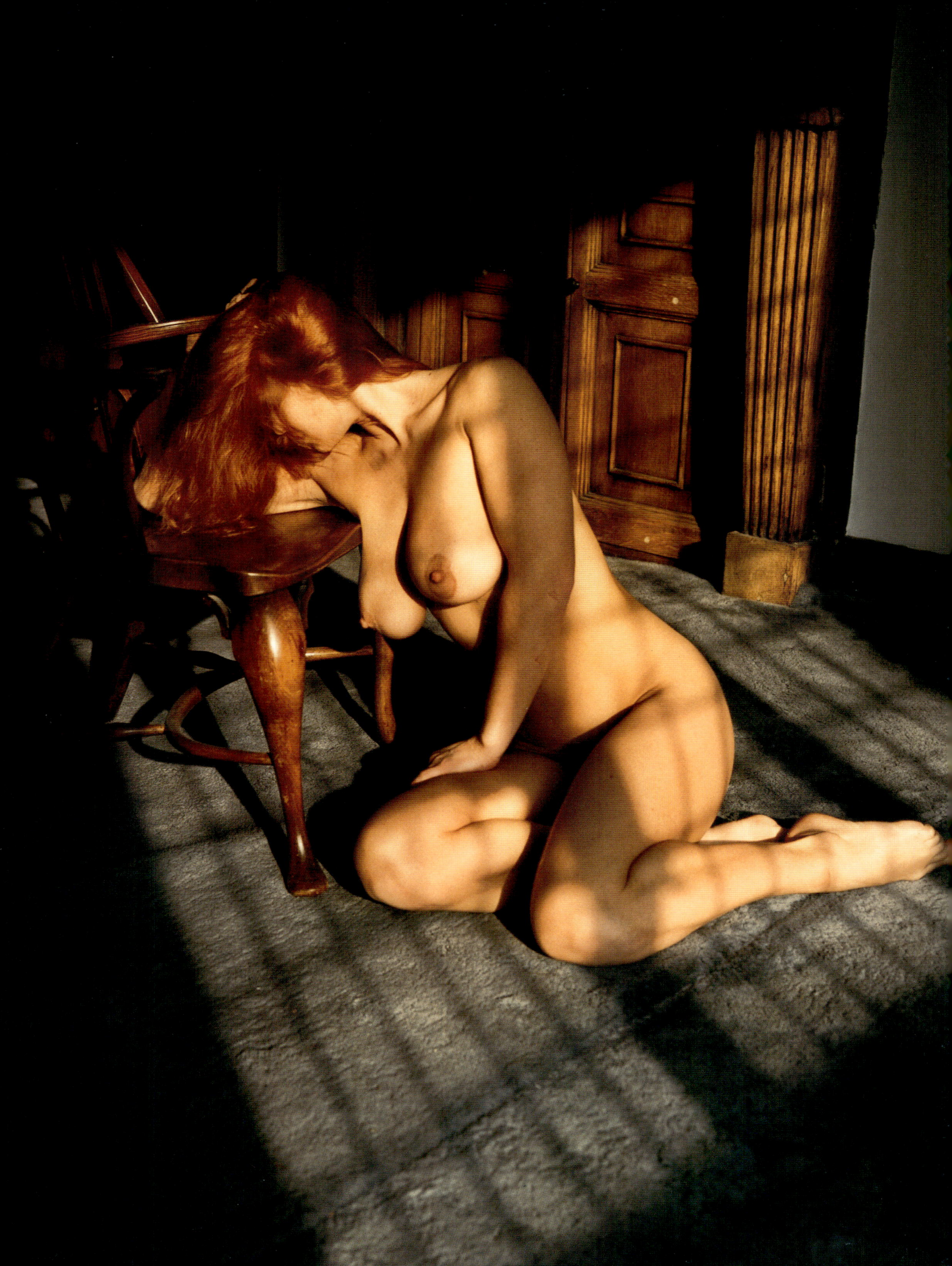

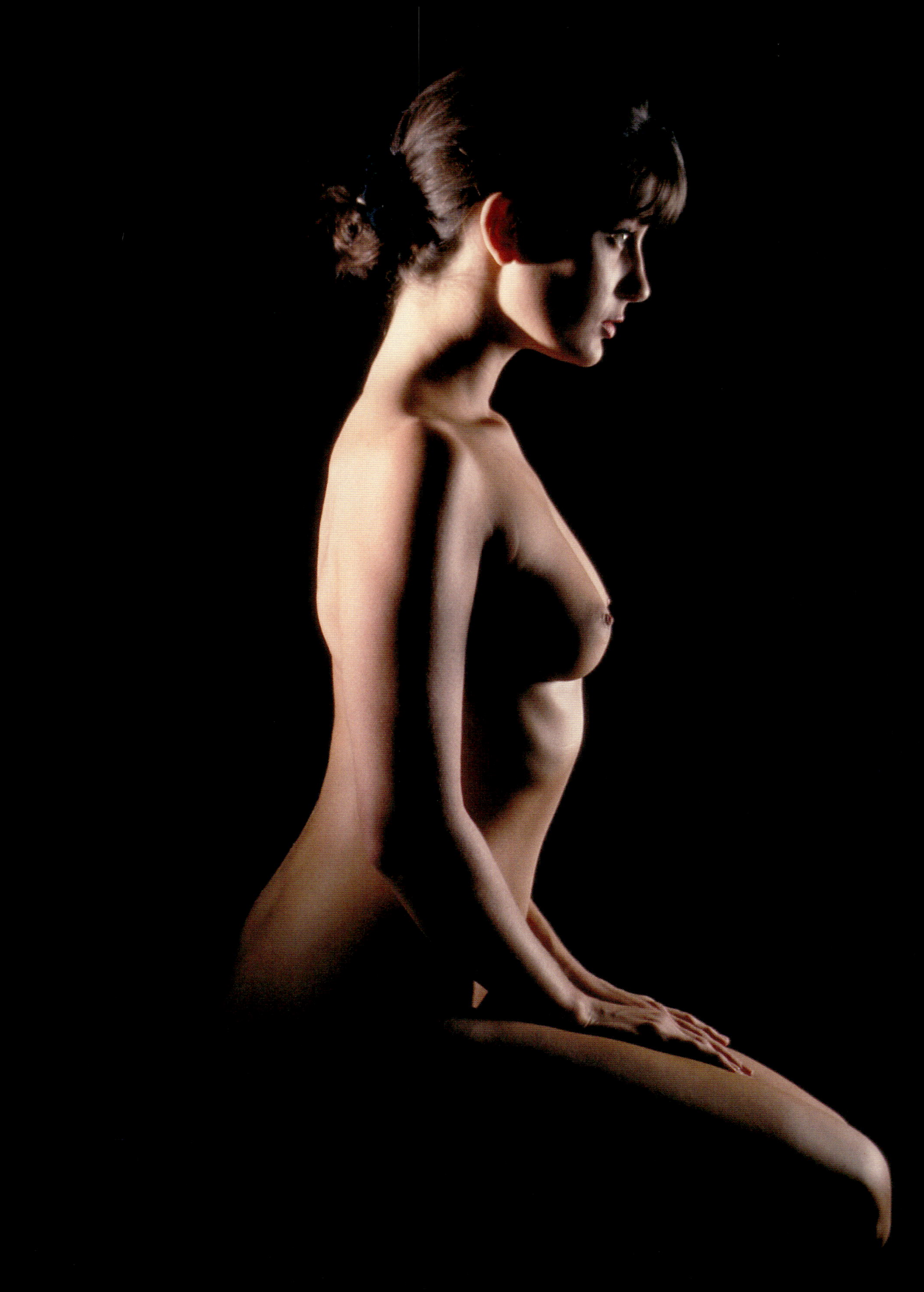

Low-key lighting

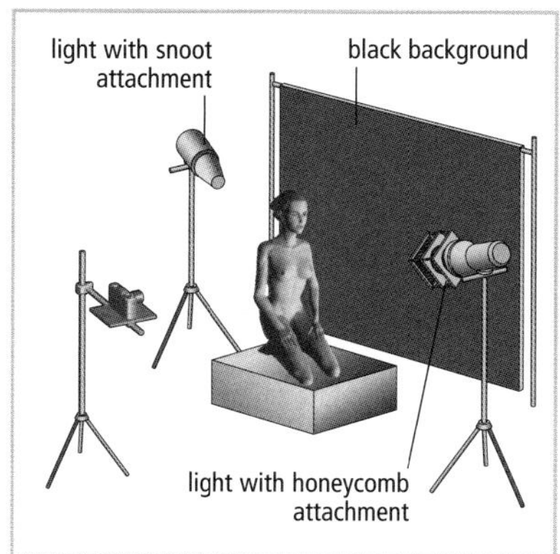

OPPOSITE: **Selective highlights.** Two lights, one with a snoot attachment and one with a honeycomb attachment, were positioned to highlight selectively the front and back of the model (see diagram). This creates a wonderfully low-key image. (MINOLTA 8000i; 35–80mm LENS; 1/125 sec at f/8; KODACHROME 64.

The type of lighting that is used to take a photograph can have a tremendous bearing on the mood and general ambience of the scene depicted. Two readily recognizable lighting styles are called high key (see pages 48–9) and low key. Photographs that contain a predominance of dark tones, colours and shadows are termed low key. These tend to give a feeling of mystery, secrecy or even foreboding. There is usually some part of the image lost in shadow, which leaves the viewer to imagine what is hidden. This style is well suited to the nude photographer wishing to convey an artistic impression of the model. It is particularly suitable for monochrome work or colour images where the colour range is limited (eg, skin tones only).

the minimalist approach
Lighting for low-key images in the studio is relatively straightforward and excellent results can be achieved with the minimum of lighting equipment. Low-key settings are often selectively lit, perhaps using only one or two lights that illuminate a small part of the model, and are characterized by a high-contrast range. To achieve this, it is best to use narrow beams of light rather than the wide-angle illumination obtained with an umbrella reflector or softbox. Attachments called barn doors, snoots and honeycombs, which restrict the flow of light in different ways, are ideal for making low-key images. Alternatively, light can be restricted with polystyrene boards or similar items. Light and expose for highlight areas and let the shadows take care of themselves. Try using coloured gels over one or more of the lights for interesting creative effects. See pages 36, 45, 53, 55, 86, 88–9 and 96 for further examples of low-key images. Many opportunities to take low-key images also arise with daylight, especially in

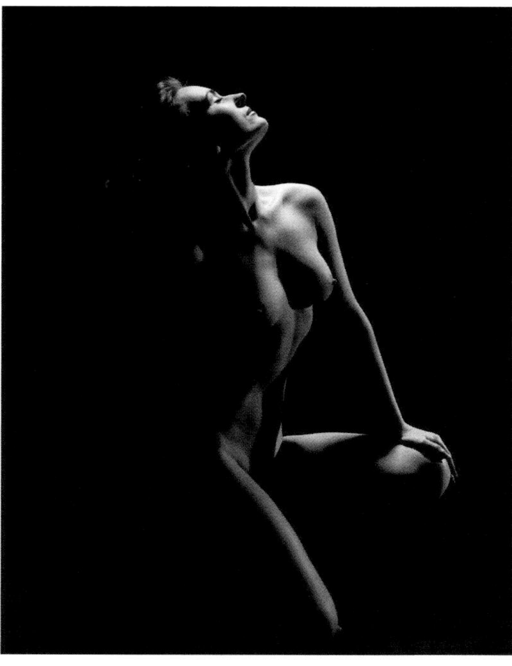

RIGHT: **Dramatic detail.** A single light fitted with barn doors was used to pick out details on the front of the model, while leaving her back in deep shadow. (MINOLTA 8000i; 100mm LENS; 1/125 sec at f/5.6; ILFORD FP4.)

situations where there is high contrast, such as when using direct window light (see pages 44–5). Allowing your camera automatically to meter a bright window scene viewed from inside the room will usually result in a fairly low-key composition, without any effort from the photographer. Ordinary scenes can take on a low-key look if you purposely meter for the highlights and ignore the shadow areas. The key of a printed monochrome image can often be controlled and manipulated to some extent in the darkroom by the use of different paper grades and printing densities.

High-key lighting

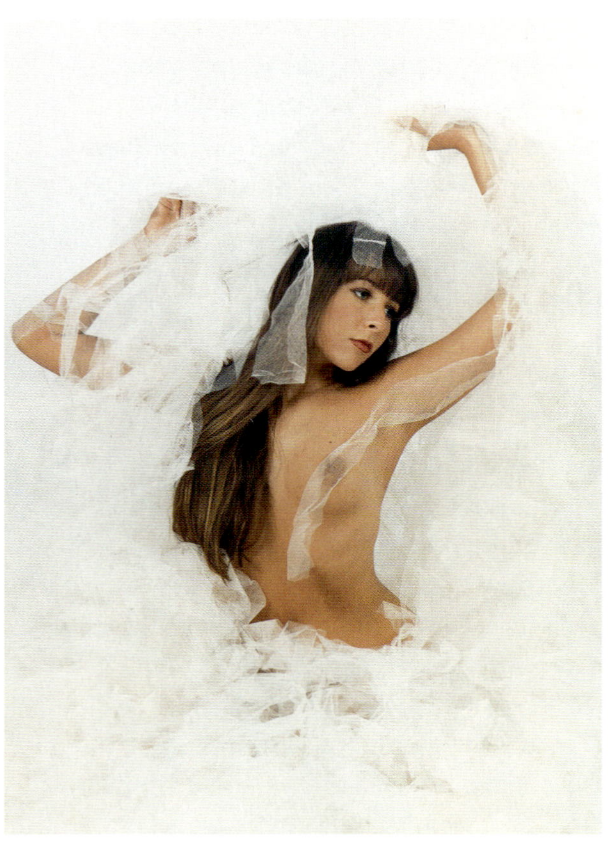

ABOVE: **Keyed-up image.** White netting cut into strips was used to reflect light and give a high-key appearance to this image.
(MINOLTA 8000i; 100mm LENS; 1/125 sec at f/11; KODAK VPS160.)

OPPOSITE: **Tent of light.** As shown in the diagram, this soft, high-key 'grooming' image was obtained by surrounding the model with a white light tent constructed from a parachute and two silver reflectors and illuminated from the outside by two lights. A softbox was used to light the front of the model.
(BRONICA ETRSi; 150mm LENS; 1/125 sec at f/16; ILFORD FP4.)

The previous section showed how low-key images can be used to convey a certain dark or mysterious mood. High-key images are quite the opposite. They are brightly lit and dominated by light tones and colours, with few dark or black tones, bringing an altogether different mood to the picture. A feeling of openness, lightness and purity are a few of the attributes of the high-key style. Here, it is the detail in the highlight areas that tends to be lost rather than the shadow detail in low-key images. This style is well suited to the photographer who wishes to impart an impression of youthfulness, prettiness and virginal beauty to the model and often works best with fair-skinned, blonde subjects. High-key portraits are popular where highlights of the face are on the verge of being lost, giving the skin a smooth white, alabaster-like appearance. This technique can do wonders if the model has a flawed skin texture. Infrared film, which tends to give soft, grainy images, is an ideal medium for high-key nudes (see page 115).

high-key imagery

In order to produce a high-key image, it is best to use soft, even light, preferably diffused through a light tent and/or bounced off reflector boards or white walls. Dark backgrounds should be avoided. Some studio photographers encase their subject almost completely in white polyboards to obtain even illumination all around the model. An incident-light meter-reading will not take account of the high reflectivity of a very white set-up. To deal with this situation, either measure the reflected light or meter for the darkest areas in the picture. If using transparency film, bracket by 1/2 to 11/2 stops depending on how reflective the set-up is. This is not so important with negative materials, especially monochrome, as much can be done in the darkroom (such as printing at different grades and densities) to achieve the desired result.

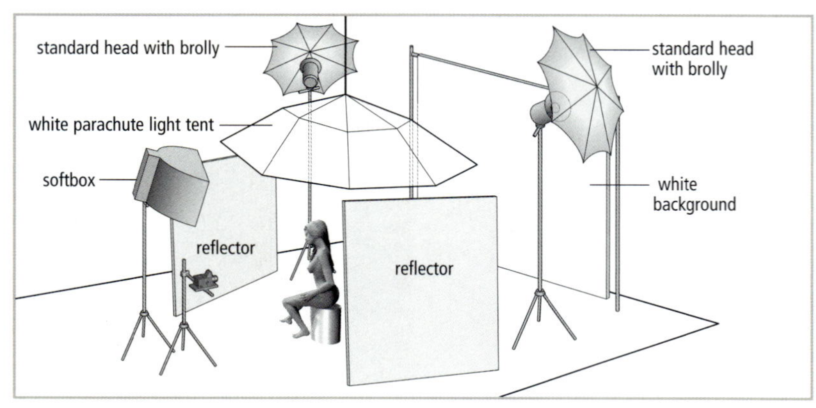

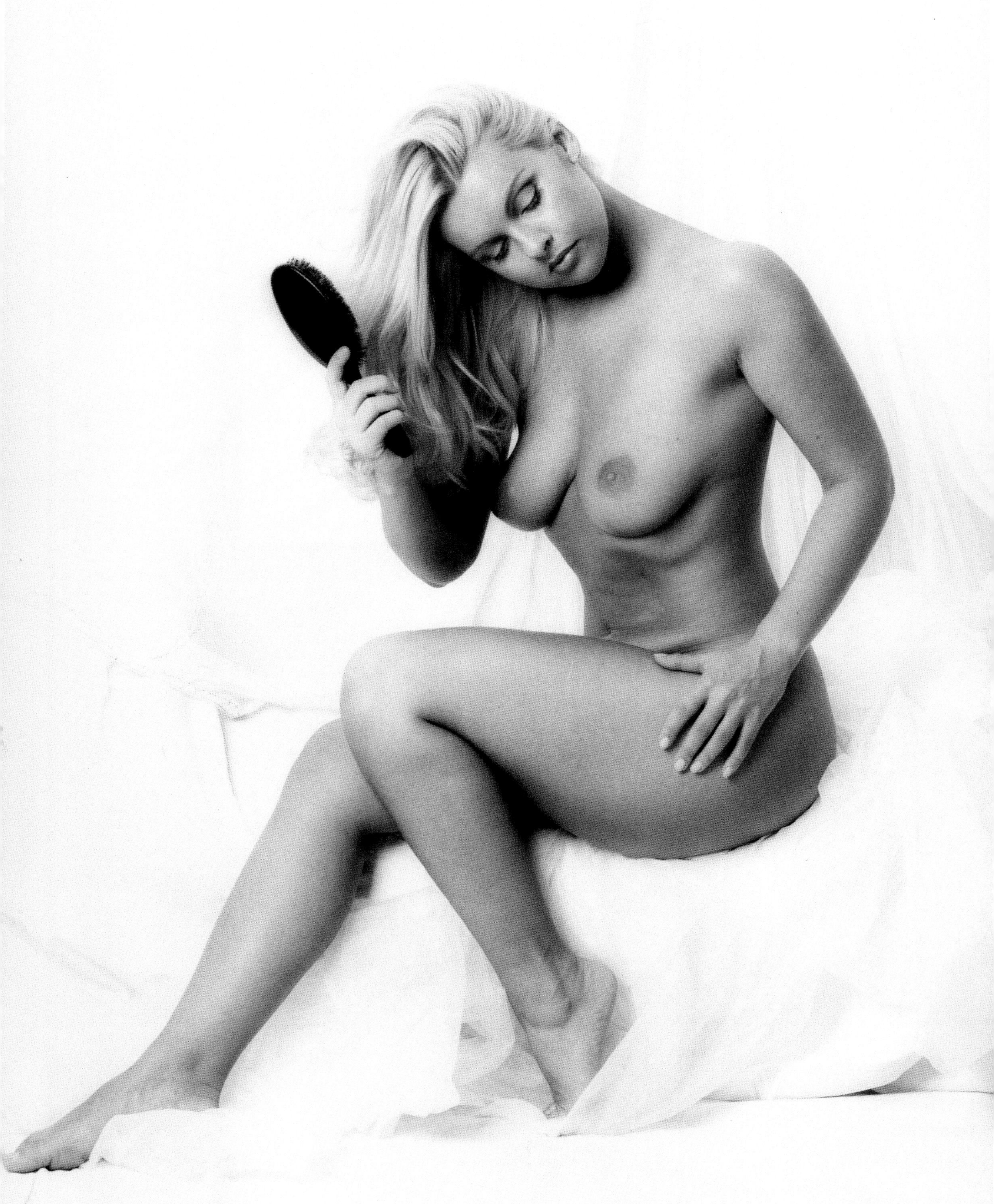

Even lighting

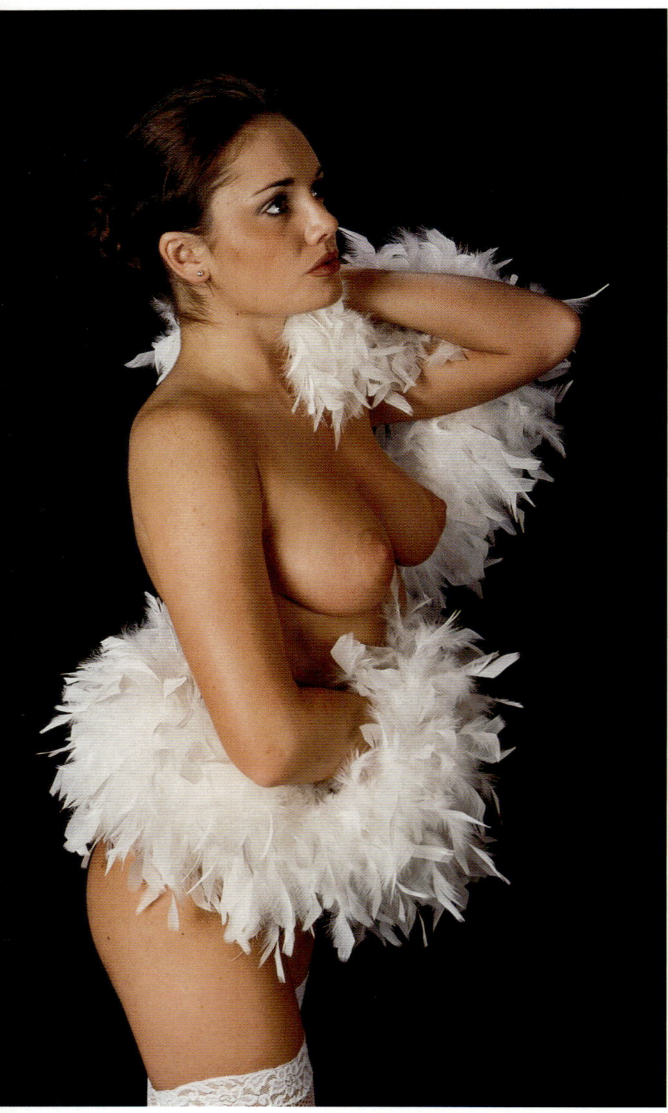

BELOW: **Filling with light.** Using one light as the main (key) light and reducing the intensity of the second light by 1–2 stops so that it becomes a fill light produces greater definition to the subject's curves.
(BRONICA ETRSi; 150mm LENS; 1/125 sec at f/8; KODAK PORTRA 160NC.)

Glamour photographers often use even lighting to light their subjects as this gives a bright, airy look to the pictures with little or no shadow. However, modelling is frequently absent and the images can look rather bland and uninteresting with this style of lighting, unless some effect lights are added, such as a hair light. Although this style can be quite flattering to a model in a beauty shot, images produced in this way may have little in the way of mood or ambience to commend them, and this method is generally not recommended to the photographer who seeks a more artistic or creative image.

Even lighting is very straightforward to set up. It generally consists of two flash units fitted with umbrella reflectors or softboxes at an angle of 45 degrees, positioned to each side of and equidistant from the model. The power output of each light is nominally set equal, which means that the same amount of light strikes the subject from both sides, cancelling out any shadow detail on the model. This type of lighting set-up invariably gives an average contrast range, so direct incident-light metering usually gives problem-free exposures. Check the reading from each light individually and then from both lights in unison. The readings should be the same.

varying the light source

Reducing the output of one of the lights by 1–2 stops or moving one of the lights closer or further away from the model will often give a more pleasing modelling effect, creating more shape and form to the subject. Move the lights, observing the effects, through different angles and distances from the model until satisfied with the results. Try varying the vertical position of the lights as well as the lateral orientation, and don't be afraid to experiment with unusual lighting set-ups from time to time. Look for and find a good combination that suits your needs. This approach will help you to develop your own personal style and technique.

OPPOSITE: **Glamour set-up.** Two umbrella flash units at 45 degrees to the subject have produced a bright, airy image with little shadow or modelling. This lighting set-up, shown in the diagram, is much used in glamour photography.
(MINOLTA 8000i; 35–80mm LENS; 1/125 sec at f/11; KODAK VPS160.)

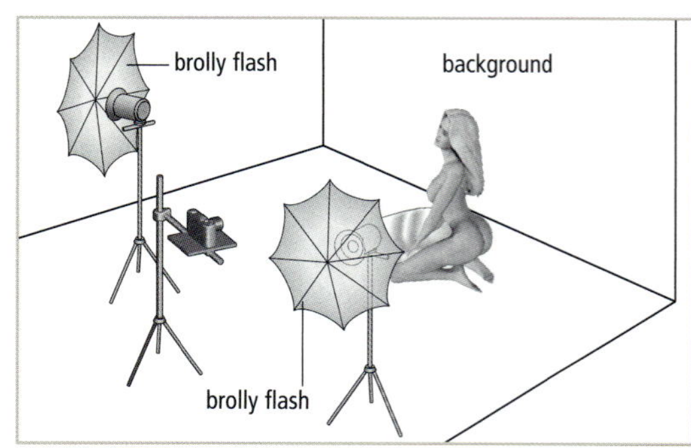

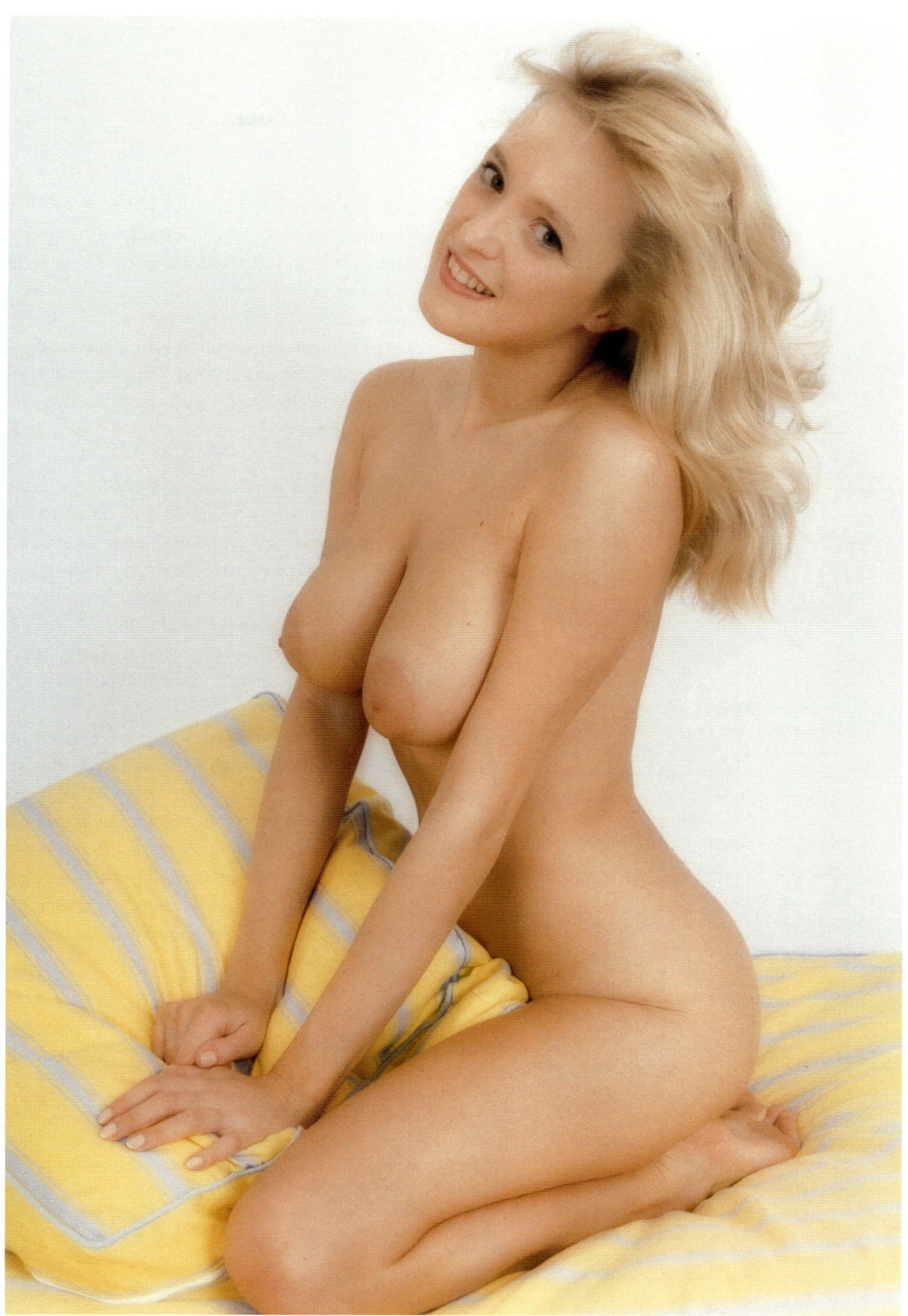

Harsh lighting

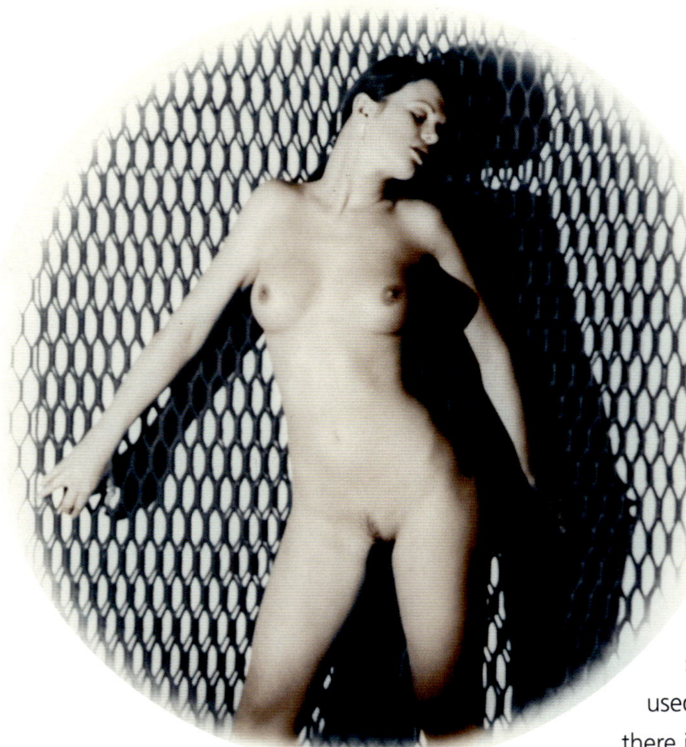

ABOVE: **Focused lighting.** Harsh light from a Fresnel lens gave a high-contrast image and hard shadow on the studio background. Texture was added to the print and contrast reduced by using a screen at the printing stage and selective split toning with sepia and iron-blue toners. A circular printing mask was also used.
(BRONICA ETRSi; 150mm LENS; 1/125 sec at f/16; ILFORD FP4.)

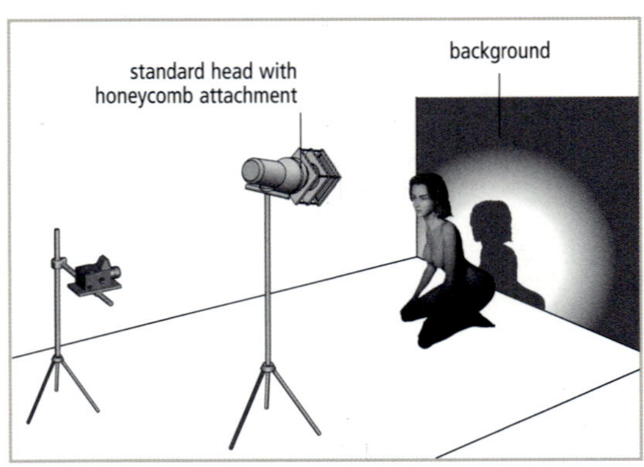

OPPOSITE: **Stark reflection.** A single light with a metal dish reflector was used to create this stark image, as shown in the diagram. The shadow on the background adds to the dark mood.
(BRONICA ETRSi; 150mm LENS; 1/125 sec at f/5.6; KODAK GPX160.)

Bright, strong directional lighting is characteristically harsh and often unforgiving, but can sometimes be used to create dramatic and unusual images. Light under these conditions can be difficult to control and the usual modus operandi is to try to reduce contrast to make the outcome more predictable. When combined with an appropriate pose, however, harsh light can be harnessed to give some very striking results.

studio Harsh lighting conditions can be created in the studio by using a single flash unit. A light with a plain-metal dish reflector will give a wide band of harsh light, while a tube or cone attachment will concentrate the light into more specific areas. This is not unlike the sort of set-up that would be used for a low-key scenario. Metering is relatively straightforward as there is only one light source. Fresnel lenses, which can be focused on the subject or background, also provide a hard light source.

open air Harsh outdoor lighting is commonly encountered during the height of summer. It is rarely useful for portrait or glamour work as strong, deep shadows are formed. However, to the creative nude photographer, shadows mean that stark, graphic images can be made, giving character and interest. Try posing your model so that she casts shadows with her body onto walls (see page 86), floors (see page 41) and other objects in order to create an image with intriguing patterns. Objects casting deep shadows across the model's body can also result in similarly striking images (see page 96).

ALTERNATIVE LIGHT SOURCES

Harsh light can be achieved in many ways for use on different occasions. Some of the light sources that can be used are projectors, with or without images (see pages 88–9), photoflood lamps, theatre spotlights and some of the more powerful torches. Car headlights are particularly effective for outdoor shots at night or during the early evening (twilight). These sources, however, are usually of relatively low power compared to studio flash, so a fast film or long exposure is often necessary when using them. Try using them with coloured gels for particularly bizarre effects.

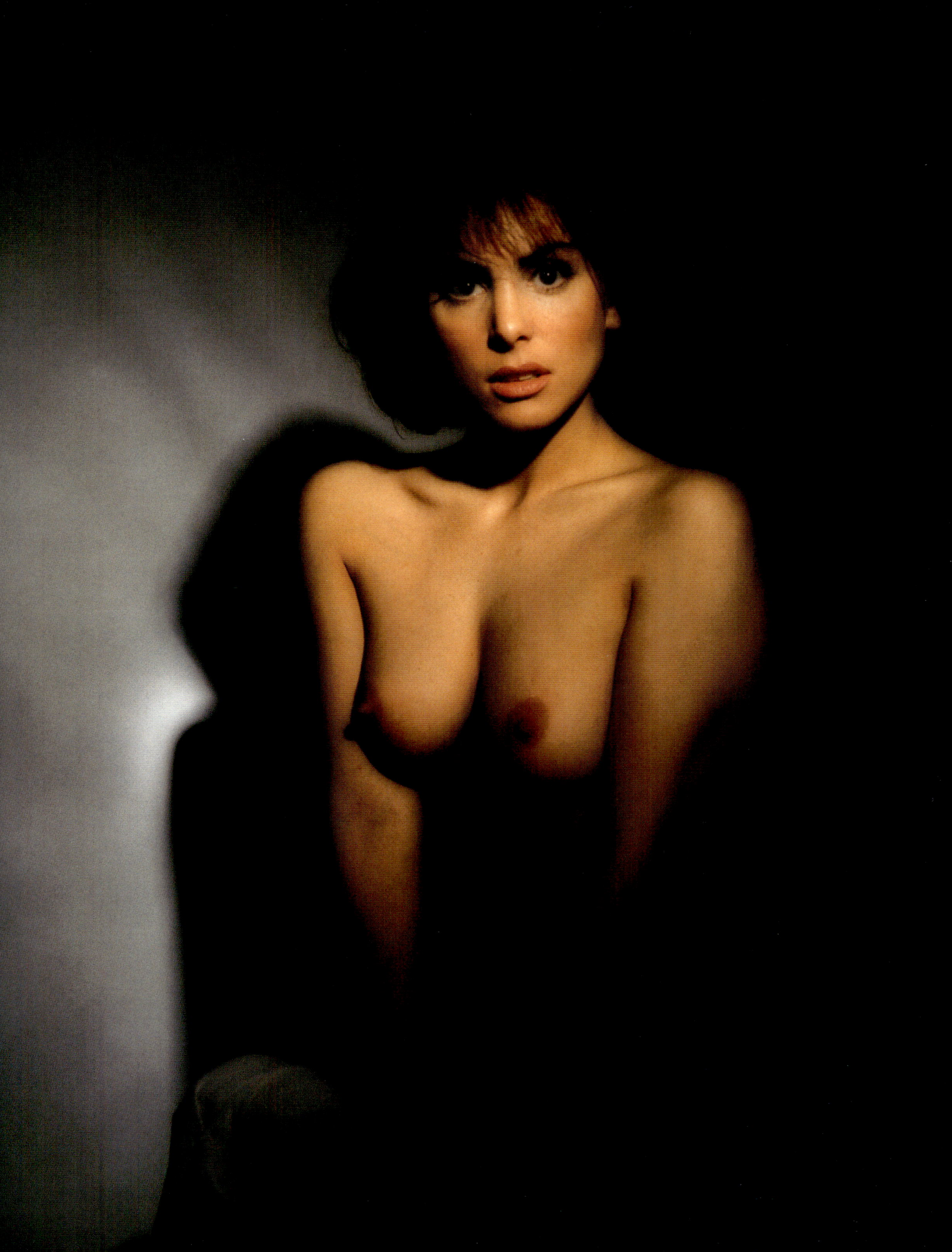

Lighting for edge effects

Beautiful effects showing the shape and form of the nude can be achieved by using outline shadow or light to illuminate the model.

black-edge effect
Outlining the figure with a black edge can be an effective tool in creative nude photography. In this case, light is prevented from reaching the edges of the body. This scenario is best attempted with a light or white background for optimum visual effect. The model is placed between two black boards, and the illumination, preferably a softbox, is directed at the model and parallel to the boards. The precise positioning of the light in relation to the boards is important if an aesthetically pleasing result is to be attained.

rim lighting
In this technique, the body is outlined with a white (or coloured) rim using a tight beam of directional light to highlight body hairs and surface detail along the edge that is illuminated.

A single flash head with a snoot or barn door attachment is sufficient to create the rim-lit effect. Decide on which part of the model is to be the subject matter (her back, for example) and position her accordingly against a black or dark background.

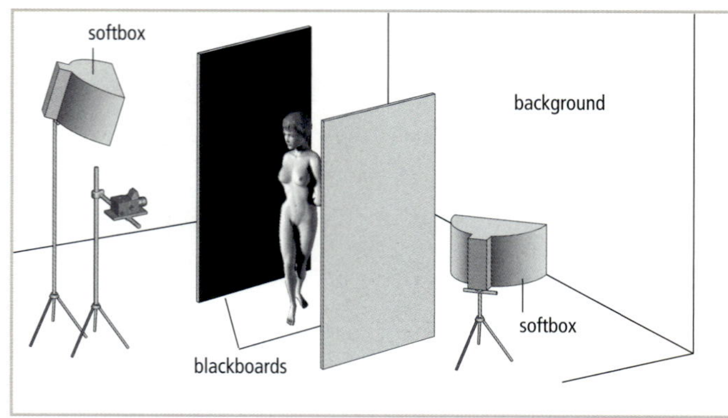

LEFT: **Black outlining.** Black boards absorb light and can be used to create the striking effect of a black edge around the model's body. (BRONICA ETRSi; 150mm LENS; 1/125 sec at f/11; KODAK GPF160.)

ABOVE: **Rim lighting.** By positioning a single snoot light low behind the reclining model – as shown in the diagram at right – a beautifully rim-lit figure study can be created. (BRONICA ETRSi; 150mm LENS; 1/125 sec at f/8; ILFORD FP4.)

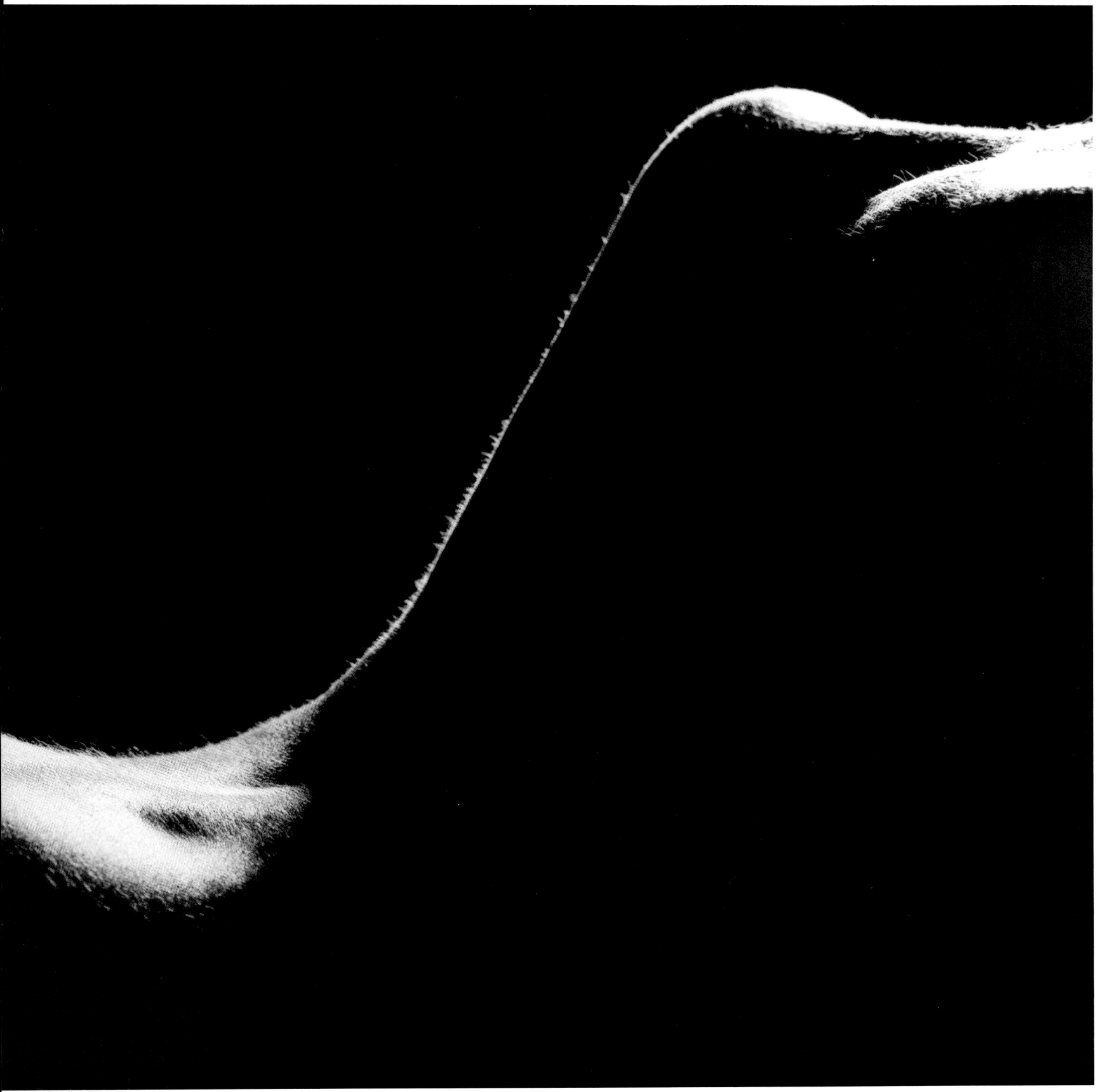

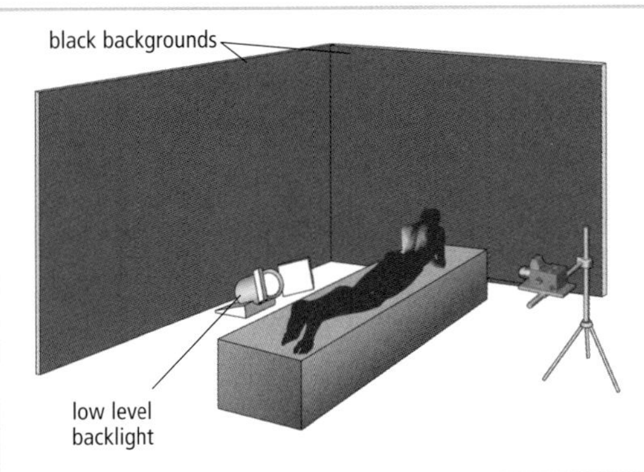

It is important that the model is placed in a comfortable position, as it may take several minutes to optimize the lighting angle. The flash head should be placed in a position behind the model so that the glancing light just illuminates the far edge of the body but does not spill over on to the front of the model. Masking any extraneous light with a black board or cloth will help to avoid lens flare. The light was placed behind, below and to the left of the model in the main image (above). Move the camera rather than the light in order to attain the optimum effect.

Lighting from above

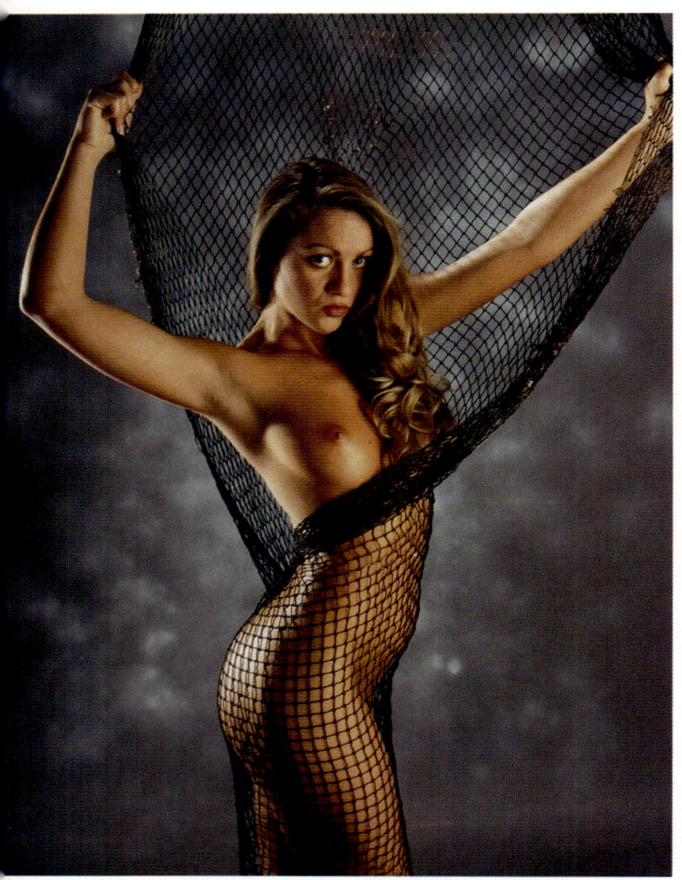

ABOVE: **Four-light set-up.** The main light source was a softbox to the front and right of the model. One effect light, with barn doors, was positioned low and left behind the model to give rim light. Another with a honeycomb was positioned high, right and level with the model to add hair detail. A fourth light illuminated the background.
(BRONICA ETRSi; 150mm LENS; 1/125 sec at f/16; KODAK VPS160.)

OPPOSITE: **Overhead sparkle.** As shown in the diagram, a large softbox was used for the main light source for this shot, with the addition of an overhead light to add a little sparkle to the hair and pick out detail in the netting. A snoot placed above and behind the model, so that light did not spill onto her face, provided the toplighting.
(BRONICA ETRSi; 150mm LENS; 1/125 sec at f/11; KODAK GPX160.)

Toplighting, as used here, is illumination from above the subject – either directly above or above and to the side, front, or back of the model. Lighting a subject solely with direct toplighting in the studio is possible using a large overhead softbox, often called a 'fish fryer' or 'swimming pool', or with lights attached to booms.

The success or failure of this technique very much depends on the pose that the model adopts. For instance, it can be used quite successfully with reclining nudes (see pages 98–9). This type of lighting is rarely flattering to a standing model because deep downward shadows are formed on the face from the nose and chin and the eyebrows can shade the eyes. This can be overcome by asking the model to look up towards the light. However, toplighting is mostly used in conjunction with other illumination as an effect light. It is especially useful as a hair light to add sparkle to a model's hair (see page 101) or to distinguish it from the background, as when photographing a dark-haired model against a dark background. Toplighting can also be used for a similar purpose on any props used in the set-up that may require highlighting.

natural light Illumination from above is frequently encountered in natural light situations – due to the relative position of the sun to the subject – and tends to look more natural than in the studio. Try using angled toplight for creative effects, such as shafts of light coming through a high window or filtered through trees. Ugly shadows formed in the midday sun have been mentioned previously and the effects and remedies are similar to those discussed (see pages 40–3 and also page 108 in this context). Alternatively use reflectors and/or fill-in flash to dissipate any unwanted shadows.

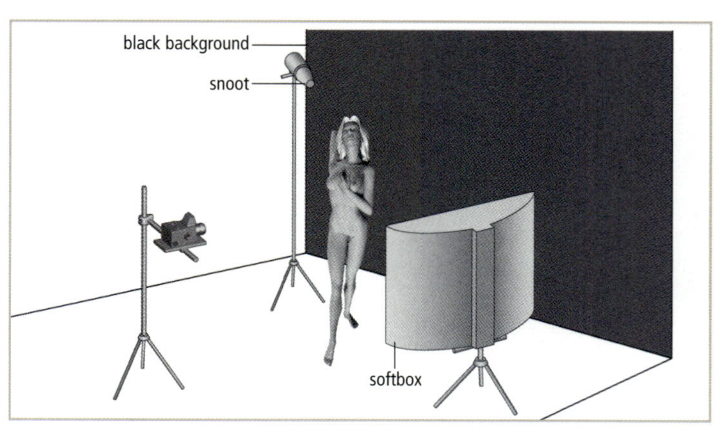

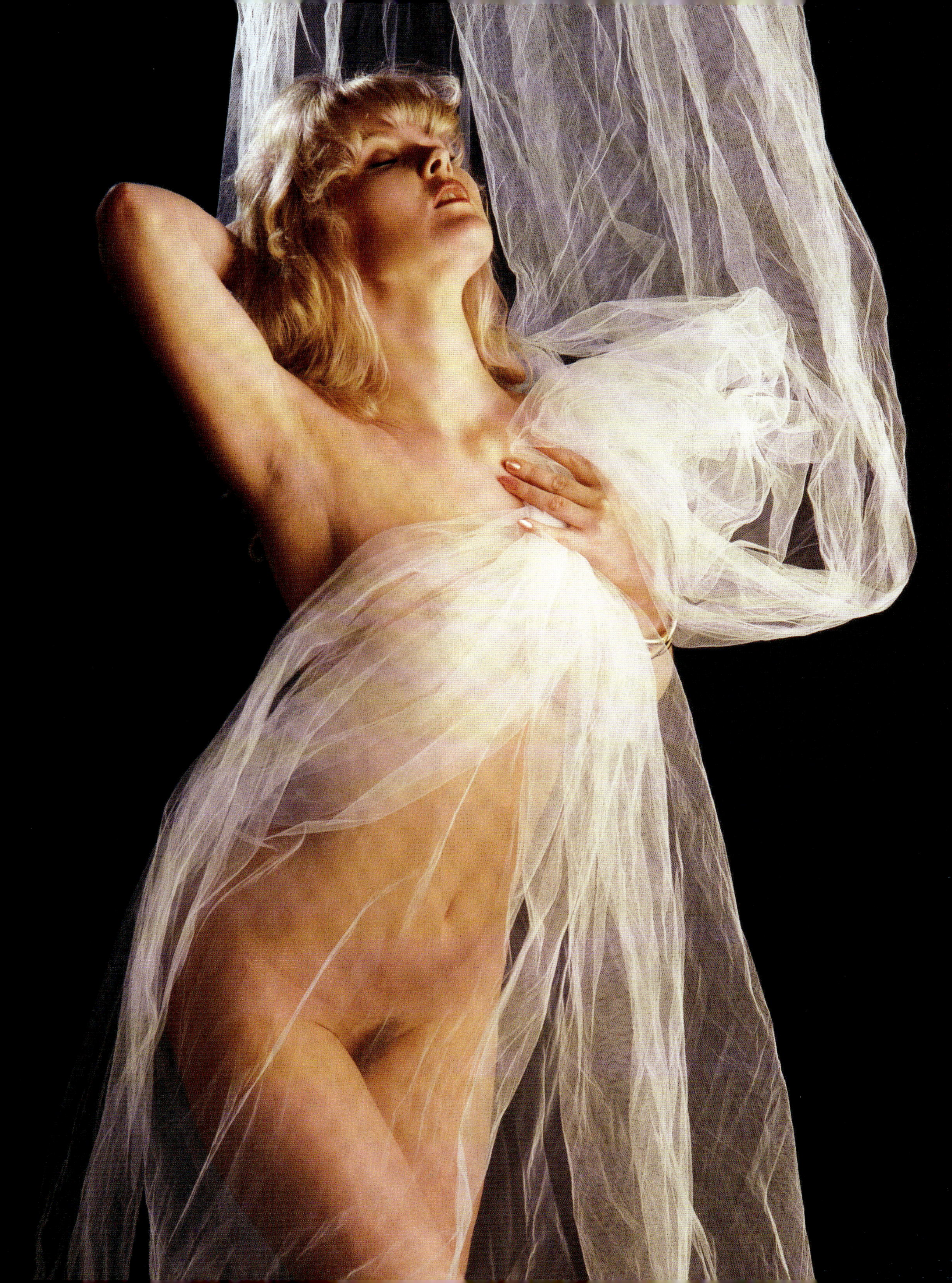

Lighting from below

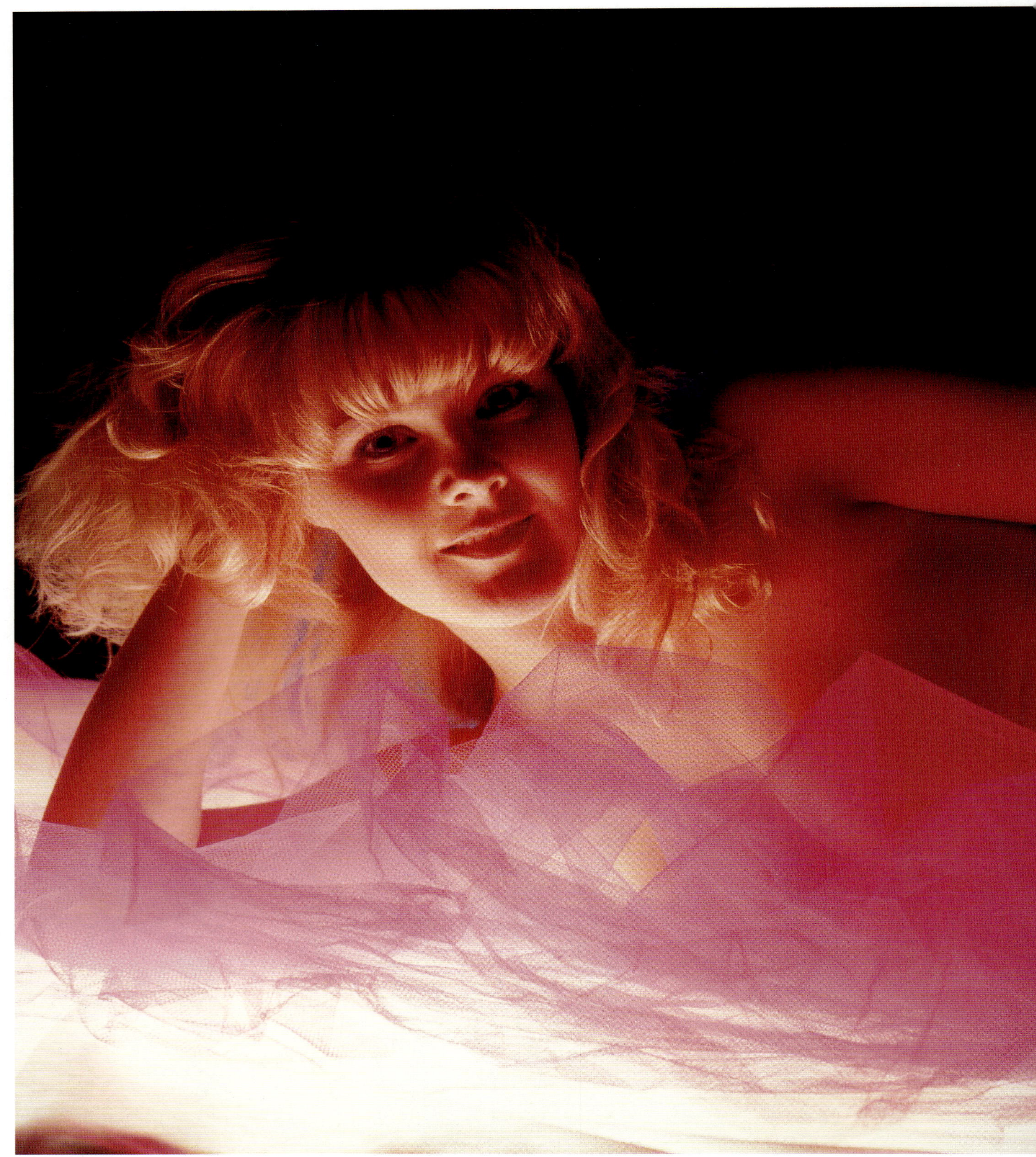

Underlighting, where the model is lit from below, is the opposite of toplighting (pages 56–7). Similar rules of thumb apply with this type of lighting in that the technique tends to work better when the model is reclining rather than standing. Direct lighting from below can give rise to rather macabre images, reminiscent of horror films, and is really only useful for special effects where this unusual type of representation is required. However, interesting results can be obtained by those willing to experiment with this lighting technique, for example, using additional light either from the top, sides, or a combination of the two.

over and under

To create the image shown here, a large lightbox was created with a translucent Perspex sheet on top and a flash unit underneath. The inside of the box was white, to bounce the light evenly underneath the model, but care was taken to ensure that little light leaked from the back and side edges of the box. A white silk parachute was used to cover the top, to diffuse and moderate the illumination, as the flash unit was close to the inner surface. The model's upper half was then illuminated with a small softbox covered with a red gel. The effects can be varied by altering the power of each light. The image on page 71 was photographed in a similar way, but the more subtle result was due to greater disparity between the toplight and the underlight.

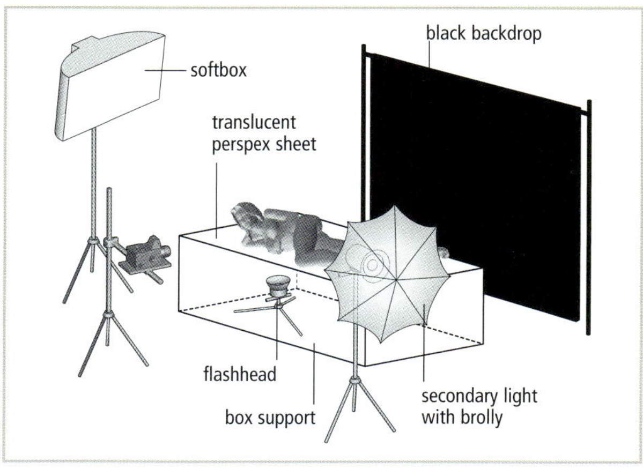

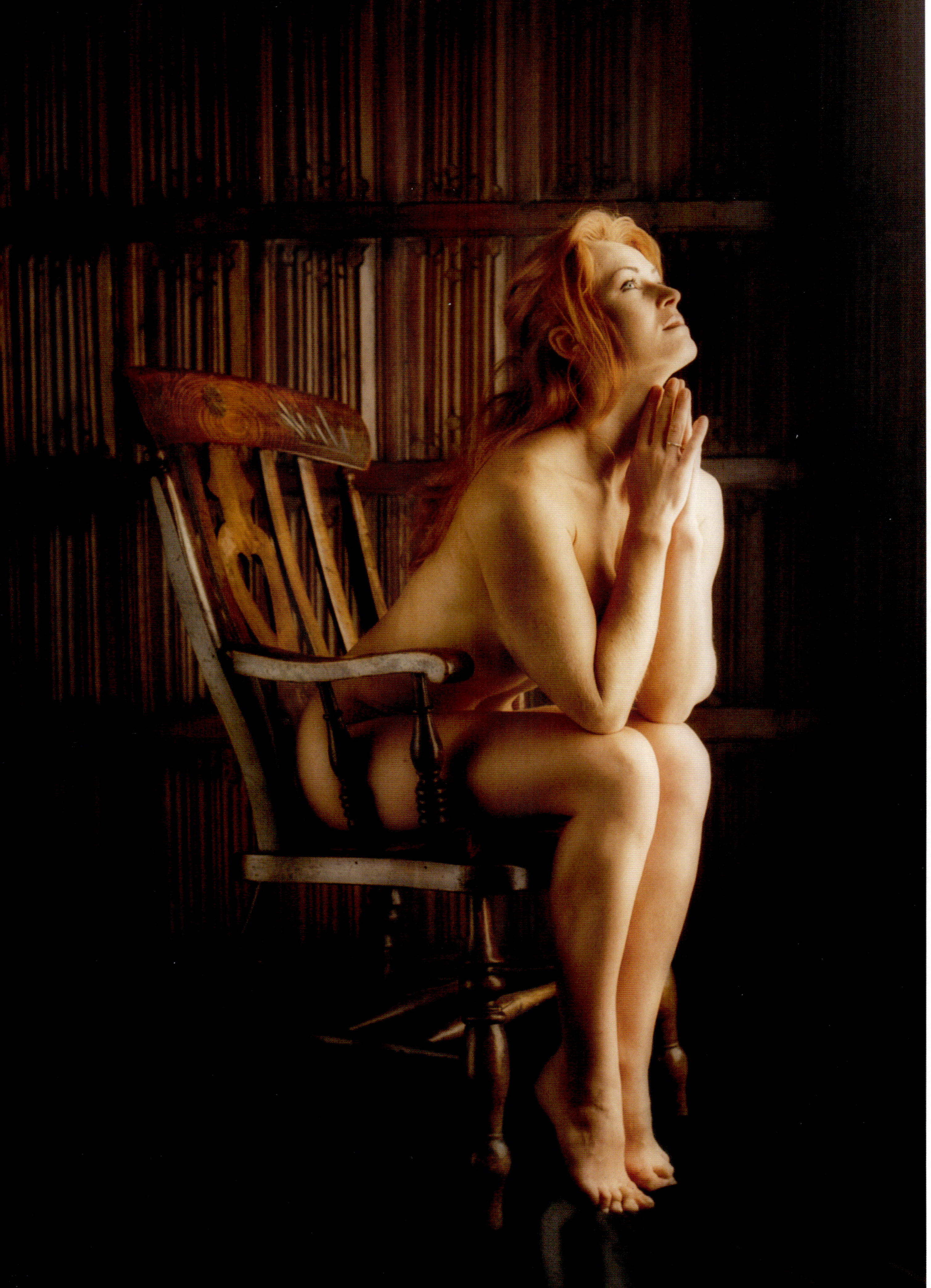

Sidelighting

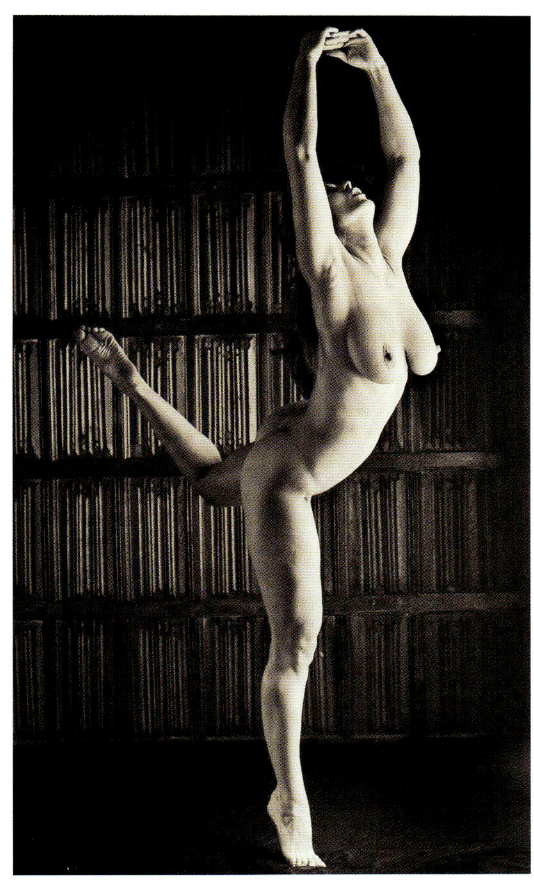

ABOVE: **Perfect modelling.** The same lighting as for the main picture was used here to model the figure to perfection. (BRONICA ETRSi; 150mm LENS; 1/125 sec at f/11; ILFORD FP4.)

Sidelighting is another option to explore when photographing the nude figure. This technique can lead to interestingly lit subjects with pleasing results. The term sidelighting, as used here, implies that the main light source comes from either the right or left side of the scene and is at right angles to the camera viewpoint, though there is some leeway with the exact positioning. A narrow beam used alone may well cause a low-key image (see pages 46–7), but a more divergent source used in conjunction with subsidiary lighting to fill in shadows and illuminate backgrounds will give a lighter, airier impression. Modelling is often good with sidelighting, especially if the light is soft, such as window lighting when the daylight is not too bright. When using a softbox for the illumination, the closer the unit is to the model, the softer the light will be. Used with a reflector, to throw light back to the unlit side of the model, this can be a very effective one-light set-up.

attention to detail
The two images shown here were photographed using the same lighting set-up in the hallway of a large manor house, which presented rather an awkward shape to light conventionally (see diagram below). The main illumination for these images was provided by a flash unit with a large softbox attachment to the right of the model. To prevent the left-hand side of the scene becoming lost in shadow, a large, silver reflector board was positioned against the wall facing the model and the softbox. This helped to fill in the darker areas. A further small softbox, behind the camera and directed at the silver reflector, was employed to bounce light into the left-hand side and reduce the overall contrast of the scene. A third light was used from a side room to illuminate the panelled wall and pick out some of the atmospheric detail in the wood.

OPPOSITE: **A simulated window.** The main light used to create this image was a large softbox, which effectively simulates natural daylight coming through a (non-existent) window to the right of the model – see diagram. (BRONICA ETRSi; 150mm LENS; 1/125 sec at f/11; KODAK PORTRA 160NC.)

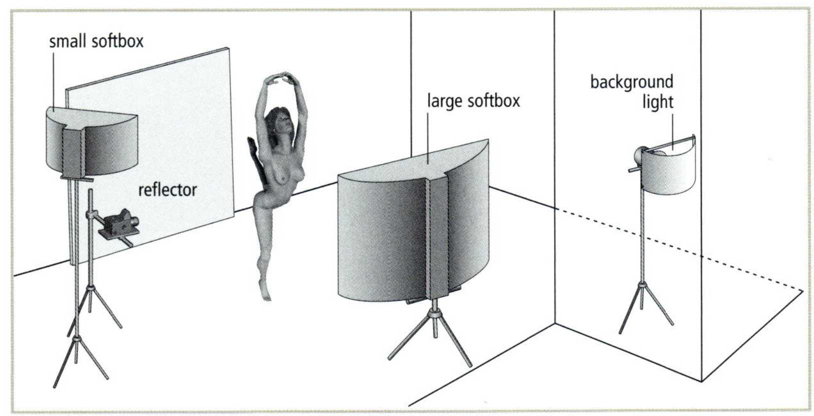

However good the photographer's technical ability and creative vision, nude photography is ultimately dependent on the model's ability to pose successfully. A beautifully composed picture will be worthless if the model strikes an awkward or ungainly attitude. If she should feel uncomfortable in front of the camera – for whatever reason – this will be painfully obvious in the final picture. Natural poses are therefore one of the essential ingredients of success. This outcome is by no means easy to achieve, but making the model feel relaxed in your presence, and confident in the photography you are doing, will go a long way towards the achievement of more natural poses – and, as a result, better pictures. This chapter suggests poses for a number of frequently encountered basic scenarios. These are analyzed and constructive advice is given to assist the inexperienced photographer to get the optimum performance from nude models.

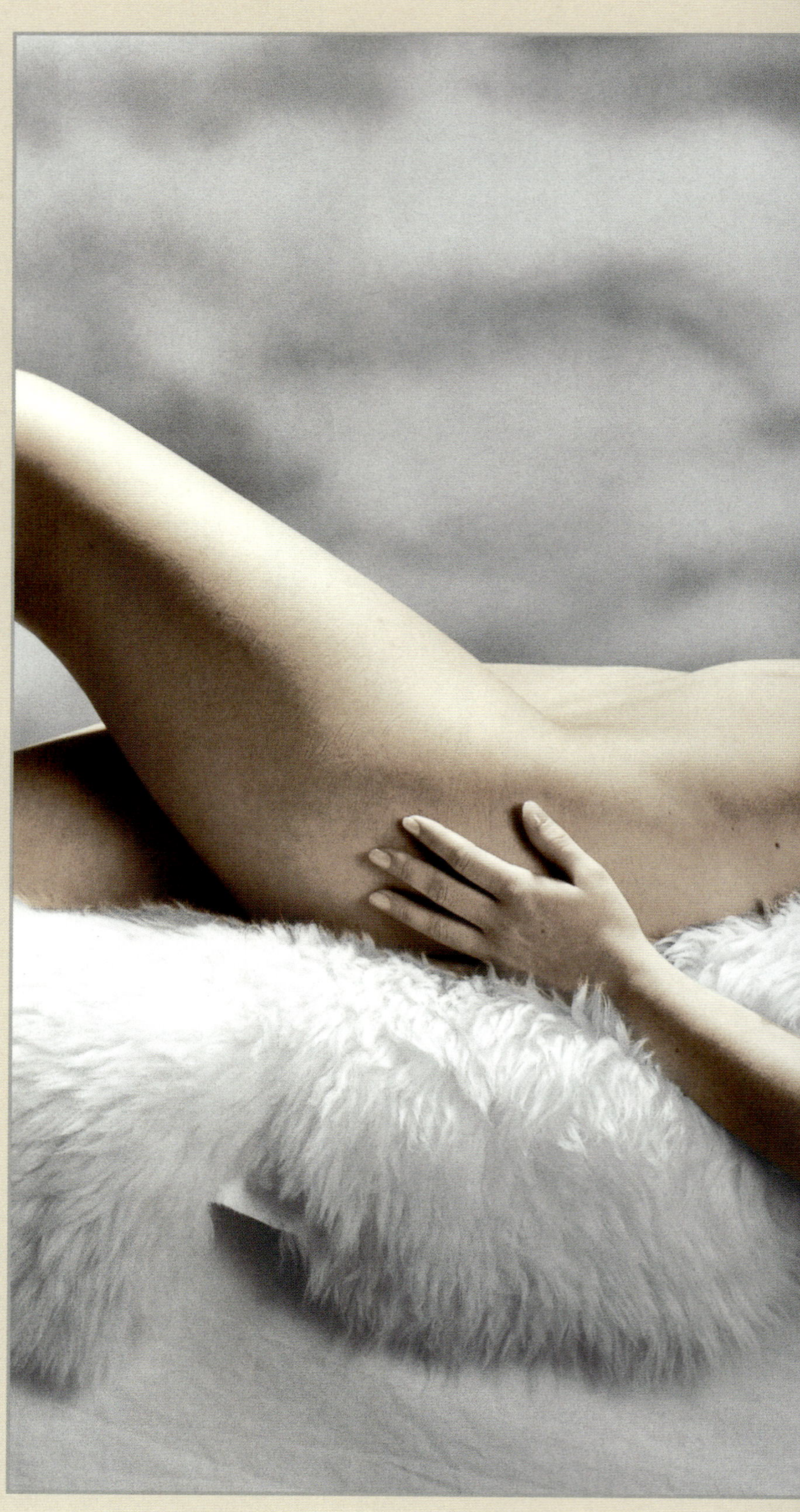

RIGHT: **Classical pose.** The success of this classical reclining nude is the result of careful attention to detail in the adopted pose. The image has been lifted from the ordinary by selective sepia toning. (BRONICA ETRSi; 150mm LENS; 1/125 sec at f/11; ILFORD FP4 PLUS.)

Arranging poses

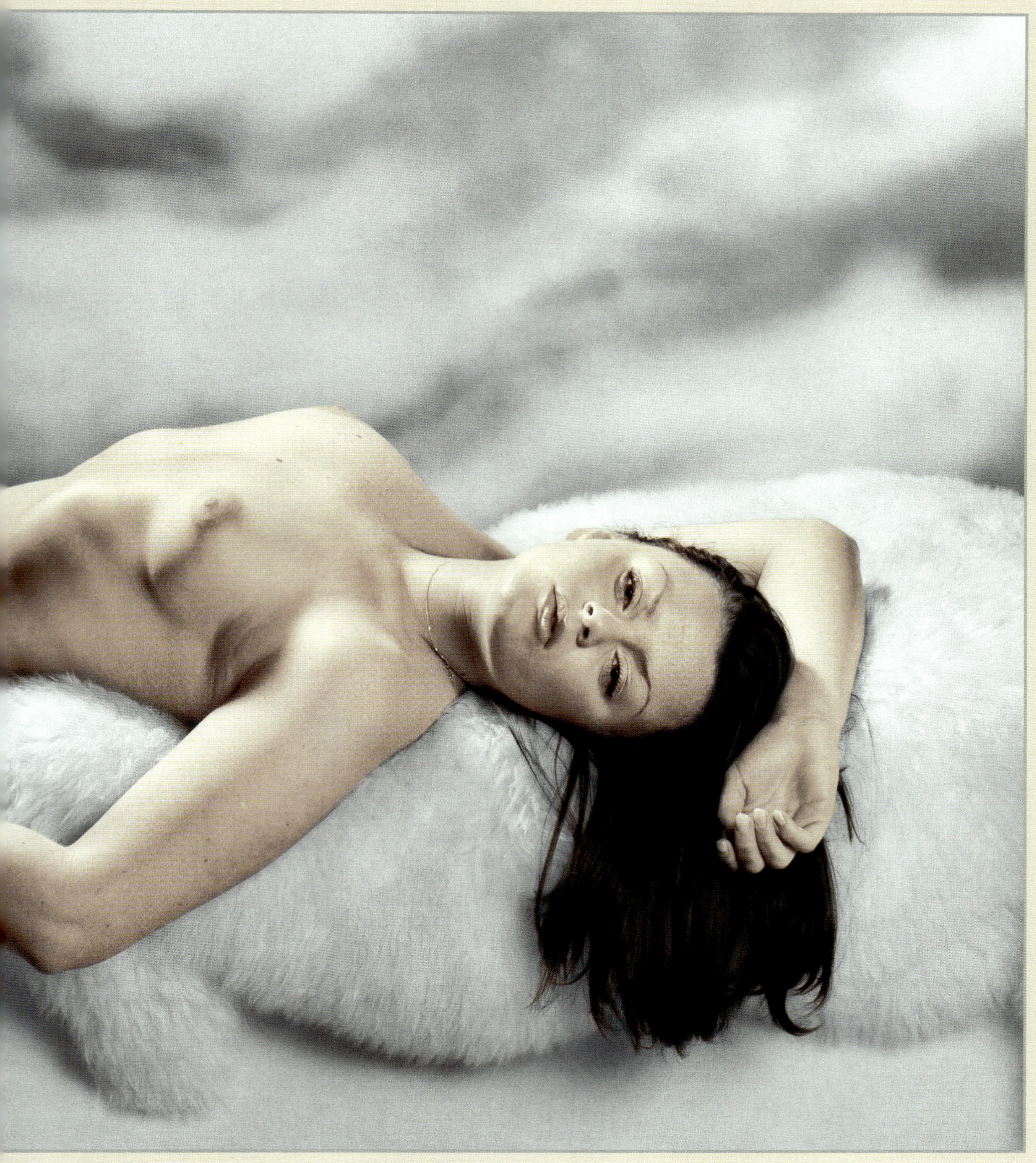

Camera angle

BELOW: **Bird's-eye view.** This image was taken from the top of a circular marble staircase and gives a striking vertical downward viewpoint of the model.
(BRONICA ETRSi; 150mm LENS; 1/125 sec at f/11; KODAK PORTRA 160NC.)

One of the first things to consider when composing a photograph is where the picture should be taken from. Making use of camera angles is one way of giving a different slant to creative nude images that will inject variety into the poses available to the photographer.

from above An elevated position gives a bird's-eye view of the subject, which can be an effective viewpoint because it is unusual and often unexpected. In the studio, a gantry or ladder can be used to gain a position above the model. On location there may be many

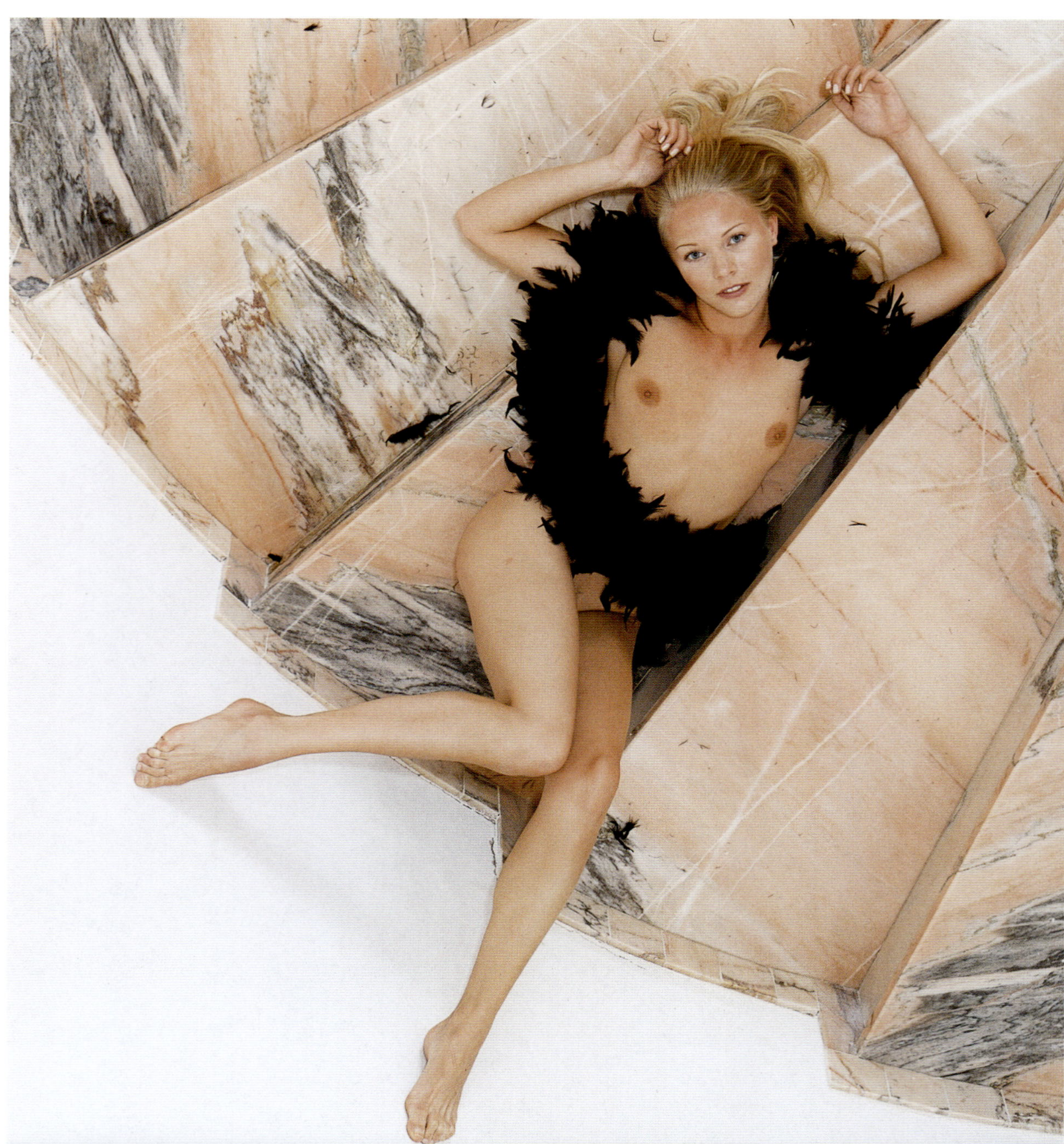

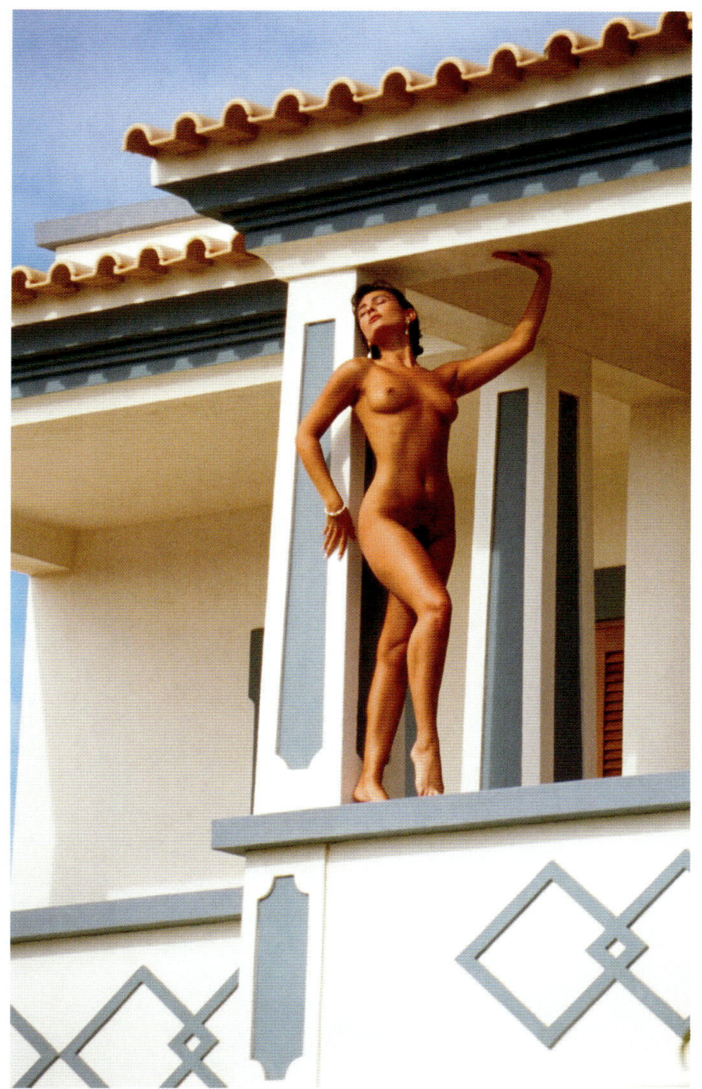

options, such as shooting from a balcony to a lower floor, from stairwells, or even standing above a reclining model.

from below Photographing from a low angle can provide a dramatic view of the model. The subject may take on a more regal or dominant appearance from below and conversely appear more submissive when photographed from above. This is purely an effect of the chosen angle. Using a wide-angle lens from a low viewpoint will also accentuate scale and perspective compared to a telephoto lens.

straight on There is nothing wrong with photographing the subject from a level position – most images will be taken in this manner. Variation in poses and composition of the picture can be used in imaginative ways to make this angle as exciting as any.

PERSPECTIVE

Photographing the subject too closely or from acute angles will distort parts of the body – particularly when using a wide-angle lens – and can lead to perspective problems. The figure may be foreshortened from a downward camera position, making the model appear fatter. If photographed from an upward angle, the legs and feet may appear over-large, leading to unflattering images. However, legs can be made to look longer by using this technique. If exaggerated perspective is not required, step back and use a longer focal-length lens, or change the pose.

ABOVE: **Low viewpoint.** The low camera viewpoint used to capture this image gives the model a regal serenity that would probably not be apparent from another angle. (MINOLTA 8000i; 75–300mm ZOOM LENS; 1/125 sec at f/16; KODAK EKTACHROME 100.)

RIGHT: **Natural pose.** This image, taken from a position level with the subject, shows the model in a comfortable natural pose enhanced by strong compositional elements. The group of flowers to the left balances the model to the right. (BRONICA ETRSi; 150mm LENS; 1/125 sec at f/11; KODAK PORTRA 160NC.)

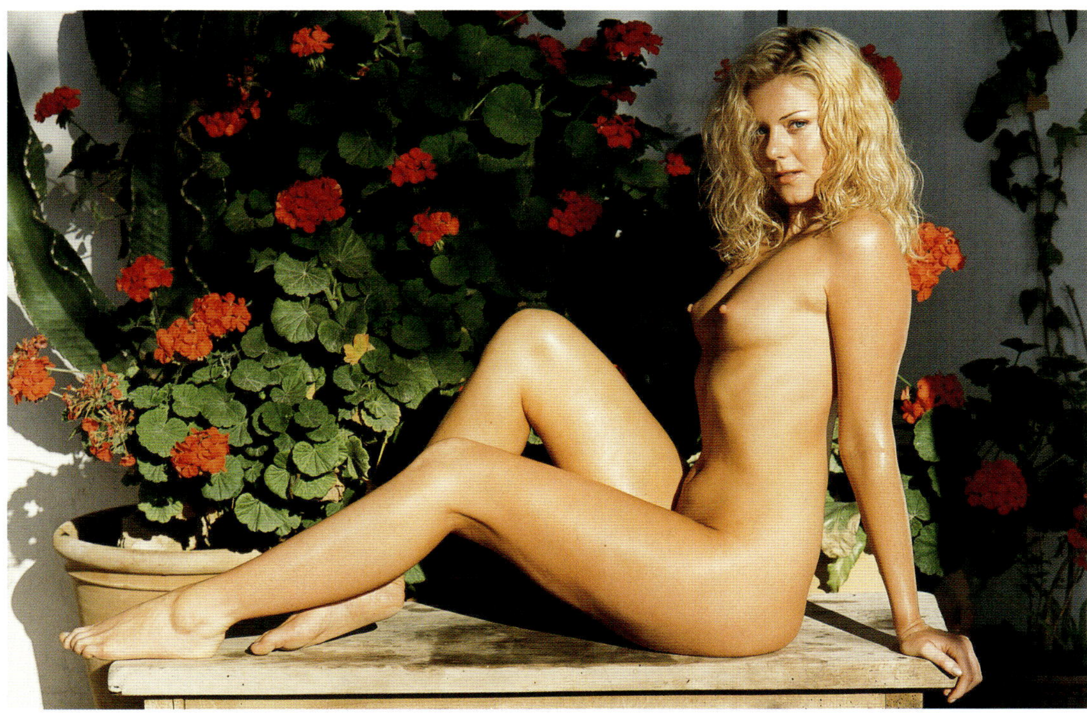

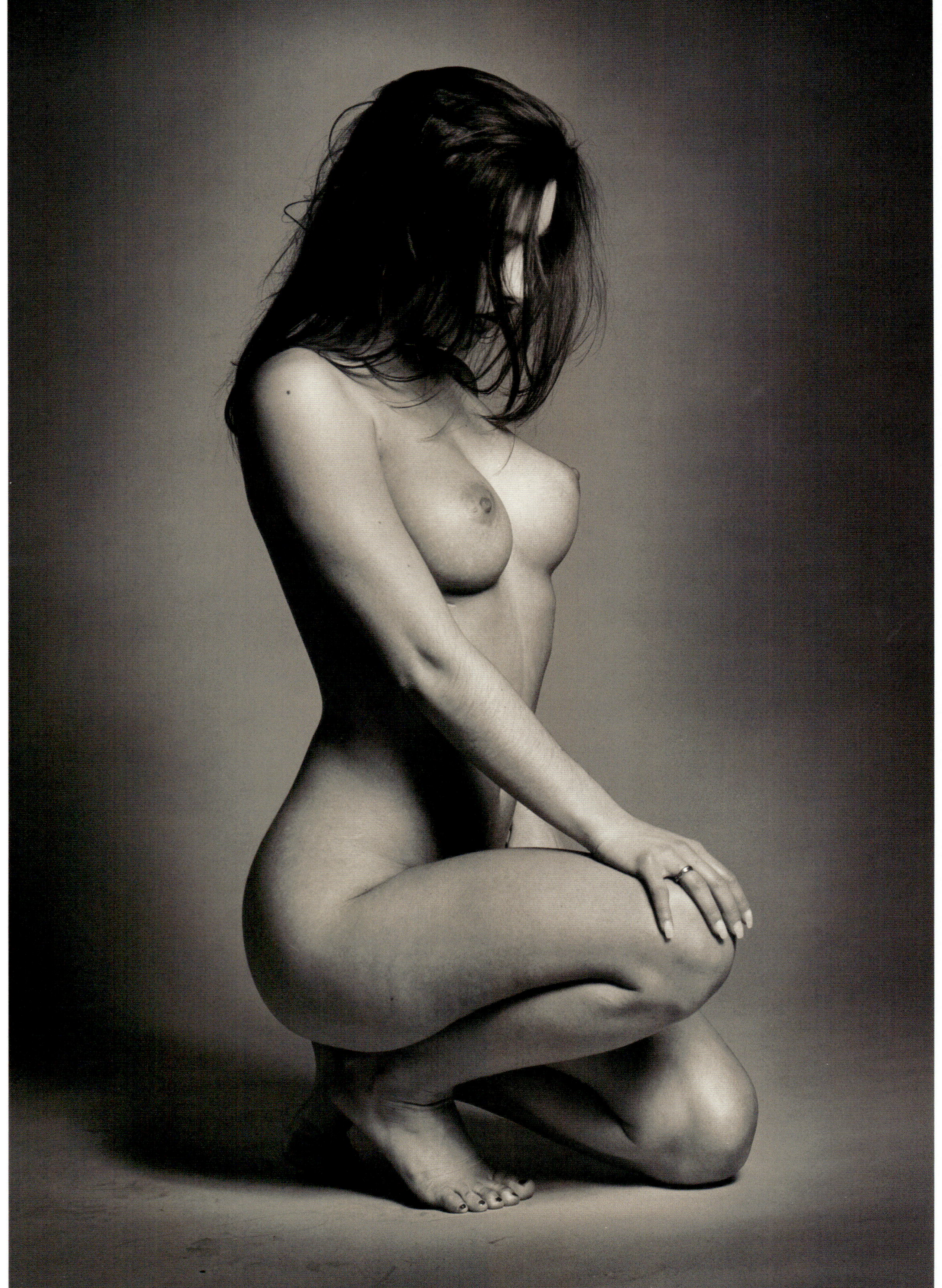

Semi-recumbent poses

OPPOSITE: **Crouching pose.** The bowed head of the model in this crouching pose suggests a subservient yet proud attitude. (BRONICA ETRSi; 150mm LENS; 1/125 sec at f/11; SPLIT-TONED SEPIA AND IRON BLUE; ILFORD FP4 PLUS.)

Photographing a model in a semi-recumbent pose (sitting, kneeling or crouching) gives many options for classical and artistic interpretation. Inclusion of props greatly expands the possibilities.

sitting
In a sitting position the model's back should be straight. A 'slouch' will tend to give rounded shoulders, an awkward head position and unsightly tummy bulges. Counter this by asking the model to stretch upwards a little, breathe in, and lean back slightly. Arrange legs carefully, ensuring that the pose looks elegant. Feet pointing towards the camera usually appear large and ungainly and the soles unattractive. When sitting in a chair, crossed ankles look more elegant than crossed legs.

RIGHT: **Simple lines.** The clean lines of this kneeling pose owe much to the absence of intruding hands and feet, plus good posture. (BRONICA ETRSi; 150mm LENS; 1/125 sec at f/11; ILFORD FP4 PLUS.)

FAR RIGHT: **Seated pose.** An elegant arrangement of legs, arms and hands is important when they are in close proximity to one another – as in this sitting image. The sunshade adds interest and helps with the positioning of the model's hands. (MINOLTA 8000i; 100mm MACRO LENS; 1/125 sec at f/8; DIFFUSED AT PRINTING STAGE; KODAK GOLD 100.)

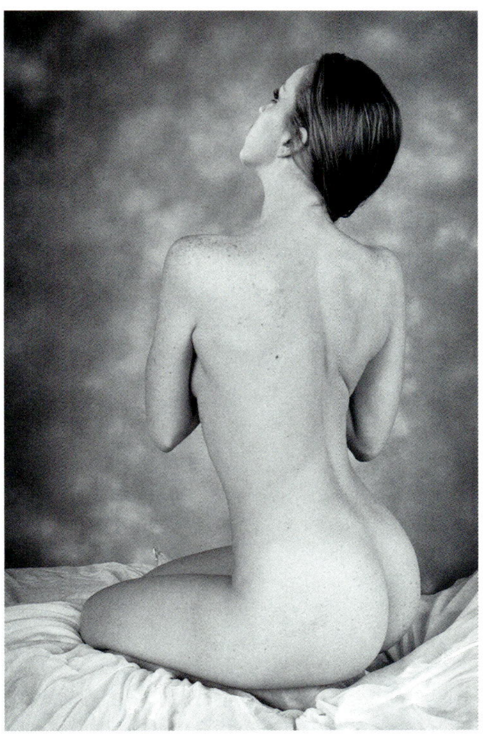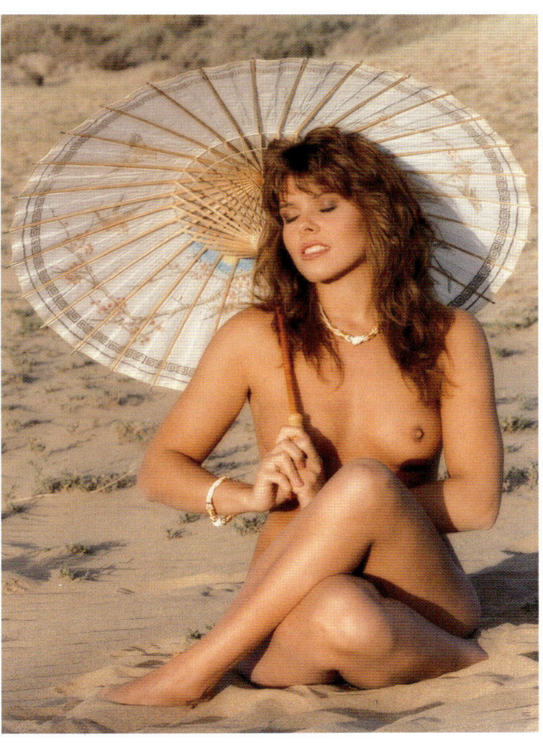

kneeling and crouching
Rules that apply to sitting positions also apply to poses involving kneeling and crouching. Hiding the model's feet beneath her legs so that she is sitting on them in a kneeling pose simplifies the composition dramatically. Hand and arm positions then tend to take on a greater importance and should be looked at carefully, making sure that all lines in the composition flow well. Crouching positions are often hard for the model to hold for extended periods, so ensure that the model appears relaxed and comfortable in what may actually be a very difficult pose.

Upright poses

Upright poses, where the model is either standing or leaning, are all about poise, posture, elegance and gracefulness.

standing and leaning

The variations are limitless, but there are some generalities that should be borne in mind when using this type of pose. The positioning of the arms, legs and head in relation to the body and each other are significant factors in ensuring that the image flows together. Leg shape is particularly important and is partly controlled by muscle tension in the calves, so standing on the ball of the foot or the toes often improves the leg shape. High-heeled shoes will have a similar

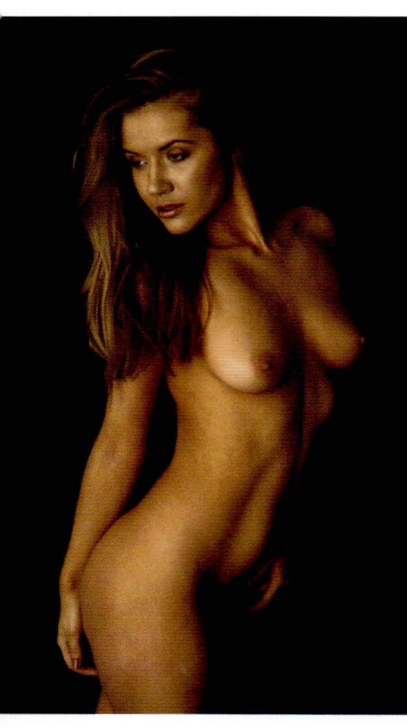

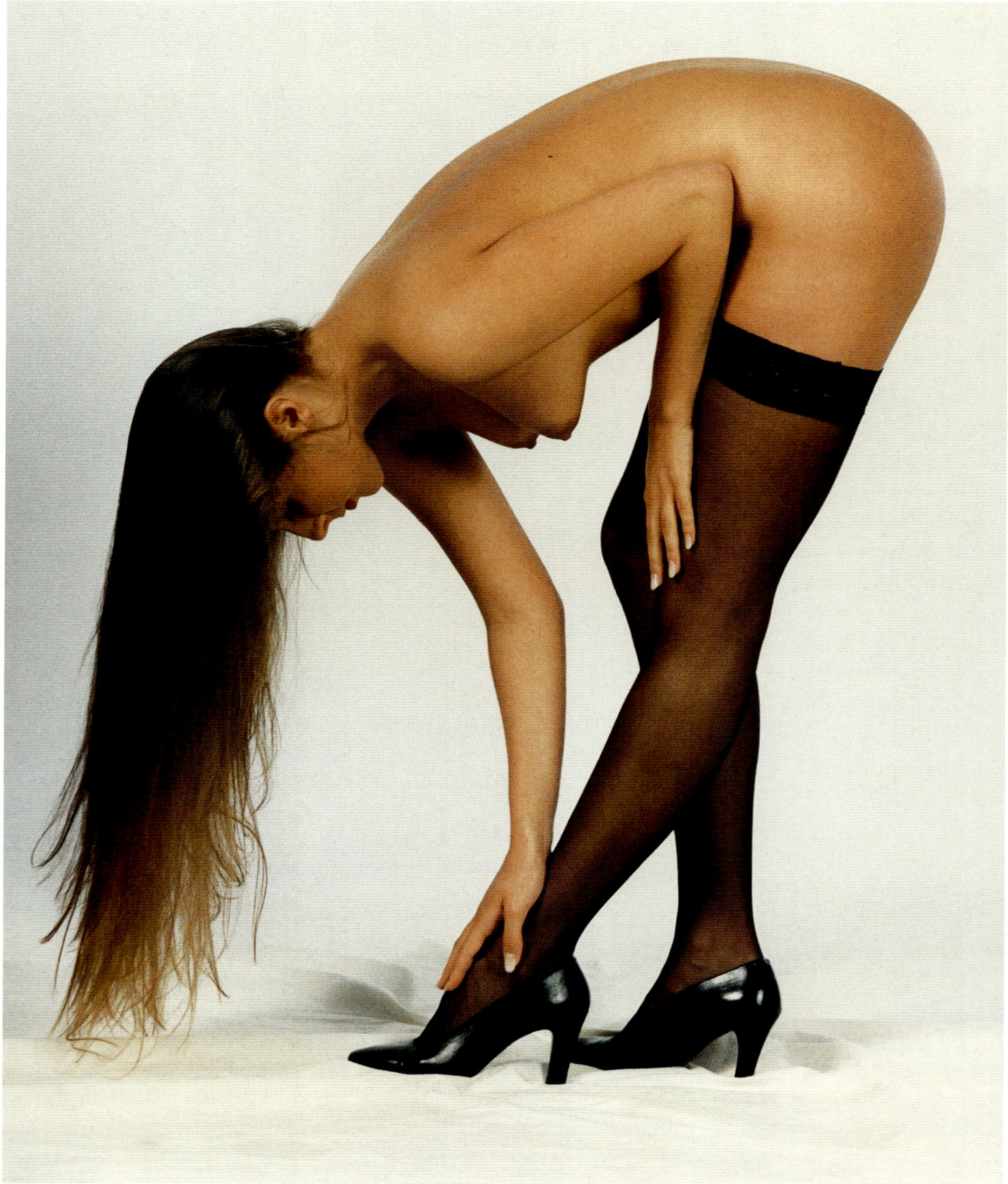

ABOVE: **Twisting.** Good posture, a slight twist in the upper torso and relaxed arm positions work together to make an elegant nude study. (MINOLTA 8000i; 75-300mm LENS; 1/125 sec at f/11; KODACHROME 64.)

RIGHT: **Curved composition.** The curve formed by the legs, body and hair is a strong compositional element in this image, which is reinforced by the arm positions. The high heels also assist in improving the model's leg shape. (MINOLTA 8000i; 100mm LENS; 1/125 sec at f/11; KODAK GOLD 100.)

effect. Placing one leg across the other improves the shape of the hips and thighs. Twisting the upper torso slightly in relation to the lower body can improve body shape – but avoid creases, particularly around the waist and neck. Relaxed, natural poses are often more effective than exaggerated, contrived poses. Small changes in posture can have a great effect, so ask the model to move a little at a time until the right pose is found.

walking Walking, running and jumping pictures are far more difficult to photograph than stationary poses. Capturing the precise moment when all the elements of a good picture come together calls for patience, split-second timing and luck. The success rate can be improved considerably if you give the model precise instructions and have several trial runs before attempting to capture the image. Predetermine the exact point at which the picture will be taken and, if possible, ask the model to do the action in slow motion.

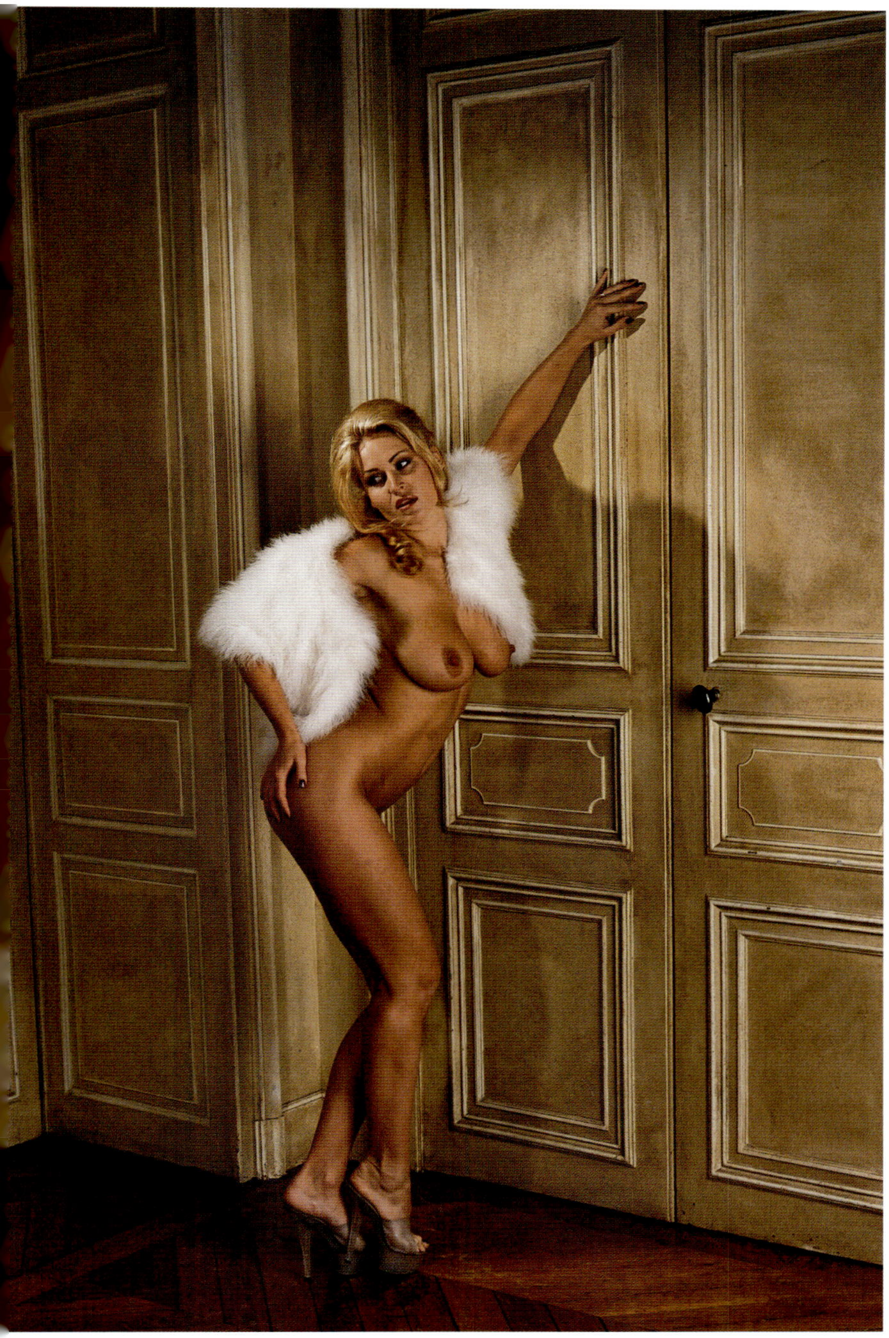

ABOVE: **Standing pose.** The arm positions of the model in this image complement and extend the curves in her body, adding to the overall impact of the composition.
(BRONICA ETRSi; 75mm LENS; 1/125 sec at f/16; KODAK PORTRA 160NC.)

RIGHT: **Moving study.** A relaxed and natural nude study captured in mid-stride. The crossed legs accentuate the curves of the hips and thighs, and the arm and shoulder positions work together to lend grace and elegance to the model.
(BRONICA ETRSi; 150mm LENS; 1/60 sec at f/11; KODAK GPX 160.)

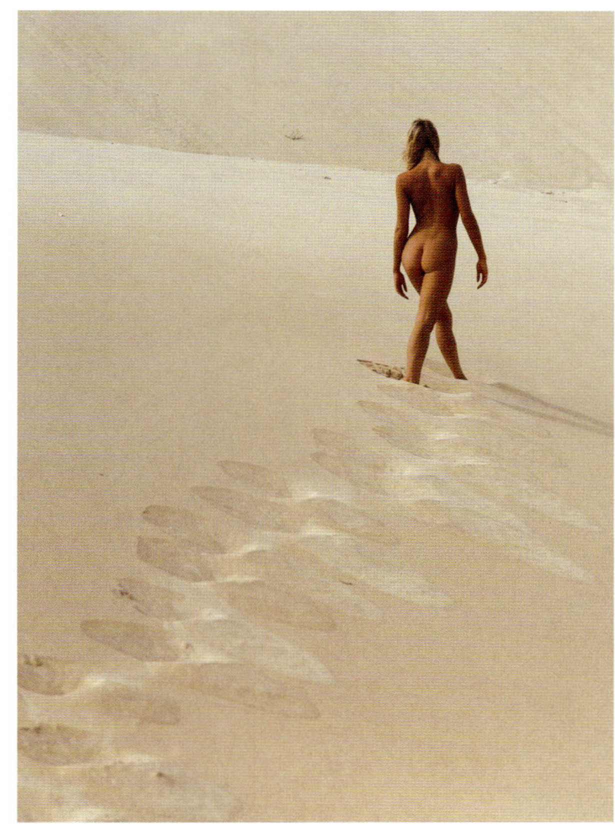

Reclining nudes

AVOIDING UNFLATTERING POSES

The model should adopt a relaxed position where the lines of her body flow and form a strong compositional image. Asking the model to breathe in or stretch just before you press the shutter will often improve the body shape dramatically. Pointing the toes is elegant and the muscle tension gives a better shape to the legs.

Photographing reclining nudes can be one of the most difficult challenges of nude photography and you will find the simplest shapes often work best. Look for strong lines and shapes, such as an S-shape or a diagonal, and position the arms and legs to complement the shape.

Pay particular attention to the position of hands, fingers and feet (see pages 72–5). Small changes can make a big difference to the overall impact, so take several photographs where small variations have been made – one will stand out when you see the final images.

Your choice of camera lens and angle can play an important role. A medium- or long-focal-length lens tends to lessen distortion of perspective, while wide-angle and fish-eye lenses may accentuate parts of the body. This, for example, can be used to make a model's legs appear longer.

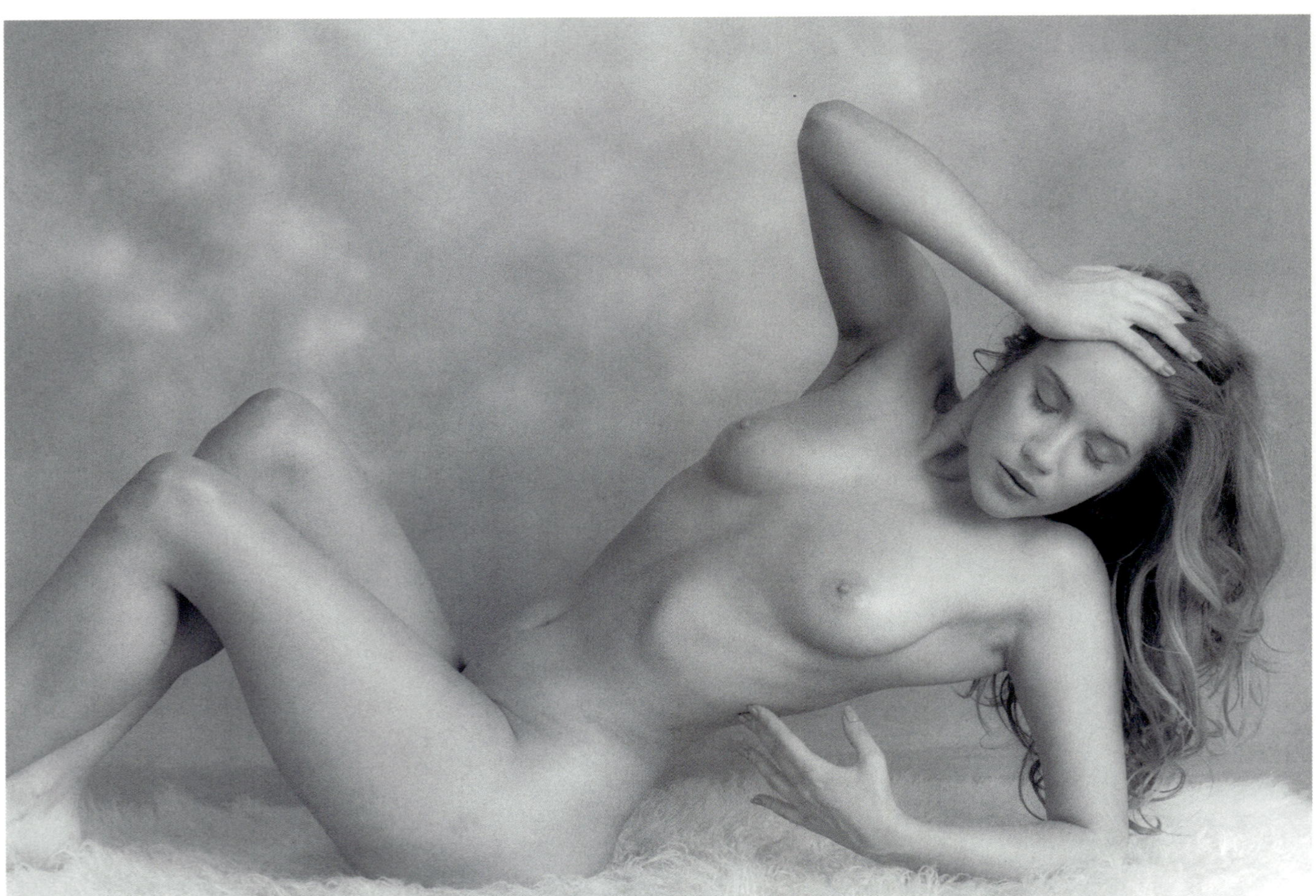

ABOVE: **Strong lines.** The main compositional elements of this image are the strong zig-zag line of the legs, thighs and torso together with the S-shape formed by the arms and hands. (BRONICA ETRSi; 150mm LENS; 1/125 sec at f/11; 120 ILFORD FP4.)

OPPOSITE: **Extended S-shape.** The shape is strong in this image. The hair has been brushed into position to emphasize the shape. (BRONICA ETRSi; 150mm LENS; 1/125 sec at f/11; 120 KODAK VPS. HIGH-KEY LIGHTING [SEE PAGES 48–9] WITH ADDITIONAL UNDERLIGHTING.)

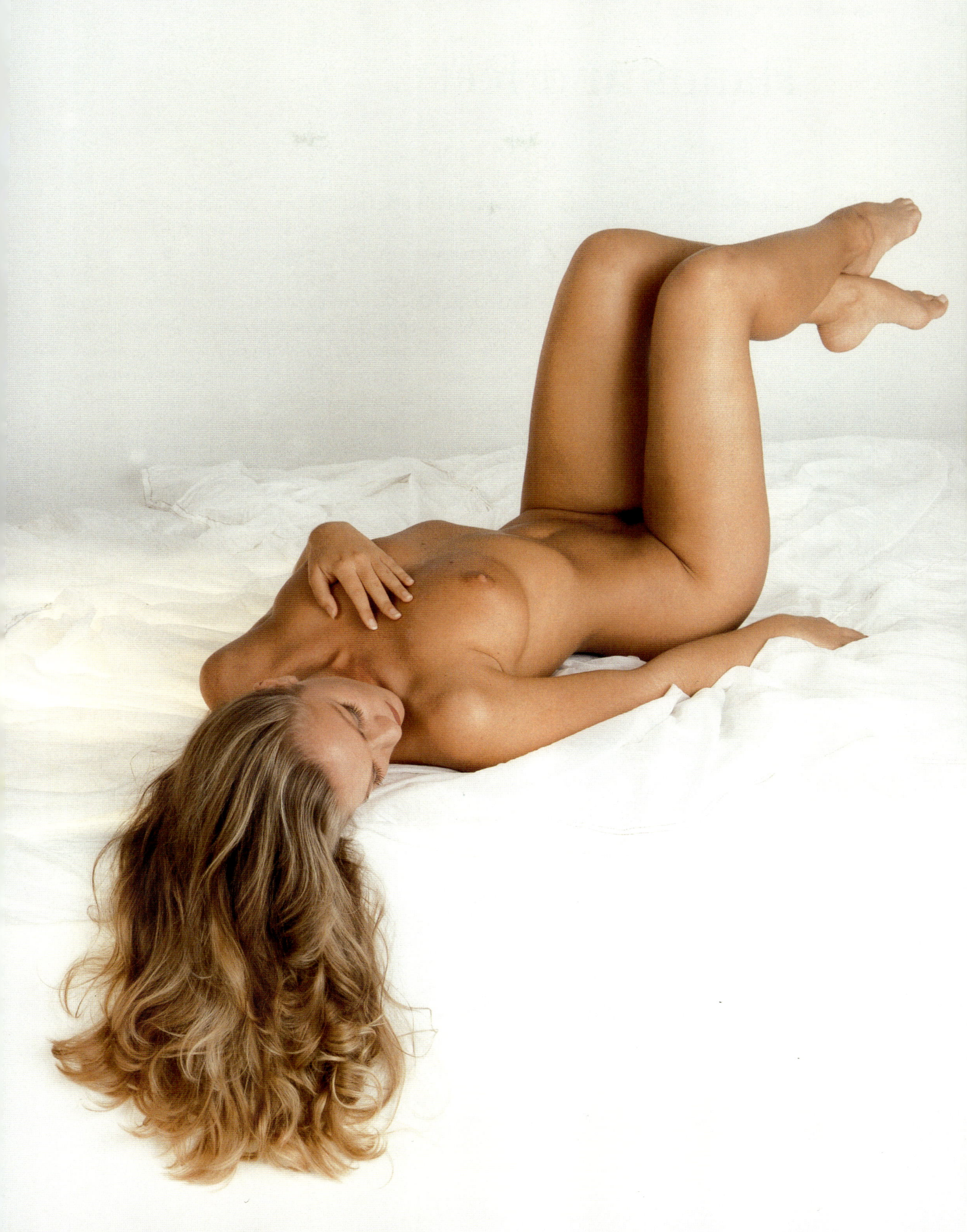

Hands and feet

OPPOSITE: **Flowing image.** The arms, legs, hands and feet in this image all flow together towards one focal point, which unifies and strengthens the overall composition.
(BRONICA ETRSi; 150mm LENS; 1/125 sec at f/11; ILFORD FP4 PLUS.)

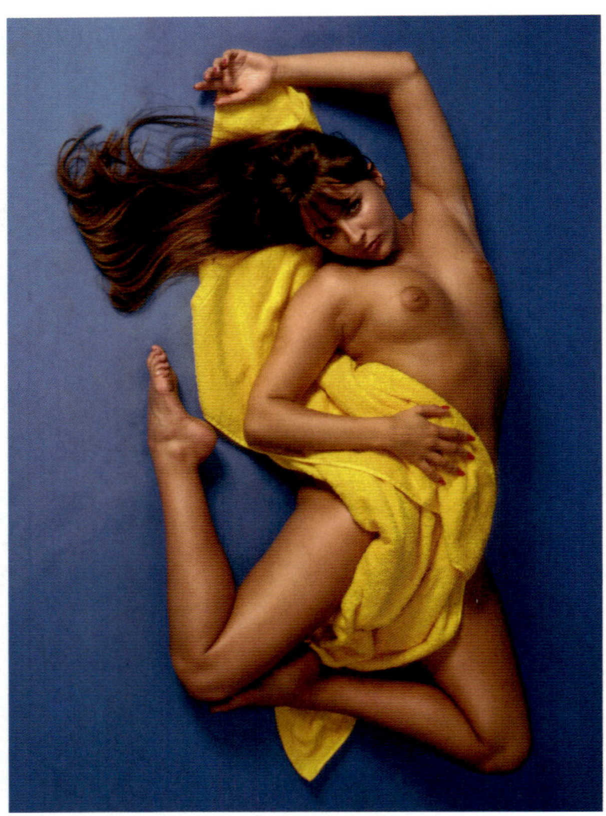

ABOVE: **Strong angles.** This image is all about shape, with strong curves and angles that almost resemble a catherine wheel. The positioning of the hands and particularly the feet of the model are vitally important to the dynamic flow of the lines in the picture.
(MINOLTA 8000i; 35–80mm LENS; 1/125 sec at f/8; KODAK EKTACHROME 100.)

RIGHT: **Elegant hands.** Relaxed hand and finger positions of the model add fluidity and elegance to this candid nude study.
(MINOLTA 8000i; 75–300mm LENS; 1/125 sec at f/5.6; KODAK PORTRA 160NC.)

Awkward hand and foot positioning can often let down an otherwise good nude photograph, so it is important to pay special attention to these details when composing a picture.

relaxation As a general rule, hands should appear natural and relaxed and not stiff, tensed or clenched into a fist – unless the image calls for such an attitude – as this can communicate nervousness or tension. Fingers and toes should look clean, elegant and well-manicured without broken nails. If nail varnish has been used, this should not be cracked, chipped or badly applied. Look out for and avoid crossed fingers, single fingers sticking out at an angle, and fingers that are too widely spread apart, as the eye will be drawn to this, detracting from the main image. This is particularly important where the hands and feet are the central focus of attention, as in the main image shown opposite.

Toes and feet that are pointed away from the shins tend to give better shape to the ankles and legs than feet placed flat on the ground or at right angles to the leg, so ask the model to point her toes or stand on tip-toe wherever possible. The feet and toes should continue the flow of the leg in a graceful manner, so avoid feet twisted in other directions. Be aware of clenched toes, crossed toes, big toes sticking out at an angle, and toes that are too widely spread apart. It is also sensible to try to avoid photographing the soles of feet. If the model does not have particularly attractive feet then it is better to keep them hidden or give them less prominence in the picture. When using a wide-angle lens do not have the model's hands and feet too close to the camera as this will make them appear rather large and ungainly.

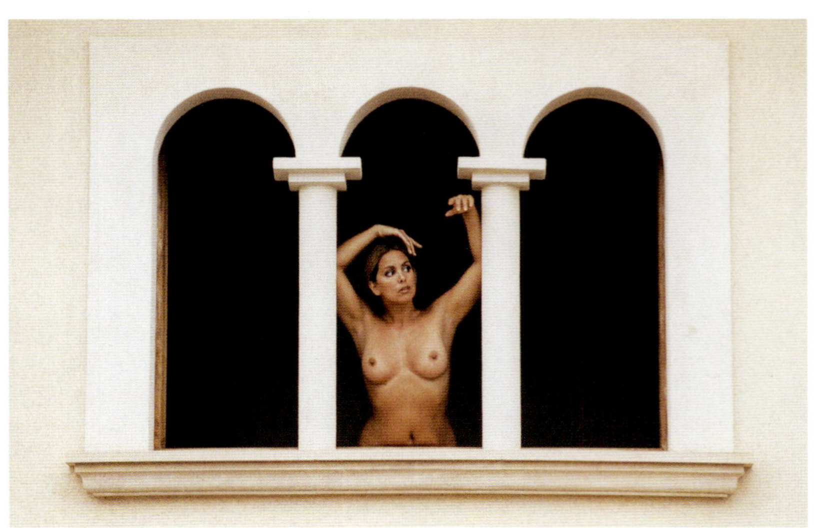

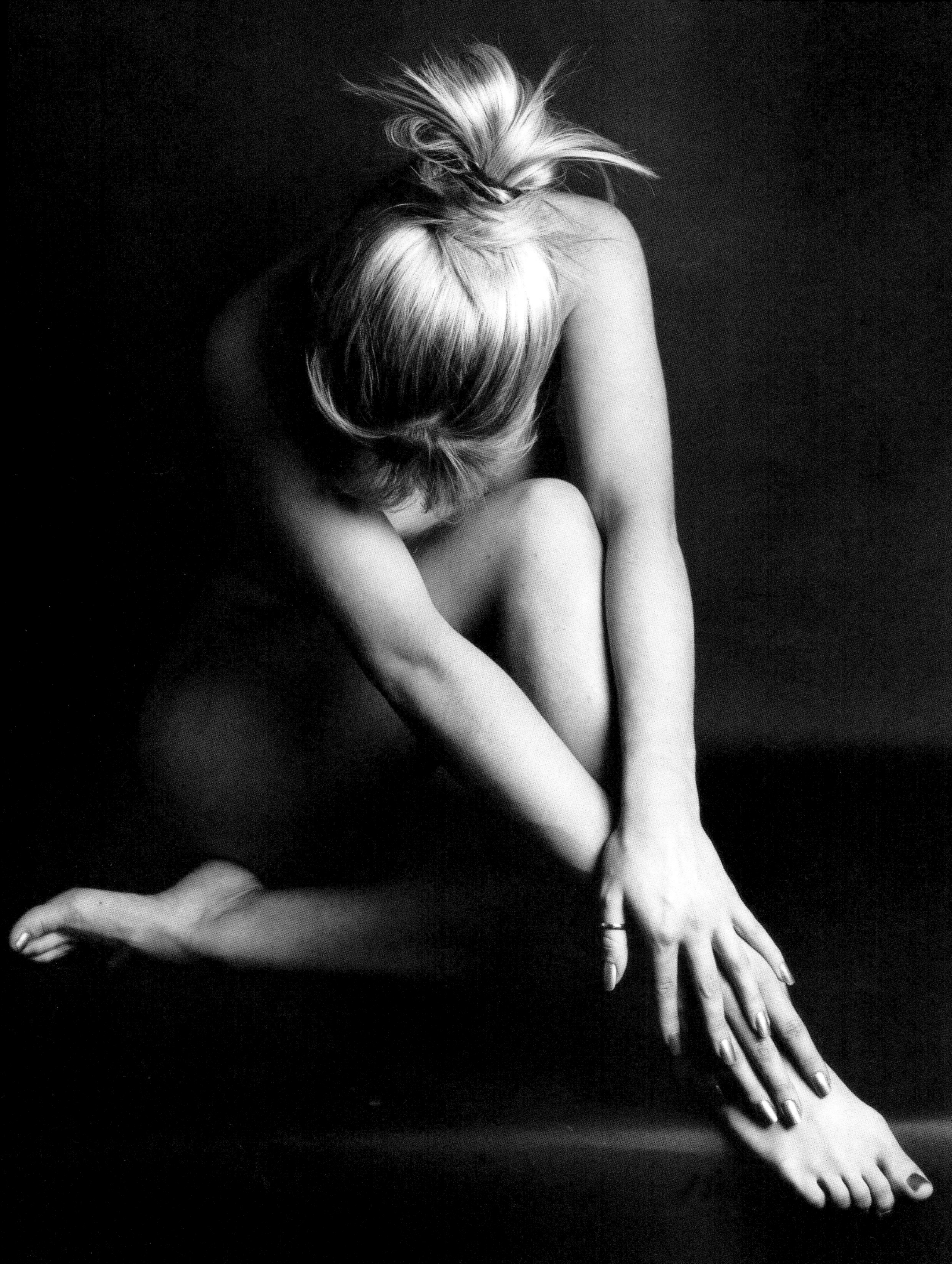

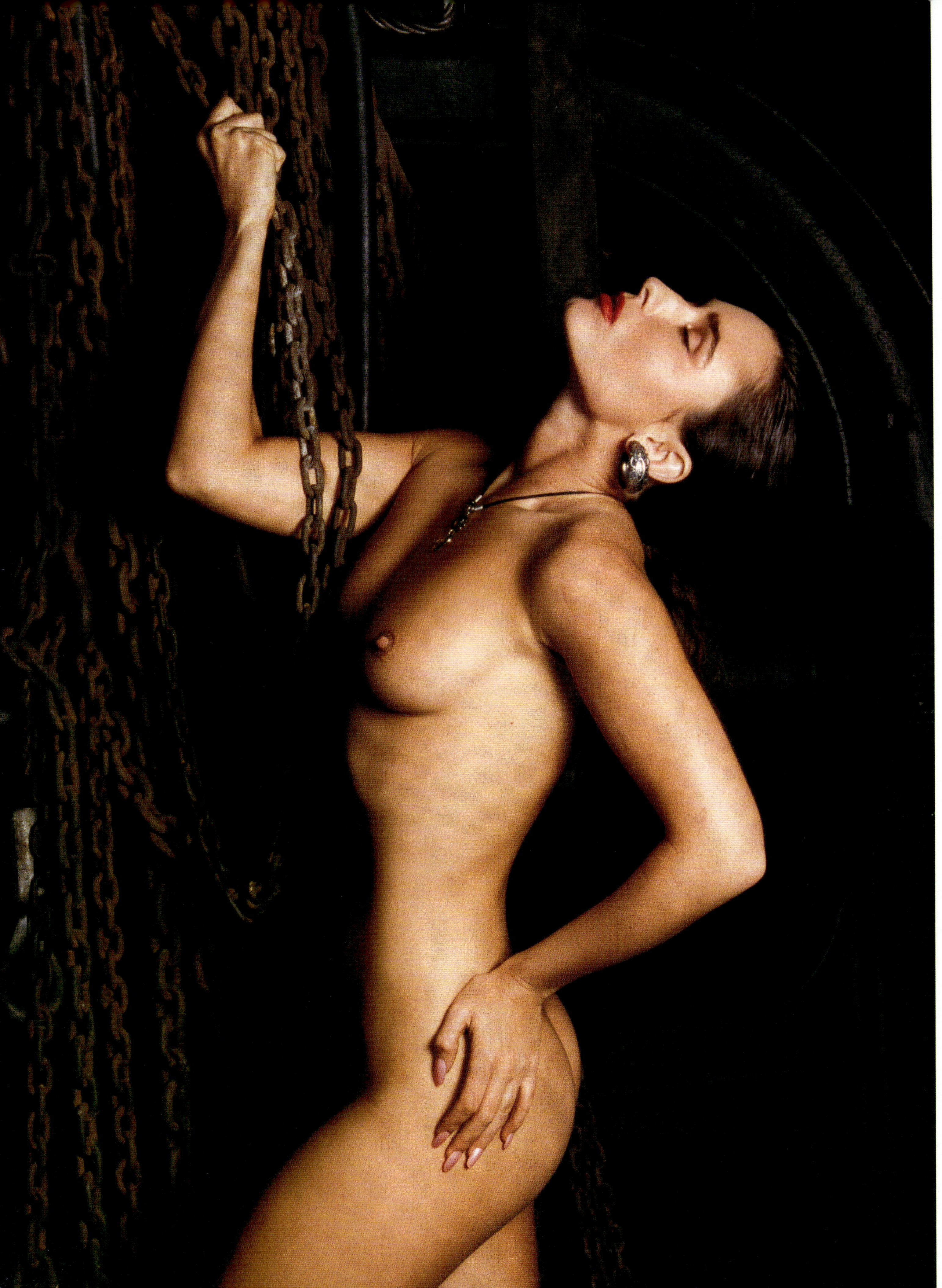

holding props
Inexperienced nude models often find it difficult to know what to do with their hands so the inclusion of a prop in a scene can be beneficial, especially if it is something that the model can hold. This does not have to be elaborate: a piece of material, a hat, or a flower are a few suggestions, but whatever is used should be in keeping with the mood of the image. Allow the model to try out a few poses that come naturally to her as well as imposing your own ideas, but keep an eye on the way the object is held and make slight adjustments if necessary. There is more information on the constructive use of props in the next chapter.

OPPOSITE: **Interactive props.** Rusty chains hanging from the set allowed the model an opportunity to use them in an interactive manner. (MINOLTA 8000i; 100mm LENS; 1/125 sec at f/11; KODAK GOLD 100.)

RIGHT: **Matching props.** Two raffia arrows are held by the model in a manner that complements the bizarre wicker headdress. (BRONICA ETRS; 150mm LENS; 1/125 sec at f/11; ILFORD FP4.)

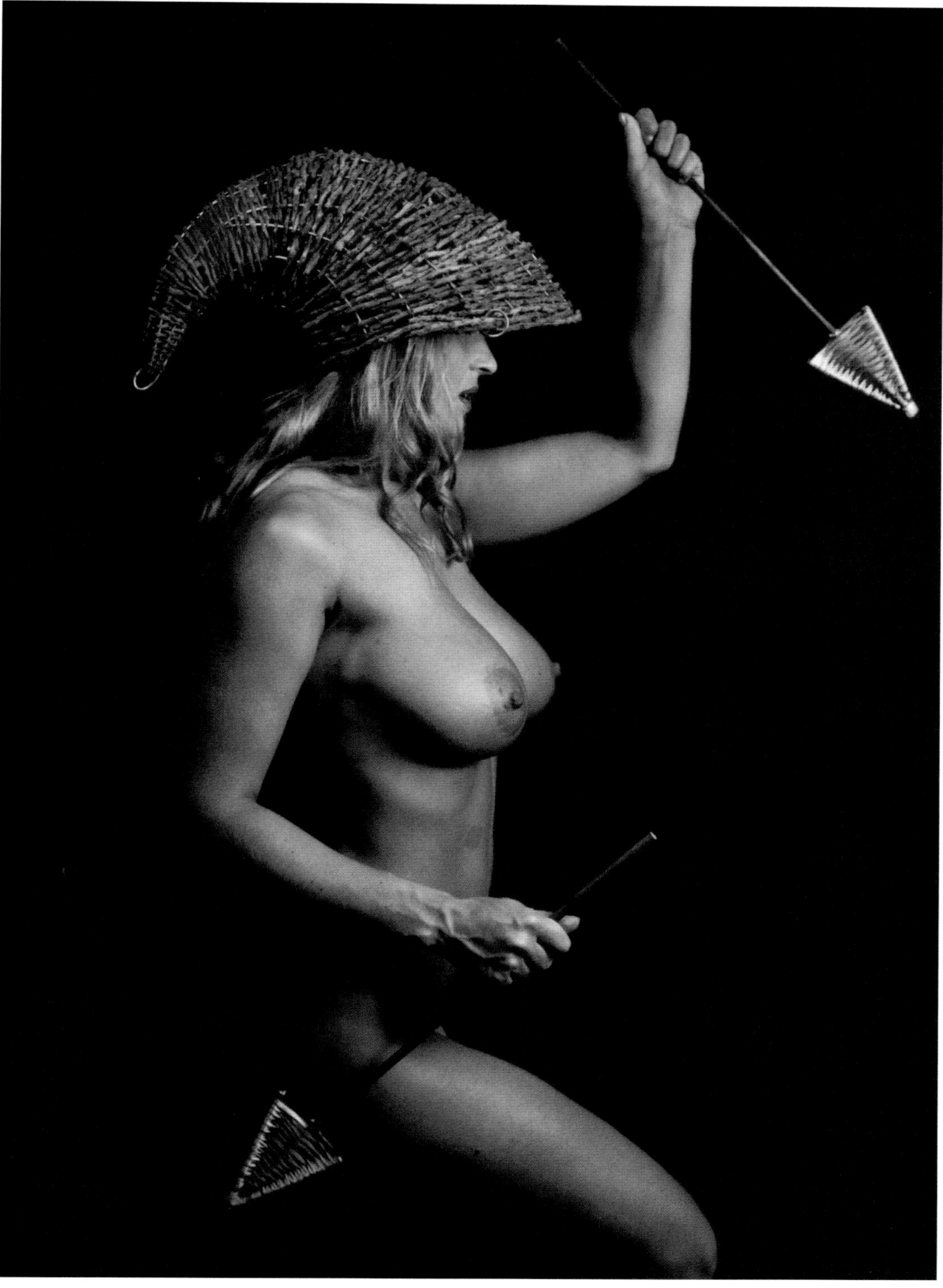

Head positions

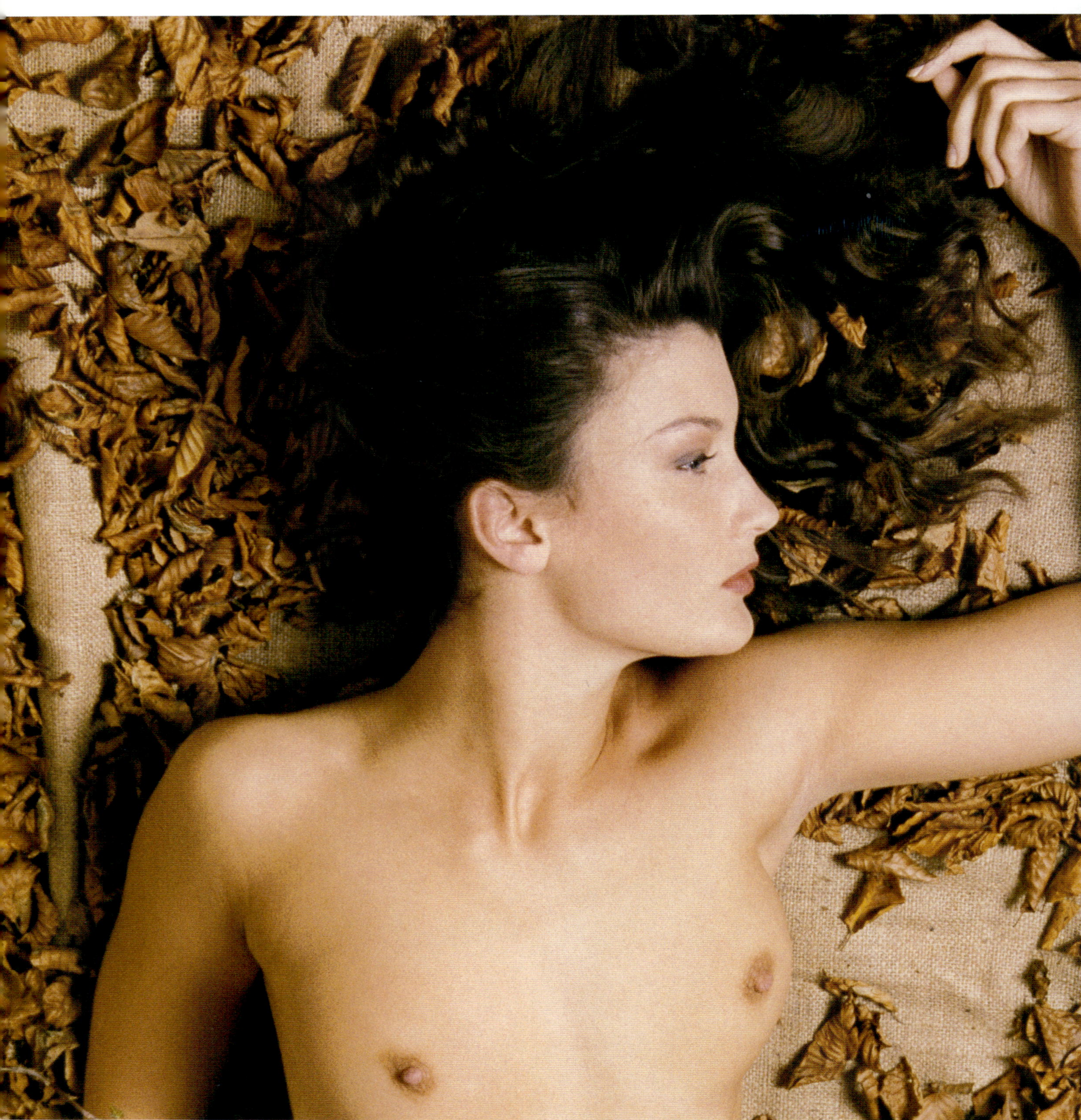

The way the model holds her head in a particular pose implies a great many things about the resulting image and a slight alteration can change the mood completely, though this is closely intertwined with the facial expression and body language that the model uses.

positioning

Choose between placing the model's head so there is either eye contact or no eye contact with the camera. Looking away is less confrontational than a direct gaze, giving a greater sense of detachment. It is therefore more suitable for classical and art poses. A confident, towards-the-camera head position is often better for glamour poses. Holding the head in an erect or elevated position may confer a confident, regal, superior or even a dominant look to the model, whereas a bowed head could imply a submissive or unconfident attitude.

LEFT: **Vertical headshot.** This profiled headshot taken from a vertical position is complemented by the mass of hair surrounding the face and strengthened by the juxtaposed arm position. (MINOLTA 8000i; 35–80mm ZOOM LENS; 1/125 sec at f/11; KODAK GOLD 100.)

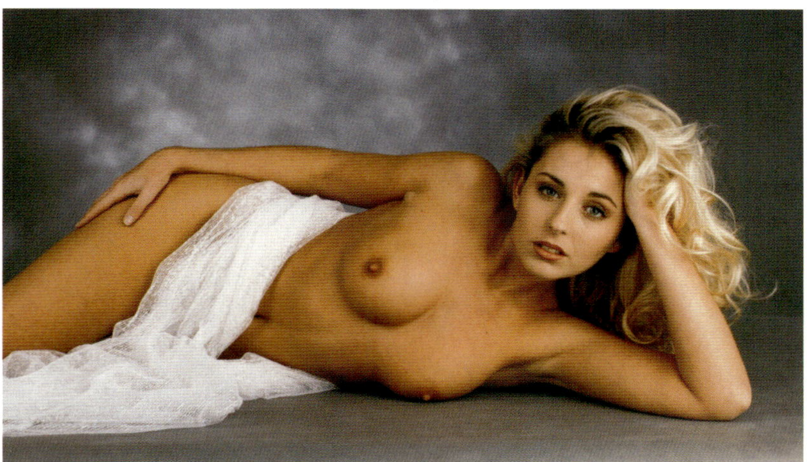

RIGHT: **Eye contact.** An inclined head supported by the left hand gives a relaxed and natural feel to this glamour shot. Direct eye contact draws the viewer into the picture. (MINOLTA 8000i; 100mm LENS; 1/125 sec at f/11; KODAK GOLD 100.)

Try to dissuade the model from leaning too far towards the camera as this is rarely a good option. A lowered-head position with the eyes looking upwards towards the photographer tends to narrow and darken the eyes and cause furrows in the forehead, which is not particularly flattering. Asking the model to tilt her head a little to one side will often allow you to create a more interesting composition than a straight-on pose. This technique is particularly useful when the picture is closer to portraiture than figure work and the head and face are important components of the image.

POSITIONING THE HEAD WITHIN THE FRAME

Head positioning can also be used to accentuate or detract from certain features of the model. If she has a large or unattractively shaped nose, for instance, it may be better to photograph her from one particular angle – perhaps the front rather than in profile. Lowering the face will tend to detract from a prominent chin and having the subject look upwards towards the camera will make her eyes appear bigger and wider. When photographing a model who is looking over her shoulder, be careful of ugly creases in the neck. Asking the model to stretch can sometimes correct this.

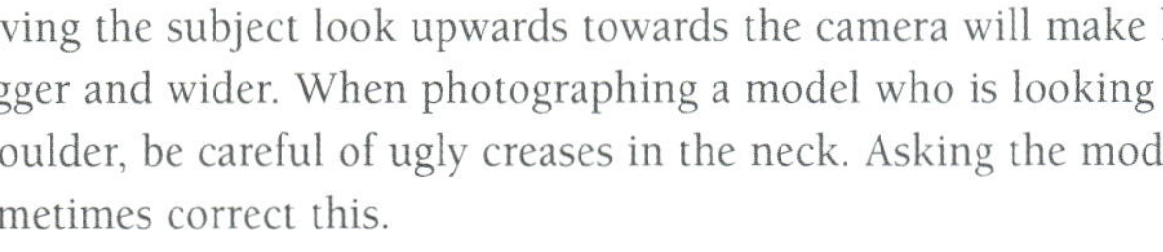

Facial expression

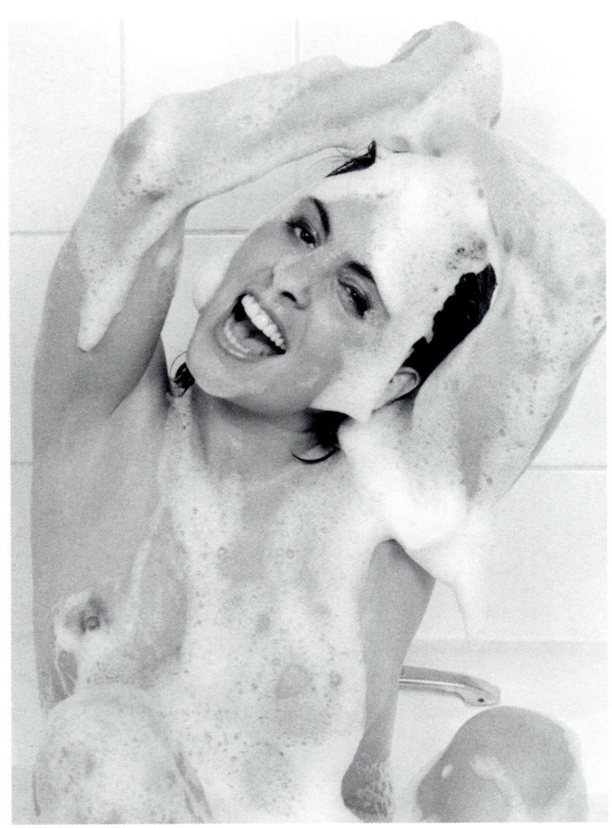

ABOVE: **Exuberant character.** A model who is outgoing and exuberant in real life shows her character very well in the realistic expression shown in this bathtub fun shot. (BRONICA ETRSi; 75mm LENS; 1/125 sec at f/11; ILFORD FP4 PLUS.)

OPPOSITE: **Setting the mood.** The model's eyes are the main mood-setters in this sultry, almost aggressive, expression which is echoed in the body language. (MINOLTA 8000i; 35–80mm LENS; 1/125 sec at f/5.6; KODACHROME 64.)

INSET PHOTOGRAPHS: **Expressions.** These three thumbnail images show how easily different facial expressions can alter the feel and mood of a photographic composition.

Facial expressions are the most dominant conveyors of feelings and emotion in pictures of people, and nude images are no exception. Such expressions communicate the quality and nature of the emotions of the subject, while body cues tell us more about their intensity. The whole spectrum of human emotions can be depicted by photography if approached in the right way, and creatively explored – happiness, joy, exuberance, flirting, sexiness, romance, love, humour, mischievousness, coyness, peace, relaxation, impersonality, sultriness, enigma, thoughtfulness, preoccupation, sadness, austerity, grief, and much more. Body language (see page 80–1) is closely related to this subject and it is often difficult to separate the two as one usually complements the other in the creation of evocative and effective pictures.

character Models, like everyone else, have their own characters. However, few are good enough actors to cover the whole gamut of emotional expressions that may be required, so don't expect it. A chatty, outgoing model will probably be able to perform much better in front of the camera at the happy, exuberant end of the spectrum, while a shy, quiet model may be more comfortable with dreamy, romantic poses. A true smile of happiness, gladness or joy is an expression in which the corners of the mouth curve upward and the outer corners of the eyes crinkle into crow's feet. For many people, a camera smile is hard to produce on demand. It is also a fact of life that some people are more photogenic when smiling and others when straight-faced. Try to gauge the types of poses and expressions that the model is most likely to be comfortable with. Above all, avoid asking for expressions that do not come naturally, as this will be evident in the final results. The aim is to make sure that your model is relaxed and understands your ideas. To achieve this, it is imperative that you adequately describe what you want your model to do and make every effort to put her in the right frame of mind. Showing her pictures similar to the scenario you have in mind, either from magazines or from your own portfolio, and good old-fashioned conversation is helpful. Playing suitable music on the stereo can also help with mood-setting.

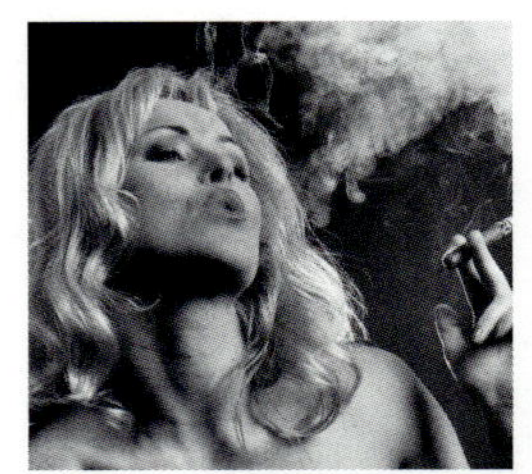

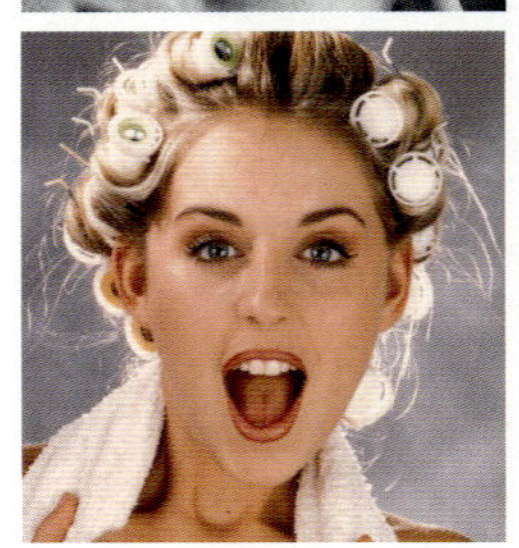

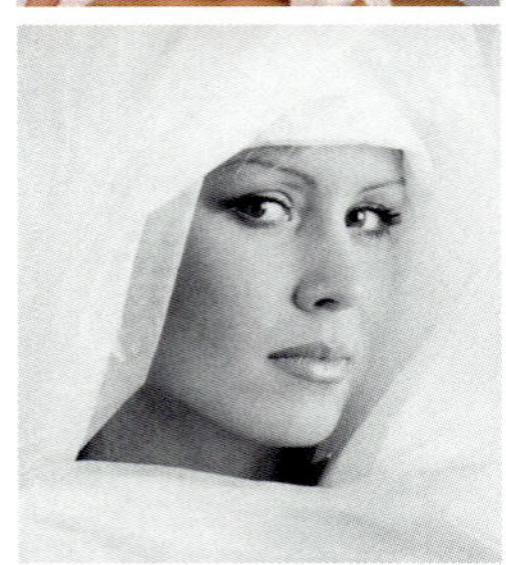

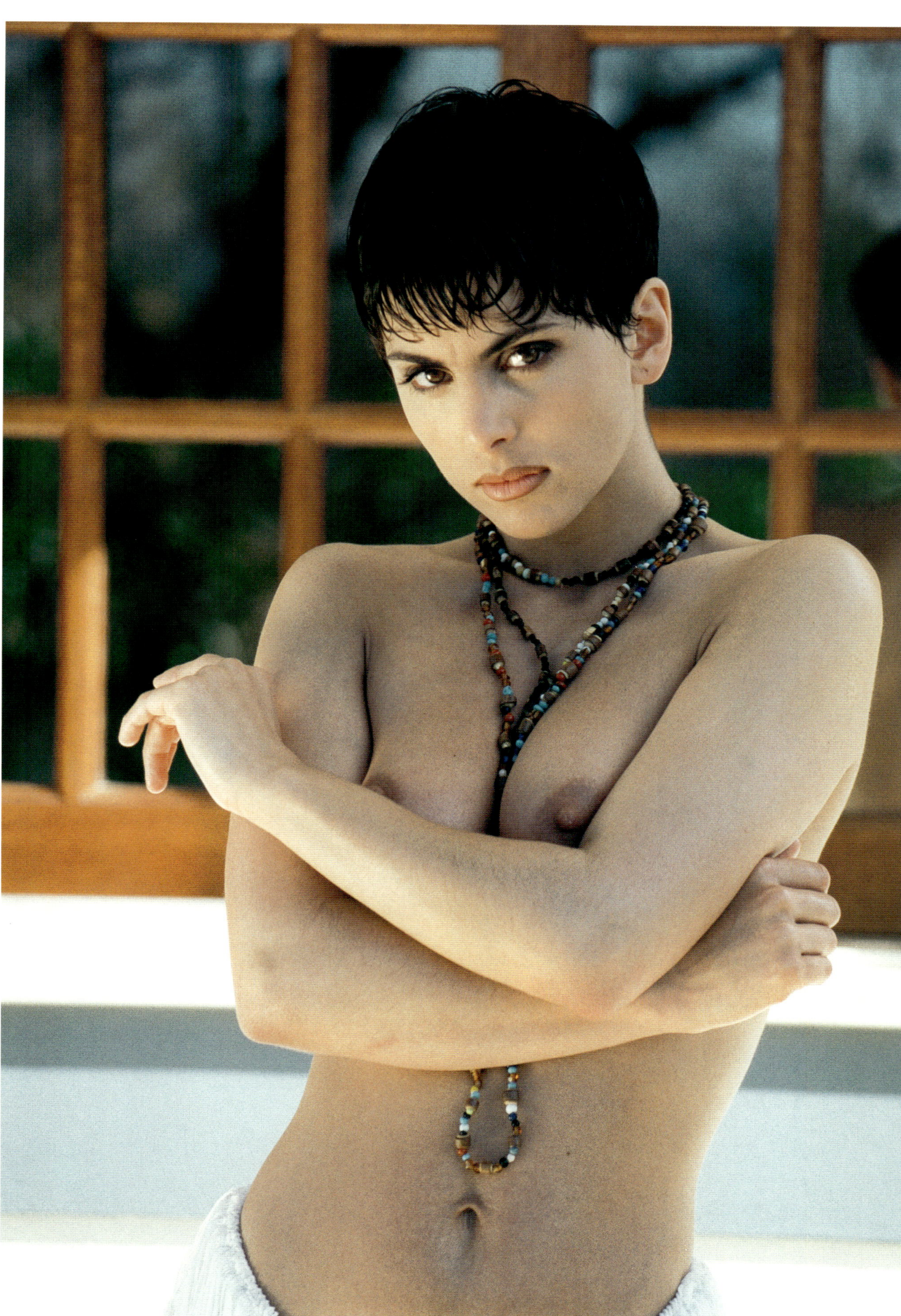

Body language

The term body language, as used in the context of this book, describes how a person can convey a particular emotion – such as feelings of anger, fear, happiness, joy, hate, love, sadness or surprise – to an image by the use of bodily gestures, postures and facial expressions.

a clear message This is particularly important in nude photography, where the message intended by the photographer must be correctly perceived and not misunderstood. We all use body language as a means of non-verbal communication, whether we are aware of it or not, and recognize it instinctively. For instance, lifting the chin and looking down the nose are non-verbal signs of superiority, arrogance and disdain, while tilting the head to one side may be used to show friendliness or coyness. Eye contact arouses strong emotions and sadness shows most clearly in the eyes. Slight postural shifts and the direction of visual focus are two extremely subtle movements that communicate a potentially changing emotional state. Crossing the arms is often decoded as a defensive barrier sign, but with arms and elbows pulled tightly into the body the gesture may reveal acute nervousness or anxiety.

Facial expression and body language are closely interrelated and usually reinforce one another. For instance, the model in the picture on the left has a happy smiling expression and the action being carried out by her body is reinforcing the assumption that she is indeed happy. The use of appropriate body language to fit the mood is imperative if the image is to be interpreted correctly. The young woman below who is about to take a bite out of the lush apple is not just eating. The expression on her face is tantalizing and seductive and the way she is holding the apple is itself suggestive of more than mere sustenance. Also, the subtle embracing of her body with her arms and her general demeanour lead us to the conclusion that perhaps the original sin is contemplated. This is confirmed by the working title of this image, which is the 'Temptation of Eve'.

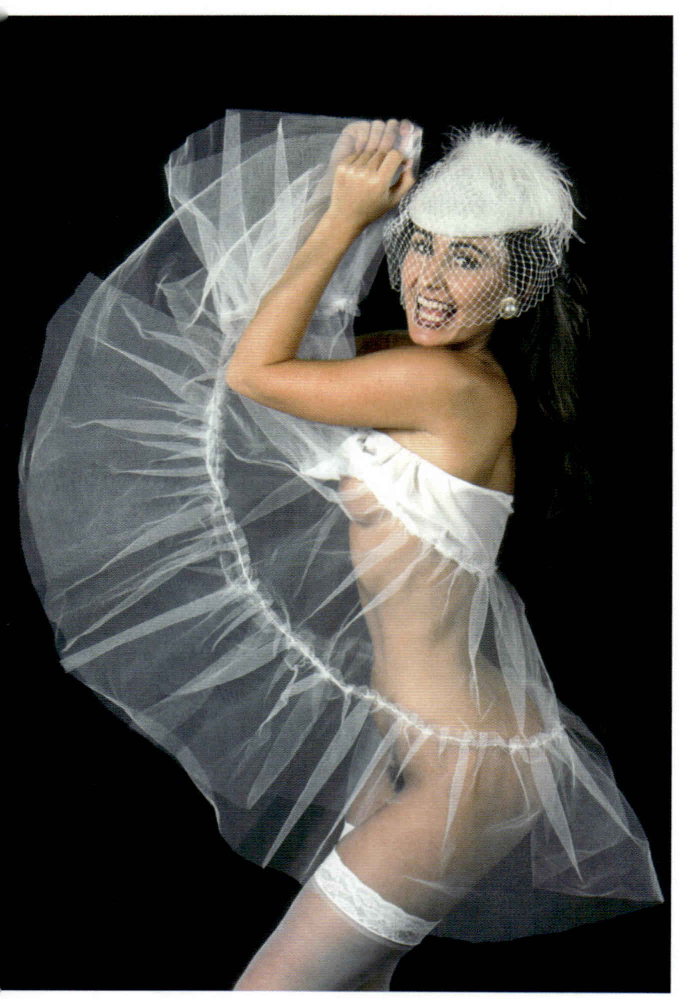

ABOVE: **Light-hearted imagery.** A happy smiling face and exuberant body language come together to produce a light-hearted fun image.
(MINOLTA 8000i; 75–300mm ZOOM LENS; 1/125 sec at f/11; KODACHROME 64.)

RIGHT: **Seductive body language.** The body language of this apple-wielding temptress leaves no doubt as to her intentions.
(MINOLTA 8000i; 35–80mm ZOOM LENS; 1/125 sec at f/8; KODAK GOLD 100.)

OPPOSITE: **Underlying sexuality.** The seemingly expressionless look on the model's face in this image belies the underlying sexuality of her body language.
(MINOLTA 8000i; 100mm LENS; 1/125 sec at f/16; AGFA RS1000.)

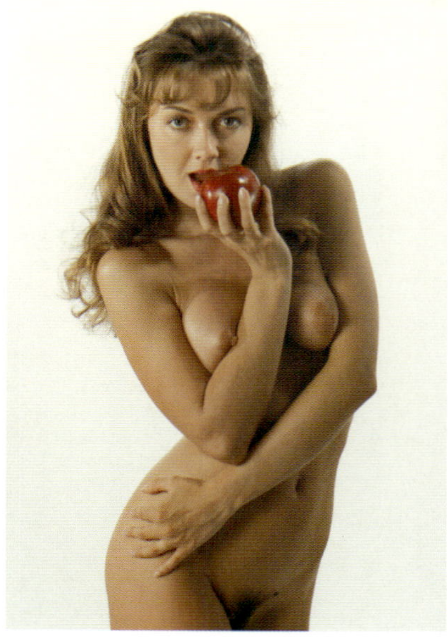

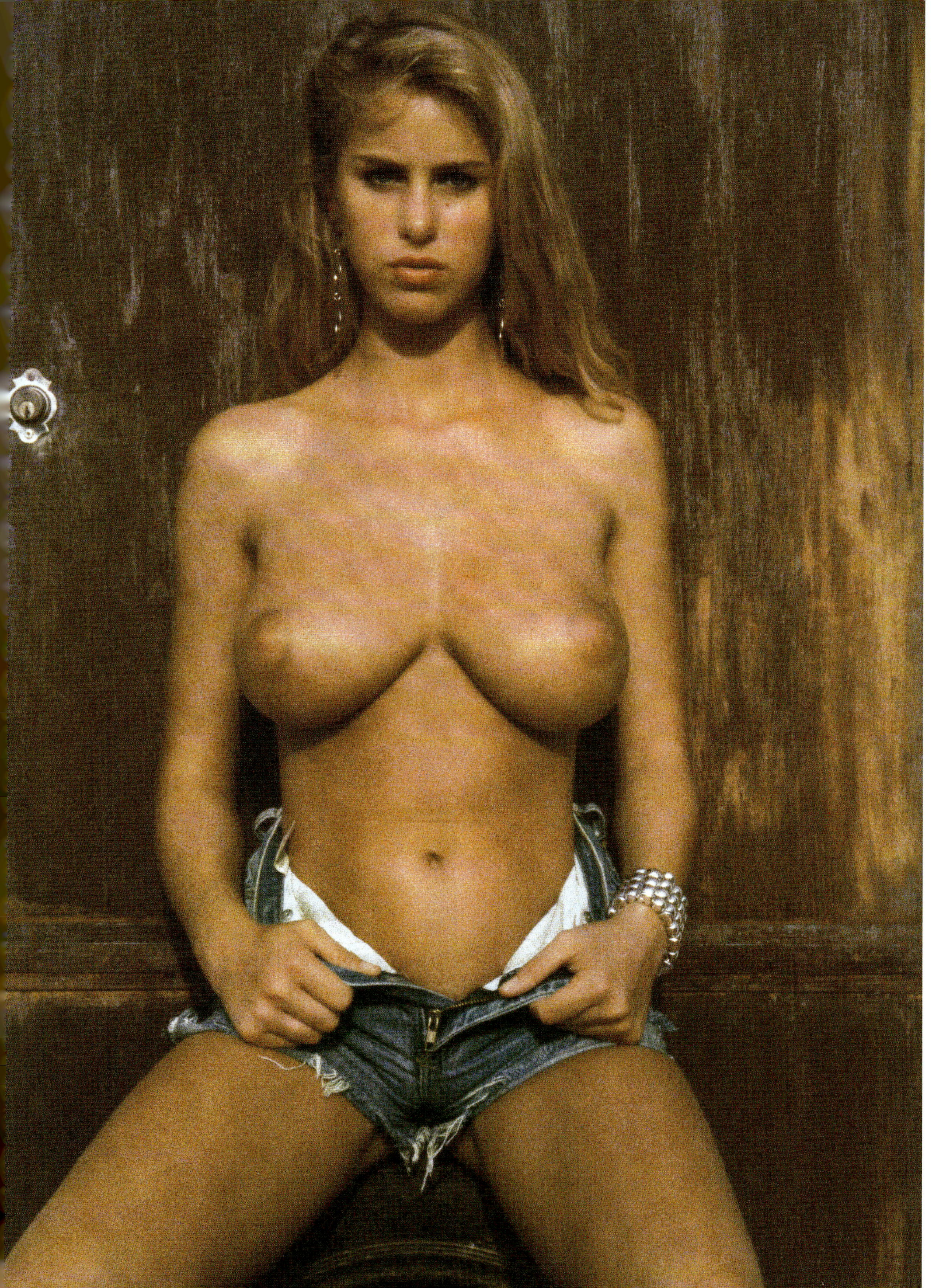

Motion

Motion, or the impression of motion, in a nude image is a tremendous way of adding impact to a picture. There are many methods of doing this, and on location classic examples are using the elements of wind and water.

making movement

A silk scarf or piece of fine material flowing in the wind behind the model can impart interest as well as elegance and often improves the pictorial content of the composition. Using a slow shutter speed will cause the material to blur and give the impression of motion. For hand-held cameras, a shutter speed of around 1/30 sec is adequate, but take extra care to hold the camera steady to avoid camera shake. A more dramatic effect can be obtained employing slower shutter speeds in conjunction with a tripod. In the studio, a wind machine can be used to add movement to a model's hair.

Water can impart dynamism to images and the sea, rivers and waterfalls are all ideal sources of moving water. Waves at the edge of the seashore, either as an integral part of the image or as a background, offer the opportunity to include movement. Use a fast shutter speed to arrest the action or a slow shutter speed to blur the movement and give a softer impression. The latter technique works well with waterfalls and fast-flowing rivers. Devices such as showers and hosepipes can also be used to add sparkling water droplets to a picture (see pages 116–7). Another way of expressing motion in an image is to ask the model to perform an animated action, such as a dance movement, walking or jumping.

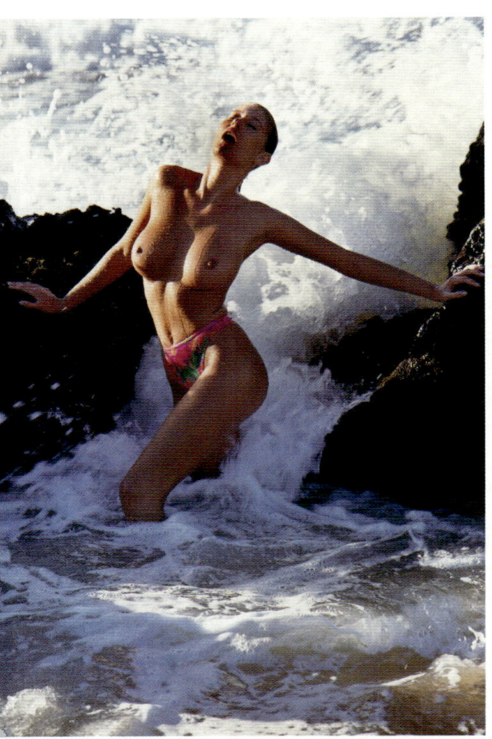

ABOVE: **Arrested movement.** A high shutter speed was used to arrest the movement of the water and show detail in the crashing waves. (BRONICA ETRSi; 150mm LENS; 1/250 sec at f/8; KODAK GPX.)

RIGHT: **Animated motion.** The use of a slow shutter speed has allowed the interplay of the wind with the silk scarf to be captured, giving the image an animated feeling. The wind blowing the surface of the sand adds to this impression. (BRONICA ETRSi; 150mm LENS; 1/30 sec at f/16; KODAK GPX.)

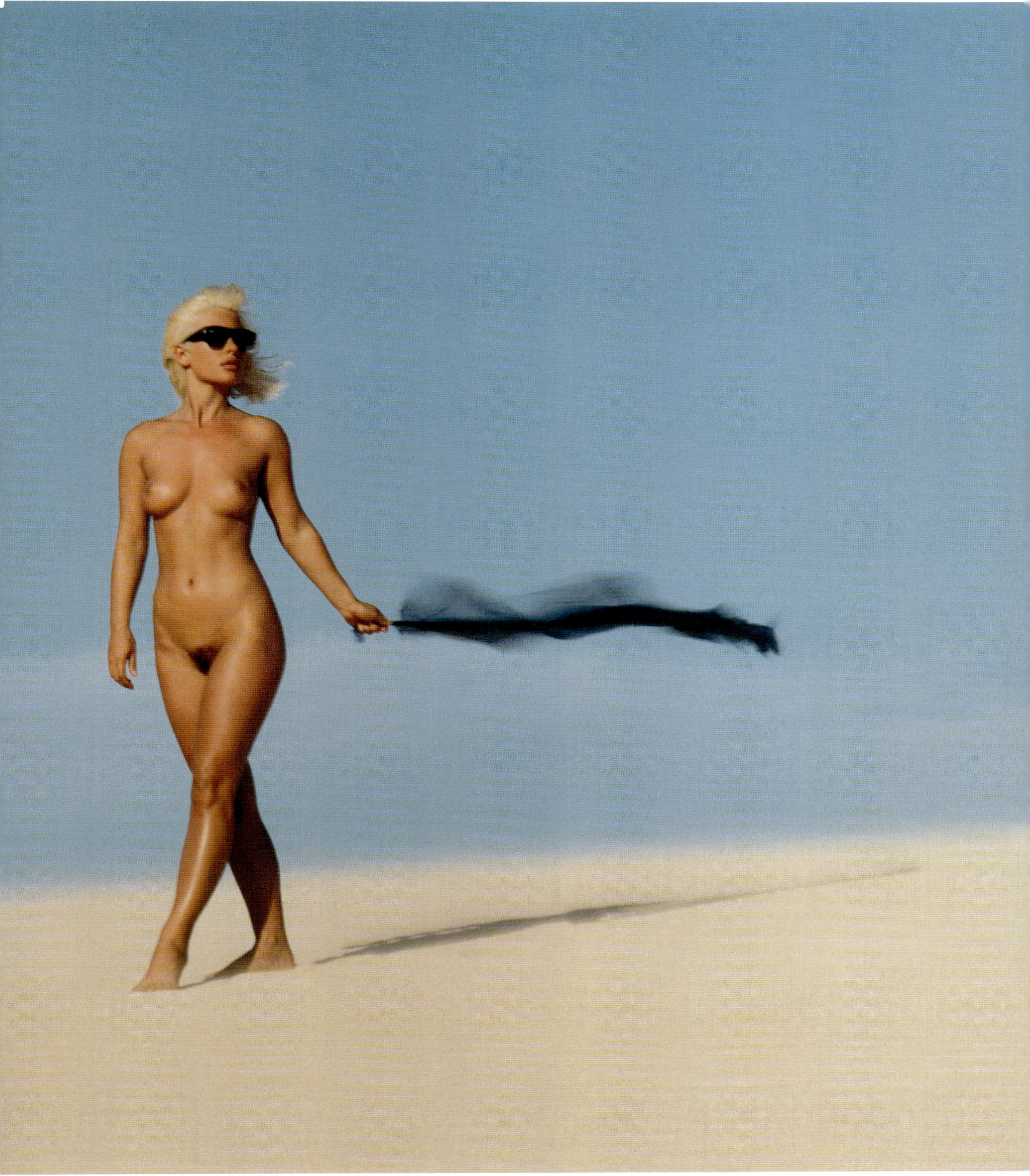

The nude has been one of the most
controversial yet most photographed
subjects since photography was
invented. At its best, the human
form has been portrayed as a
subject of beauty and wonderment,
and this chapter continues the
tradition. In the following pages, a
variety of methods and techniques
to achieve beautiful and creative
representations of the female form
are described, illustrated with a
selection of imaginative photographs
and tips. Techniques such as working
with shadows, using body projection,
making striking silhouettes, infrared
photography and using reflections or
water are simply explained. Sections
on close-up photography, textures,
shape and form show how easily
artistic nude images may be
achieved. For the more advanced
nude photographer, the sections on
working with props, locations and
multiple models provides a source of
valuable information and advice.

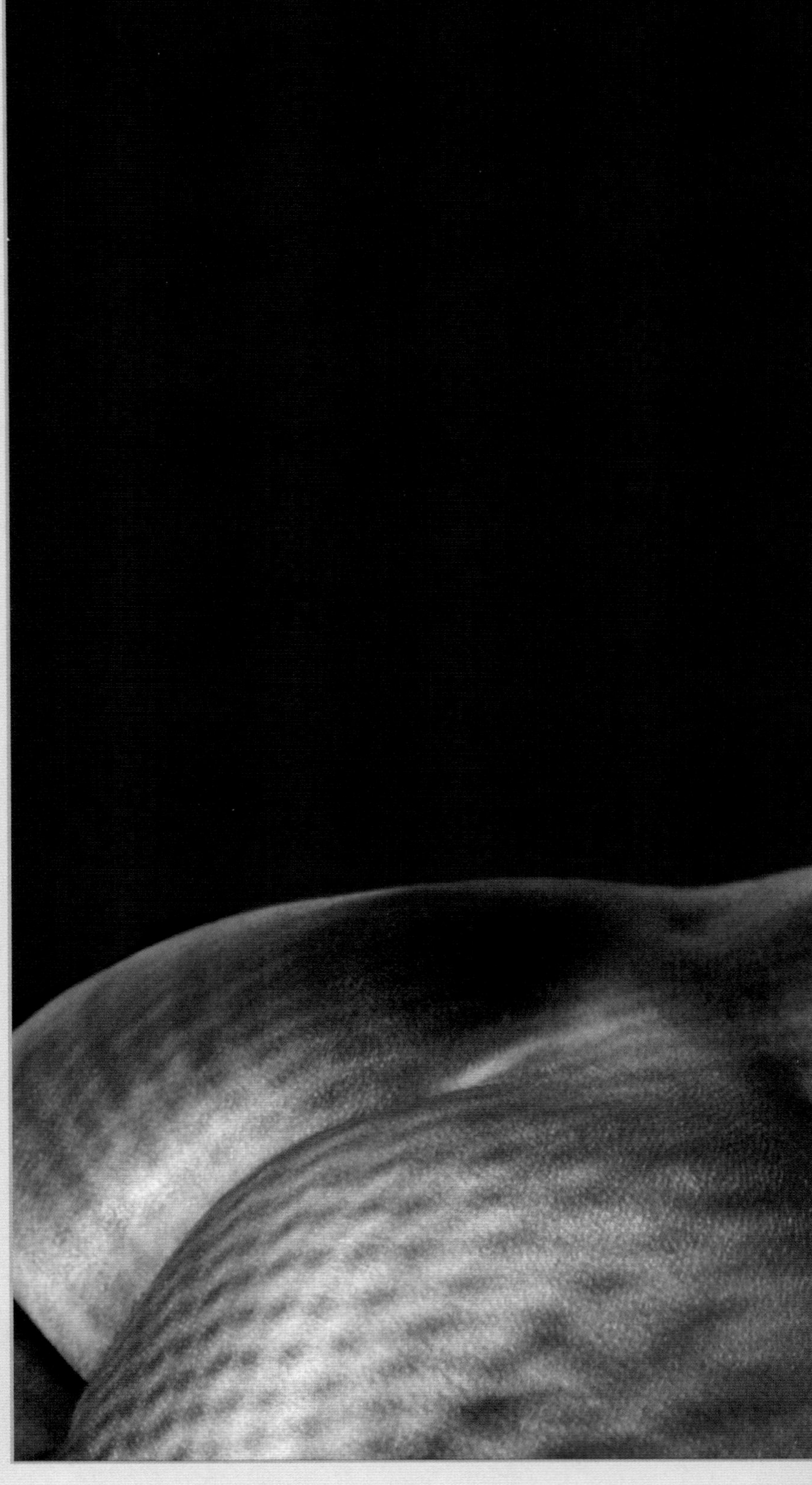

RIGHT: **Unusual patterns.** Fishing net
stretched above the model was the source
of this interesting pattern, which was
created using daylight.
(BRONICA ETRSi; 150mm LENS; 1/60 sec at f/8;
ILFORD FP4; SEPIA [THIOCARBAMIDE] TONED.)

Creative imagery

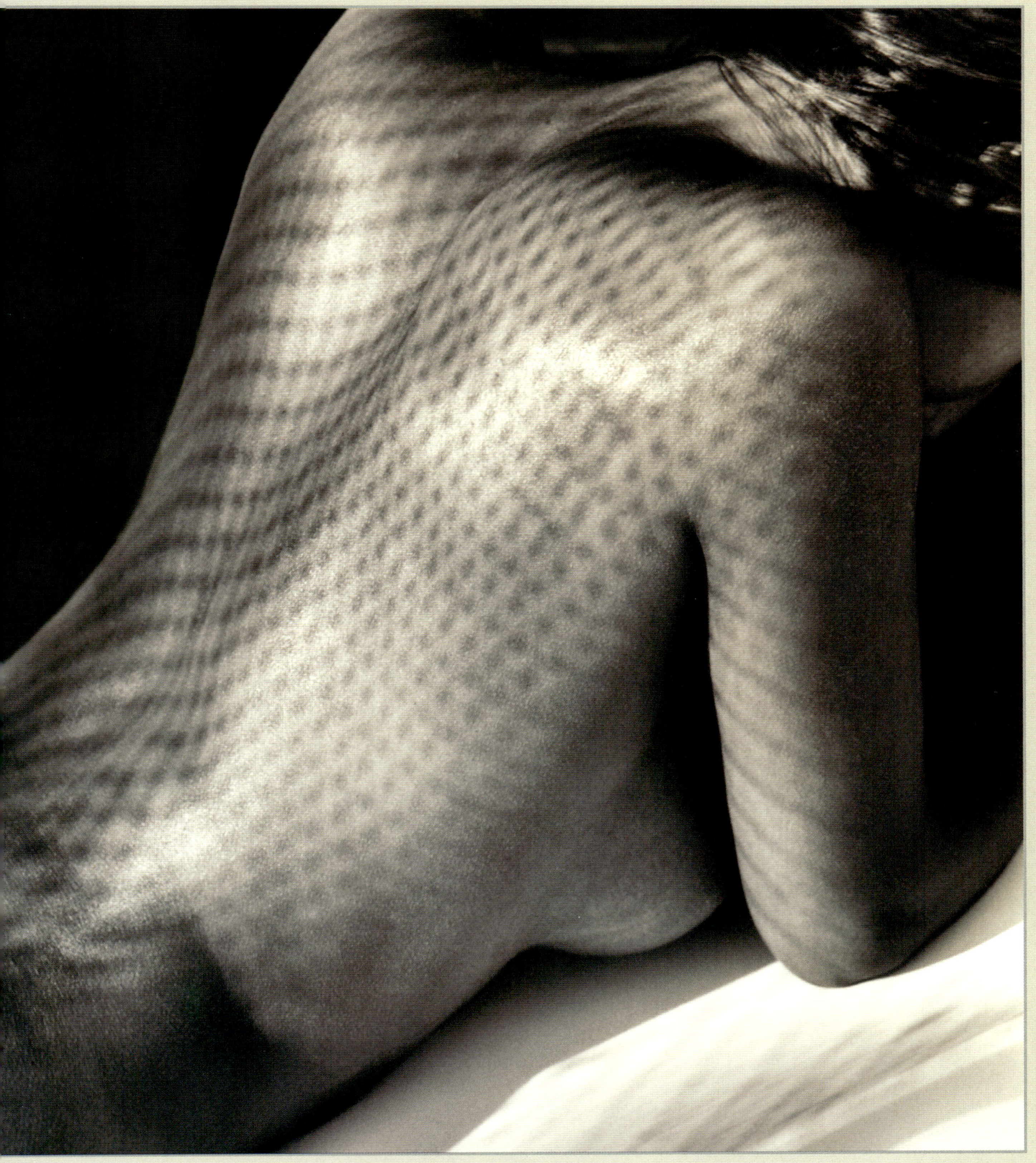

Shadows and patterns

ABOVE: **Exploiting shapes.** Look for interesting shapes and shadows and fit them to the model's body shape.
(DAYLIGHT, BRONICA ETRSi; 150mm LENS; 1/60 sec at f/5.6; ILFORD FP4 PLUS; SEPIA [THIOCARBAMIDE] TONED.)

Sunlight is an extremely versatile light source, constantly changing and capable of providing the most subtle of effects. It is also the perfect point light source and as such can readily be used to cast sharp or diffused shadows and patterns onto the human form. For this to be effective, the sunlight needs to be strong enough to give sufficient contrast between the light and dark areas of the shadow pattern. The light also needs to be directional – so early morning or late afternoon are the times of day when the most interesting patterns are likely to be formed. Midday sun, a time usually avoided by most photographers because it causes deep eye shadows, can also be used to advantage here if the object casting the shadow is above the subject.

shadow casting

Obviously, an object needs to be placed between the sunlight and the model in order to cast a shadow. This is elementary, but some thought must still be given to what is used to cast creative shadows, and the distance at which the chosen object should be placed from the subject. The closer the object is to the subject, the sharper the image will be. The further away it is, the more diffuse the pattern.

Materials with open-mesh designs – such as net curtains, lace and netting – make ideal objects to project interesting shadow patterns onto the body. These are easy to manoeuvre and manipulate, and can be hung or draped in front of the subject using a variety of methods. A few suggestions for other objects that provide interesting shapes and patterns are windows, especially if they contain grills or leaded lights; wrought-iron work, such as gates and railings; lattice-backed chairs; and various types of plants with large leaves, such as palm fronds.

The choice of materials or objects is limited only by your imagination. For the best effects, go in close and photograph parts of the body to create artistic, almost abstract, images using a lens aperture that will ensure adequate depth of field. A medium telephoto or mid-range zoom lens is recommended for creating this type of image.

USING GOBOS

Shadow effects can be produced in a studio using a focused light beam, usually called a Fresnel spotlight. Gobos, which are metal disks with patterns cut in them, can be attached to the front of these lights and focused on the subject or the background to give sharp or soft patterns. Small pieces of lace or other materials, and coloured gels can be placed in front of the lens to produce coloured patterns.

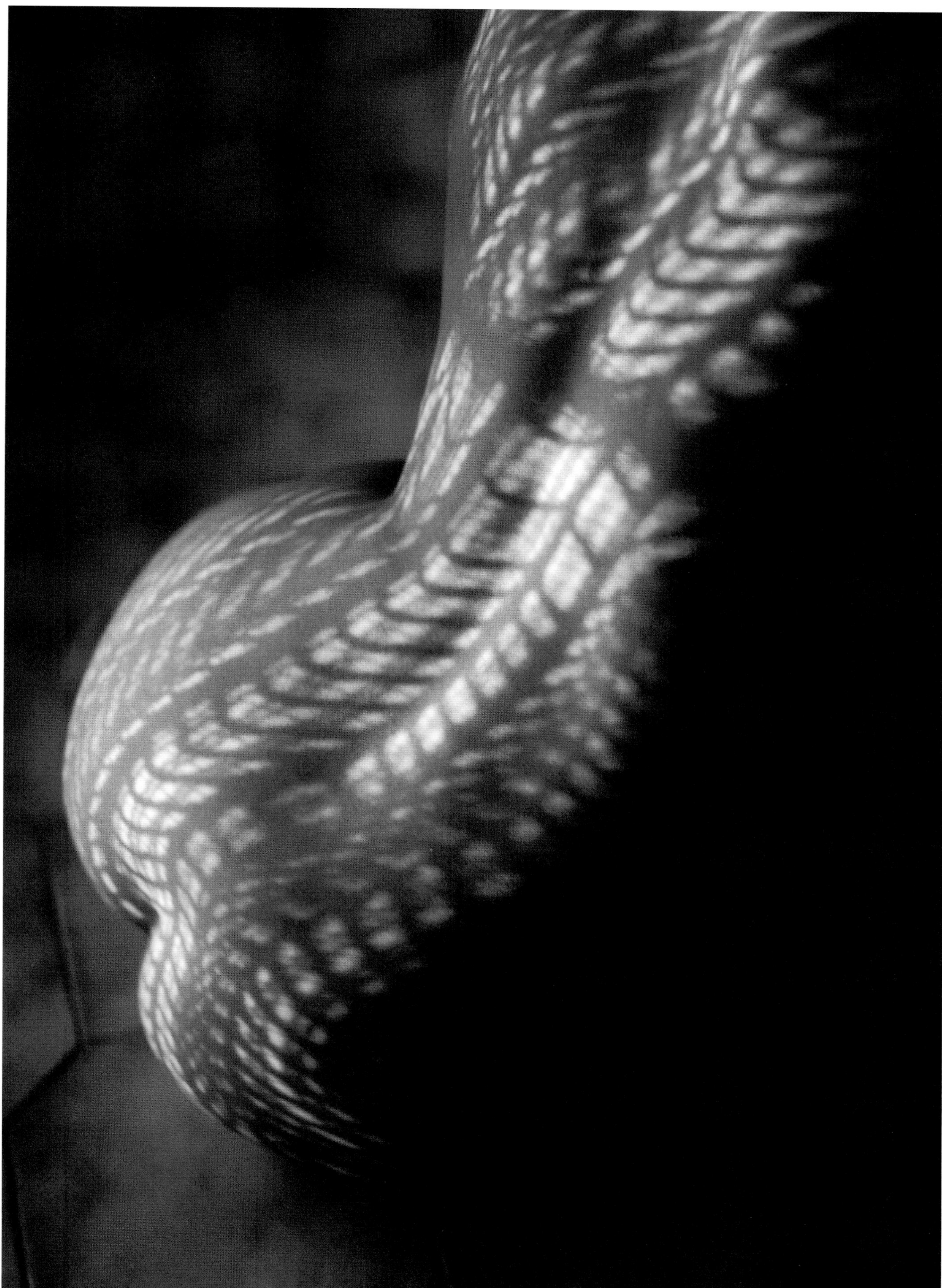

Slide projections

The previous pages have shown how patterns on the body using shadows cast by natural objects can be used to good effect. Another useful device for creating photographs of this type is to project an image on to the nude body using a slide projector.

patterns and colour By

using this method you can create not only monochromatic patterns but also coloured images using a landscape, an abstract image, or even text. A projector can offer greater creative control over the image, allowing the creation of a 'story' through the subject chosen for projection. A broad selection of slides is recommended, as it is not always obvious in advance which ones will work best. This type of photography can also be done at any time of day or night – there is no need to wait for the sun to come out.

In theory this may seem to be a fairly straightforward procedure, but in practice it

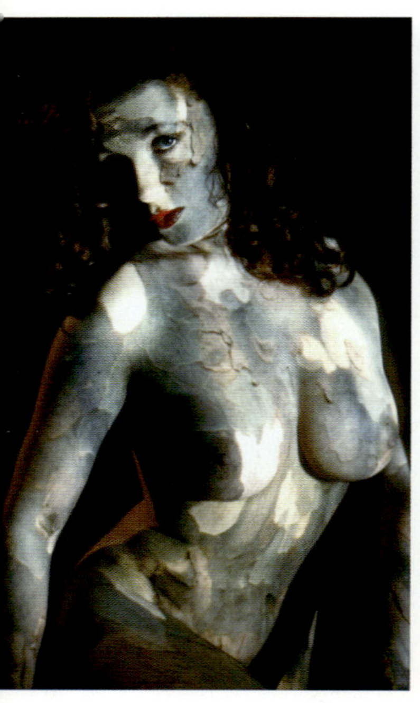

ABOVE: **Unusual texture.** A slide of cracked and broken bark from a plane tree was used to create a bizarre but effective mottled texture on the model's face and skin. (MINOLTA 8000i; 100mm MACRO LENS; 1/15 sec at f/2.8; KODAK EKTACHROME 320T.)

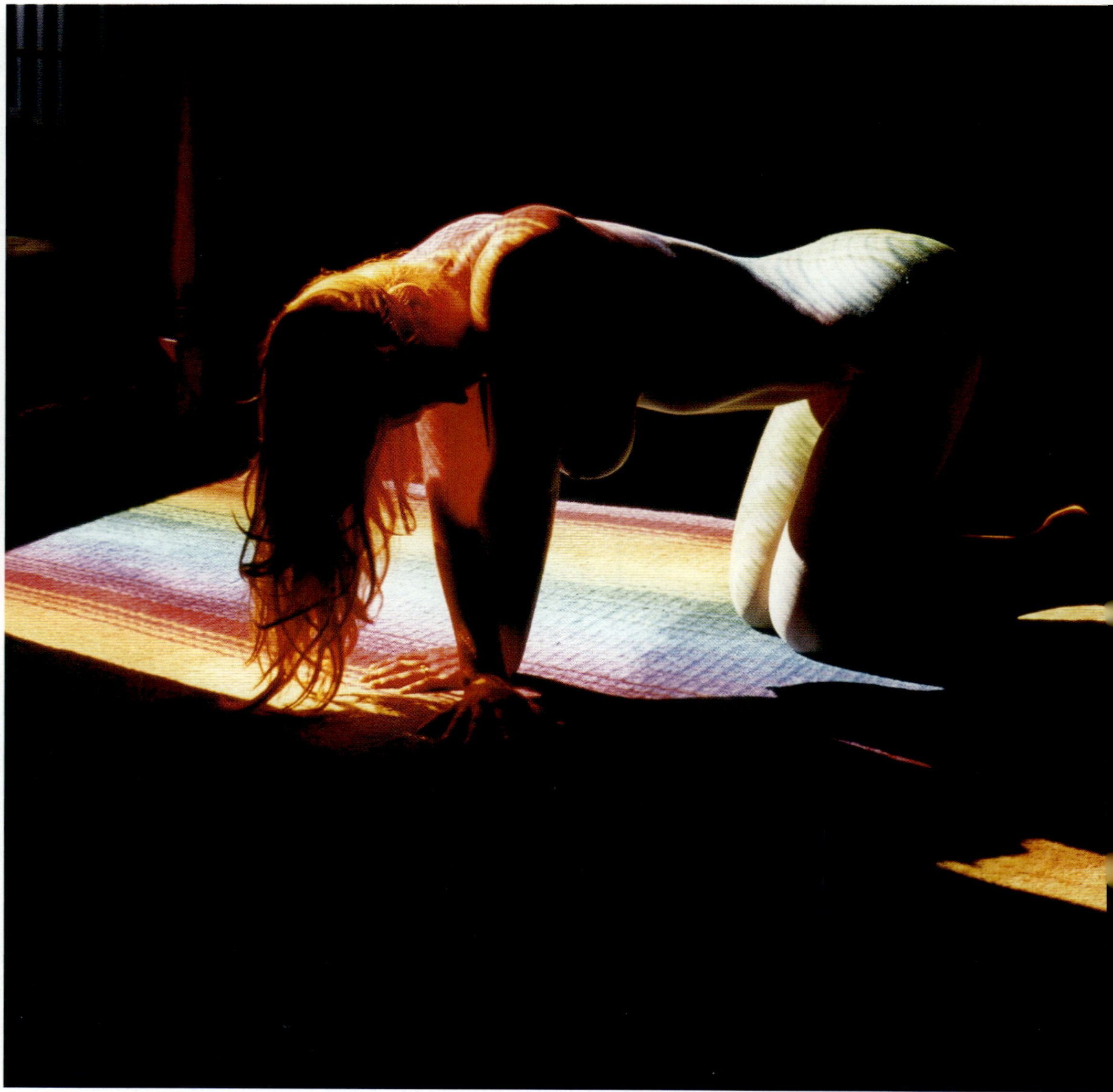

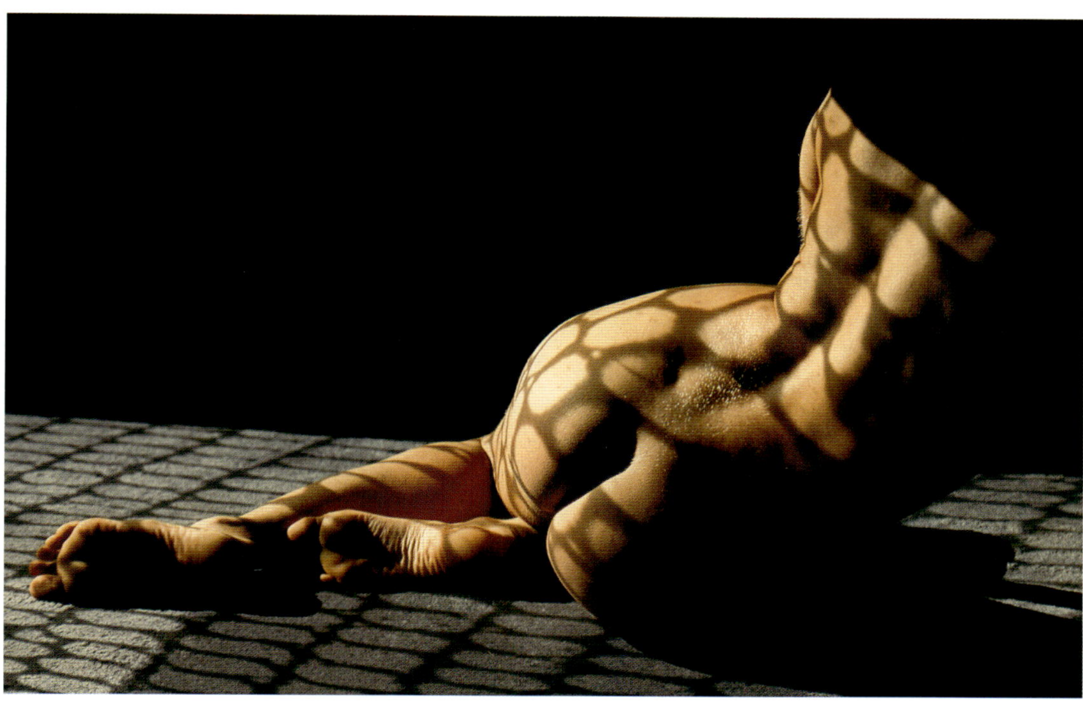

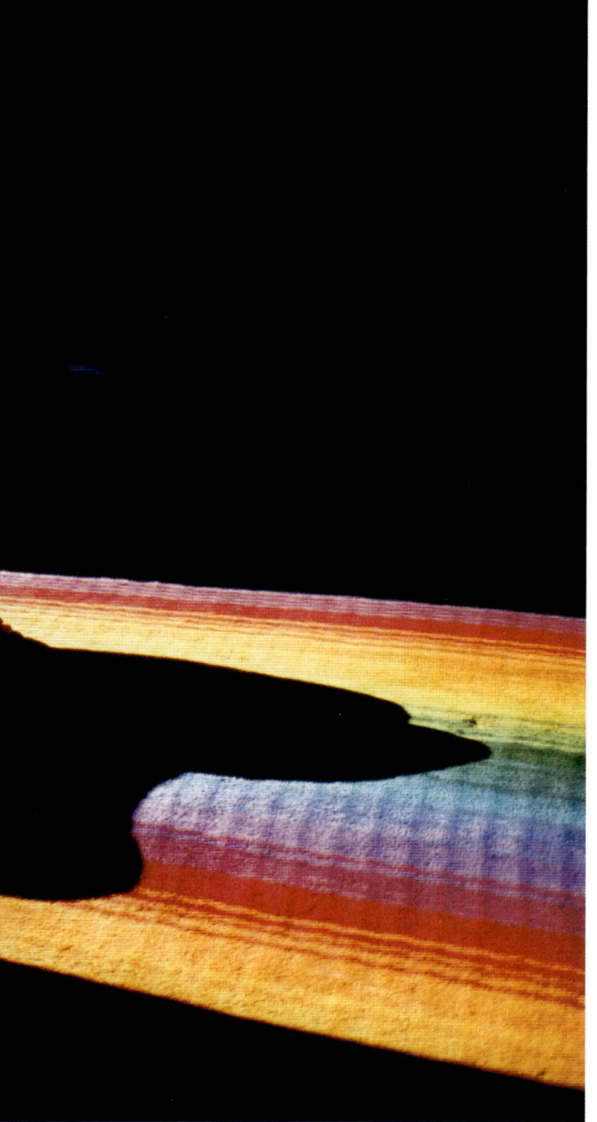

takes a lot of thought and experimentation to achieve the impressive results that are possible with this technique.

In order to cover the whole body with an image, there must be enough distance between the model and the projector, so you will need a studio or large room. Regular 35mm slide projectors do not emit a very powerful light (most use a 150-watt bulb) and light intensity falls off with the square of the distance. The closer you get to the model the better. A wide-angle lens on the projector can help. Upgrading to a 6 x 6 projector will provide more light. If space is tight, try projections on parts of the body.

quality of light

Light from a projector is warmer than daylight, so if transparency film is used, a fast tungsten film such as Kodak Ektachrome 320T should be chosen. For negative stock this consideration is not so important, as the colour cast can be filtered out during printing. Any fast negative film, ideally ISO 400 or higher, is suitable. A fast lens on the camera and a tripod, preferably with a rifle grip, is also required as exposure times are likely to be high. Projecting thin or light-coloured transparencies helps keep exposures reasonably short. Models should be positioned comfortably, as they have to hold their breath and remain still during the long exposure.

For this kind of work, a 35mm camera with through-the-lens (TTL) metering and autofocus is preferable – it can sometimes be difficult to focus manually at low light levels. A remote release also helps prevent camera movement. Sometimes an additional light is useful to illuminate a portion of the figure that is not covered by light from the projector. A modelling light from a flash unit, with a barn door or snoot attachment to localize the light, can be used for this purpose, but take care not to overpower light from the projector.

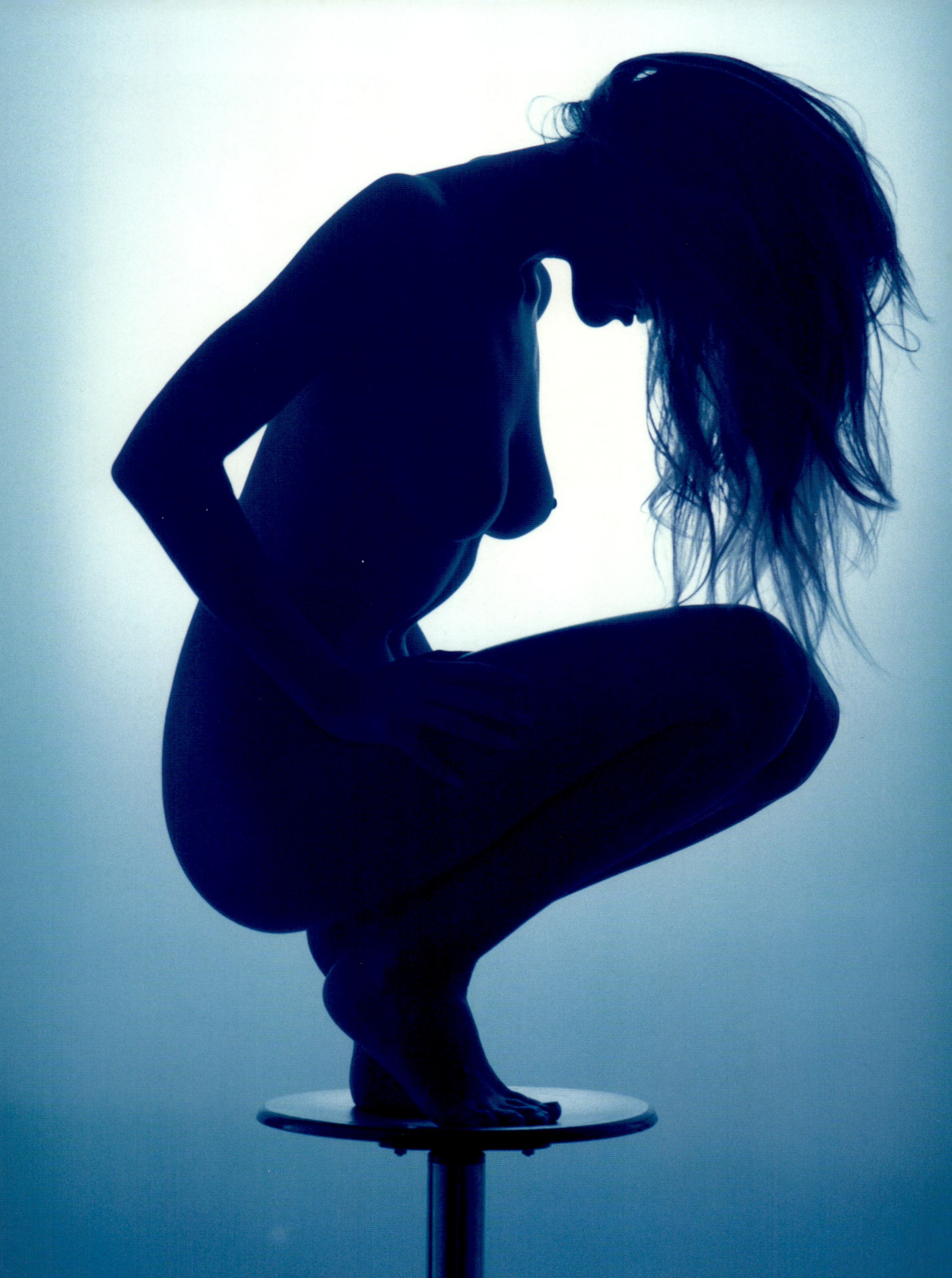

Silhouettes

OPPOSITE: **Blue light.** A blue gel placed over a light behind a translucent screen created this atmospheric semi-silhouette. White reflectors to the side bounced back some light to give the image the distinctive blue-rim effect. (MINOLTA 8000i; 75–300mm ZOOM LENS; 1/125 sec at f/11; KODACOLOR VR-100.)

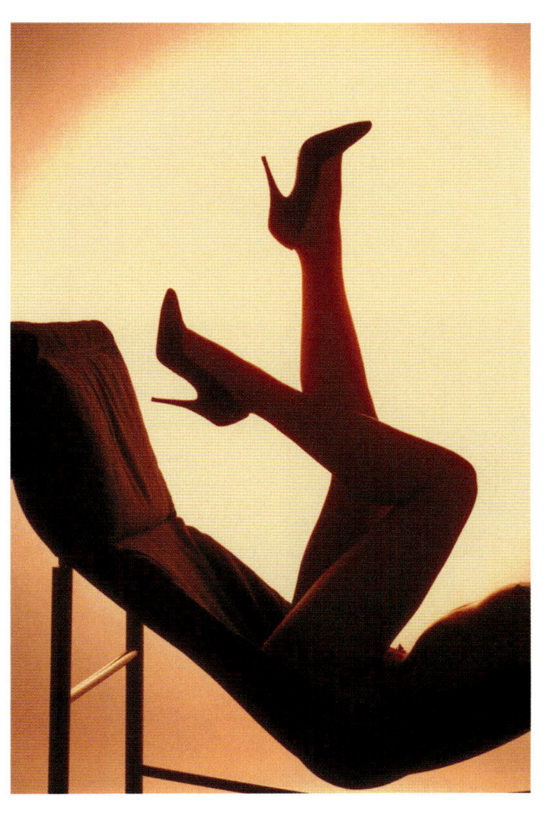

ABOVE: **Backlit silhouette.** The sun effect was obtained by backlighting through a translucent screen and the use of an orange gel. (MINOLTA 8000i; 100mm MACRO LENS; 1/125 sec at f/8; KODACHROME 64.)

Silhouettes are images that are created from extremes of light and dark to give a two-dimensional graphic representation of the subject. The background is usually very bright and the subject very dark and featureless. This technique can be a useful asset for the nude photographer to exploit. The outline of the model is the all-important feature to be aware of, and the challenge boils down to the creation of interesting shapes in two dimensions. Experiment by asking the model to adopt positions in which her arms and legs are extended, such as a ballerina-style pose.

encroaching light

Partial silhouettes are usually more interesting than total silhouettes. These can be created by permitting light to encroach around the sides of the model, thereby allowing some features to be seen. This can be achieved by using a reflector, such as a white board or a Lastolite, to reflect back some of the light on to the model's body. A good way of introducing colour interest is the use of coloured gels on the background illumination.

unintentional silhouettes

When attempting to take photographs by window light, inexperienced photographers will often produce silhouettes or partial silhouettes unintentionally. This often occurs because a subject placed in front of a bright window will appear to be relatively normal to a viewer, as the eye automatically adjusts to the differences in light level. The camera, however, will see this as a high-contrast situation and underexpose the subject accordingly, causing a silhouette. The closer the subject is placed to the window, the higher the contrast ratio will be.

LIGHTING SILHOUETTES

Lighting for silhouettes or partial silhouettes is relatively straightforward, whether you are working in the studio or using natural light. When photographing indoors, all that is needed is illumination directly behind the model and little or none to the front. Positioning a light behind a translucent screen and dimming any other studio lights readily achieves this. Take a light reading from the lit screen and set the exposure for this. To introduce more detail into the image, bounce some of the light back with reflector boards placed to the side or front of the model. A room with a large window will function in exactly the same way, as you can use daylight as the light source.

Defining details

Photographing part of your model's anatomy rather than the complete person can be a rewarding method of creating an interesting image. By getting in close, you can isolate, and focus attention on, a particular aspect of the model's body, thus adding another dimension to your picture-taking.

shape and form Leaving the

model's face out of the composition automatically depersonalizes the subject and emphasizes the figure's shapes and forms. This can be especially effective if your model has a particularly good feature, for example a pair of well-shaped legs or an attractively shaped

back. The lighting is important for this type of shot and will make or break a picture. Images like this should be considered with care and lit sympathetically, otherwise they may appear to be tacky or even crude. Soft or hard directional lighting are good options, but avoid using flat, bland lighting – an image with good modelling will have a bigger impact.

Use the viewfinder to capture the most effective compositional elements, and good images will be assured. A medium- to long-range zoom lens can be an advantage when working in this mode, as it will allow you to zoom in and out on various areas in search of the perfect composition.

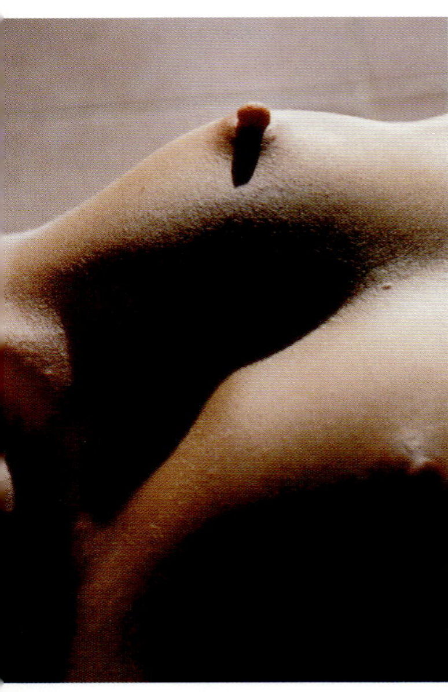

ABOVE: **Graphic detail.** Strong directional sunlight gives a graphic strength to this moody cameo shot. (BRONICA ETRSi; 150mm LENS; 1/125 sec at f/5.6; KODAK PORTRA 160NC.)

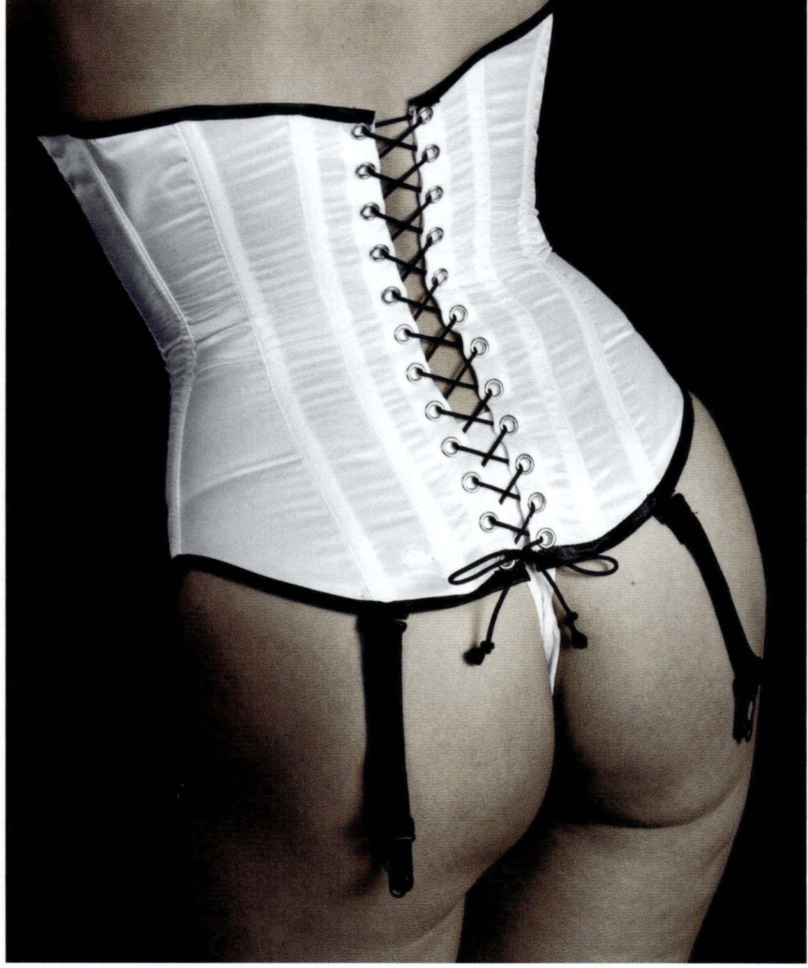

LEFT: **An added dimension.** The use of thiocarbamide toner has added another dimension to this image by emphasizing the shape of the bottom and making the white basque stand out against the body. (BRONICA ETRSi; 150mm LENS; 1/125 sec at f/11; ILFORD FP4.)

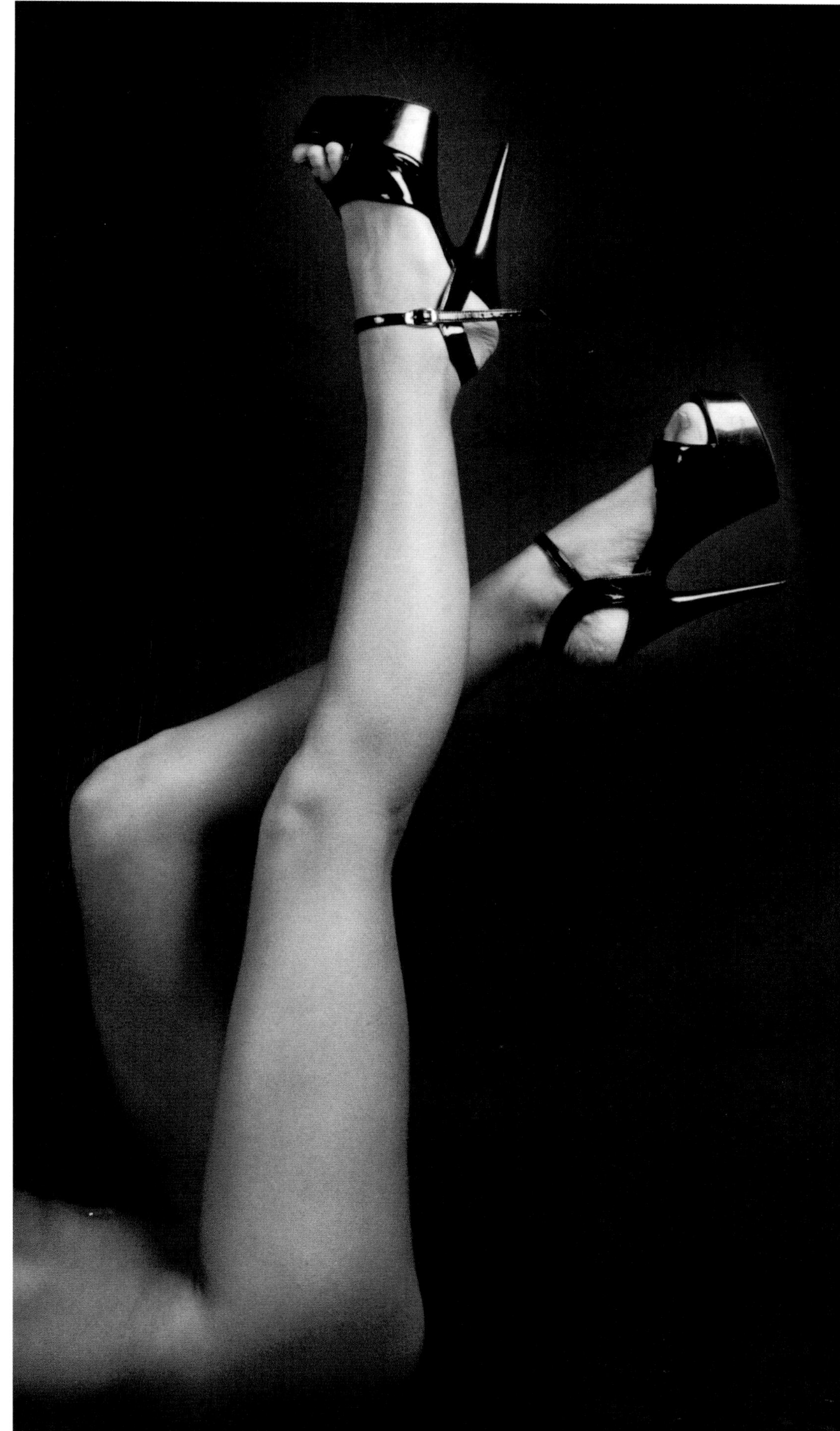

RIGHT: **Selective toning.**
A good pair of legs makes
an ideal close-up study. The
positioning of the feet and
the stiletto heels are
important compositional
elements. Selective toning
with thiocarbamide toner
adds to the effect.
(BRONICA ETRSi; 150mm LENS;
1/125 sec at f/11; ILFORD
FP4 PLUS.)

Textural contrasts

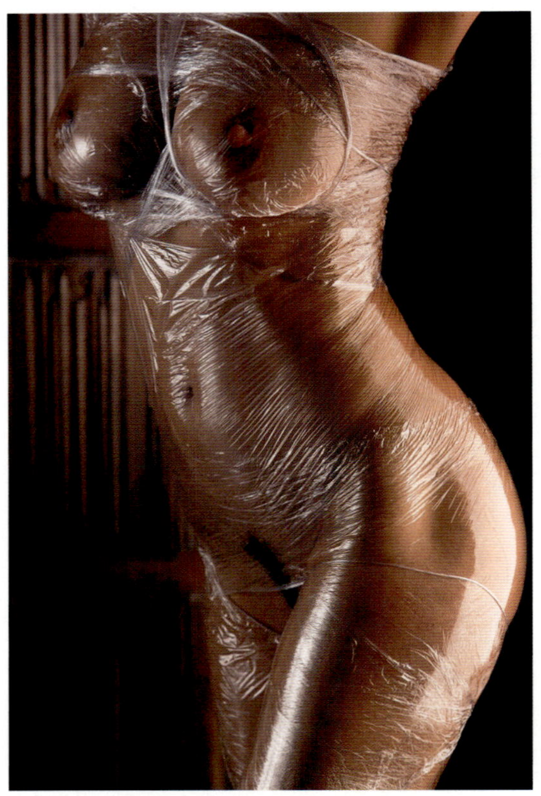

Skin has a distinctive natural texture that can be emphasized by appropriate lighting. Equally, poor lighting can be disastrous. When illuminated with undiffused light at an acute angle, all the surface details are accentuated, including pores, wrinkles and body hair, whereas softer, diffused light at a more perpendicular angle tends to suppress the surface features and gives a smoother appearance.

varied textures Textured materials and skin in juxtaposition can afford some rewarding contrasts. Materials with rough surfaces, like the rope and bark used in examples on these pages, give a sense of vulnerability to delicate human skin. Soft fabrics, such as silk or lace, tend to give a sense of comfort and sensuality. Other types of textures work equally well; for example, shiny metals, plastics and textured fabrics (eg, hessian or fur) can give distinctive images when composed and lit appropriately. Textures on skin as an alternative to those placed against the skin are also worth considering. Some of the materials that can be used on skin to give striking effects are clay, paint and soapsuds. A combination of oil and water can be particularly striking and effective (see pages 38, 102, 116).

PHOTOGRAPHING TEXTURES

It is essential that images that rely on showing texture as a main ingredient should be sharp, as any lack of detail through bad focusing or camera shake will destroy the crispness and clarity of the surface and detract from the overall impact. The ability to emphasize this pictorial quality introduces a three-dimensional quality and realism to what is a flat and two-dimensional representation. A tactile quality is the main aim here, giving the observer the feeling that they want to touch the roughness or smoothness of the surface texture. If this has been achieved, then the image has been successful in this vital aspect. Texture in black and white images is particularly effective, as the lack of colour means that there is one less subjective element for the observer to take into consideration. Going in close and photographing selected areas of the body also focuses the intent and prevents detraction from non-essential elements.

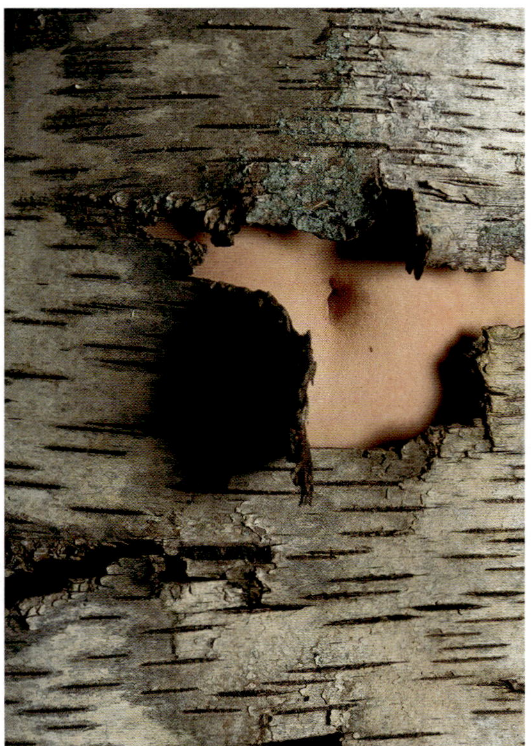

ABOVE: **Shiny texture.** Clingfilm allows the body's curves to be seen through the shiny plastic texture. (BRONICA ETRSi; 150mm LENS; 1/25 sec at f/16; KODAK PORTRA 160NC.)

LEFT: **Juxtaposed textures.** Cherry-tree bark was used to capture this juxtaposition of textures and produce a truly eye-catching image. (BRONICA ETRSi; 150mm LENS; 1/125 sec at f/11; KODAK PORTRA 160NC.)

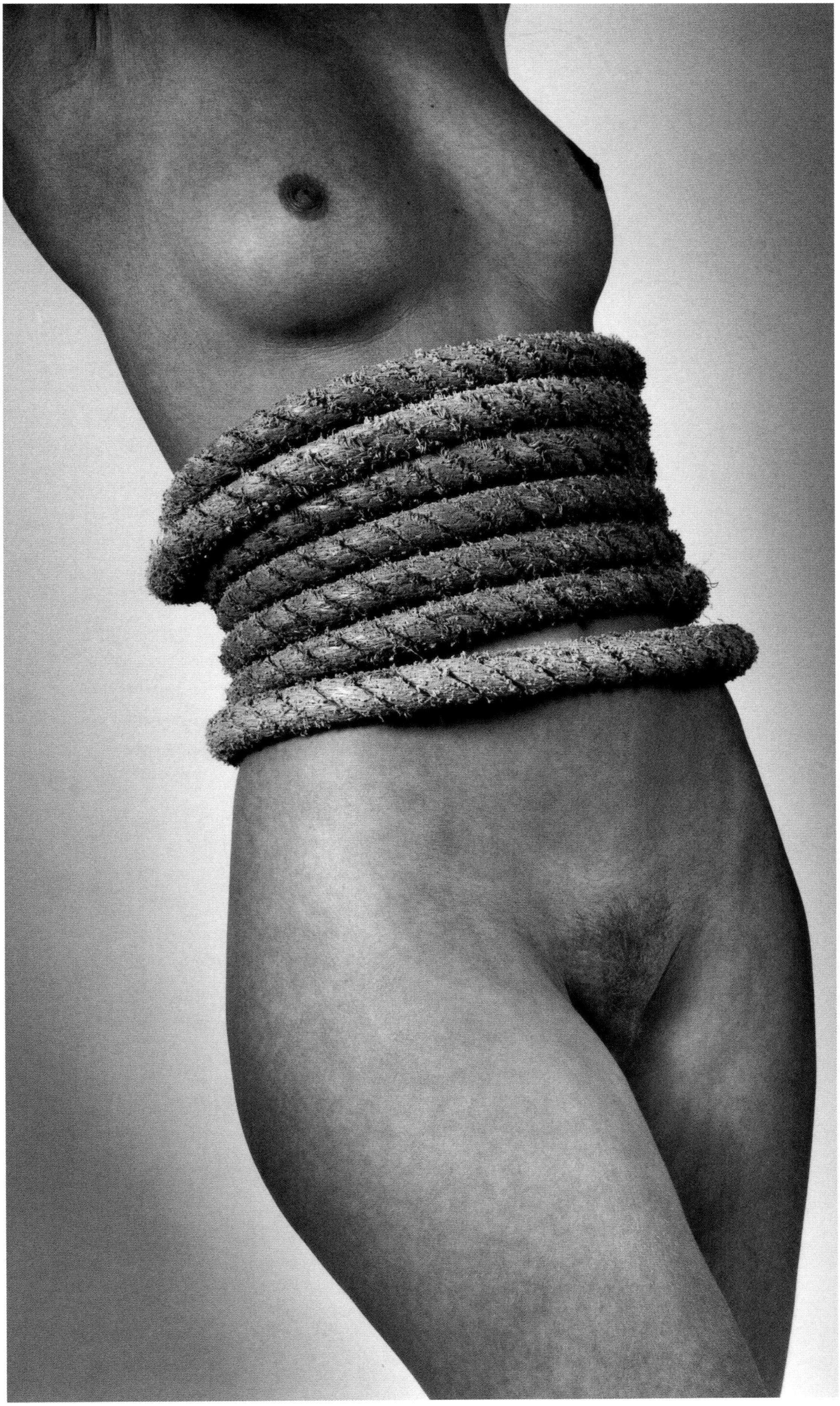

RIGHT: **Rough and smooth.** The roughness of the rope contrasts well with the smoothness of the model's skin. (BRONICA ETRSi; 150mm LENS; 1/125 sec at f/11; ILFORD FP4 PLUS; SEPIA [THIOCARBAMIDE] TONED.)

Shape and form

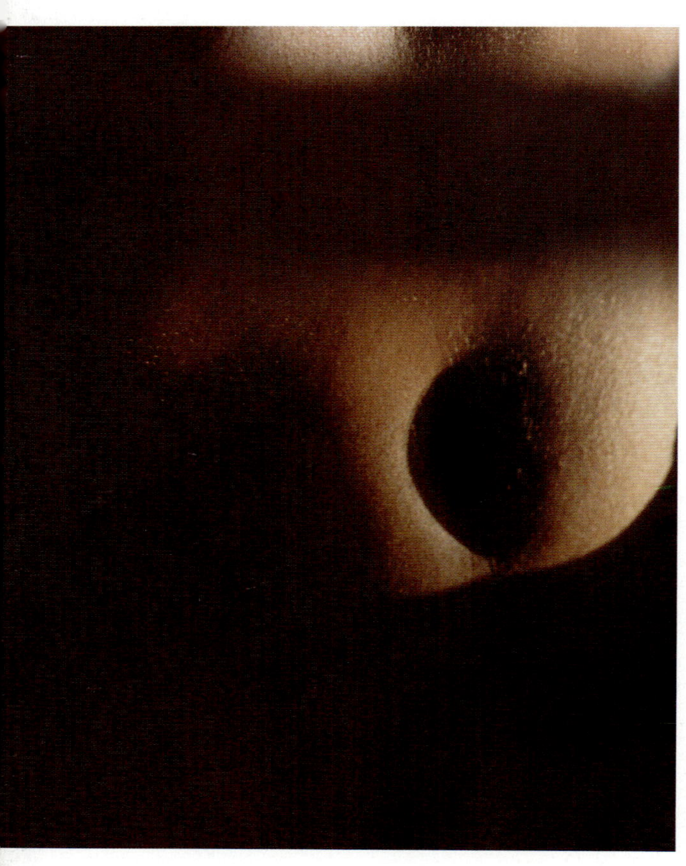

OPPOSITE: **Simple curves.** Simplicity is the key when shooting shape and form. (BRONICA ETRSi; 150mm LENS; 1/60 sec at f/8; ILFORD FP4 PLUS; LIGHT SEPIA [THIOCARBAMIDE] TONING.)

ABOVE: **Evocative shadows.** The deep shadow has reduced this image to a few subtle but evocative shapes. (MINOLTA 8000i; 100mm LENS; 1/125 sec at f/5.6; KODAK PORTRA 160NC.)

For a creative photographer, the nude human body with all its subtle curves is an ideal subject for experimentation with images involving shape and form. An identifiable but strongly abstract image is the aim. Going in close to photograph a selective portion of the body, thus highlighting a particular feature, usually gives the best results.

artistic forms

This is actually an extension of the section describing close-ups on pages 92–3, but focuses on extending the close-up to an extreme artistic form. It is important to try to show the three-dimensional aspect of the subject, such as the shape in the curve of a back or bottom, and the form, such as the roundness of a stomach or a breast. Images should always be kept as simple as possible in order to achieve the greatest possible impact.

A good tonal range between the lighter and darker areas of the composition will help to accentuate the sense of shape and form. Consider also the elimination of colour as a dimension – images of shape and form are often best rendered in monochrome. The subject must, of course, be lit sympathetically for the type of image that the photographer wishes to create. The exclusion of extraneous objects in the background is preferable to retain the purity and strength of the design. Directional or low-key lighting are useful options to give good modelling, and may be either soft or strong depending on the overall impression that is required.

zooming in

It is best to avoid the use of flat lighting, because the main purpose of this type of photography is to emphasize shape. A single-light set-up or glancing sunlight is ideal. A plain, dark or subdued background will usually be less distracting than a white or busy background, but this depends greatly on the overall effect required. Use a medium- to long-range telephoto or zoom lens and a small lens aperture (at least f/8) to maintain depth of field and keep the image as sharp as possible.

ANONYMOUS ATTRIBUTES

Not all models have perfect bodies. Going in close will help the photographer to draw attention to their best attributes and distract from their less attractive features, while still creating good images. Models who are reticent about being photographed in the nude will often be quite willing to pose for photographs of this kind, which maintain a high degree of anonymity. Explain the type of photograph you intend to take and, if possible, show the model examples of this type of work before attempting any photography.

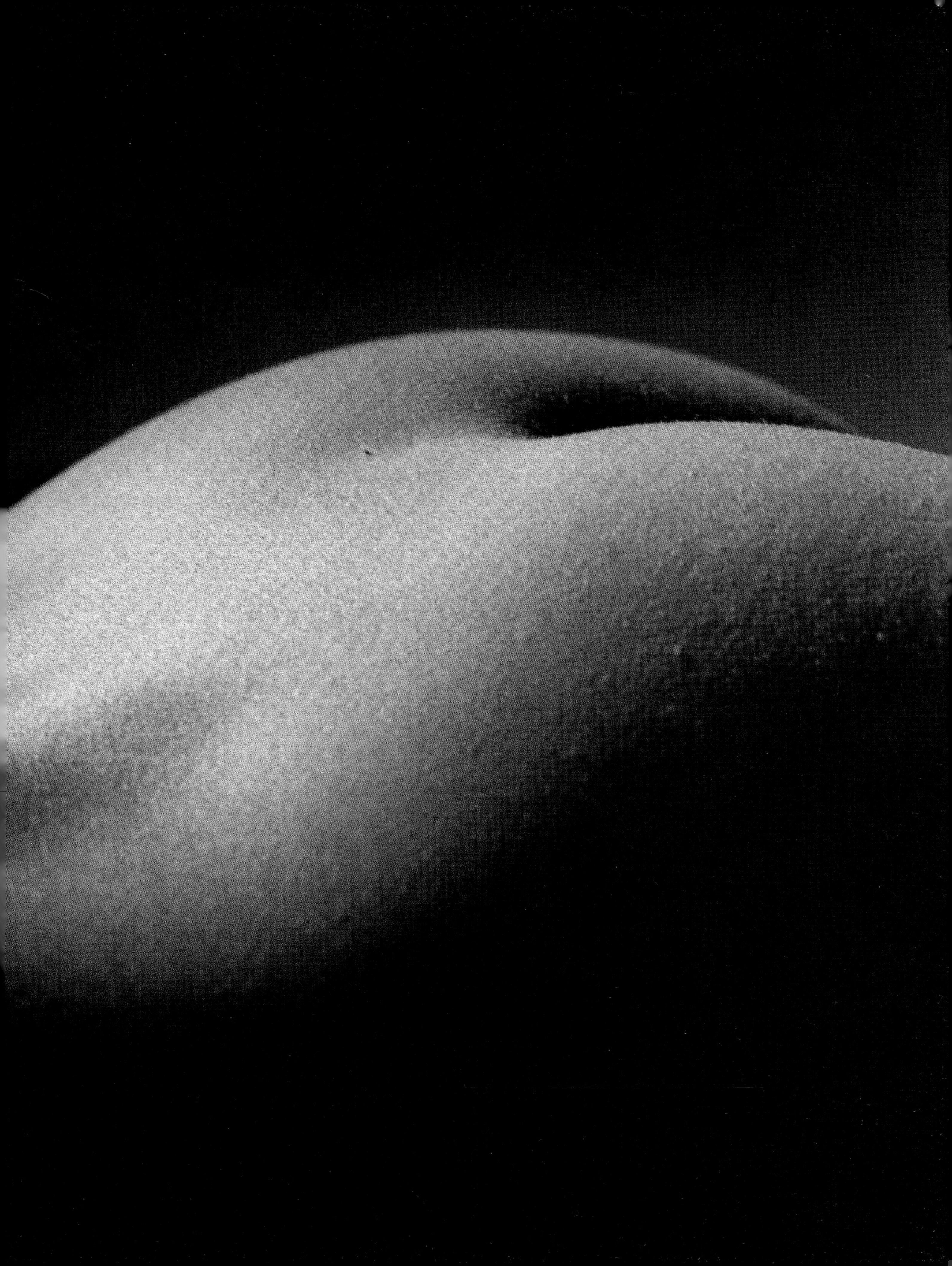

Using props

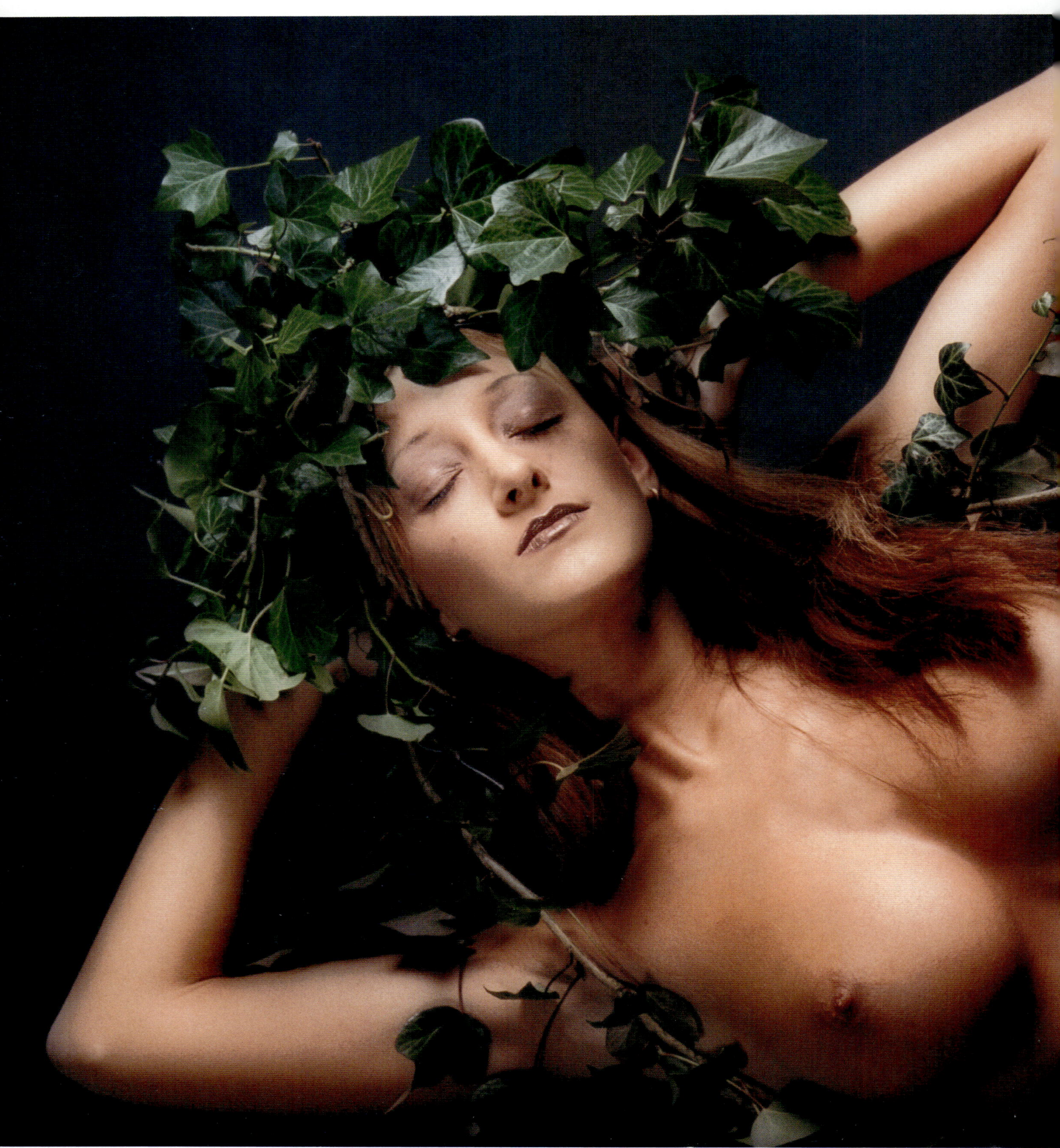

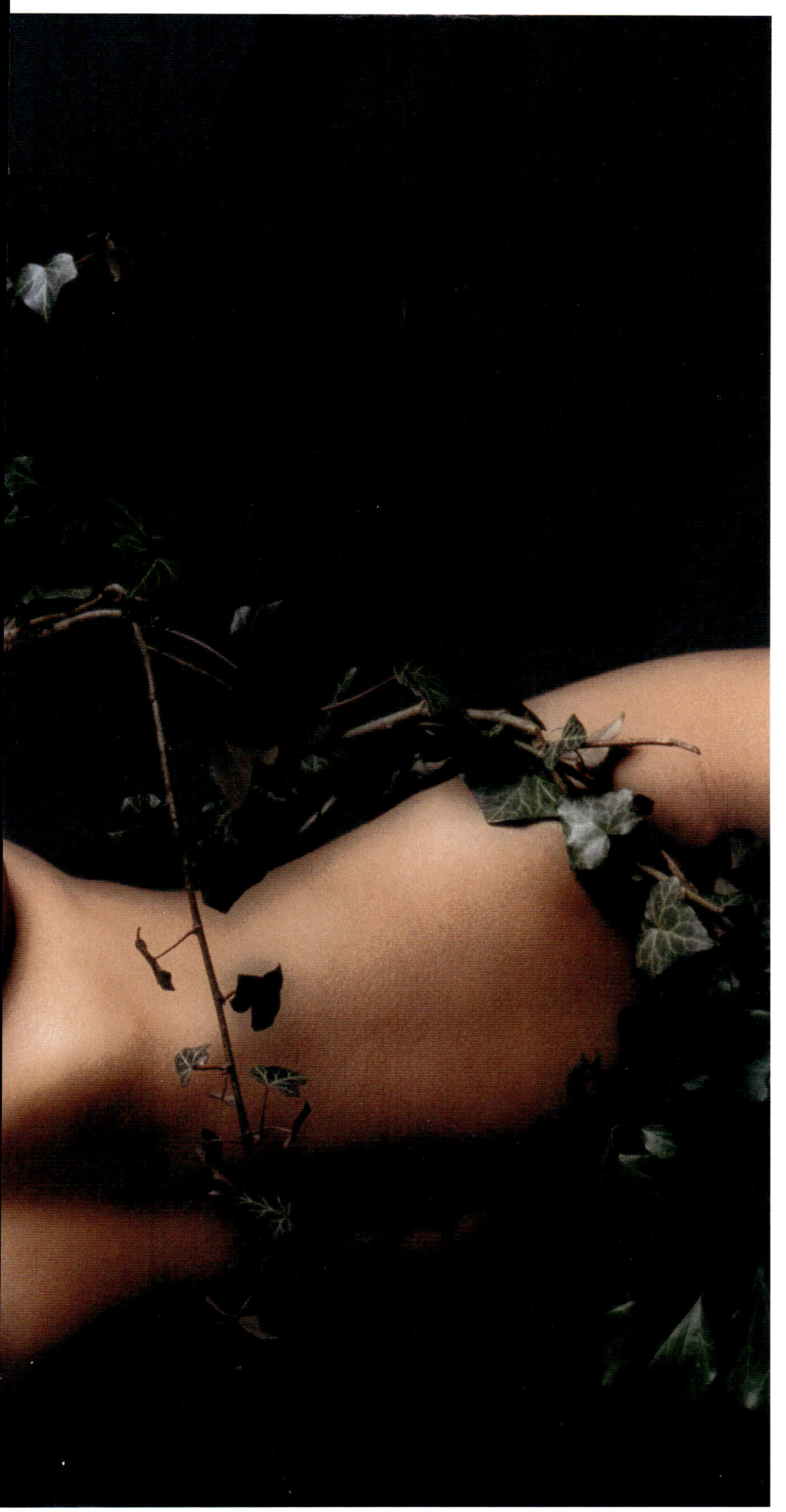

Photographing the nude without any material embellishments is the purest form of the art, but the introduction of props can open up a whole new area for experimentation and extend the range of successful new image-making ideas. Props need not be expensive or elaborate to make a big impact, and many suitable items can be found around the home. A good source of free props is the countryside, while inexpensive items can often be found in junk shops, charity shops and car boot sales. More obvious props are clothes and accessories for the model to wear, such as lingerie, hats or shoes. These can be used to great effect to enhance a nude image.

interaction One important use of props is to give the model something to interact with. A piece of material, flower, book, or other simple item can open up new avenues for poses. All it takes to create great pictures is a little imagination and forethought. Less obvious props are the surroundings in which the model is photographed. For instance, a room setting may contain a window, curtains, chairs, and so on. When arranged well and used imaginatively, such objects can become vital elements of the image. An outdoor setting such as a beach will have sand, water and rocks, which should all be considered as part of your props armoury. Props, whether simple or complex, can add further interest to a nude image and allow the model to adopt interesting poses.

LEFT: **Natural props.** Natural materials like ivy can be used as props to create images with a difference. In this instance, the image has a slightly surrealistic appearance as well as Pre-Raphaelite overtones. (BRONICA ETRSi; 150mm LENS; 1/125 sec at f/11; KODAK PORTRA 160NC.)

collaboration This process should be a collaborative effort between model and photographer as the shoot develops. Talk to your model and ask her opinions about the images you are creating – she may be able to provide new ideas. Allowing the model freedom to develop her ideas as well as yours will result in a happy model who is willing to work harder. She will feel more involved with the pictures if she has some input into the way she is being represented.

RIGHT: **Tantalizing shapes.** A tube of semi-transparent material tantalizingly clothes the model and creates an interesting shape that stands out strongly against the black background. (BRONICA ETRSi; 150mm LENS; 1/125 sec at f/11; KODAK PORTRA 160NC.)

OPPOSITE: **Classic glamour.** This glittering motorcycle makes a good prop for a calendar-style glamour shot. (BRONICA ETRSi; 75mm LENS; 1/125 sec at f/16; ILFORD FP4 PLUS.)

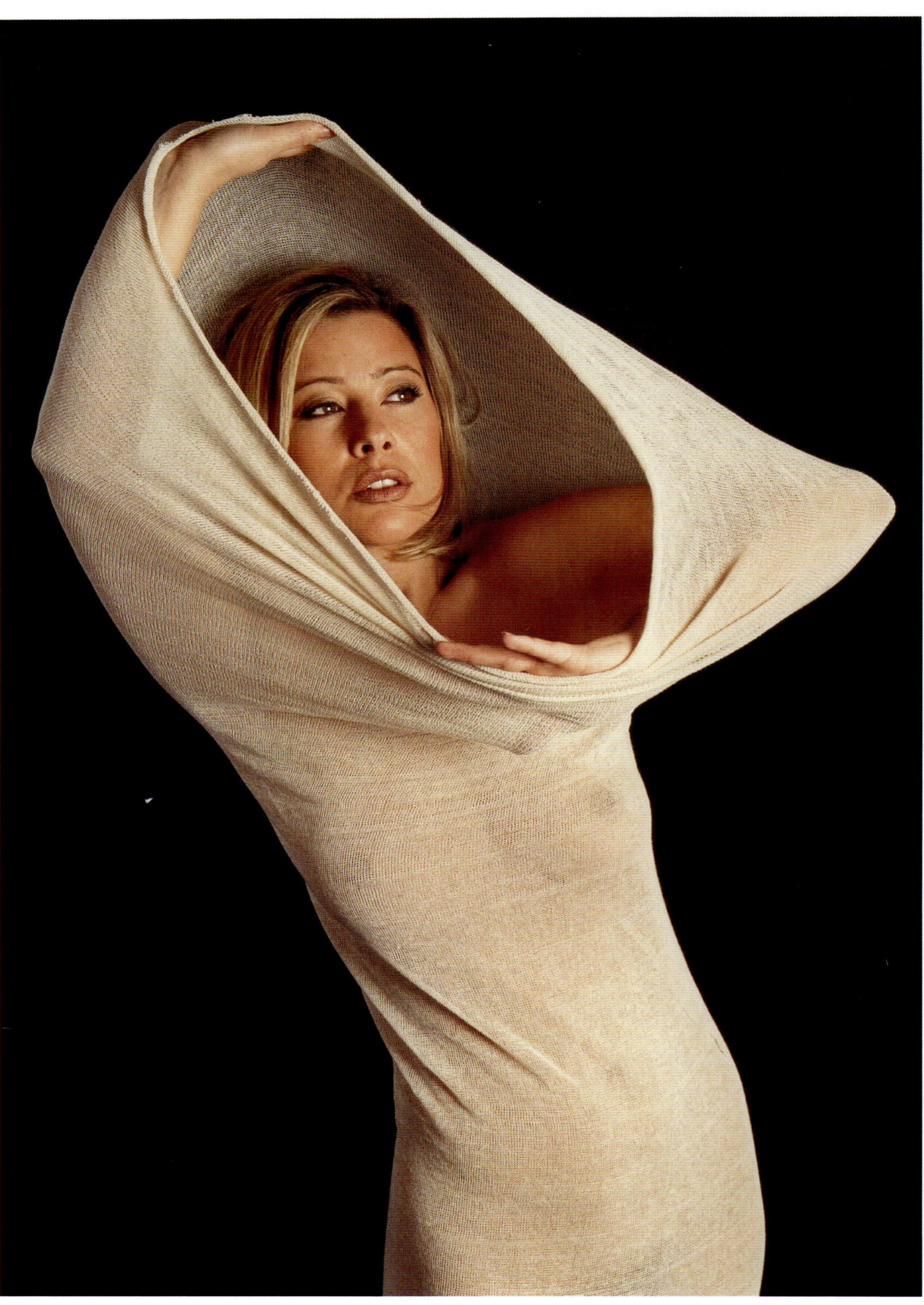

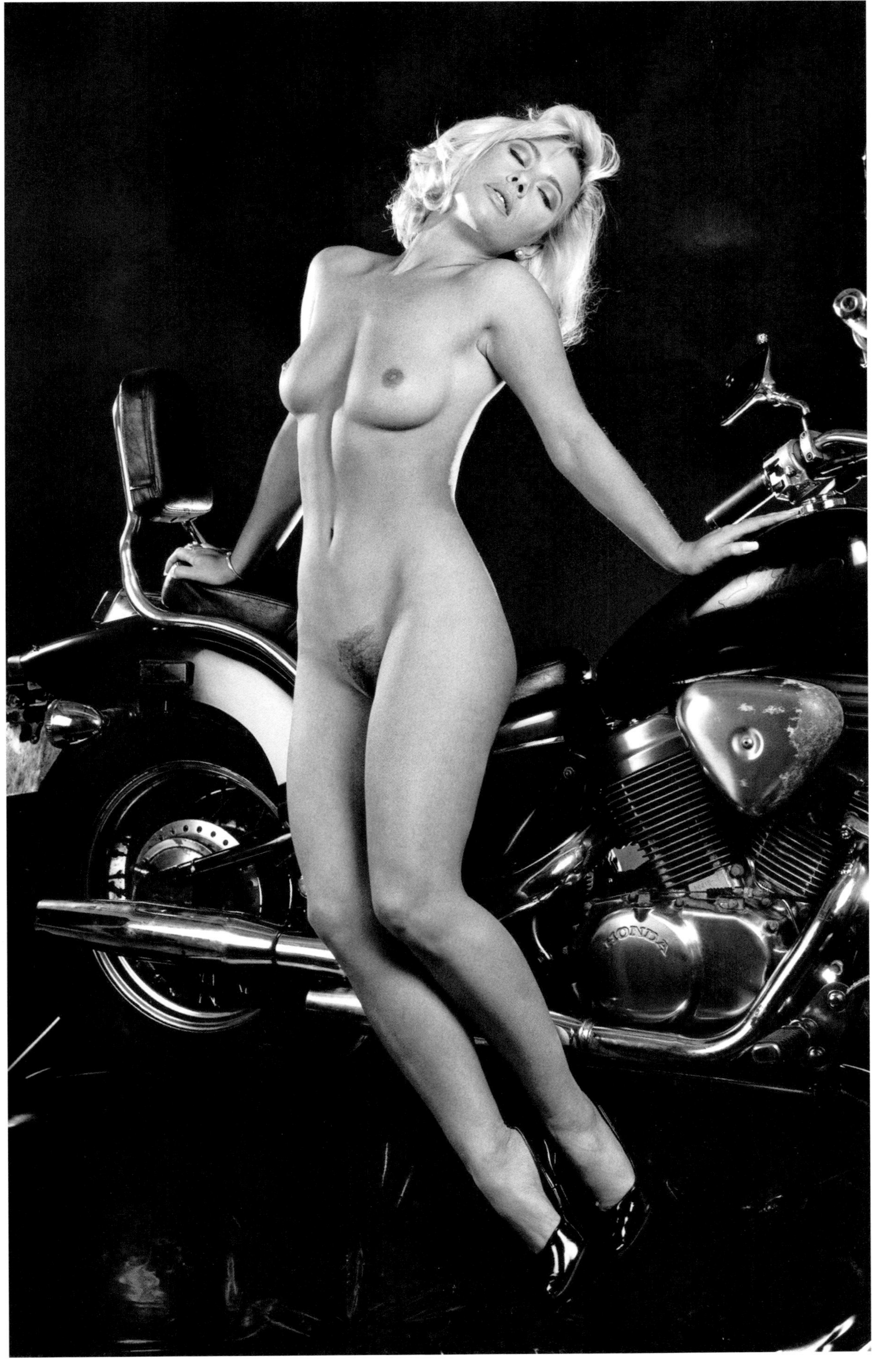

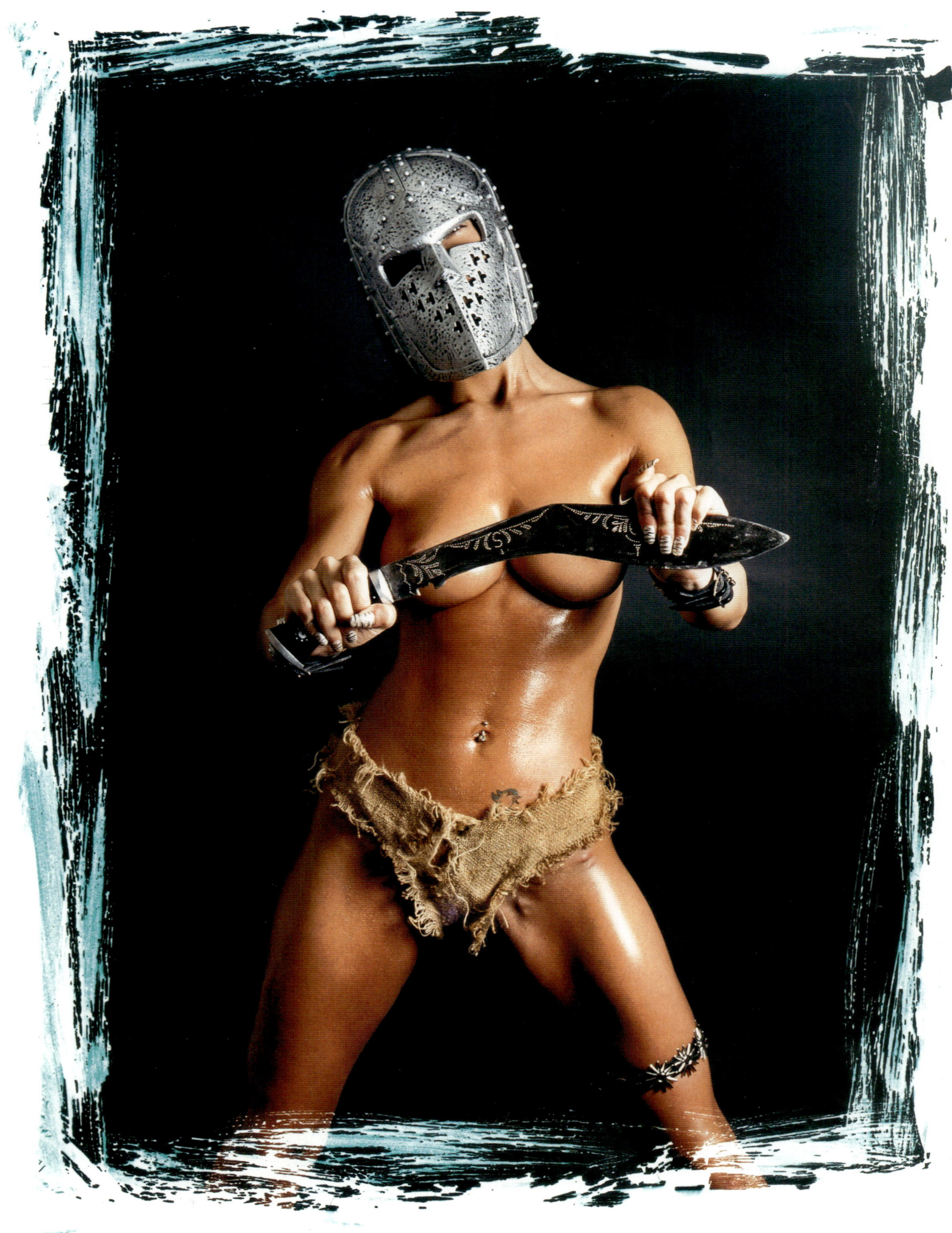

Props can help to set the mood of a photograph or convey a particular idea that the photographer may have.

drama For the 'warrior woman' shot, an aggressive pose was needed. The props used to support this were obtained at little cost (the knife from a junk shop, the helmet from a fancy dress shop, and underwear fashioned from sacking), but are essential to impart the ominous feeling required of the image. A low viewpoint, the lighting used, the flexed, oiled body, and the mystery invoked by not being able to see the model's face combine to give dramatic impact to this composition.

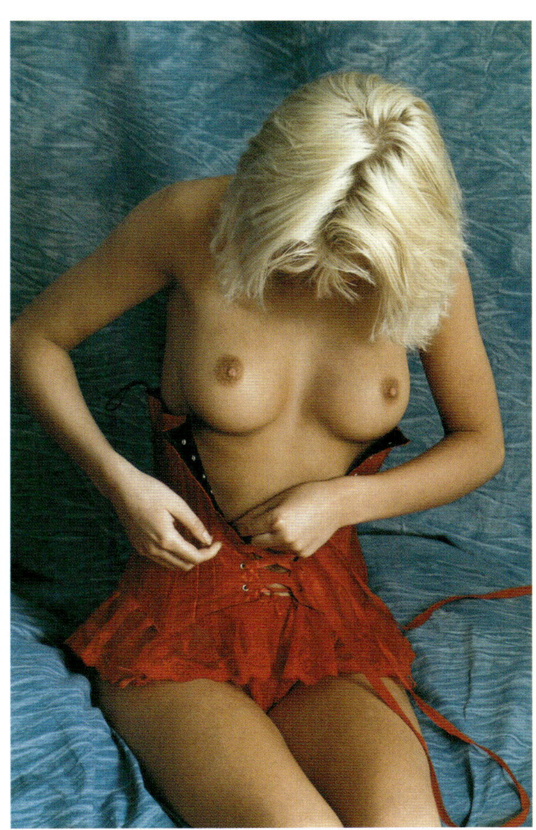

ABOVE: **Added interest.** Props can give the model something to do. Here, the model threading the laces of a basque adds interest to the image. (MINOLTA 8000i; 70–210mm ZOOM LENS; 1/125 sec at f/16; KODACOLOR GOLD 100.)

OPPOSITE: **Dramatic props.** The use of easily obtained props was the key to the creation of this dramatic image. (BRONICA ETRSi; 150mm LENS; 1/125 sec at f/11; KODAK PORTRA 160NC.)

BELOW: **Interaction.** A piece of material hanging down from the studio ceiling gives the model something to interact with. (MINOLTA 8000i; 70–210mm ZOOM LENS; 1/125 sec at f/11; KODACOLOR GOLD 100.)

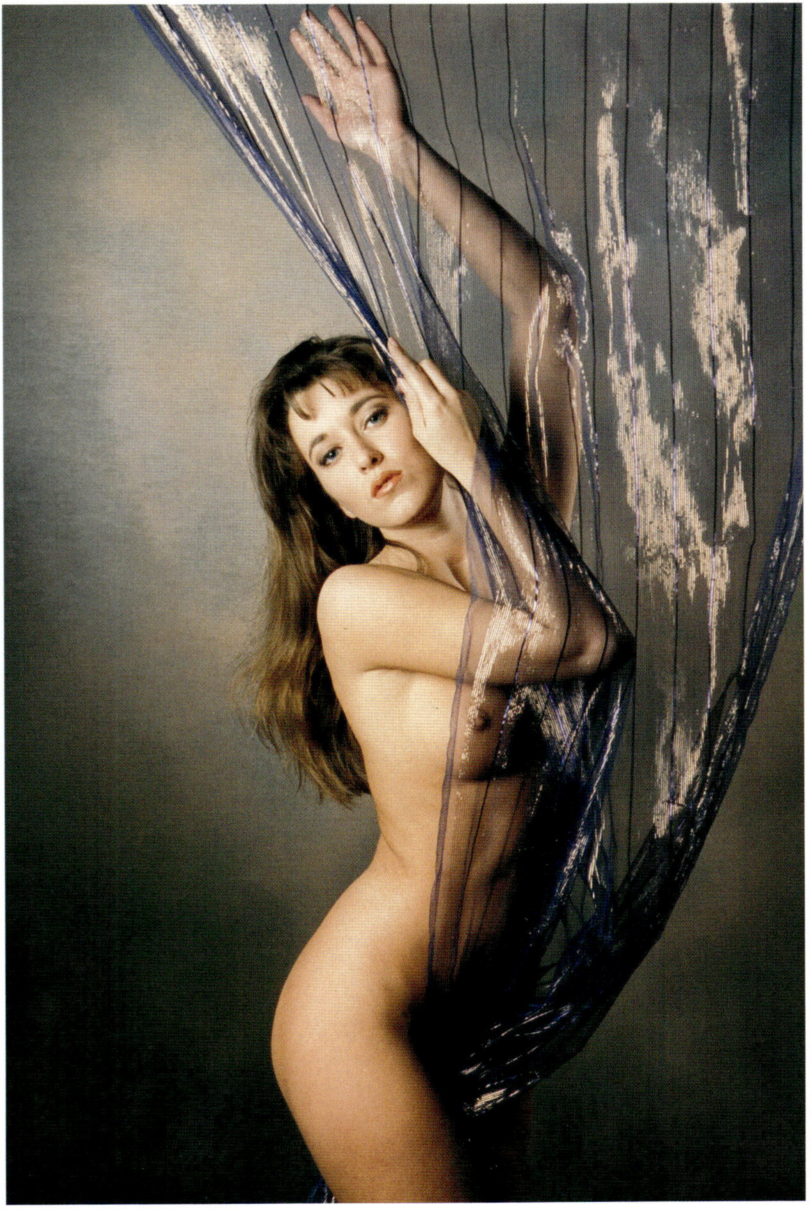

Locations

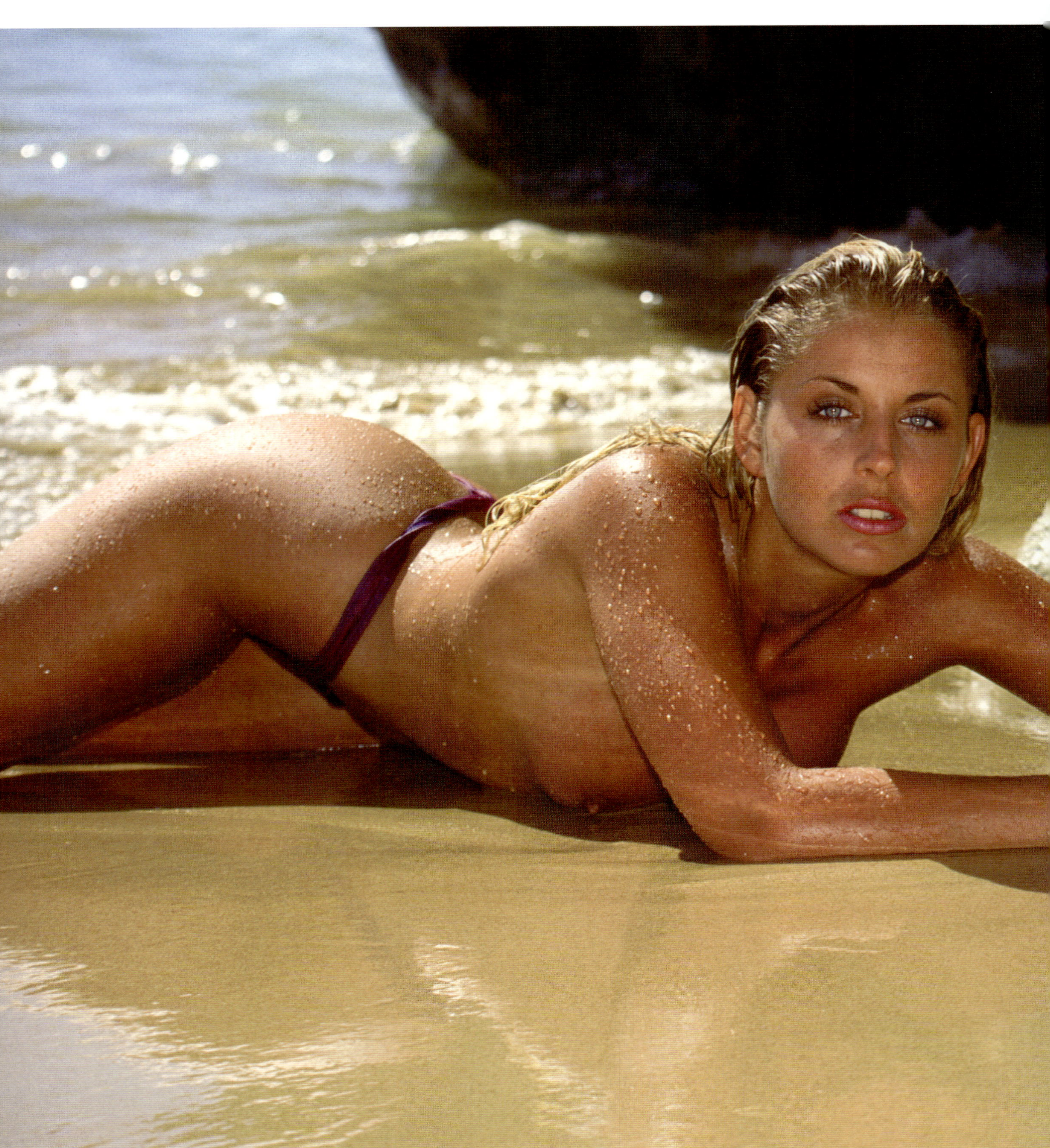

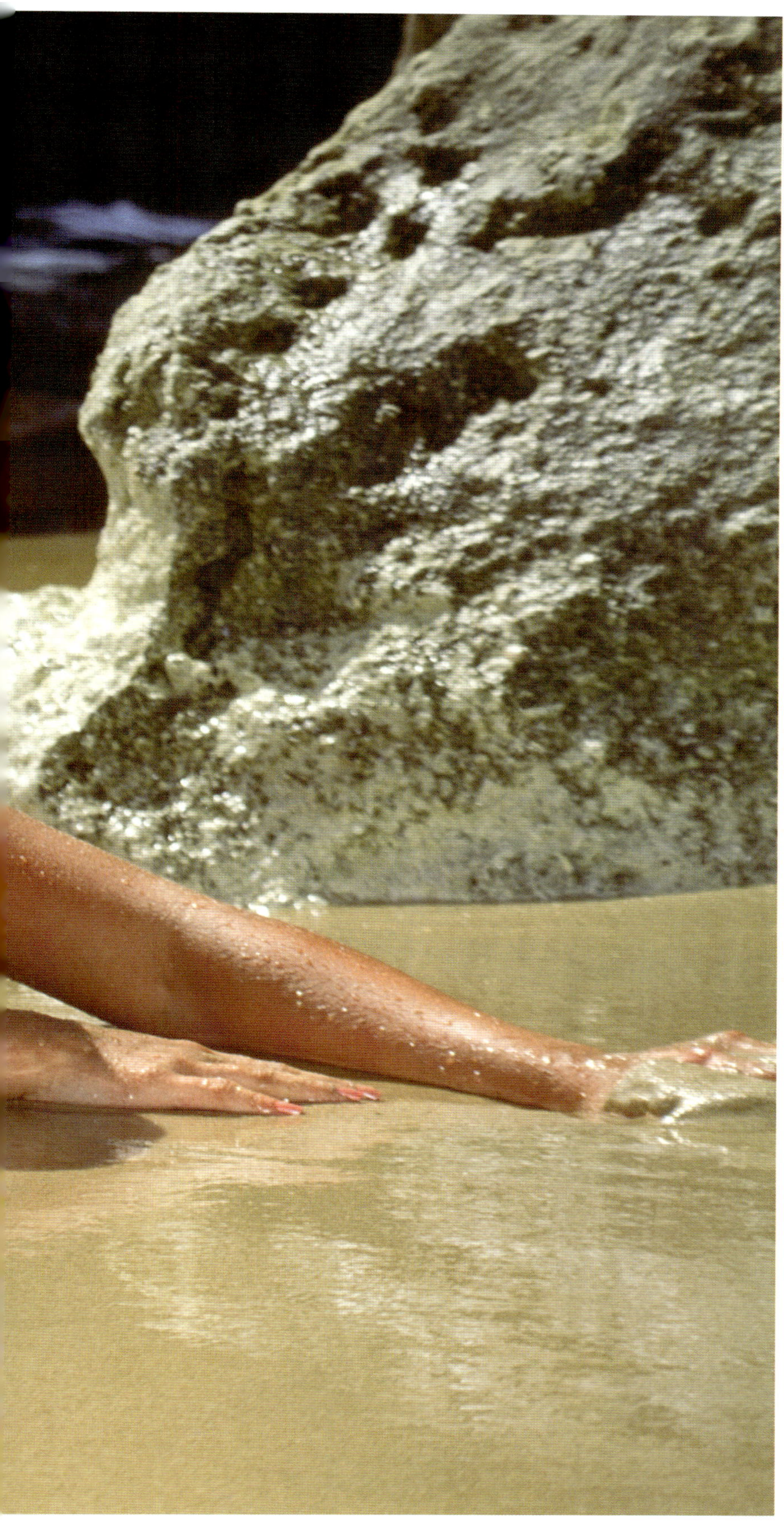

Nude photography need not be confined to the studio. Indeed, there are many locations, both indoors and out, that the adventurous photographer can utilize to advantage. For the amateur enthusiast on a tight budget, taking a model to an exotic location may be out of reach. But there are places closer to home that should be given serious consideration, because they can provide some superb photography. You may be able to use your own property, a friend's house or garden, or maybe even the model's accommodation.

imaginative thinking

If the location is fairly small, consider it a challenge. Think imaginatively and make the best of the space available. Beaches are excellent places to take nude photographs outdoors and are accessible to most people. They are often deserted early in the morning and late in the afternoon, which are the best times to shoot for the light. Woodlands and countryside can also provide excellent outdoor locations, particularly in spring and early summer before the foliage is dense enough to lower the light levels seriously. Buildings can be used to great effect, especially if they have a photogenic quality of their own. Farm buildings, such as barns, old dilapidated cottages, and – for the more affluent – villas and country houses can make wonderful locations, both inside and out. Try to find quiet areas where you can work in privacy and without undue disturbance. Above all, have consideration for your model and don't expect her to be happy about removing her clothes in a public place.

BELOW: **Using pools.** Swimming pools can be used in many ways to make creative nude images, and they can be one of the great advantages of staying in private accommodation when location shooting.
(BRONICA ETRSi; 150mm LENS; 1/125 sec at f/11; 120 KODAK PORTRA 160NC.)

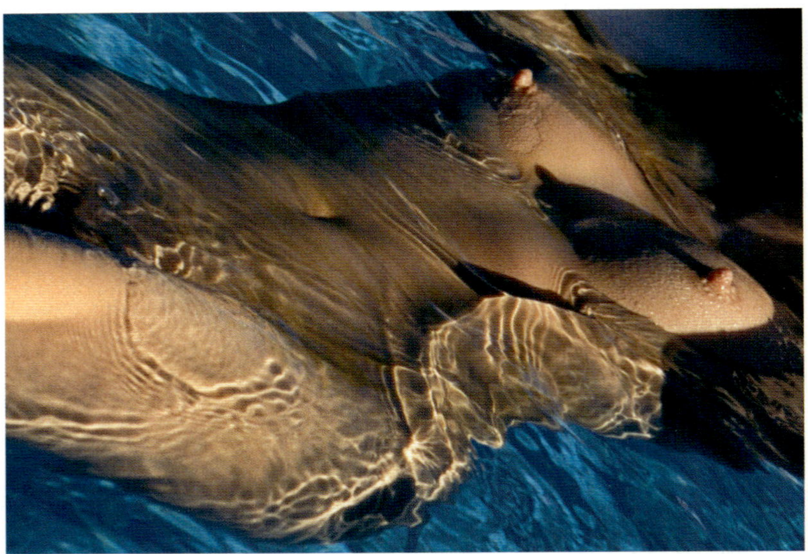

RIGHT: **Balcony setting.** This attractive villa balcony makes an ideal location setting for a delightfully framed nude study.
(BRONICA ETRSi; 250mm LENS; 1/125 sec at f/8; 120 KODAK PORTRA 160NC.)

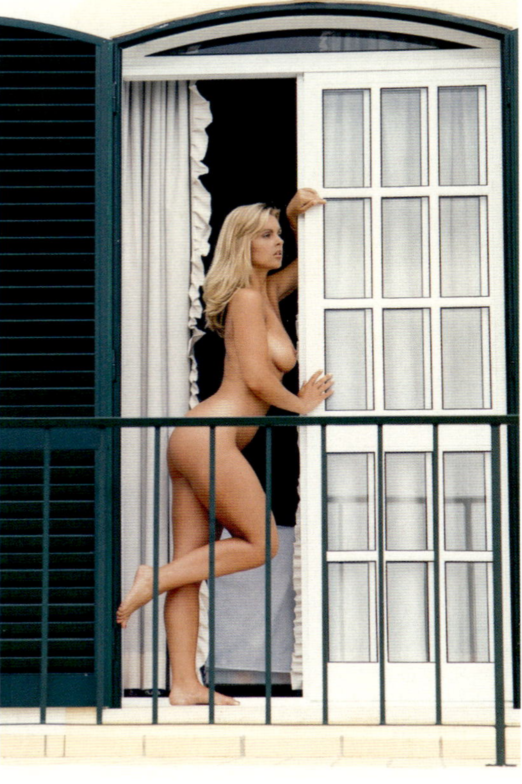

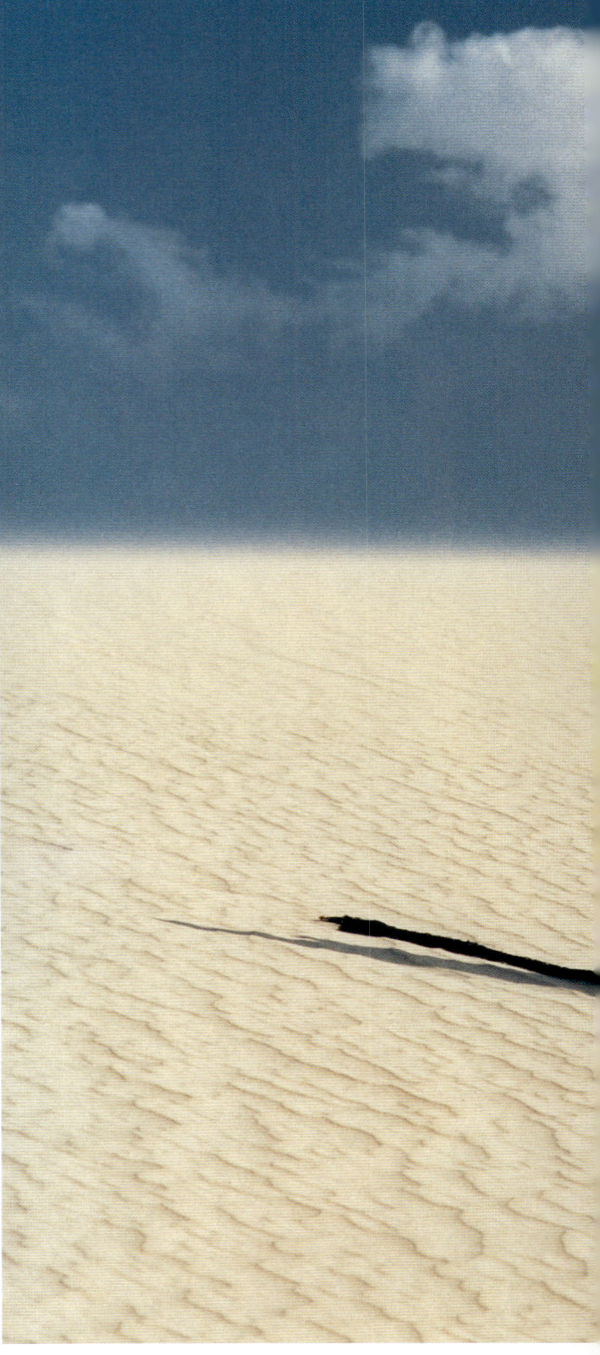

LAW OF THE LAND

When shooting nudes on location, use discretion and be aware of local laws. Nude photography on beaches is acceptable in many countries, and at the times that you want to shoot (early morning or late evening) beaches can be empty of inquisitive audiences. Out-of-the way places with some privacy are usually risk-free, but be careful when shooting in more public areas – in some countries people are easily offended by nudity.

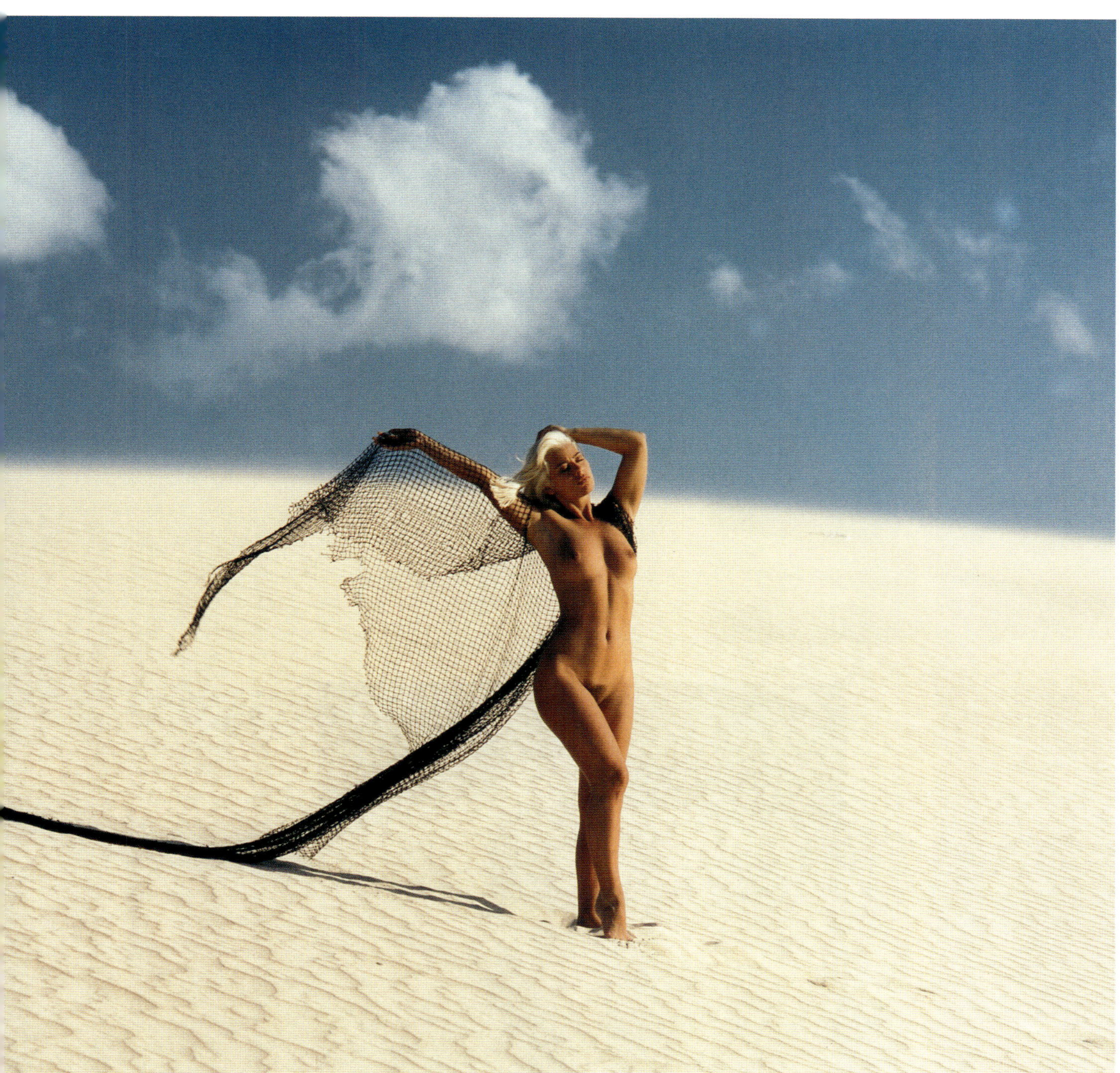

ABOVE: **Passing clouds.**
The clouds in this shot echo
the shape of the fishnet that
the model was asked to use
as a prop.
(BRONICA ETRSi; 150mm LENS;
1/250 sec at f/11; GPX 160.)

Other people are likely to appear from
nowhere and cause the model embarrassment.

exotic locations
Working in an
exotic location is every nude photographer's
dream, and island locations with sand dunes
are perfect places to shoot. White sand, blue
skies and sunshine can be combined in many
ways to make memorable images. When
photographing away from home, choose your
accommodation carefully with photography in
mind. If you can afford it, a villa or a private
house that offers some privacy is ideal for a
shoot. It can be used as a location for the
shoot itself (villas often have attractive gardens,
swimming pools and other photogenic
features) and as a back-up for indoor
photography if the weather is inclement.

Buy detailed maps of the area you are
visiting and study them for possible locations.
Make notes, paying particular attention to
features with potential and sun direction at

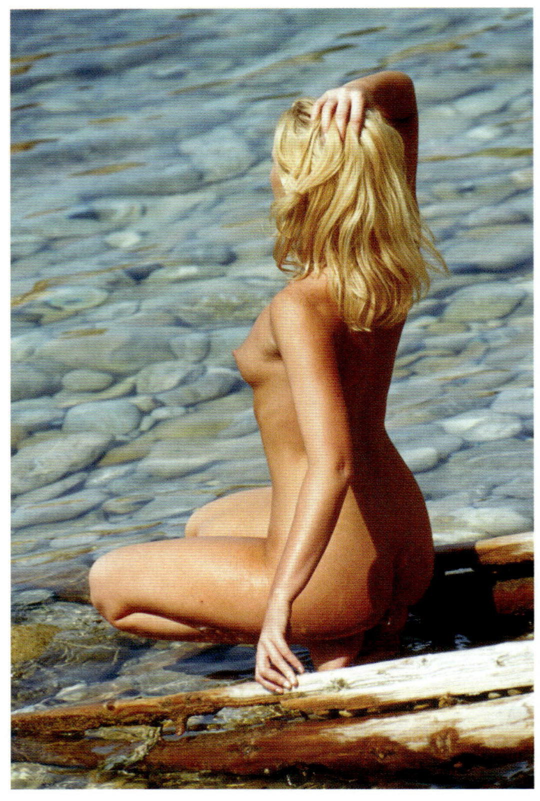

different times of the day. It will help if you can explore the area before taking your model to your chosen location.

travelling light

Many professional photographers take lights and other specialist equipment with them on a location shoot, but the enthusiast can easily work with less. It is often difficult to take all the camera equipment you would like to when travelling by air, so choose only essential items. At least two camera bodies (in case one should fail) and two or three lenses, including a wide angle, standard and medium-to-long telephoto, should be the minimum requirement.

Choose a robust carry case that can be taken onto the aircraft and use it for delicate equipment such as lenses, flash guns and camera bodies. More robust items like film backs, speed grips and boxes of filters can go in the hold. Essential accessories are a flashgun, tripod and a selection of reflectors (gold, white and silver), which can be packed in luggage. Don't forget to pack spare batteries and take a selection of clothes and props for shots you have planned. Ask the model to bring a range of modelling clothes with her. Take enough film to last for the whole trip – a minimum of 40–60 rolls is recommended, including different speeds, for a one-week location shoot. If in doubt, take more film.

ABOVE: **Beachside location.** Large pebbles in the water on this beach in Ibiza made a great background for a figure shot. (MINOLTA 8000i; 75–300mm ZOOM LENS; 1/125 sec at f/8; KODAK EKTACHROME 100.)

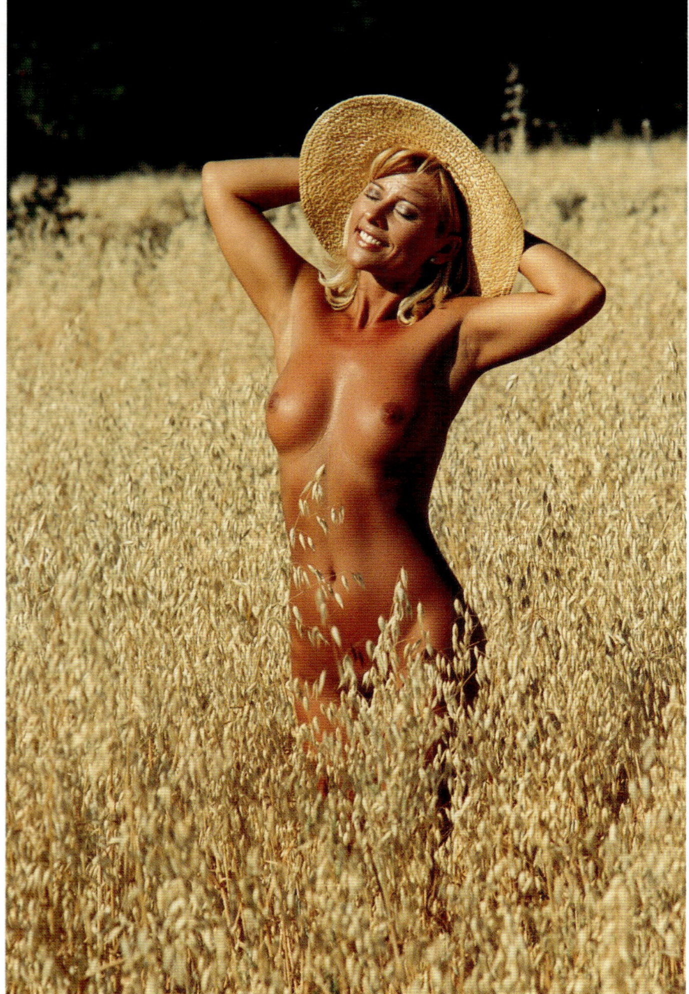

LEFT: **Secluded setting.** This secluded field of oats provided an excellent setting for a naturalistic nude study. (BRONICA ETRSi; 150mm LENS; 1/125 sec at f/8; KODAK PORTRA 160NC.)

OPPOSITE: **Striking lines.** The striking architectural lines of this Portuguese villa made for a unique nude study. Toning the figure makes it stand out from the surroundings. (BRONICA ETRSi; 250mm LENS; 1/250 sec at f/8; ILFORD FP4 PLUS; SELECTIVE SEPIA [THIOCARBAMIDE] TONING.)

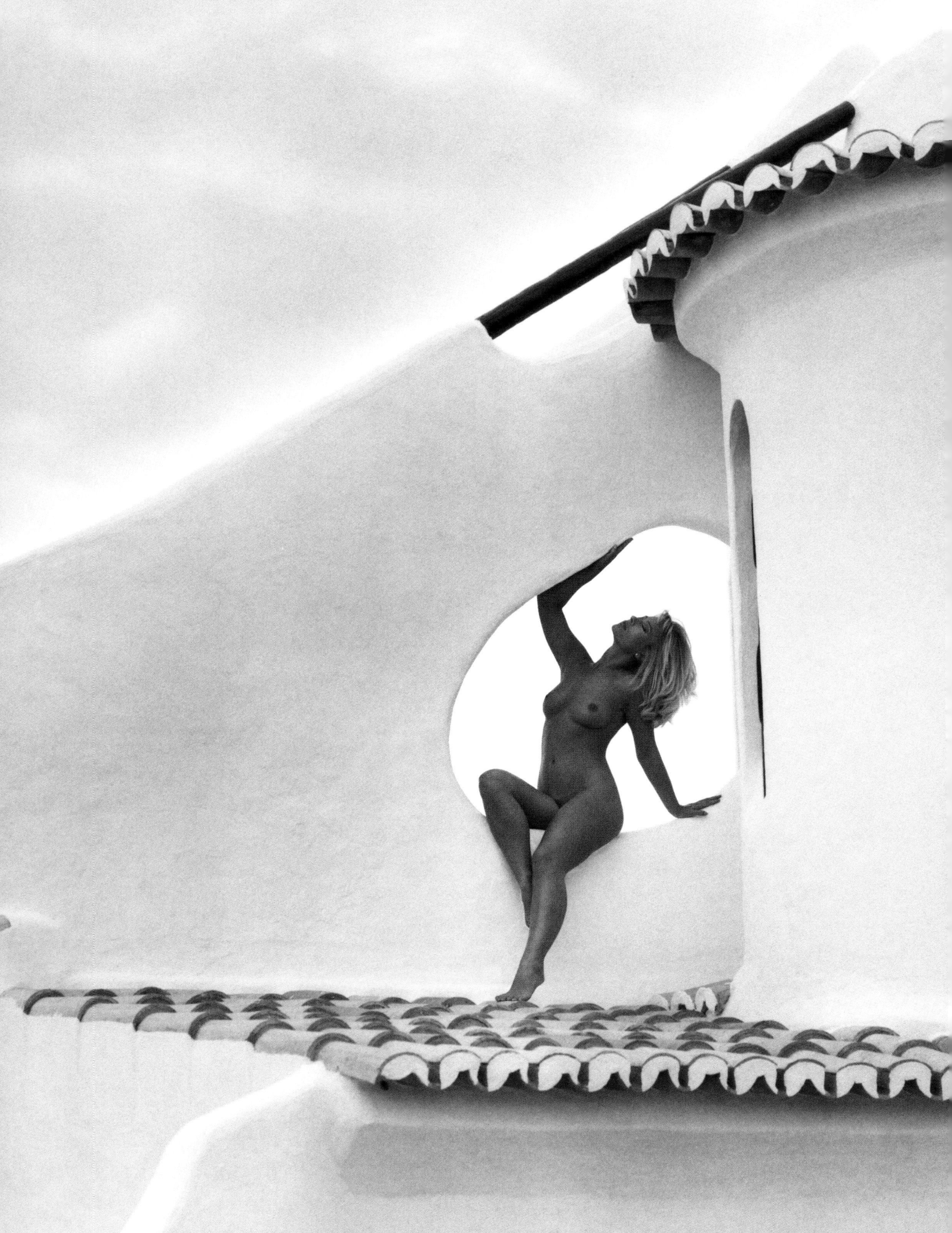

Reflections

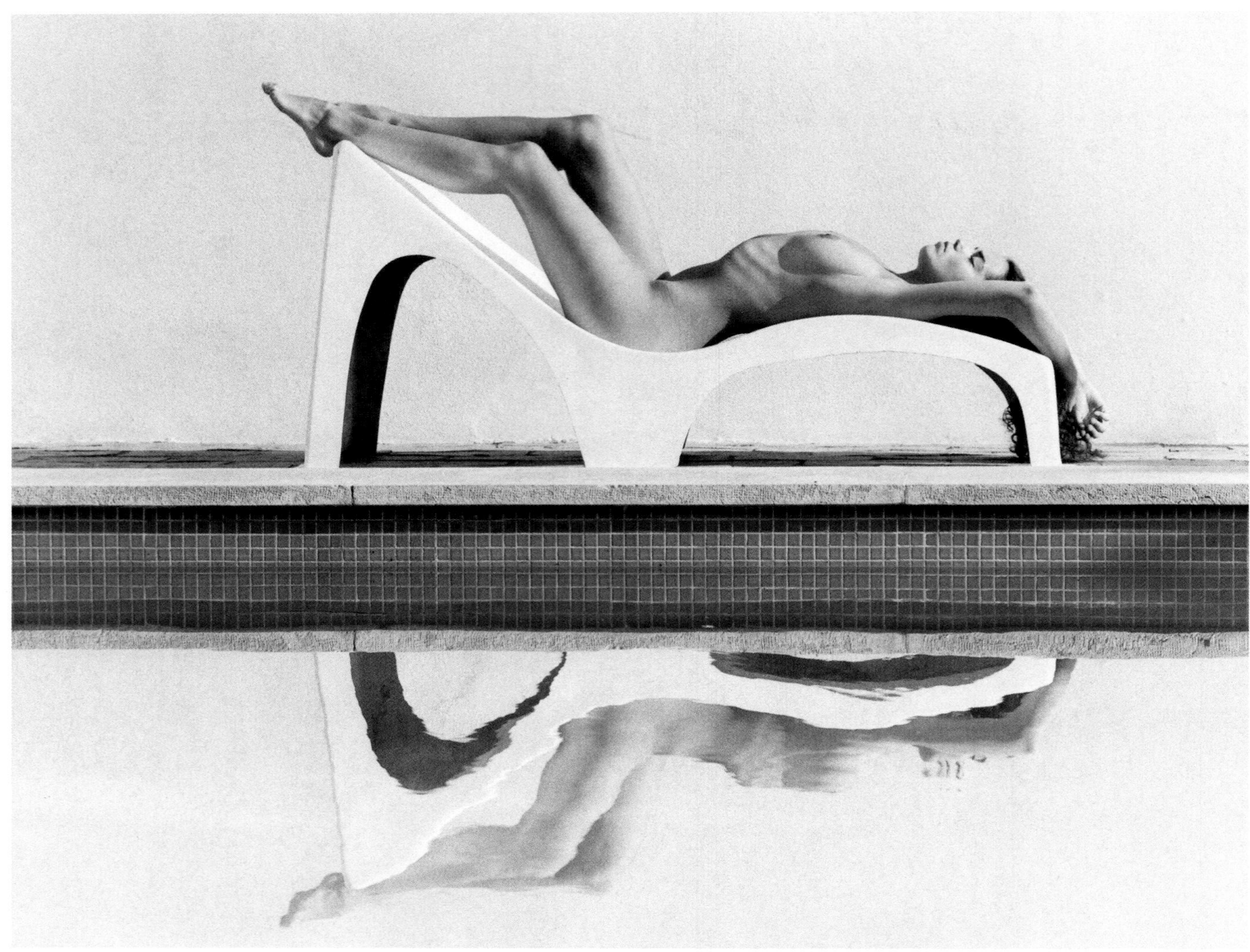

The incorporation of reflections or surfaces with reflective properties in photographs can often enhance and add another dimension to nude images – an additional virtual image of your model that can evoke a sense of mystery or set a particular mood. Mirrors are the most obvious source of reflections and are familiar to everyone as household objects, but it is also worth considering the use of other reflective materials. Water, highly polished metals, metal foils, windows and non-silvered glass, or combinations of these, are all useful reflective aids. Try photographing the reflections alone as well as the combined image of subject and reflection for unusual results.

duplication

Mirrors can be used to 'duplicate' your model or show two sides of the subject at the same time. 'Boudoir' photography often uses this technique to great effect in bedroom and dressing-room scenes. Plastics with mirror coatings are pliable and can be bent to give unusual distortions for more creative nude images. Mirrored sunglasses are easily obtained props. When used to reflect an object or scene outside the

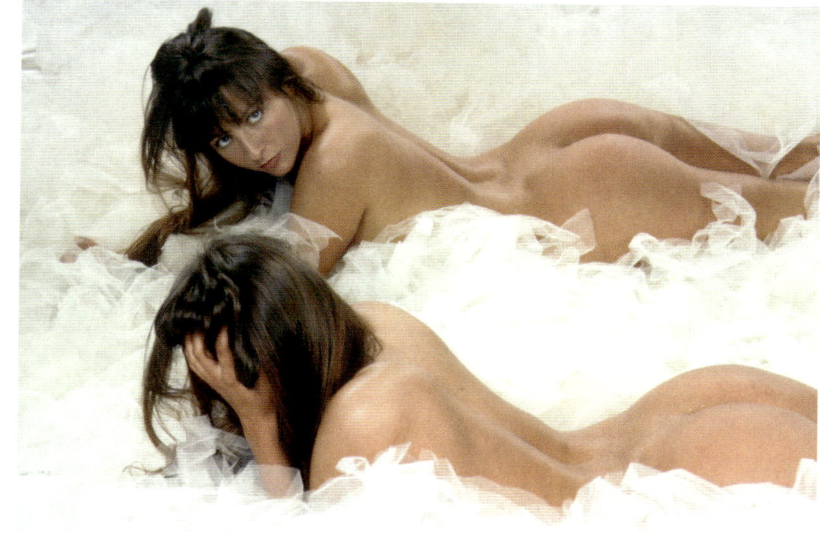

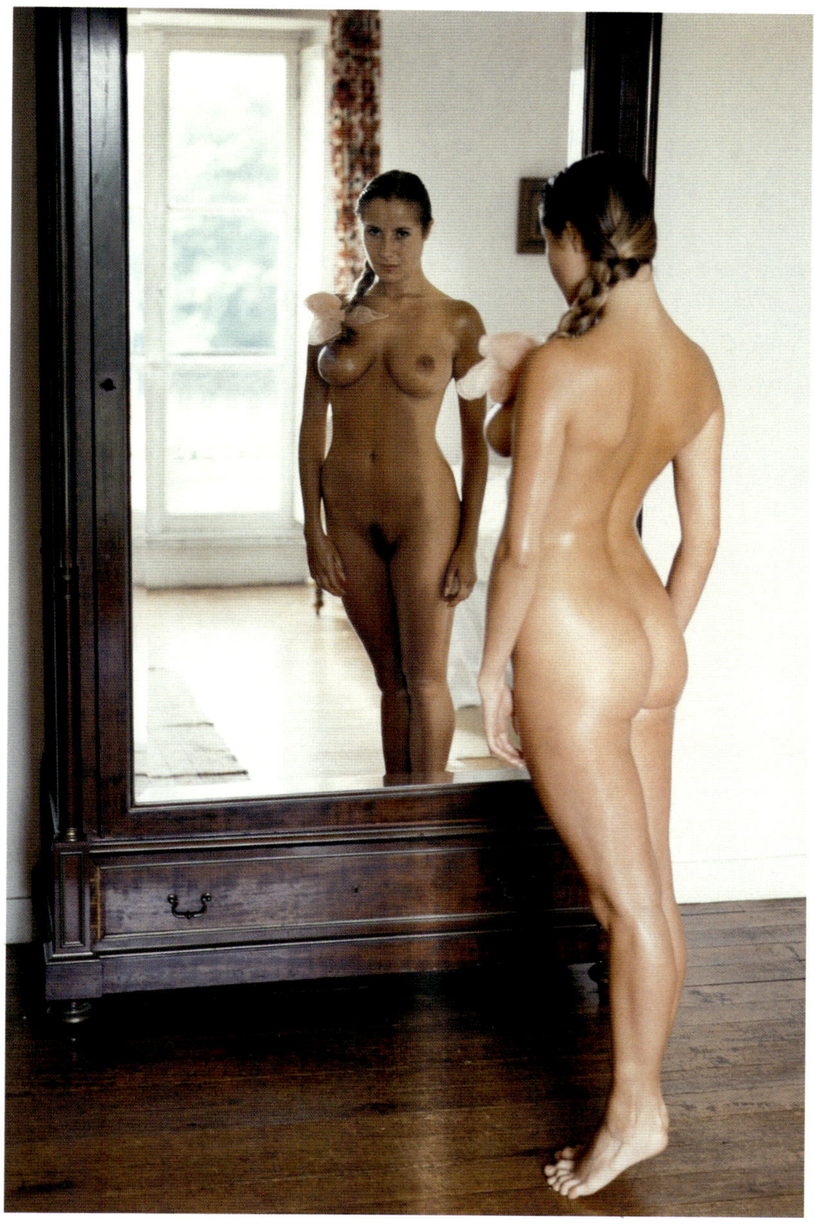

field of view, such as a sky, they can add a mysterious air to the model wearing them (as shown on page 117).

stunning images Water is a good medium that can provide a variety of excellent reflective images. Perfectly still water is almost as effective a reflector as a mirror and when available over a large expanse, such as in a swimming pool or a lake, can give the opportunity to capture some stunning images. Wet, fine sand on beaches where the tide has just receded also offers a highly reflective surface and is excellent for those early-morning or late-evening shots when the sun is low in the sky (see page 104).

USING MIRRORS

When using mirrors, the reflected image of the model is a virtual image that is the same distance behind the mirror as the real model is in front of it. Focusing on the real model with a wide aperture will mean that the virtual model will be out of focus and vice versa. This technique can be used with advantage to create pictures where one or other of the images is blurred. To make both images sharp, take depth of field into account and use a small aperture. Unless it is an intentional device, make sure that extraneous objects such as lighting equipment, unsightly paraphernalia, or your own reflection are not shown in the image, especially when using more than one mirror.

Infrared images

RIGHT: **Varied tones.**
Black-and-white infrared
film renders some colours as
darker or lighter tones of
grey than expected;
therefore the dark green of
the eelgrass in this image is
recorded much lighter.
(MINOLTA 8000i; 100mm LENS;
1/125 sec at f/8; KODAK HIGH
SPEED INFRARED (HIE) RATED
AT ISO 400; NO FILTRATION.)

Black-and-white infrared film contains an emulsion that is sensitized to both the visible spectrum, as in panchromatic films, and certain wavelengths in the near-infrared region of the spectrum. This means that it records the scene that we see, plus an additional image caused by infrared radiation that is reflected or radiated by the scene. The amount of radiation recorded is dependent on the particular sensitizers used in the film, which vary with different manufacturers' films.

diffuse images

Typically, infrared images are more diffuse than conventional black-and-white images and sometimes show a halo-like glow around subjects that are either reflecting or emitting infrared radiation. This can result in some unusual effects. It is a highly suitable medium for the fine art nude photographer, as it provides images with an ethereal quality. Good infrared reflectors, such as clouds, grass, leaves and the human body, appear much lighter or even white. Blue skies often record darker than usual because they do not emit much infrared radiation. Dark-coloured hair and water also often record darker because they absorb infrared radiation.

Because of the dual nature of this type of film, it is possible to use it in several ways. Using the film without any kind of filtration will give a relatively normal rendition of the scene, reminiscent of a grainy high-speed film. Using yellow, orange or red filtration progressively removes the visible part of the radiation seen by the film and biases the sensitivity towards infrared radiation and more bizarre effects. An opaque (black) filter (Wratten 87C) is also available; this allows only the infrared component to pass.

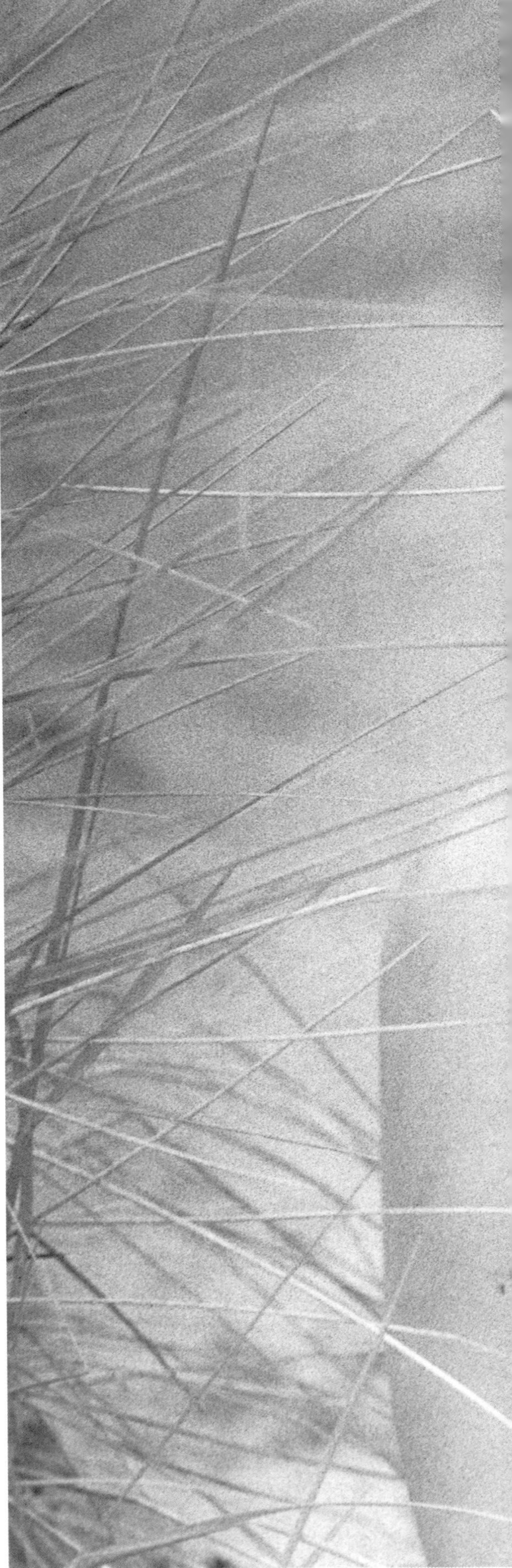

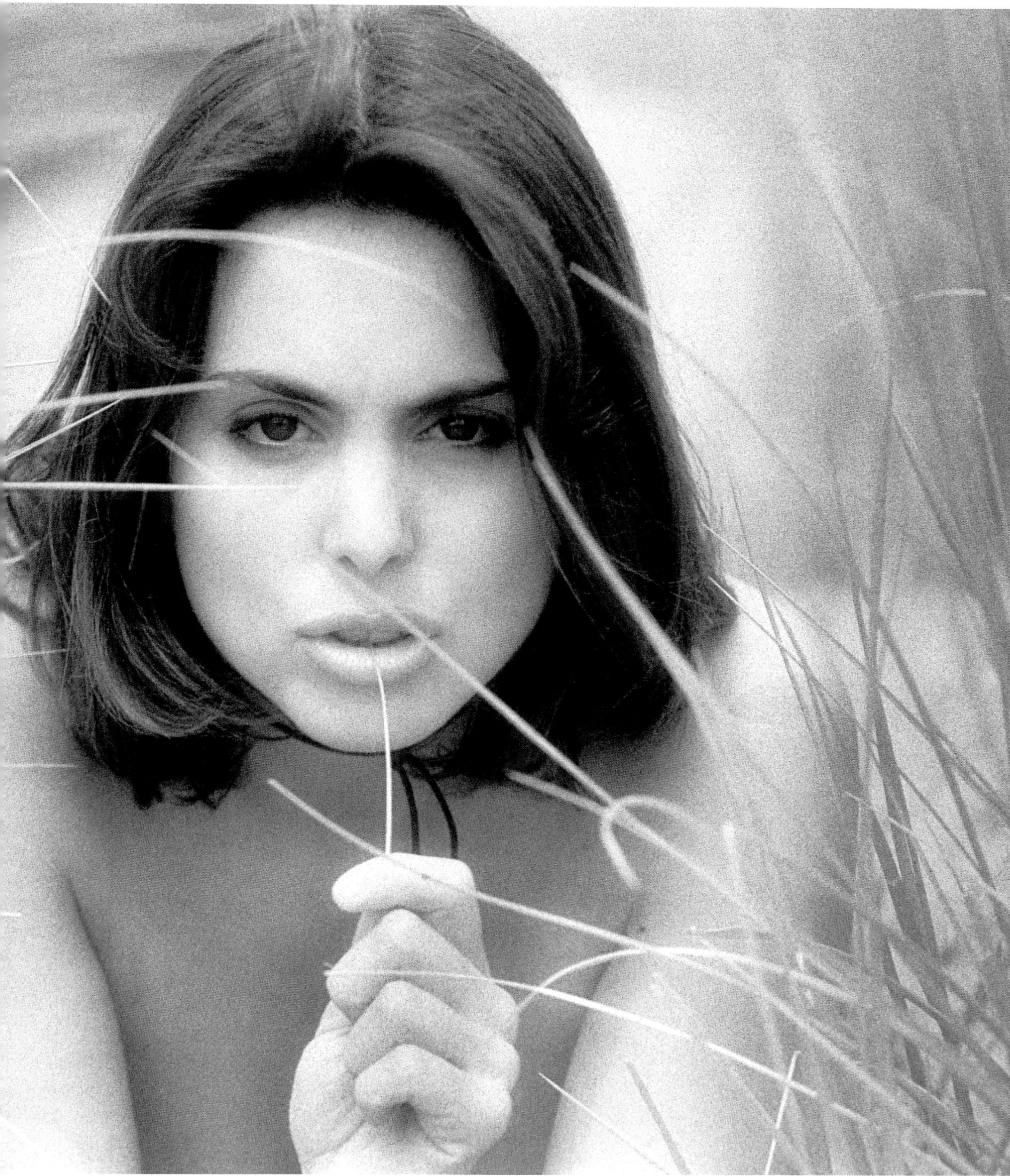

OPPOSITE: **Ethereal effect.** Black-and-white infrared film is much grainier than normal monochrome films and gives an ethereal feel to this composition. Vegetation reflects a lot of infrared radiation and is therefore rendered almost white. (MINOLTA 8000i; 100mm LENS; 1/125 sec at f/11; KODAK HIGH SPEED INFRARED (HIE) RATED AT ISO 400; ORANGE FILTRATION.)

RIGHT: **Bizarre colouring.** Colour infrared film gives bizarre colours that can be used for creative effect. The reds in this image (lipstick, nails and material) are rendered as yellow; green vegetation as magenta; and blacks take on a dark-red tinge. (MINOLTA 8000i; 50mm LENS; 1/125 sec at f/11; KODAK EKTACHROME INFRARED (EIR) RATED AT ISO 400; YELLOW FILTRATION.)

BELOW: **The artistic touch.** An artistic touch has been added to this typical glamour shot by the use of infrared. (MINOLTA 8000i; 100mm LENS; 1/125 sec at f/11; KODAK HIGH SPEED INFRARED (HIE) RATED AT ISO 400; ORANGE FILTRATION.)

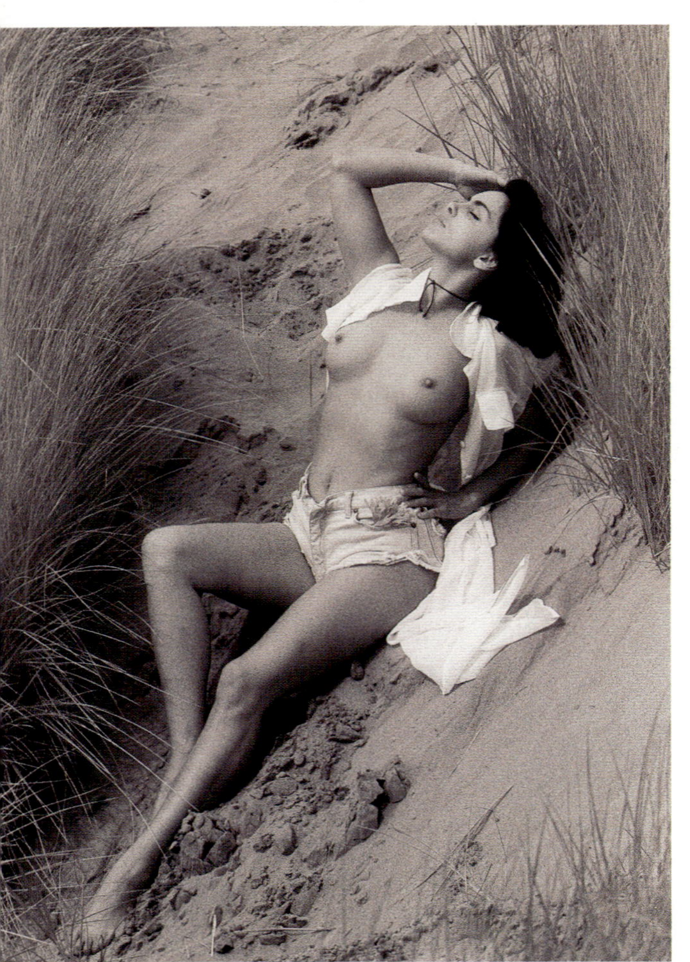

There is only one make of colour infrared film available – E6 processed Kodak Ektachrome Infrared (EIR). This is a specialist film, which gives abnormal colour rendition and can also be used to create unusual images. Infrared films are not given a specific ISO speed rating because light meters do not register infrared radiation, but recommendations for using these films under different conditions are given by the manufacturers. Always load and unload infrared film in total darkness and keep it refrigerated before and after exposure (if possible) as it is sensitive to heat.

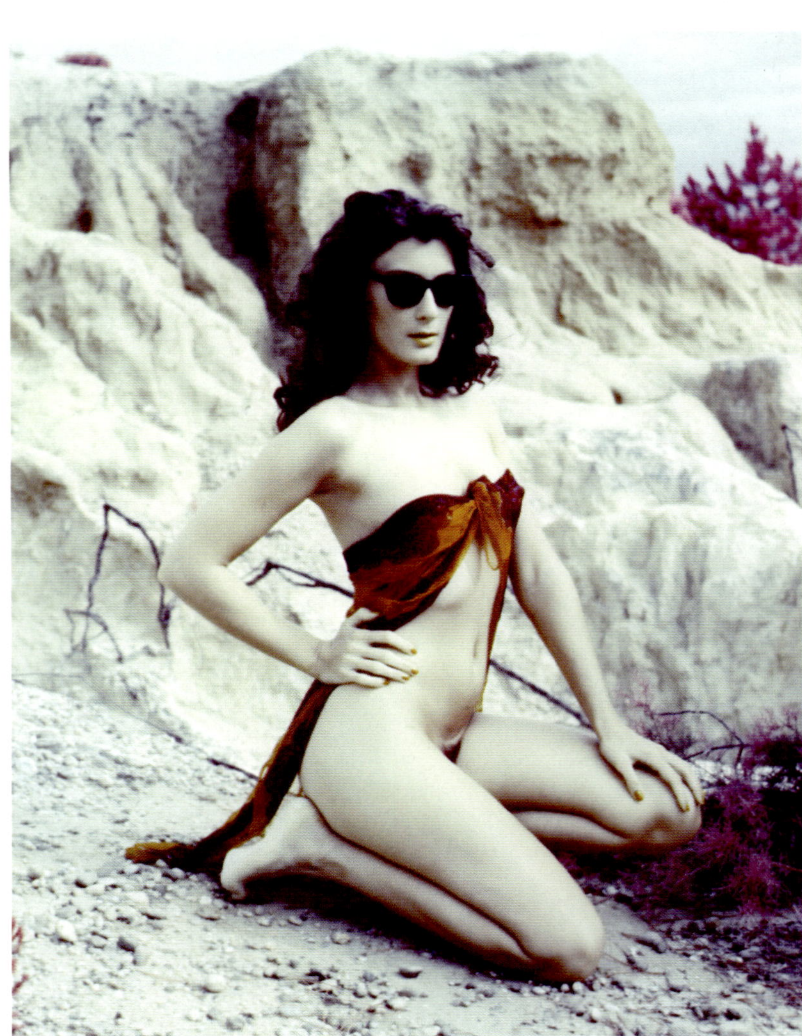

INFRARED FILM OPTIONS

For most conditions, Kodak High Speed Infrared (HIE) black-and-white film, when used without a filter or with a yellow or orange filter, performs well when rated at ISO 400; with a dark-red filter a preferable speed setting is ISO 200. Always bracket by at least one stop to allow for variability in exposure. The table shows the currently available films and formats, nominal speed ratings, and general handling conditions.

Film	Format	Speed	Type	Handling
KODAK EKTACHROME INFRARED (EIR)	35mm	400	Colour	Total darkness
KODAK HIGH SPEED INFRARED (HIE)	35mm	200/400	B&W	Total darkness
ILFORD SFX	35mm	200	B&W	Total darkness
MACOPHOT IR820C	120	100	B&W	Total darkness
KONICA INFRA RED 750	120	32	B&W	Subdued light

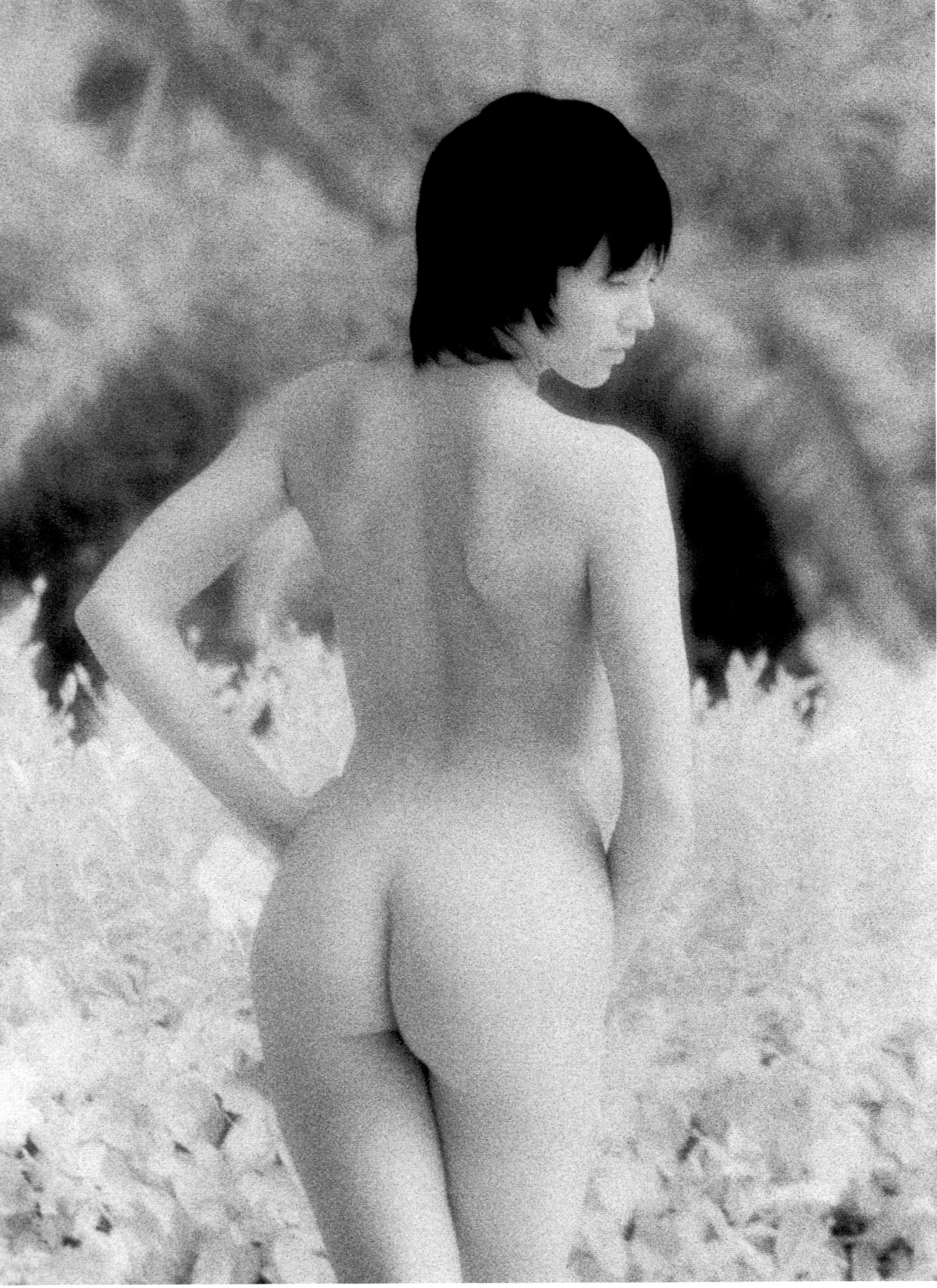

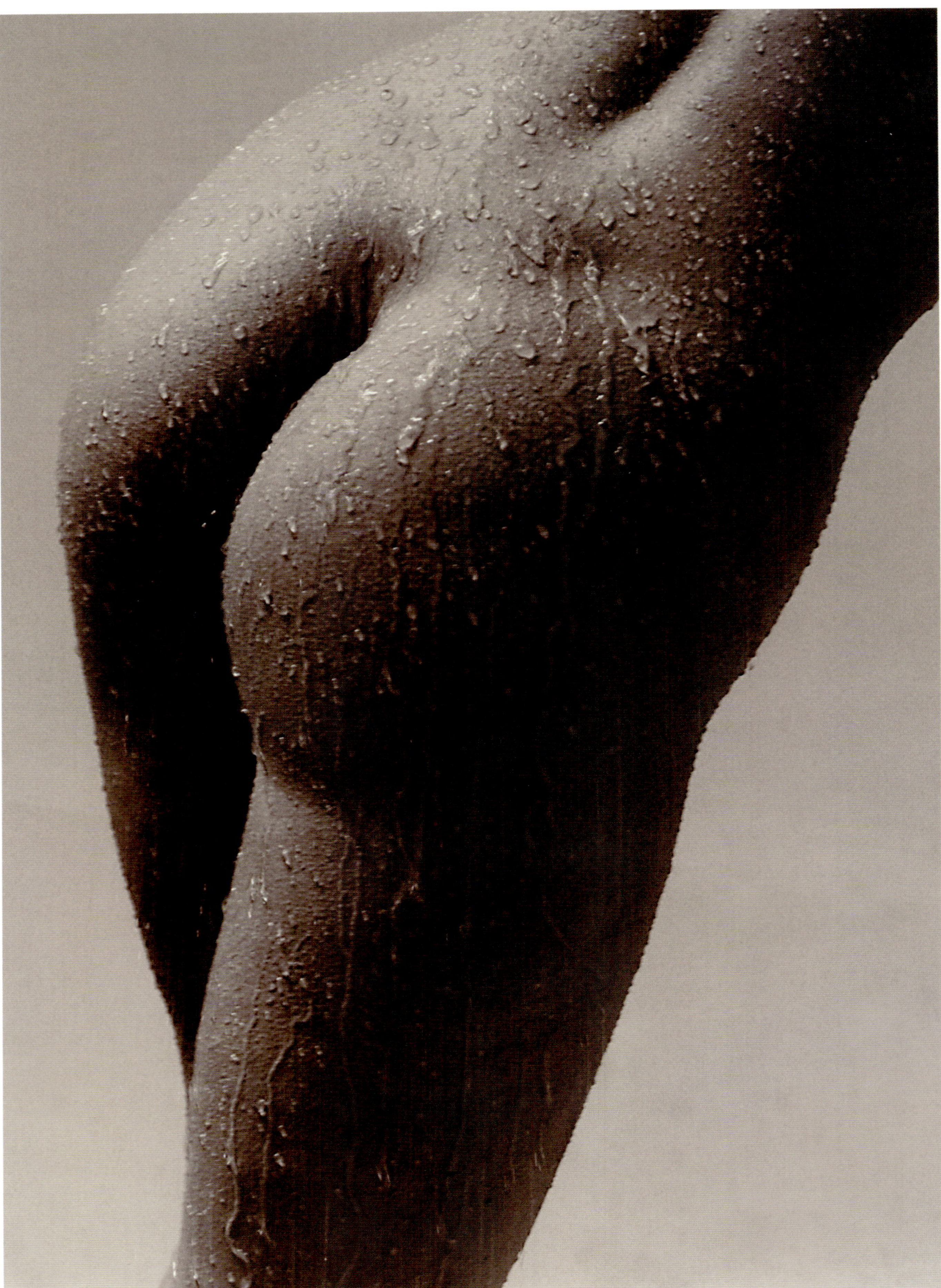

Wet shots

OPPOSITE: **An extra element.** Water droplets add another dimension to this classic monochrome figure study. (BRONICA ETRSi; 150mm LENS; 1/60 sec at f/8; ILFORD FP4 PLUS; SEPIA [THIOCARBAMIDE] TONED.)

Water and the nude can be a powerful combination that may be used in many ways to create imaginative images. Locations where you are likely to encounter water as an integral part of the scene include beaches (see pages 43, 104, 108), swimming pools (see pages 40, 110), lakes and rivers. In these environments, water may take on a secondary role, perhaps as a background, or it may be an integral part of the final image (see the partially submerged figure on page 106). Underwater photography is a specialist area but can produce stunning images, as demonstrated by the work of the American photographer Howard Schatz.

The addition of water to a figure study, using a fine spray, will result in the formation of tiny water droplets on the skin – this can be a particularly attractive effect when lit by low-angled incident light. An application of body oil before spraying will make the water droplets more pronounced.

moving images Mobility is a major feature of water and can thus impart a sense of movement to a photograph. Try taking pictures with turbulent water such as waves, fast-running rivers or waterfalls for dynamic pictures. Rain and hosepipes offer other possibilities for aquatic experimentation. Shutter speed greatly influences the way water is recorded. Using a slow shutter speed of 1/30 sec or less will blur the motion of the water, while a fast shutter speed of around 1/1000 sec will freeze the action.

RIGHT: **Rain effect.** To create this rain effect, the model was positioned under a tree. An assistant directed water from a hosepipe over the foliage while another directed sunlight at the model with a gold reflector. A slow shutter speed was used to accentuate the sense of movement in the water. (MINOLTA 8000i; 100mm LENS; 1/15 sec at f/8; KODACHROME 64.)

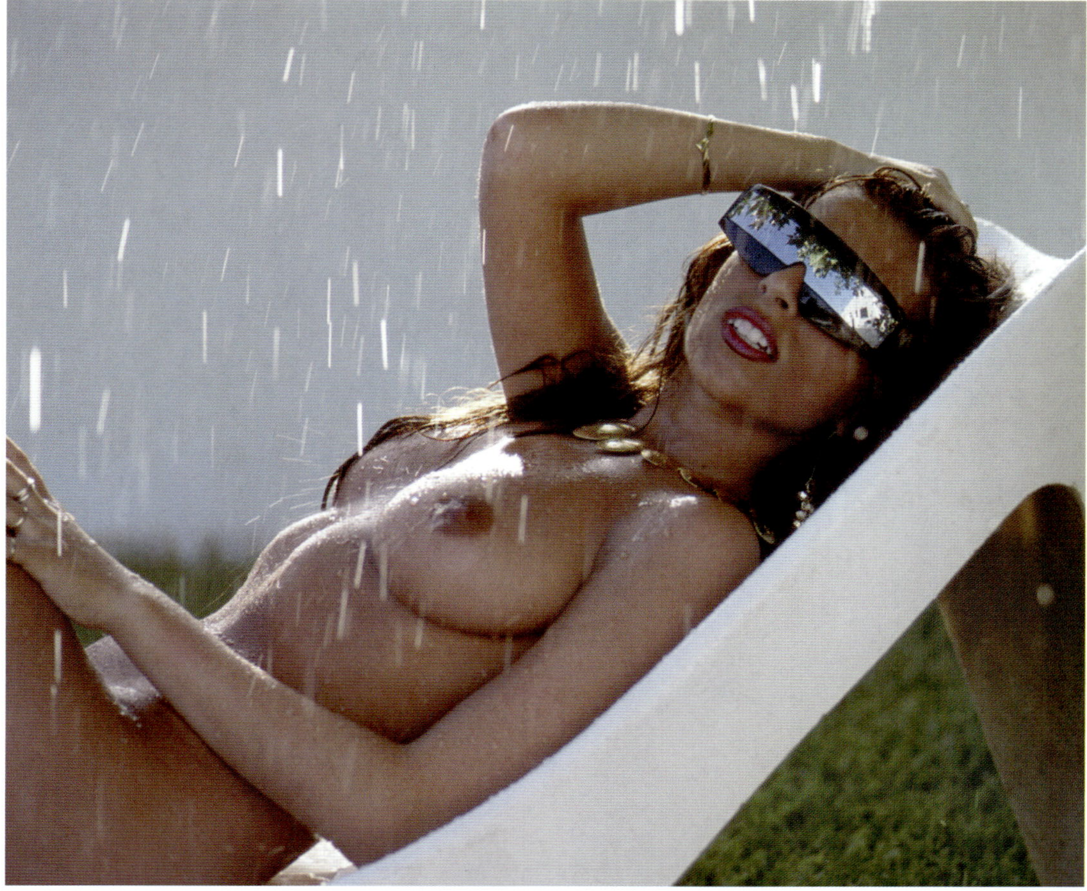

Two or more models

BELOW: **Pleasing symmetry.** Photographing two nude models in an elegant and tasteful composition is challenging. The similarity and symmetry of the two poses works well here. (BRONICA ETRSi; 150mm LENS; 1/125 sec at f/11; KODAK VERICOLOR 160.)

Photographing a single nude model and obtaining an aesthetic pose is challenging in its own right, but working with two or more models requires even more thought and skill if the desired effect is to be achieved. It is important that the models, whether they are male, female or both, are comfortable with each other – especially if the image requires any physical contact.

good relationships

Often you can find models who are friends, couples or family members and will happily model together – such as the two sisters in the image shown below. Each model needs to be directed individually and considered as an element of a complete composition to give a strong interrelationship between the subjects. The

OPPOSITE: **Triple pose.** Working with three models at the same time is not recommended for the beginner or faint-hearted. Each pose has to be worked on individually and related to the others to create a well-balanced image. (BRONICA ETRSi; 150mm LENS; 1/125 sec at f/11; KODAK PORTRA 160NC.)

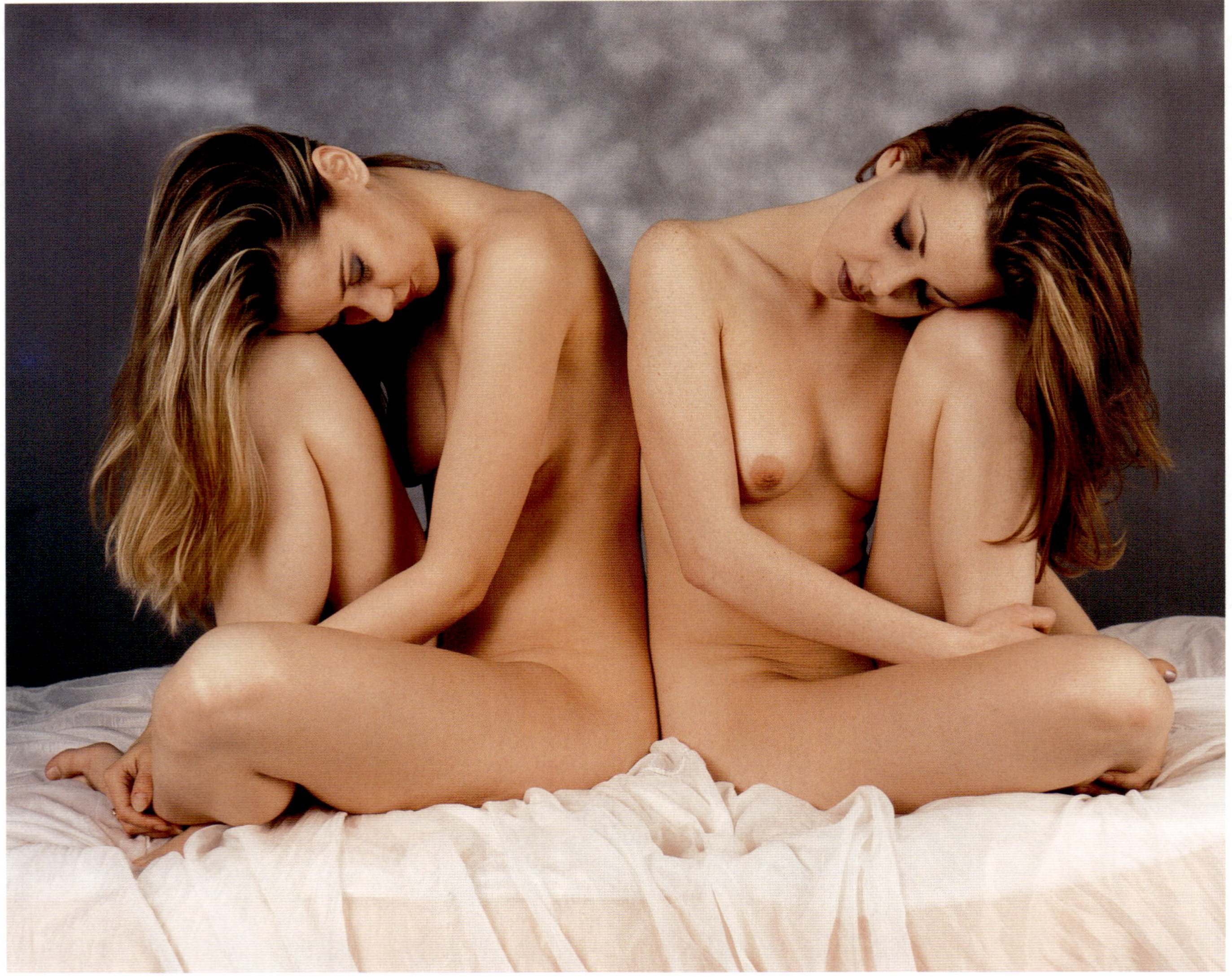

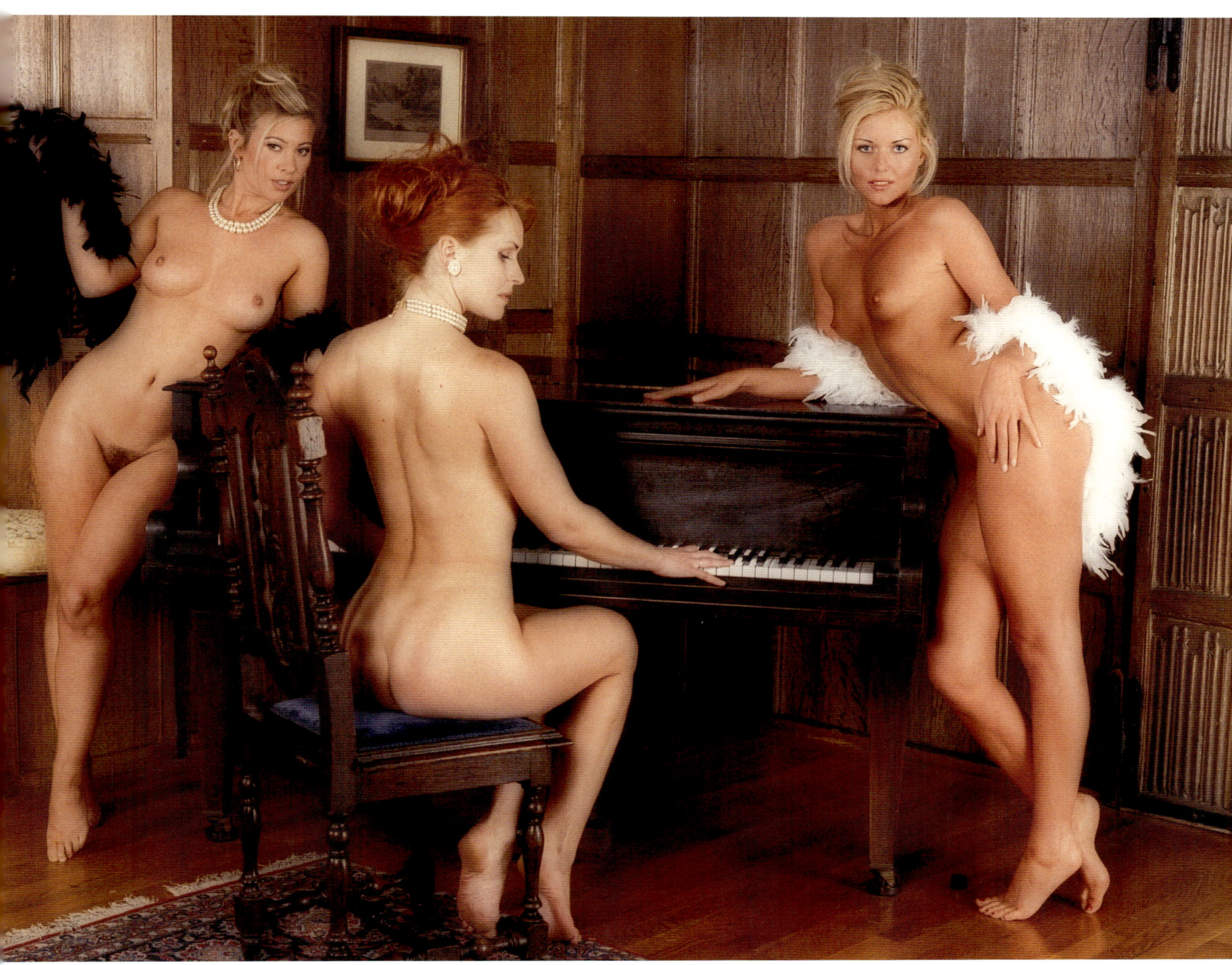

more models used, the more complex this task becomes. Direction from the photographer is critical in such a situation. It is important that each model should know what pose is wanted and what facial expressions or body language are required to unite them into an integrated image. Take time over this aspect and don't be afraid to make changes in each model's pose to obtain the desired result.

Lighting several models at once is complex because each model casts a shadow. It is important that the shadow of one person should not unintentionally be cast on to another, spoiling the overall image. In the studio, check where the shadows fall by using modelling lights. Each model should be lit for optimum exposure, using extra lighting if necessary. With limited equipment, soft diffused light or bounced flash can help overcome any problems of this sort. For more dynamic images, try highlighting one member of the group or placing one model at a different distance from the camera and selectively focusing on them.

GROUP COMPOSITION

Strong composition is paramount to a successful group picture, which is demonstrated by the images shown here. The strength of the sisters' image lies in the similarity of the two poses, their expressions, and the mirror-like symmetry of the whole composition. The three models around the piano also have a strong, balanced compositional element. The two outer models leaning inwards focus attention on to the seated model and hold the group together. The placement of the seated model's hand on the piano keys and the right-hand model's arm on top of the piano also give essential connectivity to the grouping. Having a common prop that all the models can interact with, such as the piano, is often beneficial to a group composition.

Capturing the image is the first step
for the majority of people in the
creative process of making a picture
– and often the last step. But the
advanced photographer will at some
stage be drawn to methods that
create unique images, stamped with
his or her personal style. One way of
achieving this is to take your images
into the darkroom. This chapter is
designed for photographers who like
to work in the darkroom, and
it includes some of the techniques
that can be used to enhance nude
images. Knowledge of basic printing
methods, split-grade printing,
dodging, burning, and the like is
assumed, so attention can be
focused on a selection of creative
techniques that could improve the
quality of your nude photography.

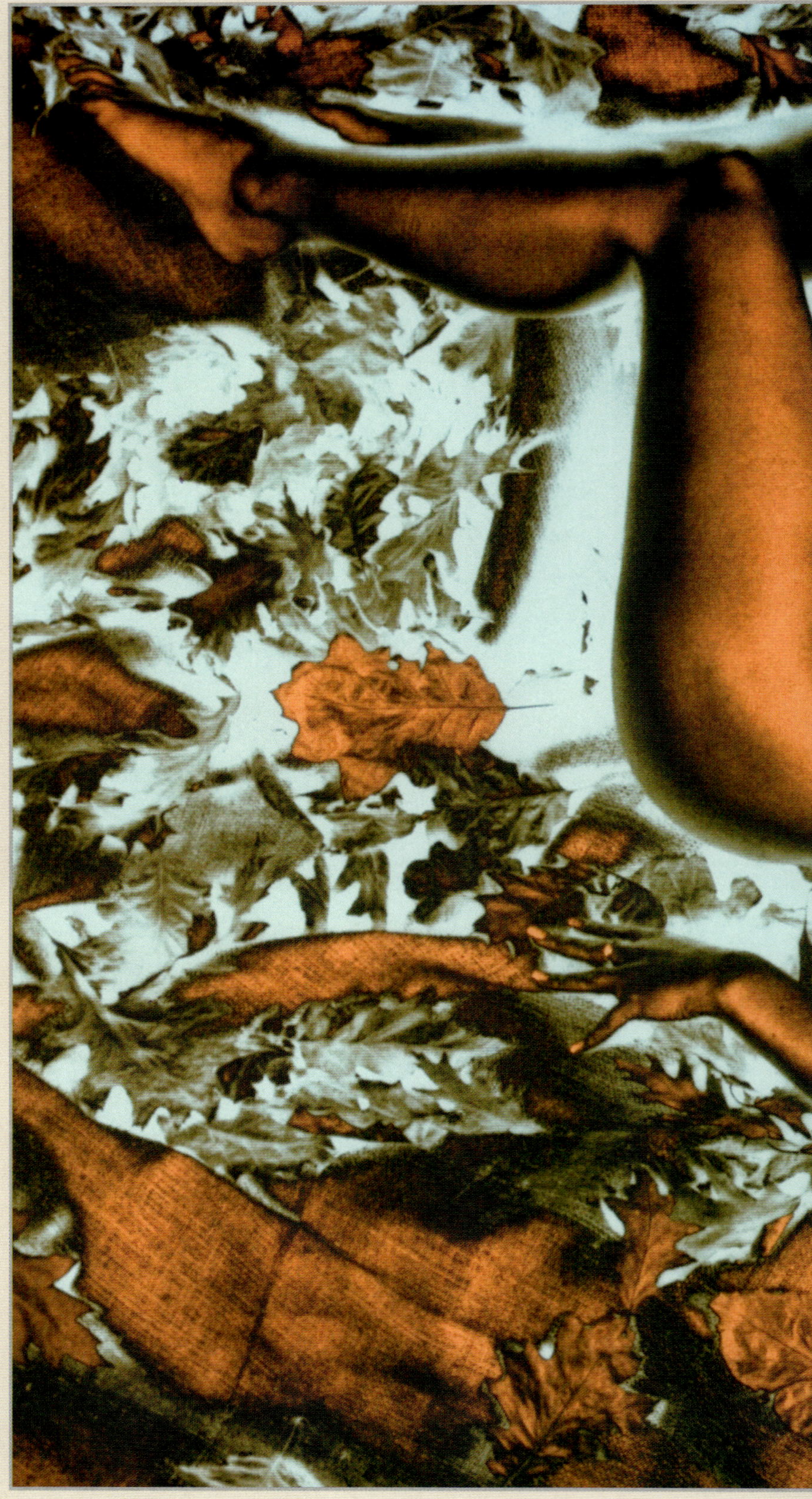

Darkroom know-how

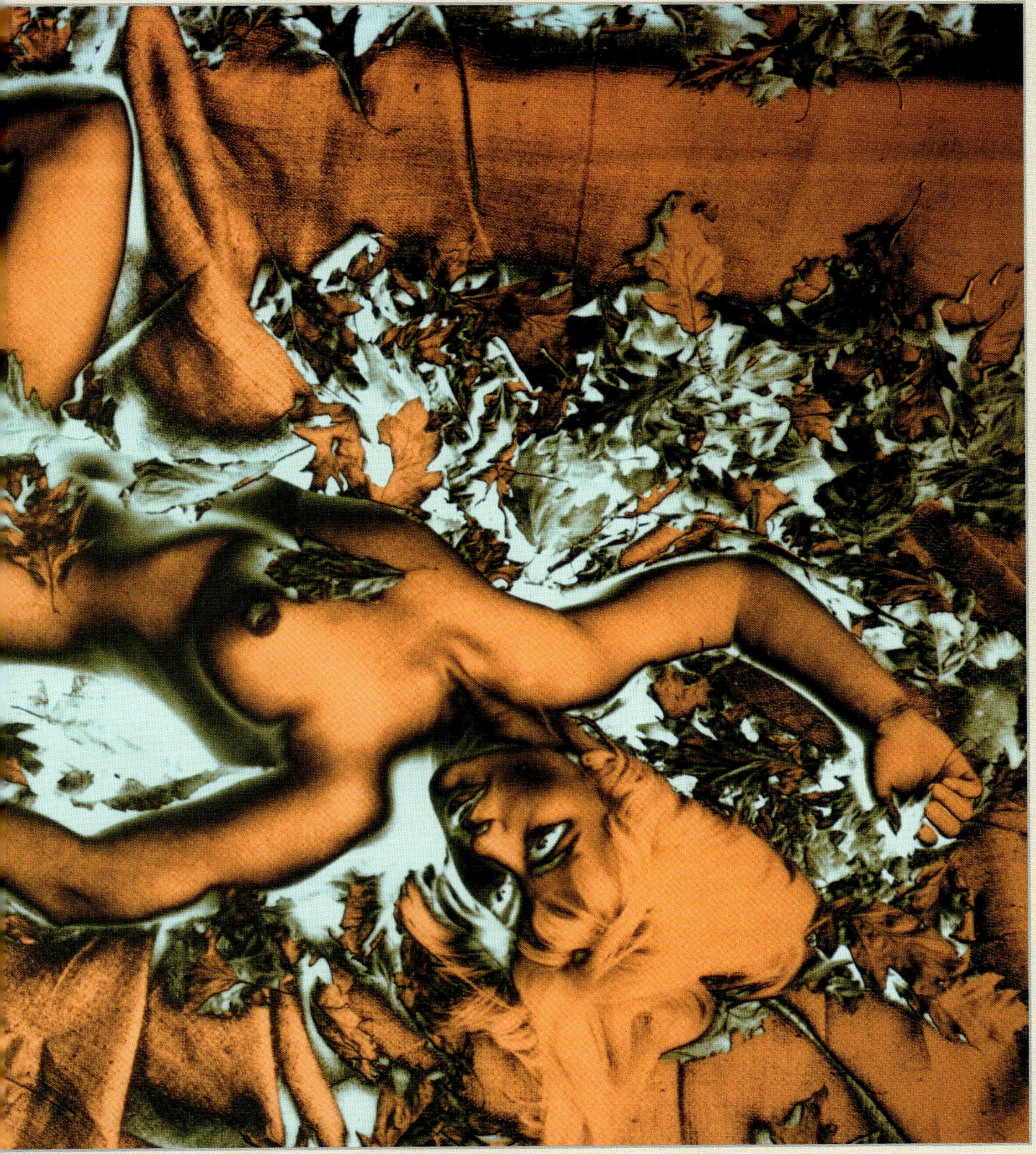

Borders and edges

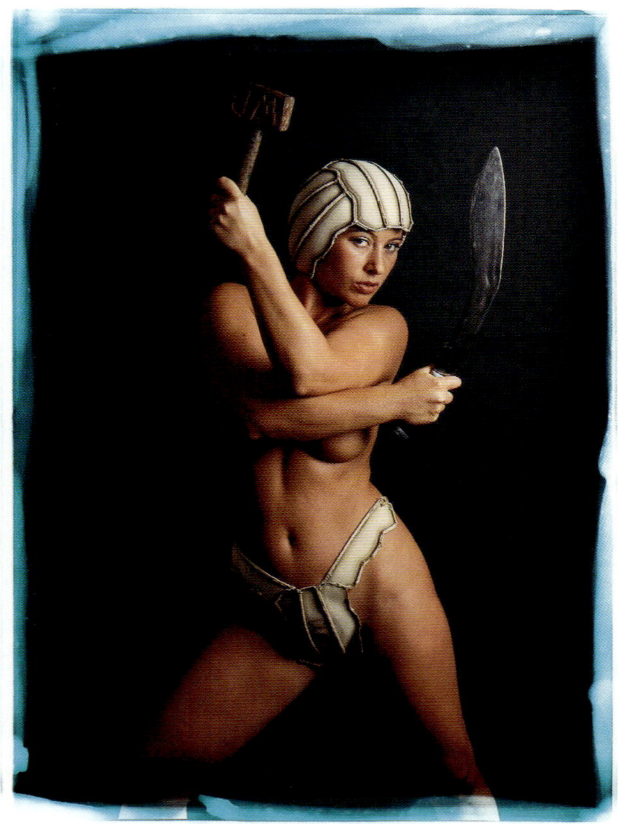

ABOVE: **Mask in enlarger carrier.** The blue
edge to this print was generated using a
carrier mask. Take care not to use the
technique too frequently and only use it on
images that will be enhanced by the effect.
(BRONICA ETRSi; 150mm LENS; 1/125 sec at f/11;
KODAK PORTRA NC.)

When making prints for an exhibition or a portfolio it is worth considering what can be done at the printing stage to enhance the chosen images. Borders and edges can be used to make a print into an individual statement. The simplest border that can be applied to a print at the printing stage is a plain white border, and this can have a profound effect on the viewer. A picture printed with a wide border is more isolated from its surroundings and commands greater attention. Border width can be varied using a standard masking frame.

baseboard masks A thin black line around a black-and-white image is easily created using a mask made from line film. The photograph is exposed normally and the mask is then placed on top of the paper and exposed with white light through the thin line of transparent film. Line film is a low-speed, high-contrast black-and-white negative film obtainable from specialist photographic suppliers. Torn or ragged-edge prints can be generated in a similar way, using a paper mask. I use black resin-coated photographic paper (exposed to white light and processed), which can be marked up for a particular print and the image area carefully torn away to leave a ragged edge. The mask is placed over unexposed paper in the masking easel and the print made through the hole in the paper mask. The border on the edge can be increased by carefully lifting off some of the black resin coating, leaving a thin layer of semi-transparent white paper that will allow some light through during printing. These masks work best with prints that have black or dark backgrounds. See also page 127.

carrier masks Another method uses a film mask, which is sandwiched with the negative being printed in the negative carrier. I use a piece of clear, unexposed and processed black-and-white film the same size as the negative being printed. Place this over the negative and use it as a guide to apply photo opaque from just inside the printing area to the edges of the film frame, leaving the central area as clear film base. Using this kind of red-brown mask for printing onto colour negative materials will produce a cyan-blue-coloured edge in thinner areas. Photo opaque is a quick-drying red-brown pigment-based fluid, which can be painted on film to block the passage of light. Other opaque materials such as inks and paints can be used to provide alternative edge colouration. Preformed black/transparent masks can be purchased from specialist photographic retailers, but I prefer the homemade variety, as each is unique and can be made in a few minutes. See also page 128.

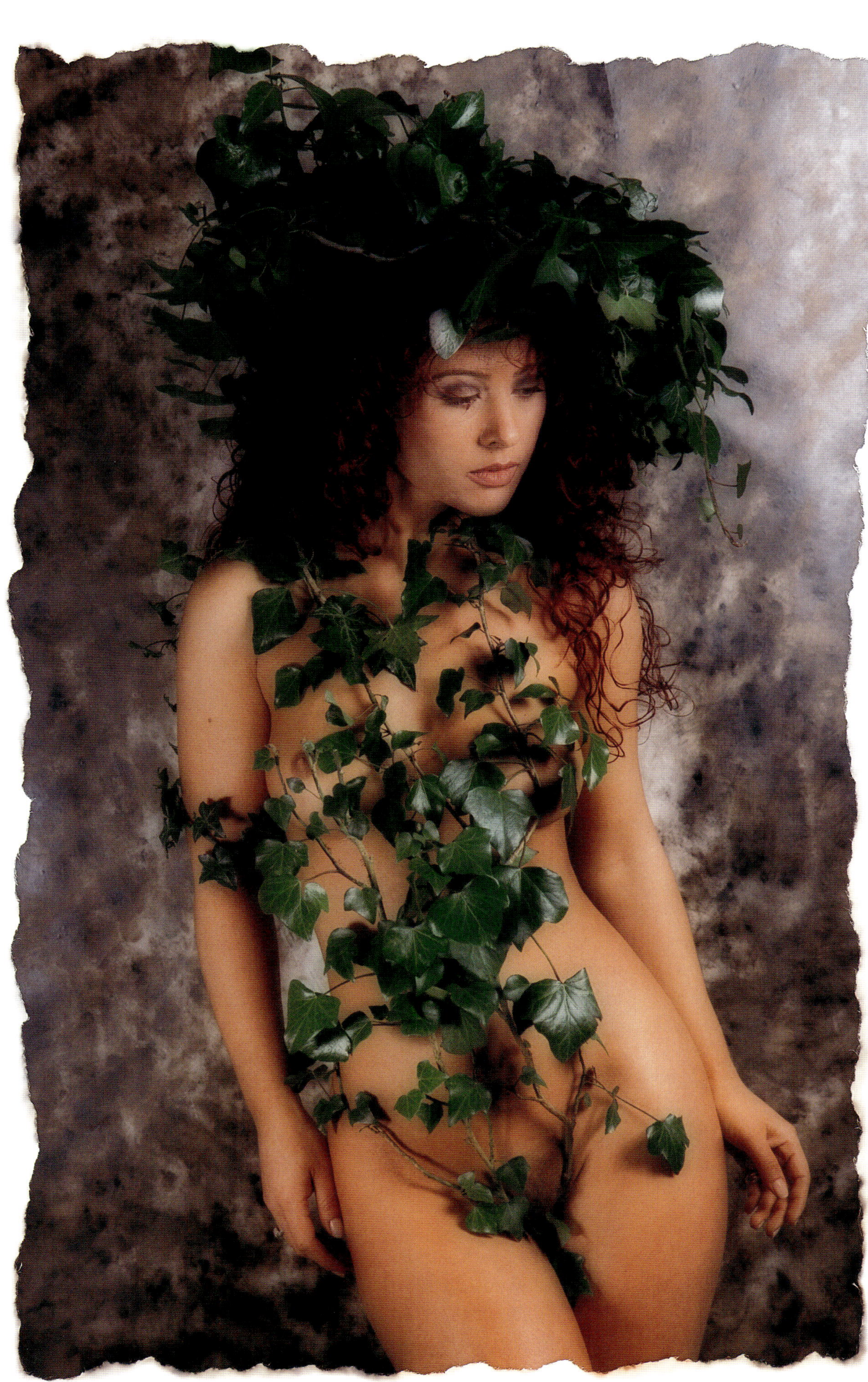

Image softening

Diffusion filters and screens are very useful devices for the manipulation of images. They should have a place in the darkroom of every creative photographer.

diffusion

It is sometimes desirable to give a picture a softer look. Perhaps the mood requires this, or the image structure is just too sharp. Softening an image can be done during a shoot by using on-camera diffusion filters (see page 17), but this is irreversible. If you leave the decision about diffusion to the darkroom stage, you have the option to use the image sharp or soft. Darkroom diffusion is achieved by using a diffusion screen under the enlarger lens during printing. It can be attached to the lens or, preferably, hand held under the lens. A sheet of anti-reflection glass from a picture frame (tape the edges for safety) is ideal for this. The degree of diffusion can be controlled by the amount of time the diffuser is left under the lens during exposure. As a rough guide, 20–50 per cent of the exposure time using the diffuser will be sufficient. If overdiffused, the blacks tend to 'bleed' into lighter areas; with on-camera filters the whites 'bleed' into darker areas. This technique is particularly suitable for nudes, portraits and 'boudoir' photography.

screens

Textures can be applied to prints, but use them sparingly as they become tiresome if overused. The method is similar to that used for printing edges. A rectangular card frame is made to fit in the baseboard masking easel and a piece of semi-transparent material with a fine-textured weave, such as calico, is stretched over it and fastened with tape. The image is then printed through the screen onto the photographic paper. Slight adjustments to exposure times must be made to compensate for the light absorption of the material, and it is sometimes desirable to print through the screen for only a portion of the exposure time. As well as adding a texture, the overall contrast is reduced, so the method is best suited to higher-contrast images. This technique can also be used in the sandwich method. Grain screens can be used in a similar way to impart a granular texture to the image, mimicking the effect of fast film. You can buy these screens from photographic outlets or make them yourself by photographing grainy subjects such as fine sand. Another example of printing with a screen can be seen on page 52.

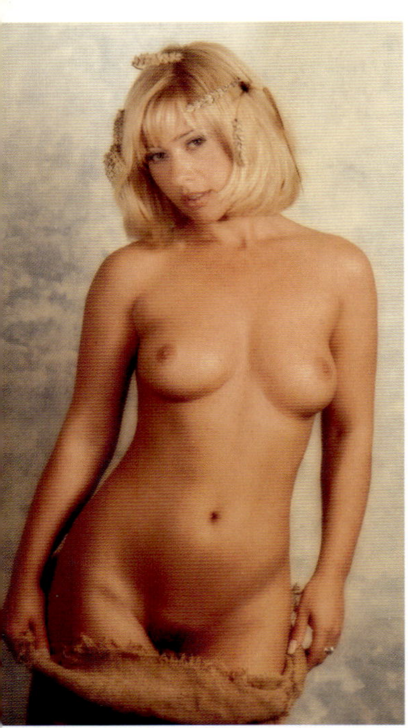

ABOVE: **Reduced sharpness.** The original image for this print was just a little too sharp. Using about 30 per cent diffusion at the printing stage reduced the sharpness to a more pleasing level. (BRONICA ETRSi; 150mm LENS; 1/125 sec at f/11; KODAK PORTRA 160NC.)

RIGHT: **Soft diffusion.** A soft, dreamy mood was required for this print, so the image was diffused at the printing stage using approximately 25 per cent diffusion. (BRONICA ETRSi; 150mm LENS; 1/125 sec at f/8; KODAK GPX.)

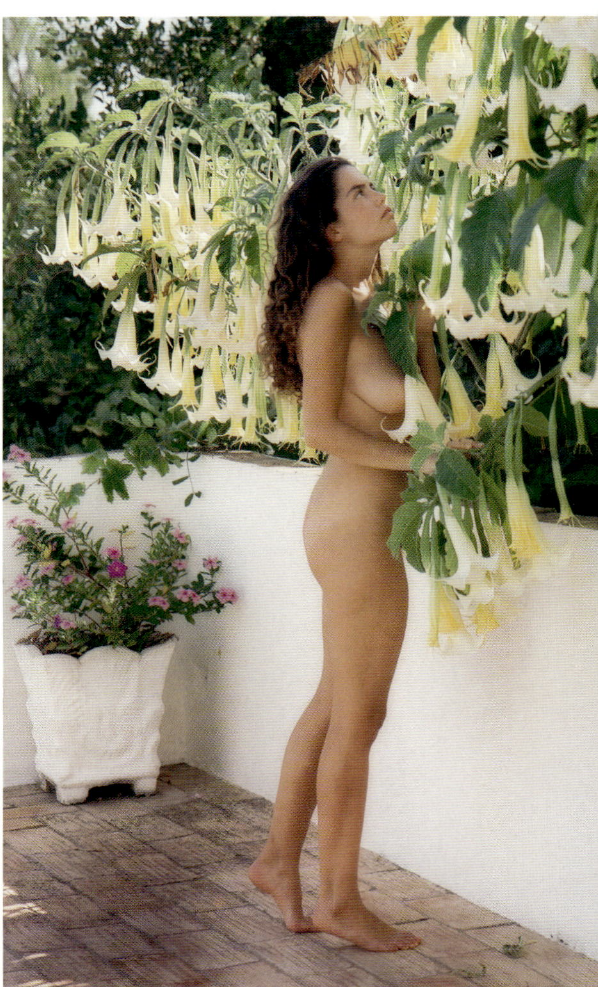

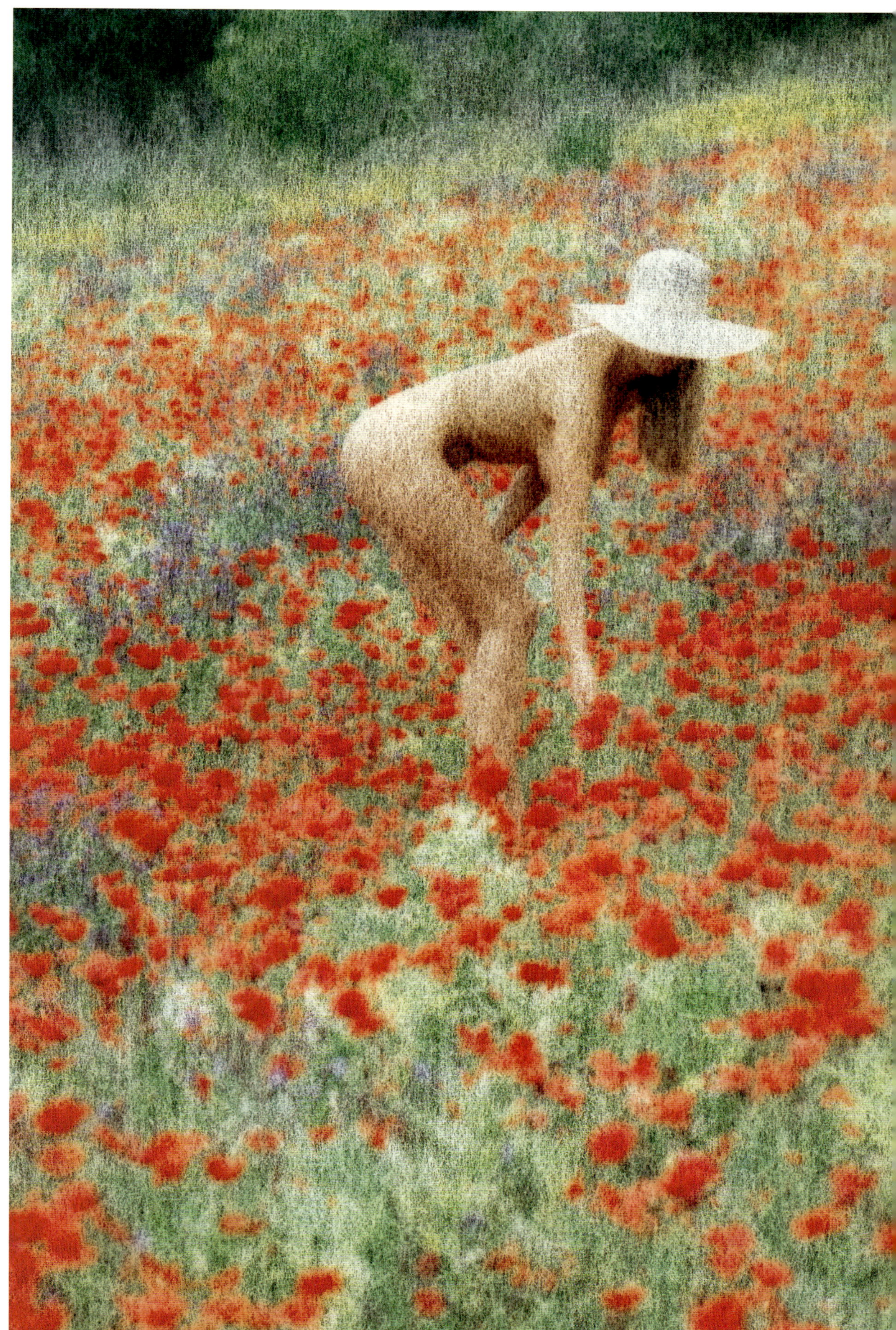

RIGHT: **Textured finish.** A light texture was added to this image of a nude in a poppy field, giving the photograph the appearance of a painting. A fine material screen was used for 50 per cent of the printing exposure time. (BRONICA ETRSi; 75mm LENS; 1/125 sec at f/8; KODAK 400VC.)

Toning black-and-white images

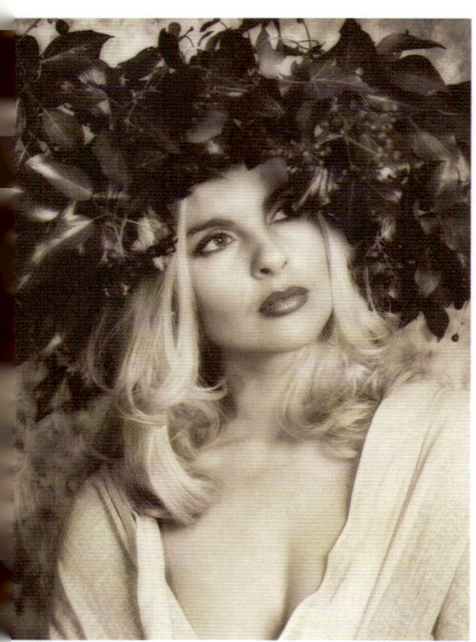

ABOVE: **Added warmth.**
Light bleaching of highlights and toning with thiocarbamide toner has added a little warmth to this black-and-white print. (BRONICA ETRSi; 150mm LENS; 1/125 sec at f/11; ILFORD FP4 PLUS.)

RIGHT: **Split toning.** Partial bleaching before toning gives a print split-toned in sepia and silver. Here the image was bleached until the mid-tones started to disappear, but the blacks were retained. (BRONICA ETRSi; 150mm LENS; 1/60 sec at f/8; ILFORD FP4 PLUS.)

OPPOSITE: **Selective toning.** Selective toning can give a dramatic finish. In this print, areas of the silver image were carefully bleached back with stock ferricyanide bleach using a fine paintbrush, washed, and then toned with thiocarbamide toner. (BRONICA ETRSi; 150mm LENS; 1/125 sec at f/11; ILFORD FP4 PLUS.)

Silver images can be manipulated to give varied visual effects and chemical toning of black-and-white prints is one way of adding individuality and colour to a monochrome image. Techniques include sepia, selenium, iron blue and copper toning. Chemicals can be bought individually and mixed according to the formulas in the Appendix or purchased in kit form from specialist photographic suppliers.

sepia Warm images can be obtained from sepia toners. Modern sepia toners use a two-bath procedure with odour-free thiourea (thiocarbamide) as the toning agent. The colours obtained can be controlled by manipulating the alkalinity of the toning solution. The print is first bleached in a ferricyanide and bromide bath to convert the silver image to silver bromide, washed well with water, and then immersed for a few minutes in the toner solution to convert the image to silver sulphide. Addition of small amounts of sodium hydroxide to the toner bath gives yellowish-brown tones. Larger quantities produce colours ranging from red-brown to rich chocolate brown. Partial bleaching before toning gives a split-toned print in sepia and silver, often producing a more pleasing result than full toning. Selective toning is another option where only selected areas of the image are bleached and toned.

selenium Toning with selenium is a one-bath process that can also give colour changes, depending on the paper used. Bromide papers tend to give black tones so there is often little colour change, whereas high-chloride papers tend to give a warmer reddish tone. Selenium toner works on the higher-density areas first, depositing silver selenide on top of the silver with the result that an increase in contrast is often observed.

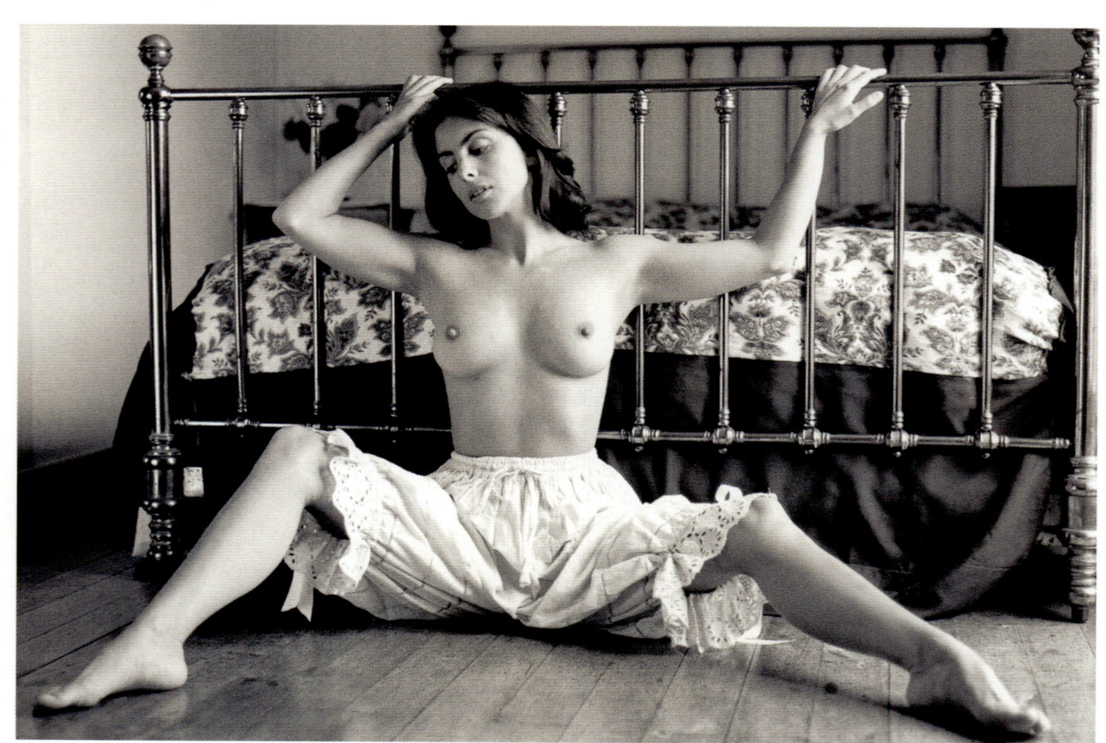

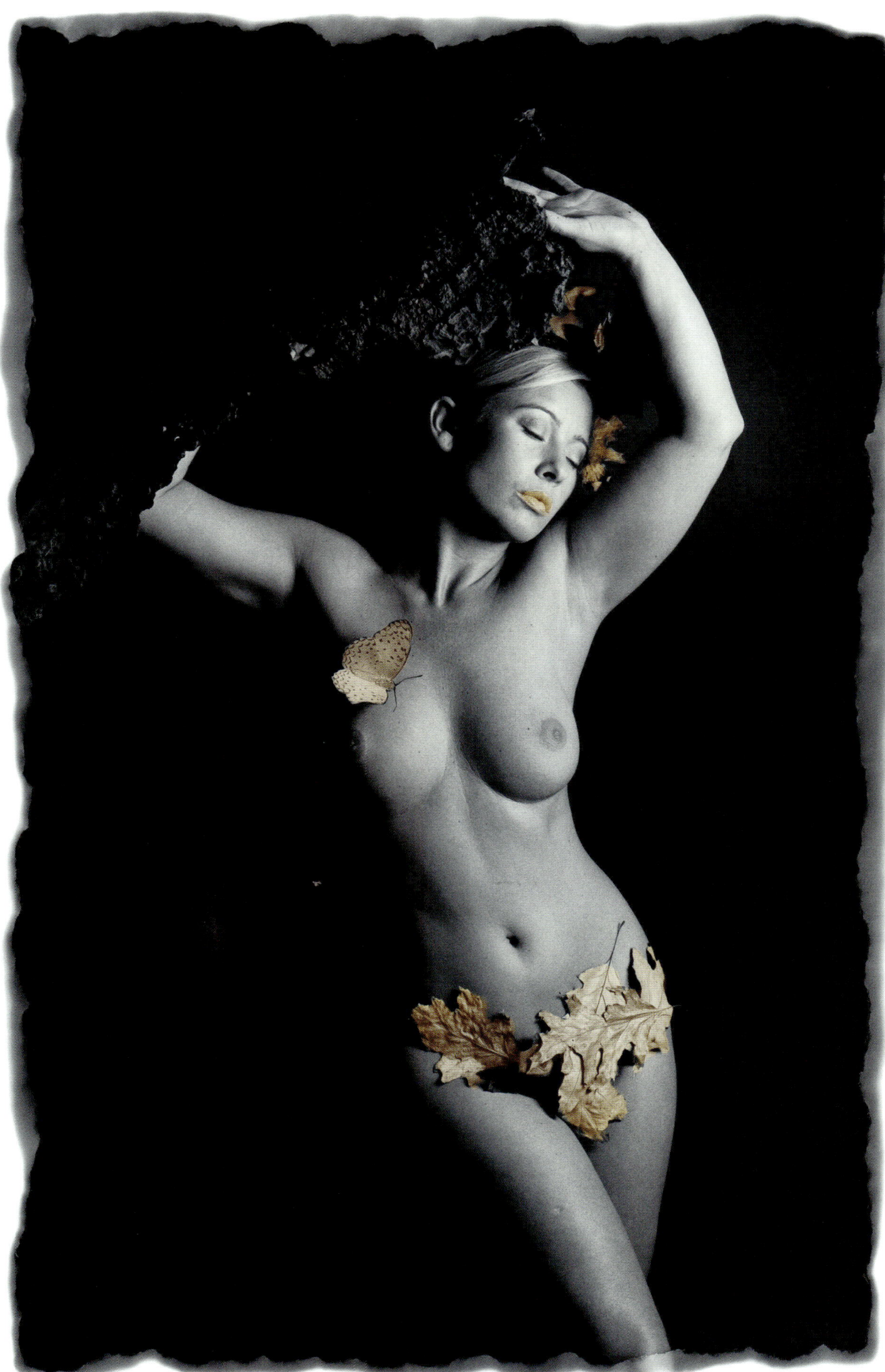

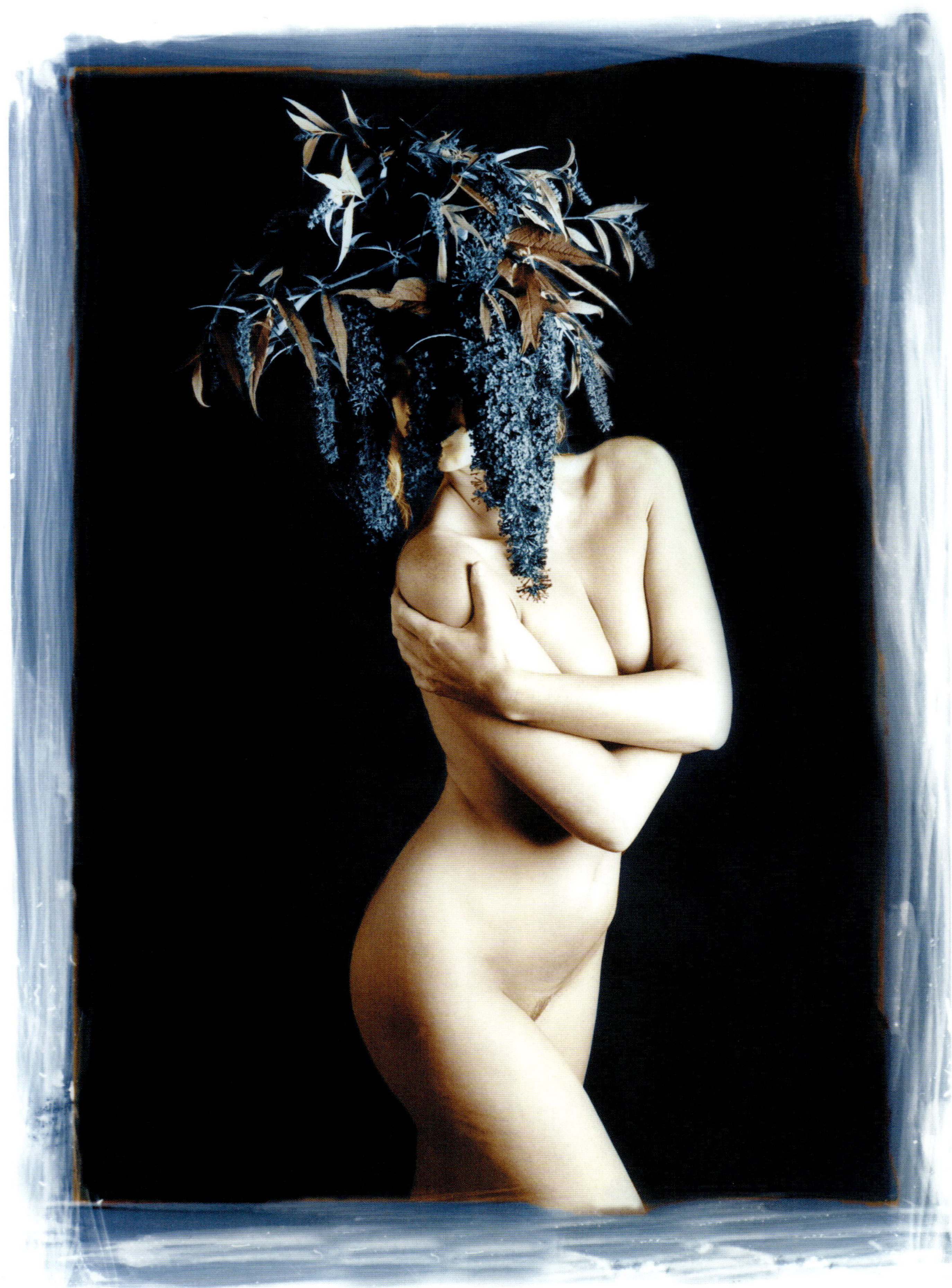

iron

iron Blue images can be obtained using iron-based toners. The most common type is a one-bath solution. This toner is available commercially and provides a vivid blue pigment (Prussian Blue) that is deposited on top of the original image, giving rise to image intensification. There is also a (non-commercial) two-bath iron toner that uses separate bleaching and toning baths and provides a more aesthetically pleasing steel-blue colouration, though prints must be thoroughly washed between steps to avoid contamination. Extensive washing can lead to removal of the colouration in images made by the one-bath method, whereas the blue colour formed by the two-bath method is relatively resistant. White print borders contaminated by blue stains can be restored by carefully wiping with a slightly alkaline solution (very dilute print developer can be used for this) and over-toned prints can be reduced in intensity by soaking in salt solution.

copper Toners containing copper give warm brown to distinctly red and sometimes purple-red images. Formulas for these, some of which are available commercially, are invariably single-bath solutions with a limited lifetime and should be used rapidly to avoid contamination. Part-used solutions may deposit a film of metallic copper on the print, which can be removed by gently swabbing with a soft cloth under running water. Toning has little effect on image density, and toned prints last fairly well, although are not as stable as sepia- and selenium-toned prints. Extensive toning of heavily printed images sometimes leads to images with a metallic copper sheen.

split toning Images can be toned with more than one toner to give a range of colour effects, though not all can be used together successfully. This process is generally referred to as split toning. Two of the most successful combinations for split toning are sepia and blue, and sepia and copper. Sepia toning destroys blue tones and has to be carried out first. Interesting mirror-like effects can sometimes be obtained with copper-toned sepia prints.

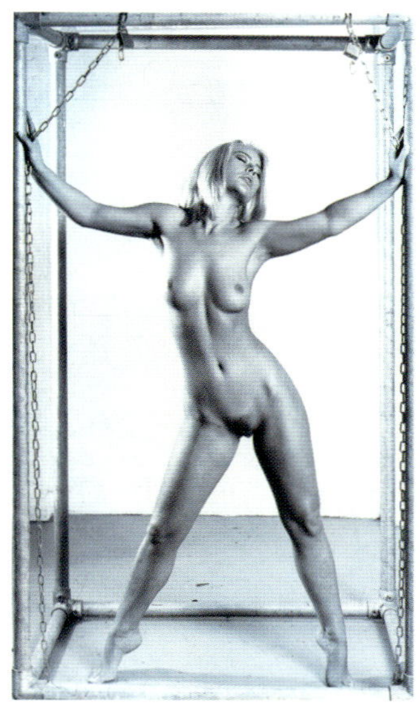

ABOVE: **Iron-blue toning.** Straight blue toning tends to give a vivid blue colouration if taken too far, so it is better to stop at the silver/blue split-toned stage, as here. (BRONICA ETRSi; 150mm LENS; 1/125 sec at f/11; ILFORD FP4 PLUS.)

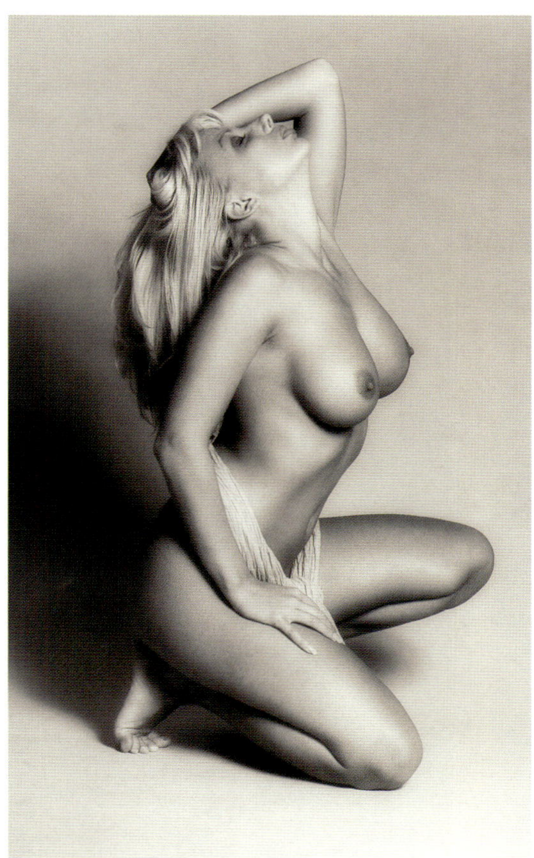

OPPOSITE: **Iron and sepia toning.** Selected areas of the silver image were completely bleached and toned with thiocarbamide toner; the remaining silver was then blue-toned. (BRONICA ETRSi; 150mm LENS; 1/125 sec at f/11; ILFORD FP4.)

RIGHT: **Iron and light-sepia toning.** Light-sepia toning followed by the briefest of blue toning gives this print a very subtle colour effect. (BRONICA ETRSi; 150mm LENS; 1/125 sec at f/11; ILFORD FP4 PLUS.)

FAR RIGHT: **Copper and sepia toning.** This copper-toned image shows the warm reddish-brown colouration obtainable with this toning method. (BRONICA ETRSi; 150mm LENS; 1/125 sec at f/11; ILFORD FP4 PLUS.)

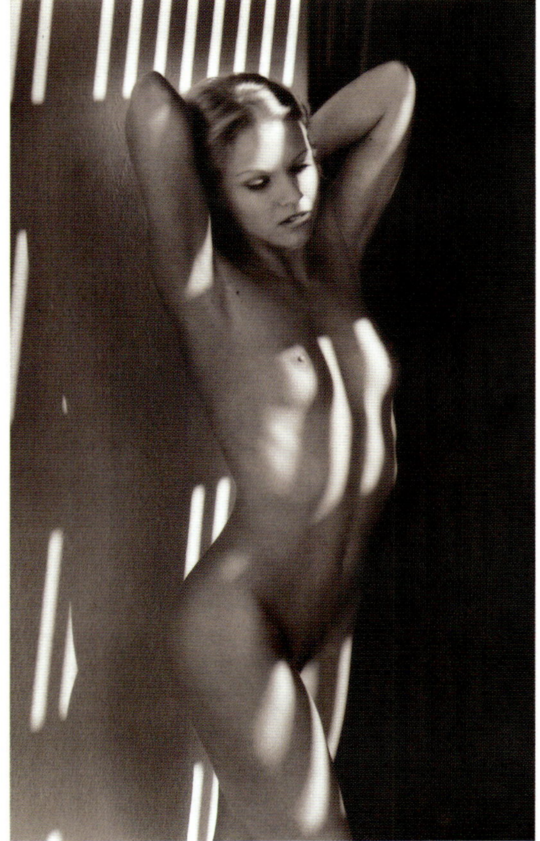

Creative darkroom processes

Applying standard darkroom techniques to negatives and transparencies can transform and revitalize an image, generating unusual and visually stunning pictures. Two of the best-known techniques are explained here.

pseudo-solarization
The complete reversal of an image by acute overexposure to light (1,000 times or more) is called solarization. Partial reversal, which is the result usually obtained by

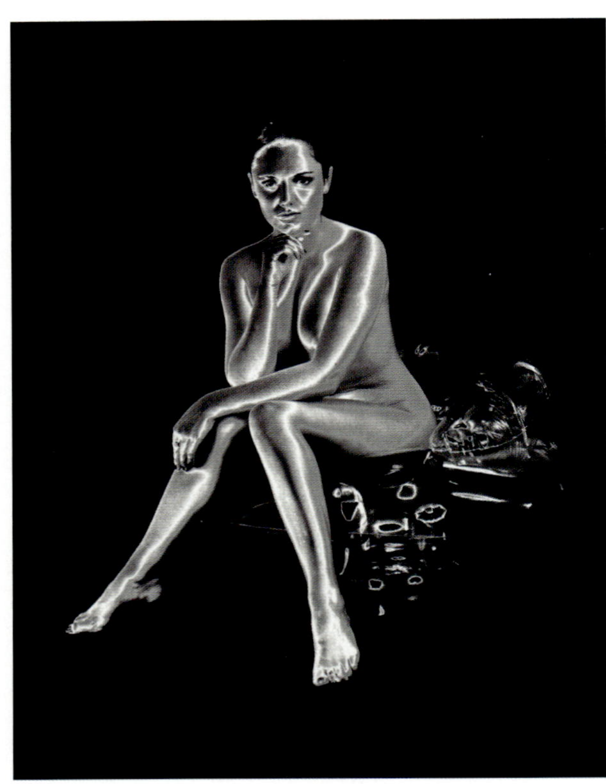

ABOVE: **Solarization.** Images with well-defined edges and a good tonal range, as in this nude study, are ideal subjects for pseudo-solarization. The positive/negative image obtained by the method described in the text was reversed by copying onto film and then printed to give this dramatic final image. (BRONICA ETRSi; 150mm LENS; 1/125 sec at f/11; ILFORD FP4 PLUS.)

RIGHT: **Bas-relief imagery.** Printing the dark-blue colour through the black-and-white negative image and the pink colour through the positive black-and-white image onto colour paper gave this effective colour bas relief. Light and dark lines are formed at the edges due to the misalignment of the images. (ORIGINAL IMAGE SHOT ON BRONICA ETRSi; 75mm LENS; 1/60 sec at f/8; ILFORD FP4 PLUS.)

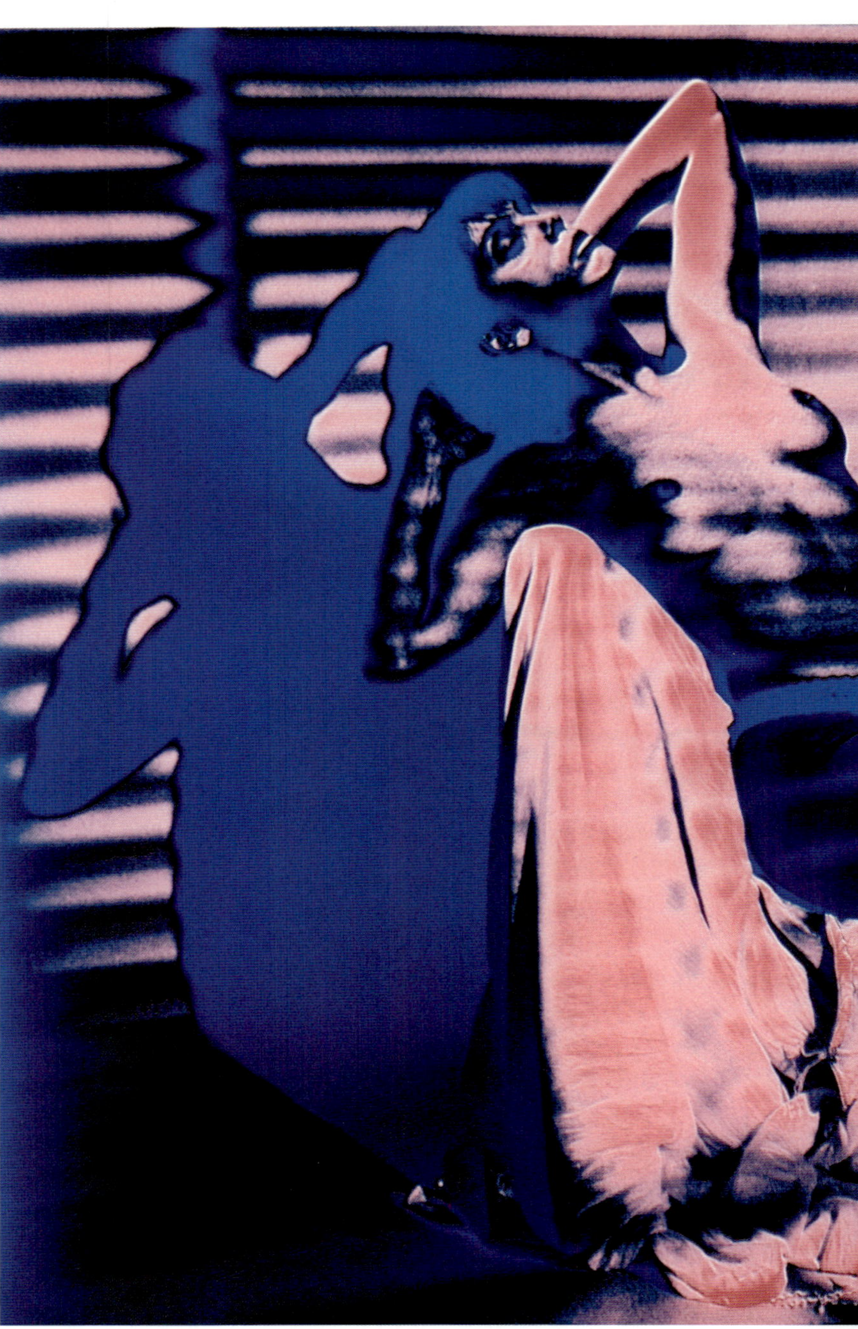

deliberately fogging a film during development, is more correctly called pseudo-solarization or the Sabbatier effect. This technique results in an image with both positive and negative elements. Where the two meet there is an undeveloped line called a Mackie line, named after the discoverer. There are several ways to produce a pseudo-solarized image, but the following is my preferred method. The chosen negative is enlarged onto a sheet of 5 x 4 lith film to form a positive image. The best exposure time is determined using the test-strip method and development in a proprietary lith developer. Another sheet of film is then exposed at this setting and developed for half the development time with agitation. After a brief stop and wash to arrest development, surplus water is removed from the film surface and the film placed under an enlarger. It is exposed again to white light, exposure being determined by trial and error. Continuation of the development, without agitation, achieves the final positive/negative image.

bas relief

A bas relief is obtained by printing a negative and a positive of the same image, sandwiched together slightly out of alignment. The effect is not unlike a shallow carving. In its simplest form, a black-and-white negative/positive sandwich is used. Other techniques include combining a colour slide with a black-and-white negative or printing through each component onto colour paper with different colour filtrations. The bas-relief image shown on this page (and page 121) was made by the latter method. The original black-and-white negative was enlarged onto 12 x 16 black-and-white paper speed film to give a positive image. This was contact printed onto another sheet of 12 x 16 film to give a negative image. The sheets were taped together at the edges, with the images slightly out of register, and holes made along the side with a four-hole punch to act as alignment guides. These fit a homemade registration device (see diagram) that consists of laminated chipboard with four inset metal rods. A sheet of colour paper was then punched along one edge, placed on the registration device, and each negative/positive placed in turn on top of the paper and exposed to light on the enlarger baseboard using different colour filtration values and the paper processed in standard C-41 chemistry.

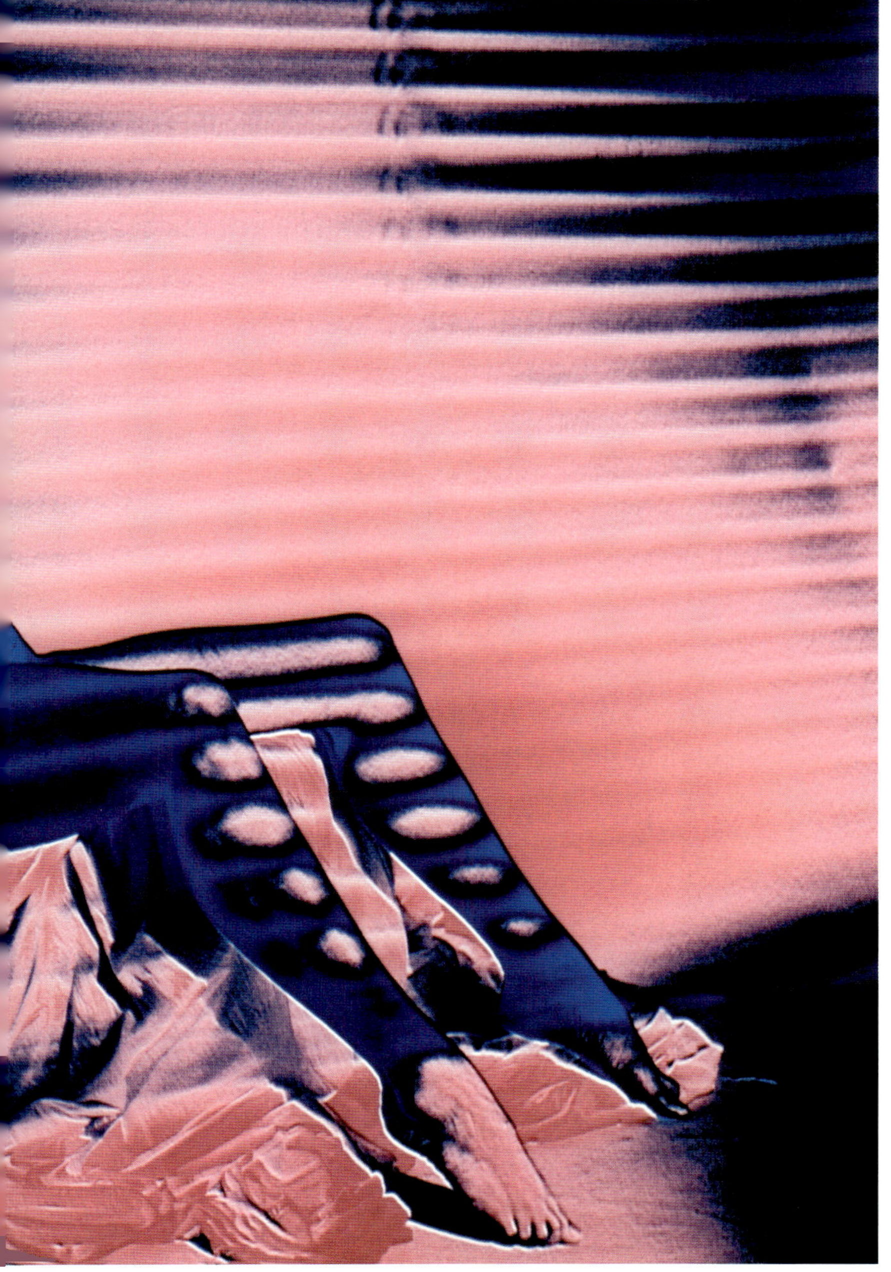

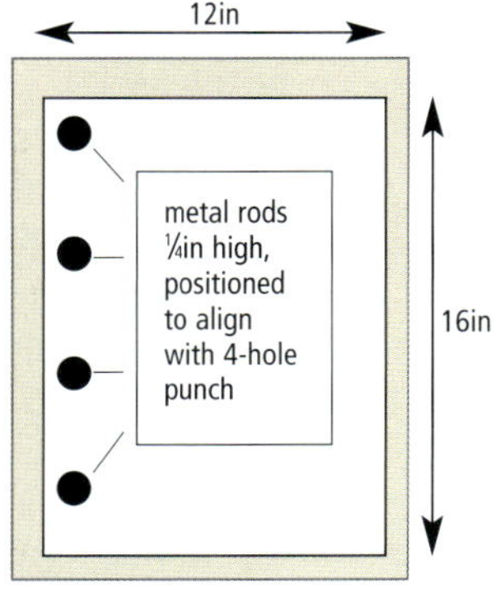

Registration guide for making bas-relief images.

DEVELOPER PRETREATMENT

The results of initial processing in a lith developer can be disappointing, giving only weak colouration. However, the more prints that are processed in the same solution, the better the colours become. The optimum lith effect is obtained when the developer is part used, so it is a good idea to keep some used developer solution from a previous darkroom session to add to a freshly prepared solution. If no old developer is available, season the fresh developer by making up the working solution about an hour or so before required and process a couple of sheets of paper that have been exposed to white light.

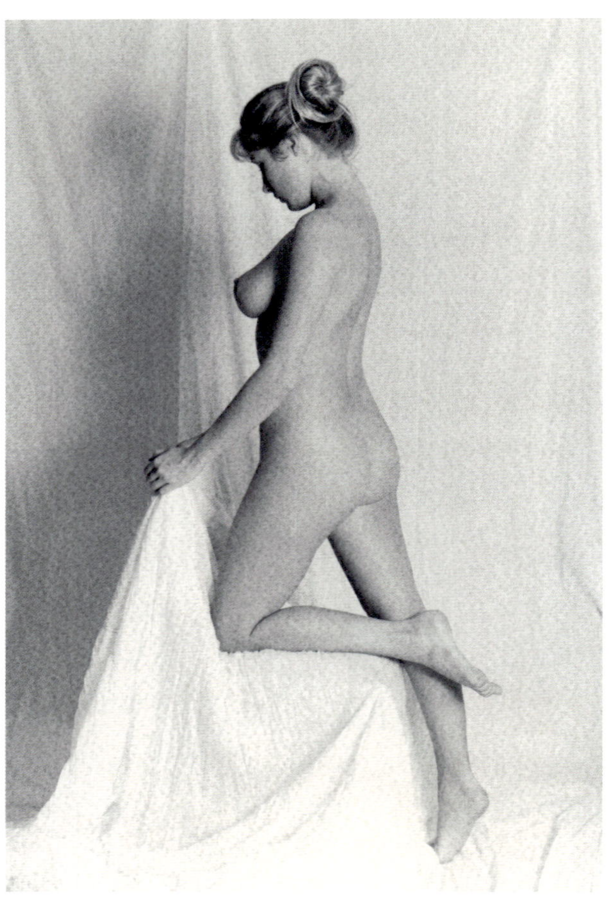

ABOVE: **Comparison print.** Regular print developer was used to make this comparison print on the same paper as that used for the lith print opposite. Fotospeed Tapestry paper using Kodak Dektol 1+9, 1.5 minutes' development at 20 degrees.

OPPOSITE: **Lith development.** The delicate pinkish-brown colours in this image were obtained by development in dilute lith developer for 30 minutes. This was the third print through the solution and subsequent prints became more intensely pink. Paper exposure was four stops more than that used for the comparison print. Fotospeed Tapestry paper using Speedibrews lith developer, 30 minutes' development at 20 degrees.

lith prints
Lith printing is a special black-and-white printing process that produces distinctively coloured images with different tonal distribution characteristics from normal black-and-white prints that cannot be obtained by other methods. Combined with chemical toning, this is a powerful method for the introduction of colour into prints. High-contrast negatives, lith film and graphic arts materials have nothing to do with this technique, but lith developer is an essential part of the procedure. It is a highly creative process, well suited to the fine-art nude photographer aiming for an artistic interpretation of an image and willing to spend time experimenting in the darkroom. The procedure is time-consuming as development times are typically around 15–30 minutes. This process sometimes gives unexpected results, and often cannot be reproduced unless detailed notes are taken. The results, however, can be very rewarding and are certainly worth pursuing.

In essence, the process of lith printing involves printing a normal negative onto a suitable black-and-white photographic printing paper at a much higher exposure level than usual and partially developing the paper in a dilute lith developer solution. Overexposure by two, three or even more stops is not uncommon. Little development activity is observed at first, but after some time density builds up in the shadow areas and then the mid-tones. At some point infectious development sets in, where silver is formed in an exponential chain reaction, and image formation becomes increasingly rapid. This is the important stage of the process and the print must be carefully observed, particularly for highlight detail, and snatched from the processing solution at the optimum point of development. This will provide a print that has black shadow areas, delicately coloured mid-tones and white highlights. Creams, caramel-browns, yellow-browns, pinks and reds are some of the colours that are typically produced by this method – depending on a number of factors. Different manufacturers' papers respond to lith developers in different ways and tend to give a variety of colours. Some do not respond at all. Exposure, temperature and development times also have a bearing on the final result, as does the age of the developer solution. Wet colour is often different from the dried-down colour, so prints should always be judged only when they are dry.

Colour negatives as well as regular black-and-white negatives can be used in this process. Infrared negatives have a particular affinity with lith printing because the highlight rendition is readily controllable and provides delicate tones in these areas of the print. A wide variety of black-and-white printing papers are now available that respond well to lith printing, and some, such as Sterling Premium F Lith, are dedicated to the process. Standard dish development is all that is required in the darkroom, along with an appropriate safelight for the paper in use. Lith developers, which are hydroquinone-based, are available from specialist photographic suppliers and come either as two-part solutions or powders.

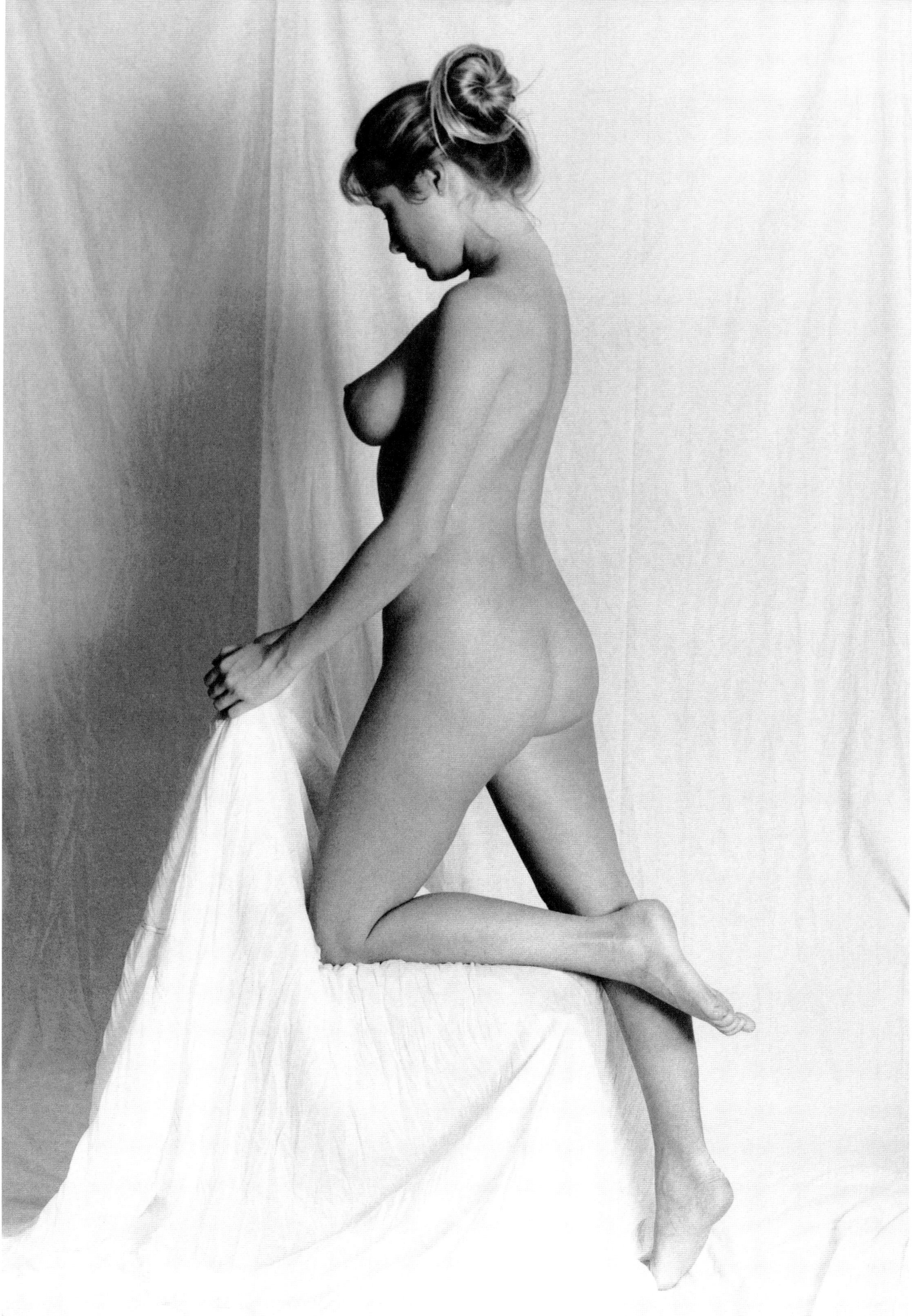

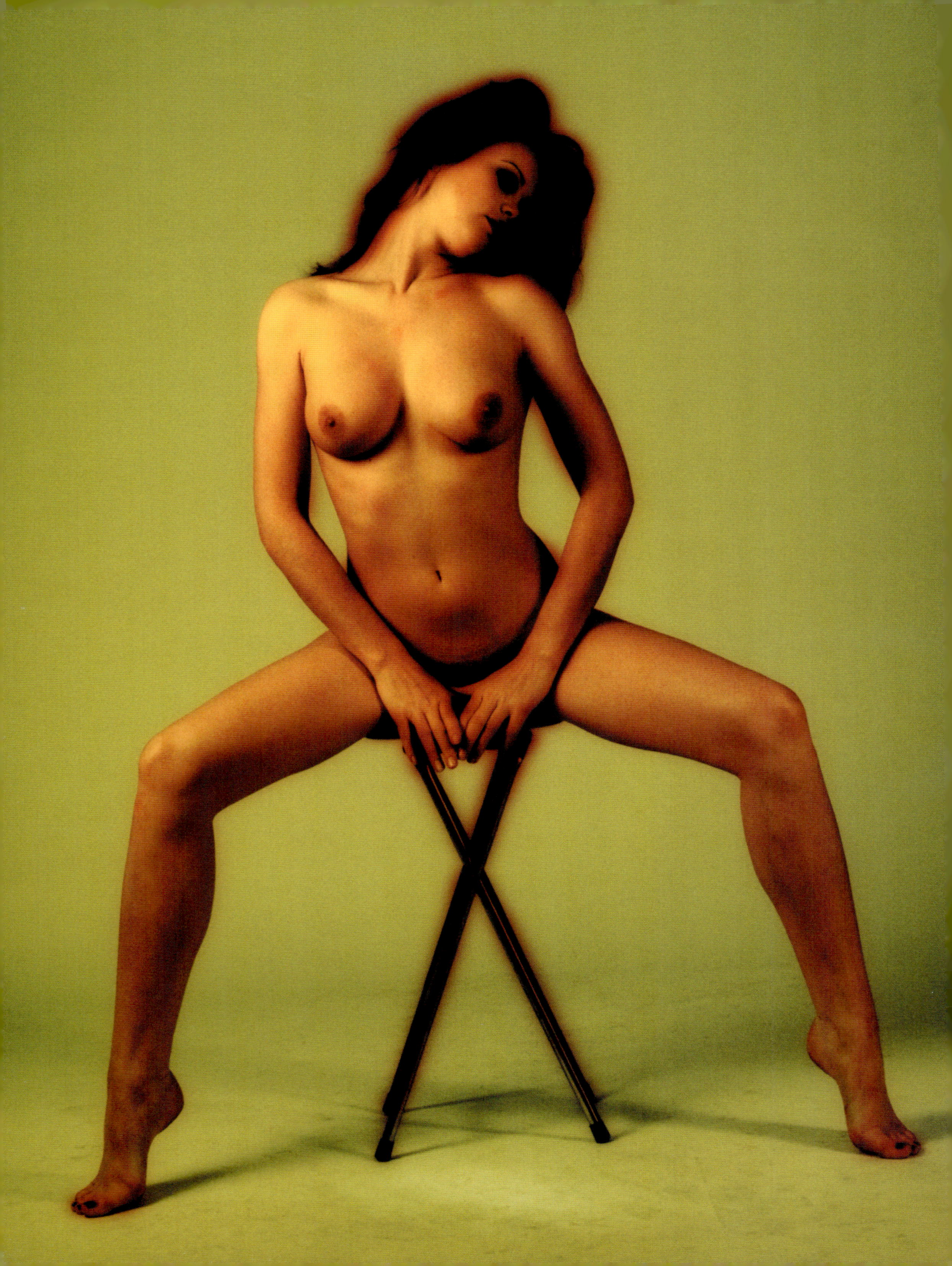

Cross processing

Cross processing is the development of colour films using the wrong chemistry. This may sound like a strange thing to do but it is a technique worth experimenting with. By taking the risk, you can occasionally produce some extraordinary creative effects.

dramatic colour changes

When employing this technique, colour negative films are processed using E-6 chemistry to give low-contrast transparencies and colour transparency film using C-41 chemistry to give high-contrast negatives. You will find that the results are often bizarre, unpredictable, and sometimes quite startling. Some colours may change dramatically whereas others do not. Different brands and speeds of film, when subjected to this process, will each give a different result. It is advisable to test a particular film thoroughly before embarking on any project of importance to learn the characteristics and usage of that film. Due to its current popularity, most professional labs now accept films for cross processing.

EXPOSING FILM FOR CROSS PROCESSING

Getting the exposure right for cross processing is a matter of trial and error, as the nominal ISO ratings will not apply. It is recommended that an initial investment should be made in ascertaining the correct exposure ratings for each particular film that is used. This can be done by photographing a subject under the same conditions and bracketing widely (±3 stops in one or 1/2 stop increments should suffice). This is important for processing negative film in E-6 chemistry as the film latitude is minimal, but not so important for processing slide film in C-41 chemistry as here a one- or two-stop error in exposure can easily be accommodated at the printing stage.

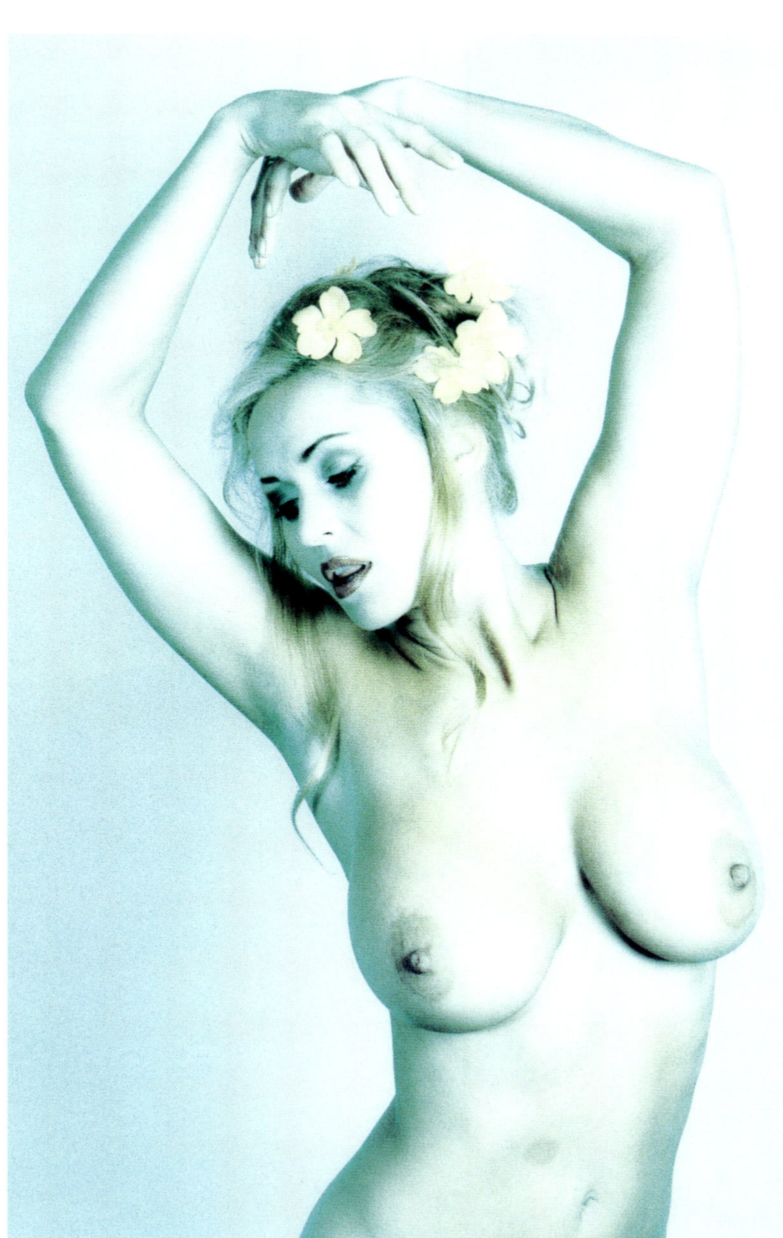

LEFT: **Bizarre colouration.** The high contrast and bizarre colouration shown in this image is typical of the effects given by cross processing colour slide film in C-41 chemistry. The film was rated at a nominal ISO 100 and processed under the standard conditions.
(BRONICA ETRSi; 150mm LENS; 1/125 sec at f/11; KODAK EKTACHROME 100SW.)

Slide sandwiches

MAKING SLIDE SANDWICHES

All those overexposed 'mistakes' that have been kept over the years after escaping the rubbish bin can be resurrected on dark winter evenings to make stunning slide sandwiches. Place a selection of images on a light box and superimpose suitable candidates until a match is found that works well, rotating or reversing the images as necessary to fine tune. Then remove each image from its respective mount, tape the slides at the edges to keep the images aligned in the chosen configuration, and remount them in a reusable slide mount. To keep a more permanent record of the image, copy the sandwich to film using a slide copier or scan to a digital file.

Making composite images from transparencies – slide sandwiches – is not really a darkroom technique as the only equipment required is a light box, slide viewer or projector. However, this topic has been included to illustrate how creative nude images can be readily created, simply by combining two images on reversal film.

two into one The first consideration for this exercise is subject matter, and the skill is in choosing component images. Nude images and abstract or semi-abstract images are well suited and should be chosen carefully to complement each other. The main compositional elements that should be looked for are the areas of high and low density in each of the slides. Silhouettes (or their reverse) are often good starting points for slide sandwiches as they contain areas of extreme densities and few mid-tones – the image of the kneeling model below is a good example of this. The area occupied by the model is light in colour and overexposed, whereas the surrounding area is black. Any image placed under this will only be visible through the lighter areas. In this case a normally exposed, uniform abstract image fills the lighter area, resulting in good overall density. If both images have an average tonal range across the frame, the best slide sandwiches are obtained by combining thin or overexposed transparencies. Combining normal or underexposed transparencies tends to give combinations that are too dark.

BELOW: **Slide sandwich 1.** A light-coloured, overexposed nude figure study taken against a black background (left) was combined with the picture of a tray of baking beans (centre). The resulting sandwich (right) shows the fill image only where required in the lighter areas.

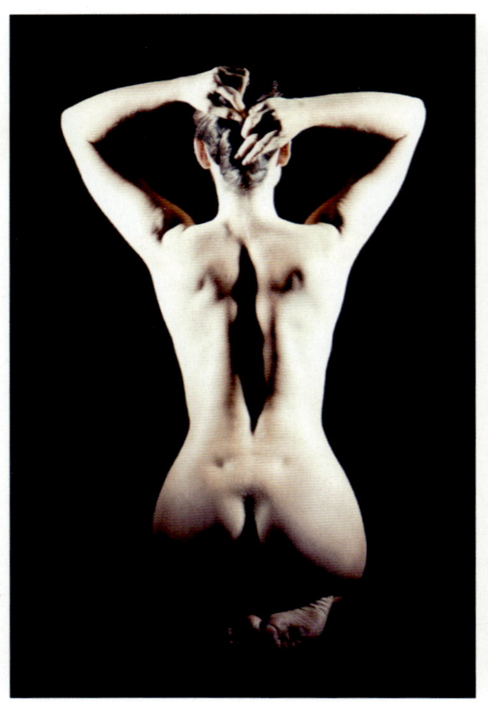
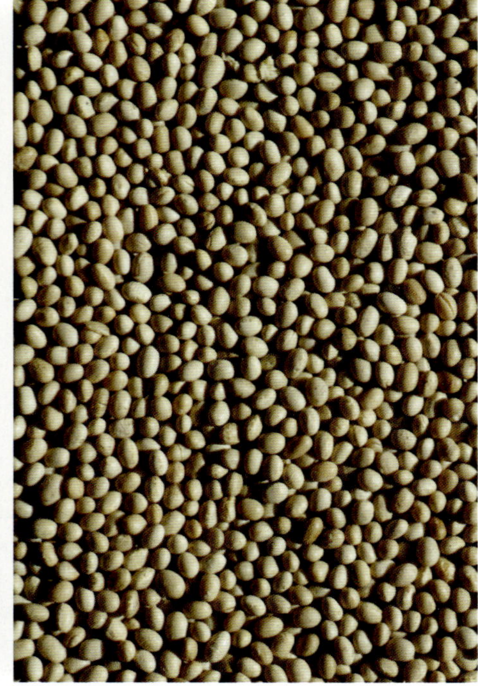
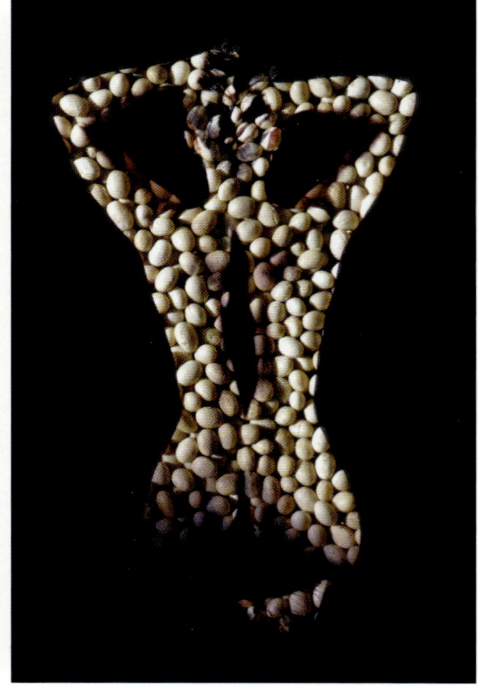

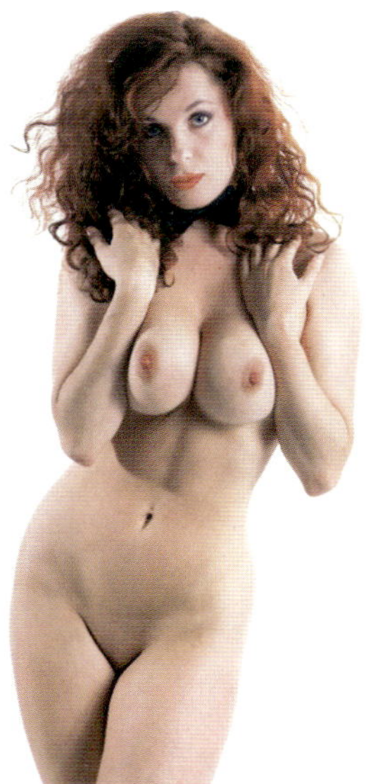

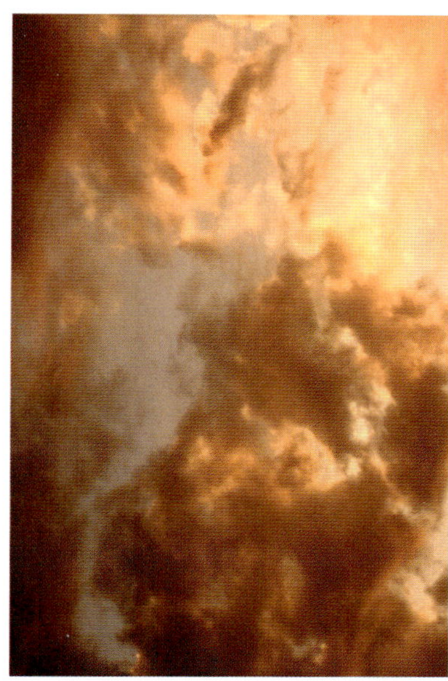

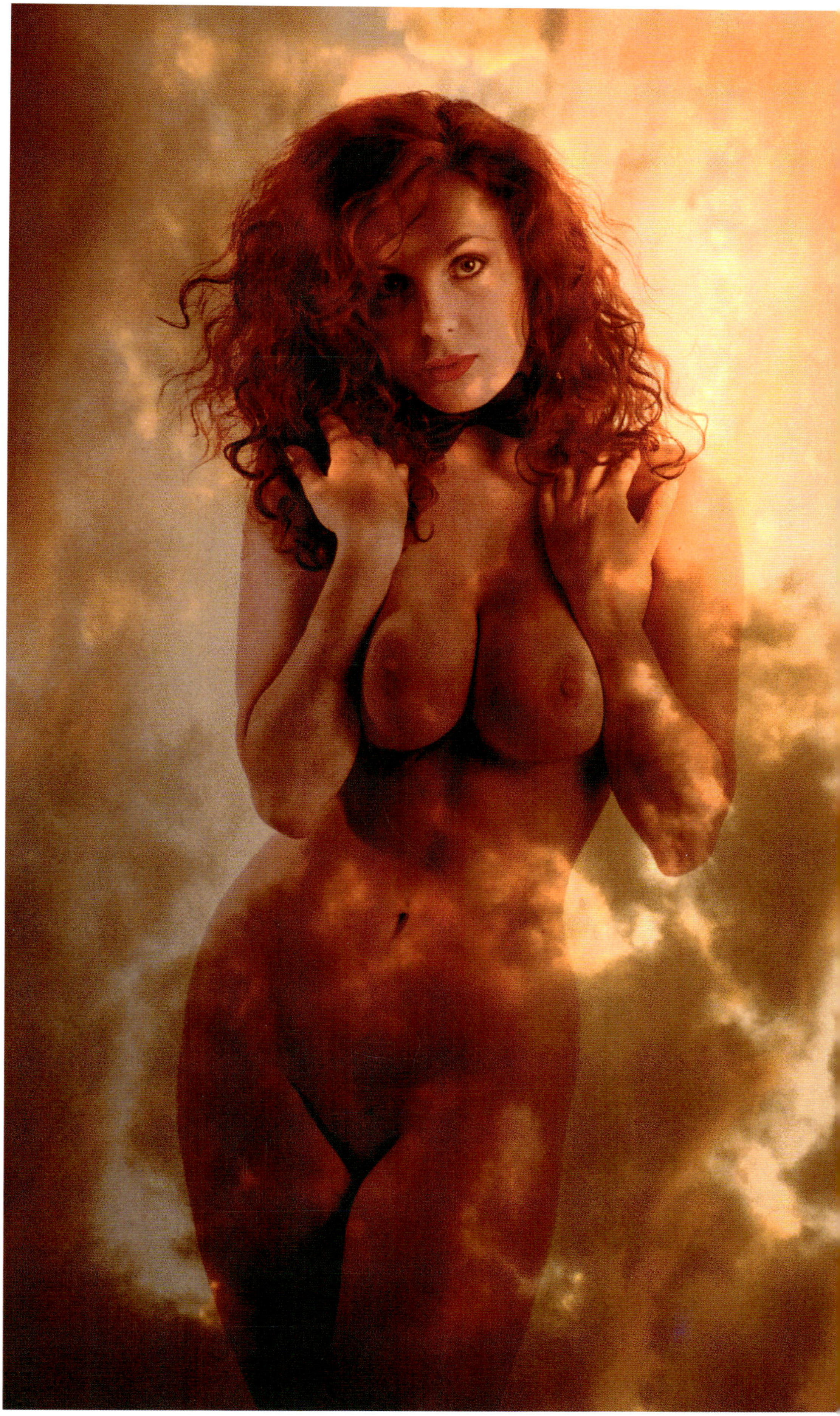

RIGHT: **Slide sandwich 2.** A studio nude taken
against a white background (above, top) and
a picture of clouds at sunset (above, bottom)
were combined to make this interesting slide
sandwich. The figure study was a 1/2 stop
overexposed and the original cloud image
rotated 90 degrees counter-clockwise.

Digital photography has had its infancy
and is fast growing up to become a
tool that is competing effectively with
the more traditional forms of creative
image-making that use silver halide
photography. Huge strides have been
made in this area in a few years and
digital technology is now available
both at an affordable price and also
with the high quality expected by the
discerning artist. This can only improve
further with time and should therefore
be embraced as a welcome addition to
the nude photographer's armoury of
image-making methods. This chapter
aims to introduce the novice to a few
of the basic digital manipulations that
can be used to create some of the
traditional photographic effects and a
few that would be difficult or
impossible to reproduce in the
darkroom. The industry standard
imaging software is Adobe Photoshop,
and all the manipulations described in
this chapter were made using this
powerful software package.

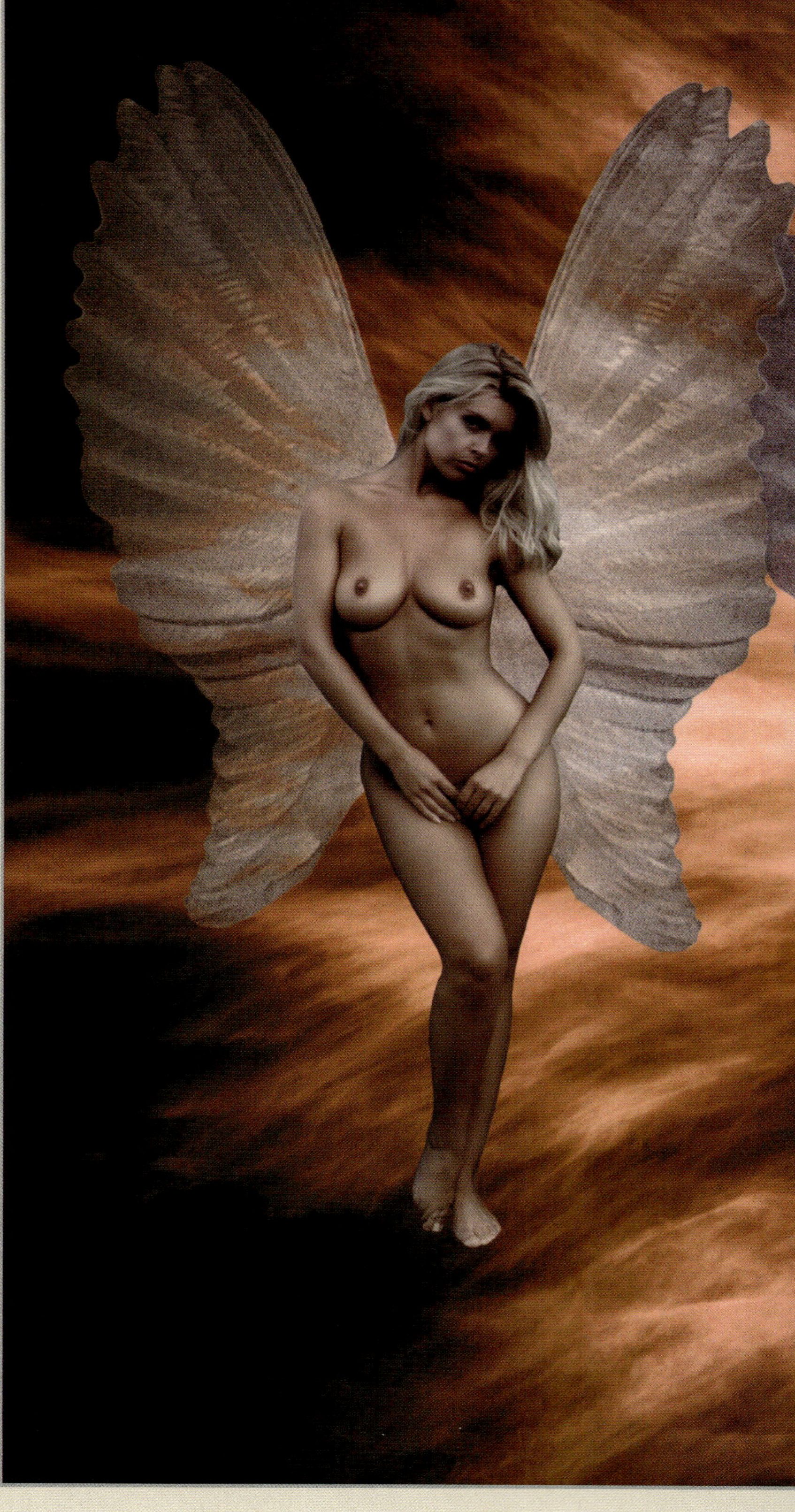

RIGHT: **Composite angels.** This is a digital
composite image made from three separate
images: a nude study, a skyscape, and the
wing of a bird. See page 154 for more
details of how this was created.

Digitizing the nude

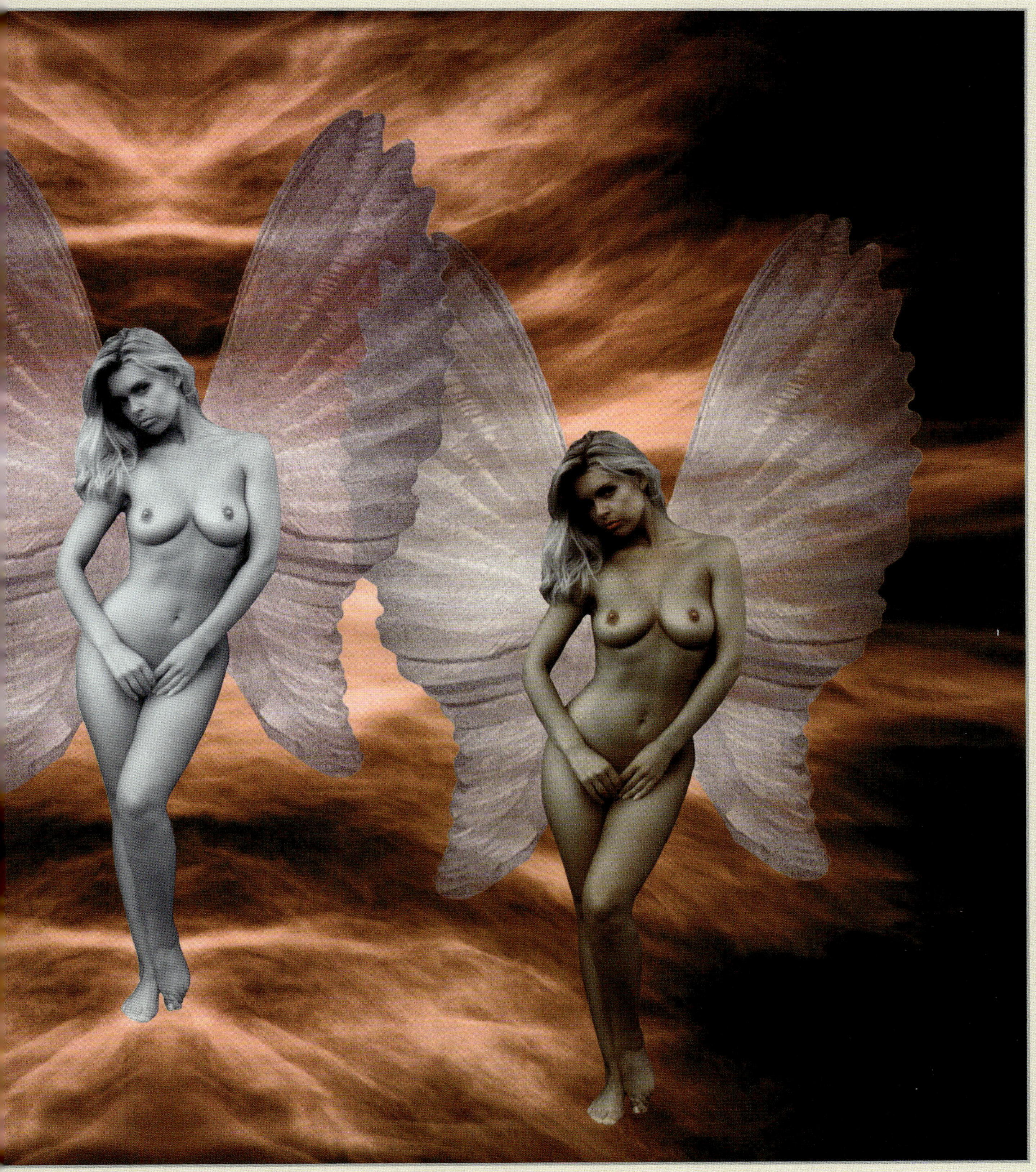

Image manipulation

Image cleaning to remove dust marks, small hairs and scratches is a process that should be completed on each image before any other manipulation is carried out and ought to be done as a matter of habit. Some scanning devices automatically clean images and some do not, so it is worth checking each image at the pixel level to ensure it is free of blemishes. Imperfections should be removed using a dust and scratch filter and the rubber stamp (or cloning) tool. This works by selecting a group of pixels in close proximity to the blemish and copying them over the offending area. In Photoshop the dust and scratches filter is located in the Filters menu under Noise.

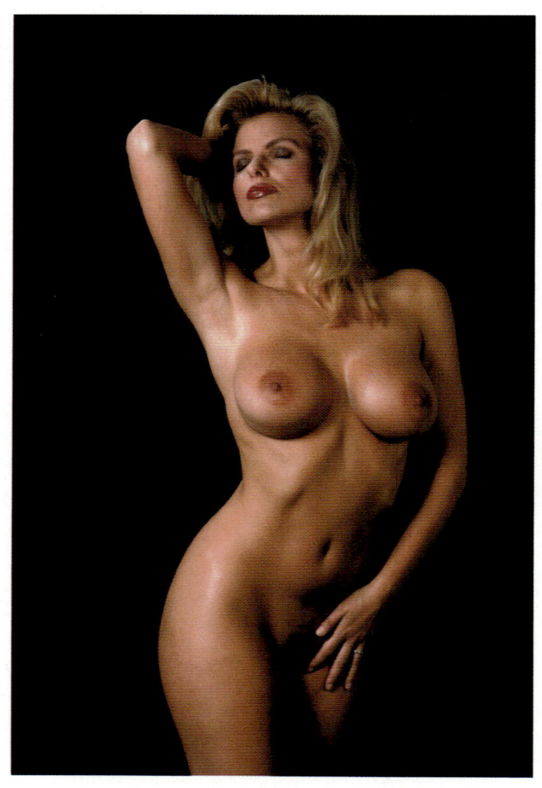

ABOVE AND OPPOSITE: **Changing colour.** The main image (opposite) shows the effect of one simple digital manipulation operation on the original image (above) – the hue was changed by +180 degrees.

There are some basic requirements before starting to create digitally manipulated images: the hardware that is needed to set up a digital workstation; software to do the actual manipulations; and some knowledge of how digital imaging tools and techniques work.

equipment

The first consideration when setting up a digital imaging workstation (the equivalent of a darkroom) is the necessary equipment. The heart of the system, the computer, must be chosen with image manipulation in mind. A powerful processor is essential. A computer with 64Mb of RAM and a 400MHz processor (CPU) is the absolute minimum recommended for fast working. A hard disk drive with plenty of space for storing images in progress is advisable. Computers with 256Mb of RAM, 1GHz CPUs and 20Gb of hard drive storage are now commonplace and affordable. A system for capturing images is required: a film scanner, flatbed scanner or digital camera; software to perform image manipulation; and an optional output device such as a printer. Buy the best printer you can afford if you want quality prints. Digital images use a lot of space, so invest in hardware that allows file storage off the computer, such as a DVD drive, CD writer or ZIP drive – also vital for back-up purposes. The industry standard imaging software is Adobe Photoshop, but there are other suitable software packages.

preparation

Before starting work, decide on the final image you want. Determine the final size and quality of the image that is wanted and make sure that all the component images are available to complete it. For instance, an image destined to be an exhibition print will need different specifications from an image for a website. For commercial reproduction, it is best to work at a minimum resolution of 300ppi (pixels/inch) with tagged-image-format files (TIFFs), which do not have any compression algorithms applied to them. This means that a file size of approximately 25Mb is required for an A4 print and a 50Mb file for a 16 x 12 print at this resolution. If the component images are acquired by scanning a print or a transparency, they must be scanned at a resolution that will eventually be appropriate for the final image.

colour space

Digital images are made up of pixels (picture elements), and digital manipulation is about changing the characteristics of those pixels, either individually or en masse. To understand how this works it is necessary to understand how an image is defined in terms of colour space, which is made up of three terms: hue, saturation and lightness.

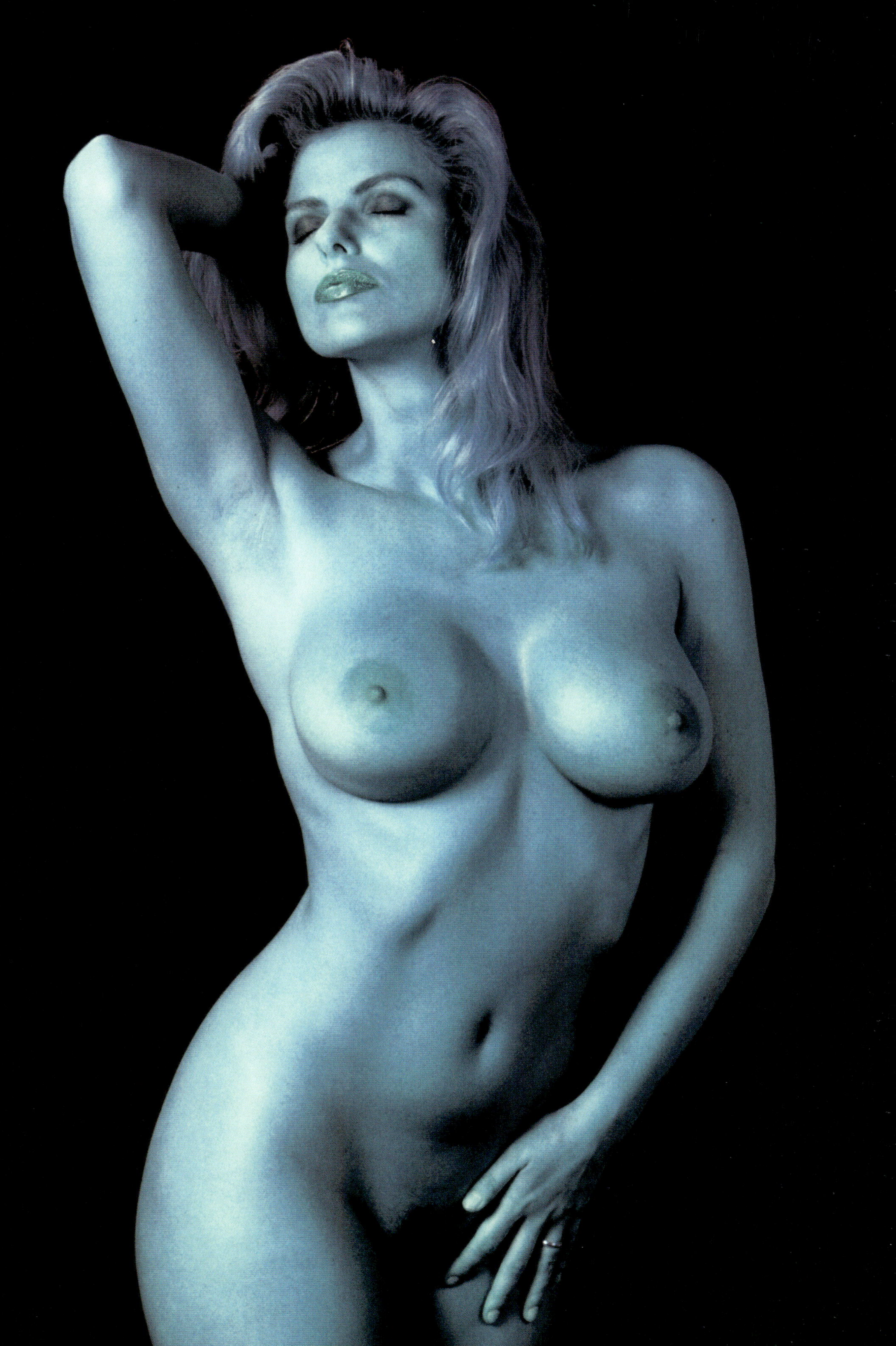

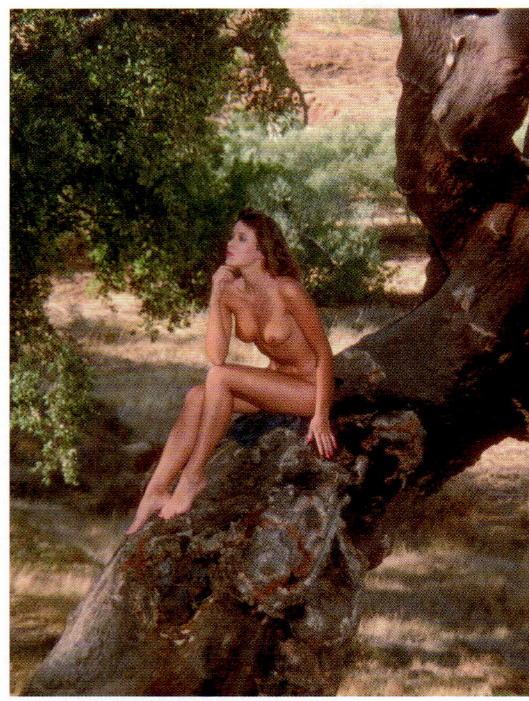

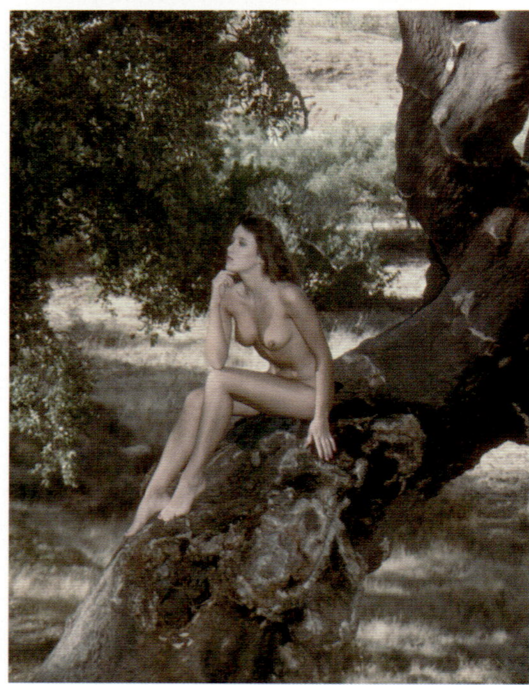

ABOVE: **Saturation changes.** Decreasing the saturation of a colour image can give a result reminiscent of a hand-coloured black-and-white image. The saturation of the original image (above, top) was reduced by −70 to give the tinted image (above, bottom).

Hue determines the colour of the image (eg, red, blue, green, etc); saturation how colourful or pure that colour is; and lightness is the intensity or brightness of the colour and ranges from black to white. By changing these characteristics of the individual pixels the whole gamut of the colour space can be covered. The pairs of pictures shown on pages 140–3 illustrate the different effects of changing the hue, saturation or lightness of original images to create simple yet interesting variations. Photoshop contains several means of adjusting hue, saturation and lightness, which operate in slightly different ways. These can be found in the Image menu under the Image > Adjust heading.

tools

In order to perform changes in pixel characteristics, it is necessary to use software tools. These can be divided into three main categories: selection tools; artwork tools; and viewing tools. Selection tools, such as the marquee, lasso and magic wand tools, are used for selecting groups of pixels to work on. Artwork tools perform a specific operation on pixels. Examples of these are the airbrush, brush, pencil, line drawing, rubber stamp (cloning), paint bucket, gradient, dodging/burning/smudging and eraser tools. Before using an artwork tool, attributes must be chosen that define how that tool operates on the selected pixels, and each tool will have a wide variety of options to choose from. For example, if the pencil tool is chosen, options for the colour, width and style of the line to be drawn will be available. In Photoshop, selection tools and artwork tools are found in the floating toolbox palette. In addition, further selections can be made from the Select pull-down menu. Tool attributes are chosen from one of the attribute windows, such as the Options window, the Brushes window and the Color window. Viewing tools, such as the zoom tool and the hand tool in the toolbox, make moving around and working on the image easy. Further view options are available from the View pull-down menu and the Navigator window.

filters

Dust and scratch filters have already been mentioned for cleaning images, but there are many more options that can be used. Sharpening filters are used for edge effects and improving image sharpness. Special-effect filters can be used for a multitude of artistic effects – a topic that is explored later in the chapter.

ADJUSTING COLOUR AND CONTRAST

After acquiring and cleaning an image it is good practice to correct the colour and contrast before performing further manipulations. In most cases this can be done by using the Auto Contrast, Auto Levels, Levels, or Curves options in the Image/Adjust pull-down menu. Use the option that best suits the image by visual inspection of the result. Make sure that the computer monitor is calibrated first (choose Preferences>Monitor Setup from the File pull-down menu to do this) in order to achieve printed output that is close to the screen display.

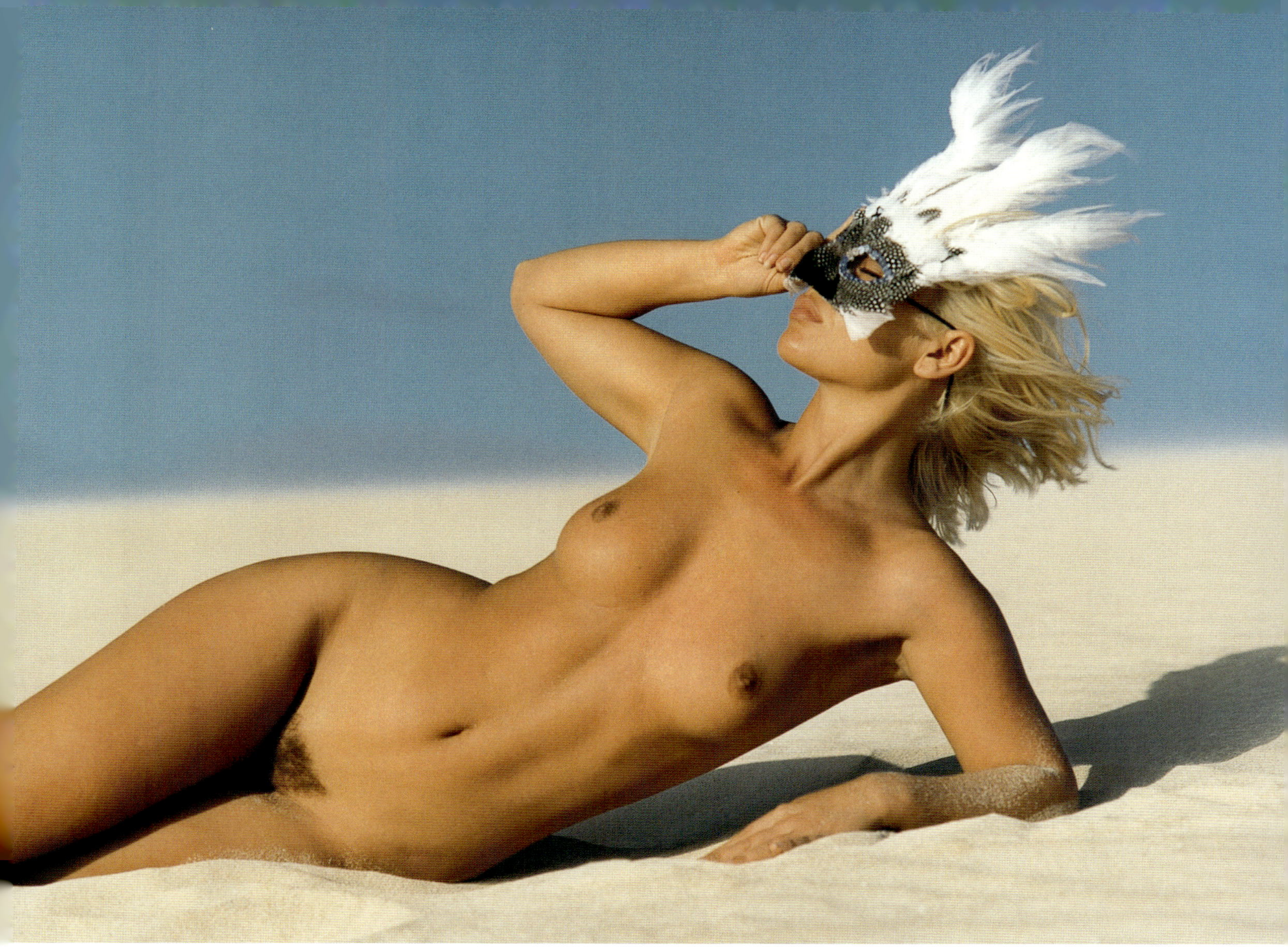

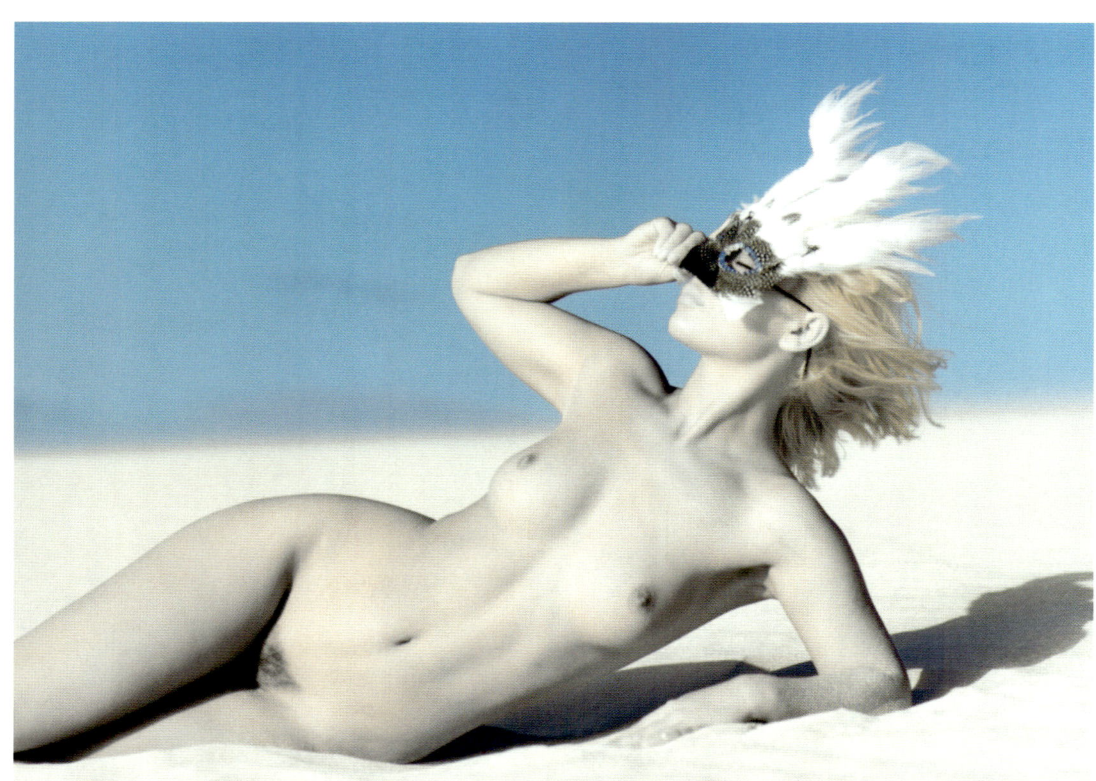

ABOVE AND RIGHT: **Red record.**
In this image the lightness
of the red record was
changed by selecting it in
the Hue/Saturation window
and manipulating by
changing the lightness to
+90. Note that only those
areas of the image that have
a red component are
lightened: the blue sky is
completely unaffected.

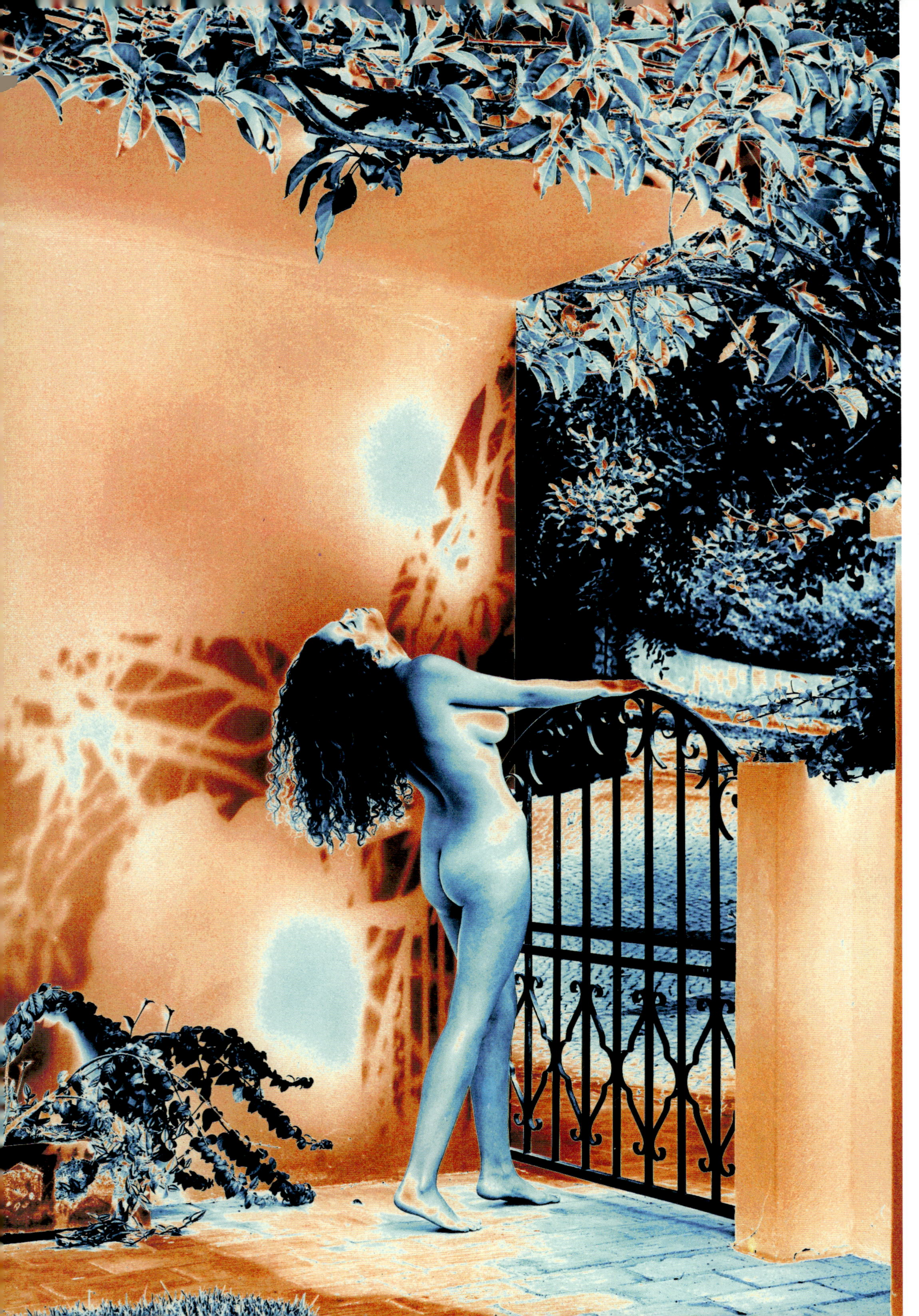

Colour from monochrome

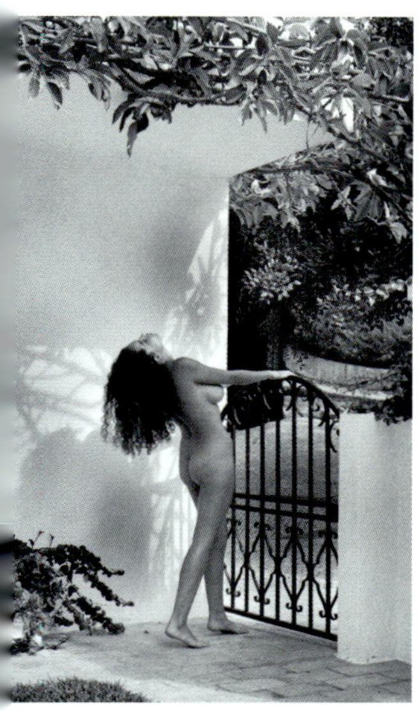

Solarizing and saturation. The monochrome print (above) was scanned in RGB mode and then solarized, using the Solarize filter. The neutrals were changed to blue and the highlights to orange in the Selective Color options window, leaving the shadows black. Adjusting the colour saturation gave the final image (opposite).

RIGHT: **Split-toned effect.** A scan of the original monochrome print (right) was manipulated using Selective Color to give the blue and sepia split-toned effect (centre). The neutrals were adjusted by −20 per cent cyan and +10 per cent yellow and the blacks by +15 per cent cyan and −5 per cent yellow. The pseudo-lith effect (far right) was obtained by using the method and values described in the main text.

A useful tool in the creative artist's armoury of techniques is the addition of colour to monochrome images. Traditionalists use toners to add colours to prints, but similar effects can be obtained by introducing digital colour into a monochrome image file. Two examples of replicating traditional darkroom styles are given here, but there are many more possible methods, limited only by willingness to experiment with the digital palette.

split-toned images To create a digital split-toned image, a monochrome image is first acquired, either by scanning a black-and-white print or negative in RGB mode to the size and final resolution required. Choose Image > Adjust > Selective Color from the Photoshop Image menu to display the Selective Color window and change the Colors pull-down menu to display Neutrals. Adjusting the colour sliders to the left or right will change the grey mid-tones of the image to a colour value. For instance, moving the cyan slider to −20 per cent and the yellow slider to +20 per cent will change the mid-tones to a

yellow-brown colour reminiscent of sepia-toned prints. The shadow blacks and white highlights are retained as in a traditional split-toned print. The shadows and highlights can be similarly changed to different colours by selecting Blacks to change shadow colour and Whites to change highlight colour.

psuedo-lith images Nothing can compare to the delicate beauty of a real lith print, but it is still possible to achieve interesting approximations by digital techniques. The pseudo-lith effect shown below right was created by deploying two different colour manipulations. The scanned image (below left) was first adjusted from within the Image > Replace Color option window in Photoshop. A mid-tone was selected with the eyedropper tool and the lightness increased to +60 at a fuzziness value of 125. Then, using the Image > Selective Color option, the highlights and mid-tones were coloured a pinkish-cream colour by changing the whites by −92 per cent cyan and +32 per cent yellow and the neutrals by −5 per cent cyan.

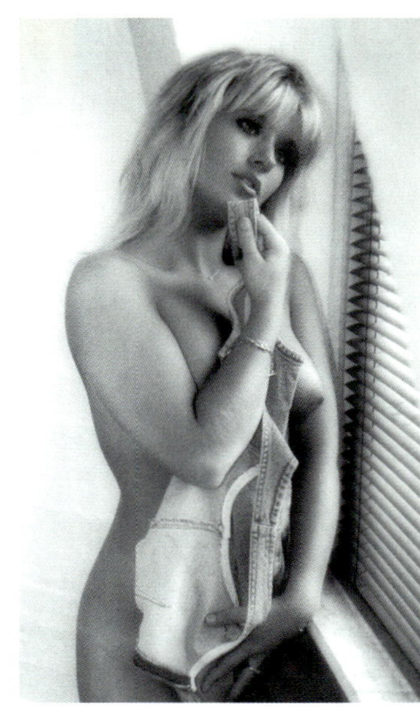
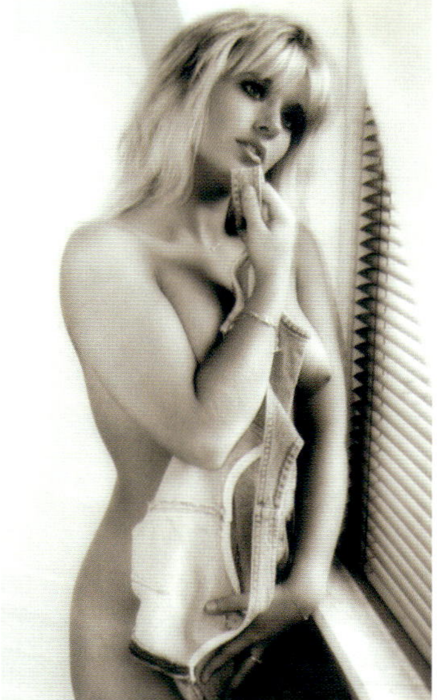
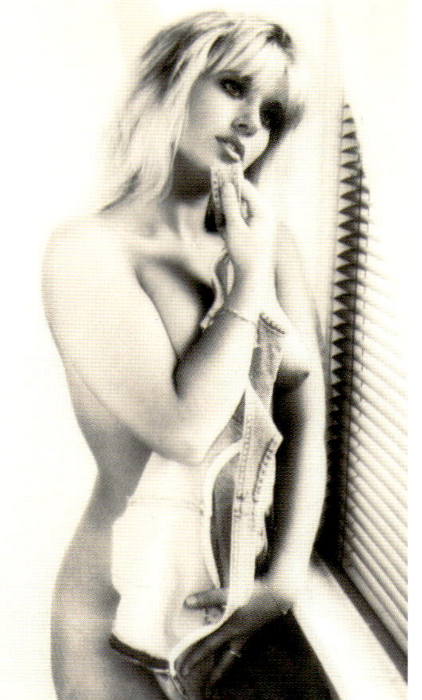

Filters for artistic effects

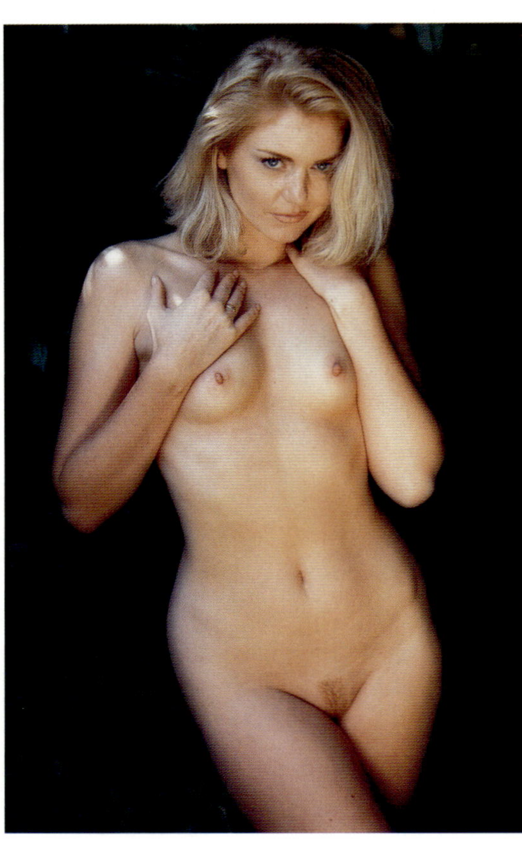

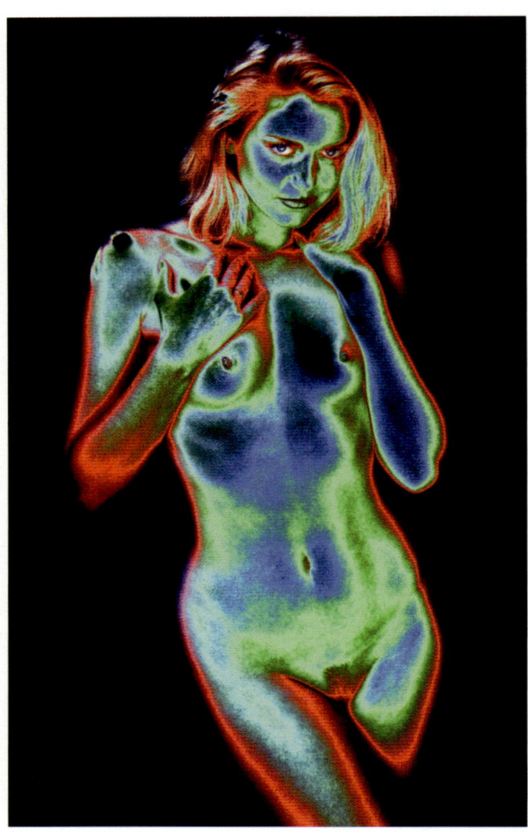

One of the most useful aspects of digital manipulation is the application of a mathematical algorithm to an image to create a particular effect. In common parlance these are called filters. These cover a wide range of uses and applications, but they can be loosely categorized into two groups: the utility filters and the artistic filters. Examples of utility filters are Noise filters, which are used to clean pictures, and Sharpen filters, which are used sharpen the edges of images. Some of the more popular artistic filters replicate traditional techniques such as solarization, bas relief and embossing. These can be found within the Filter > Stylize pull-down menu of Photoshop. Other effects such as Posterize and Equalize are found in the Image > Adjust menu. Many artistic filters create the effect of a particular

medium; these include paint and draw effects that can turn the image into a representation that is reminiscent of an oil painting, a watercolour painting or a charcoal drawing. A few examples of these filters are the Colored Pencil, Dry Brush, Palette Knife, Watercolor, Crosshatch and Chalk & Charcoal filters. Further options can be accessed from within the Filter > Artistic/Brushstrokes/Sketch pull-down menus in Photoshop. When using these, it is best to perform the transformation on the full-sized image, as the effects will often differ markedly if applied to a smaller image.

solarization The Solarize filter (Filter > Stylize > Solarize) can be used on monochrome or colour images to give partial reversal effects similar to those obtainable by

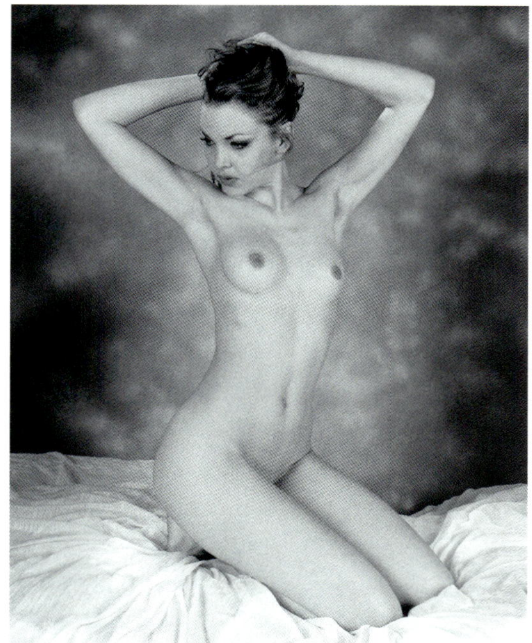

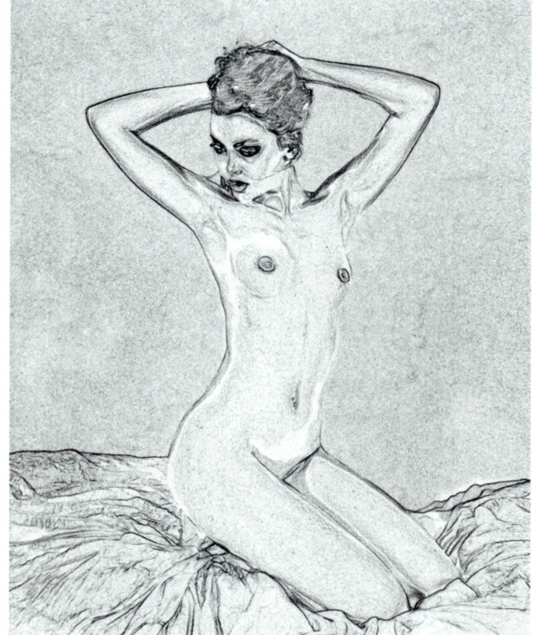

LEFT: **Find edges filter.** Find edges filter was applied to the original black-and-white image (far left) to provide the pencil-drawn rendition (left).

BELOW: **Filter effects.** This block of six images shows the effect of applying various filters to a single image. Top Row: (left) original image – sepia toned; (middle) Emboss filter; (right) Find edges filter. Bottom Row: (left) Solarize filter; (middle) double solarization; (right) Equalize command.

traditional techniques (see pages 130–1). In a darkroom the process is time-consuming, labour-intensive and complicated – especially for colour solarizations – and even then may not give the anticipated result. The digital method, however, can be achieved in seconds and is easily controlled by the adjustment of contrast or image reversal. Solarized black-and-white images tend to work better than colour, but sepia-toned monochrome images are also quite appealing, giving an attractive blue and brown colouration (lower-left image of six). A solarized image can even be resolarized digitally to give a double-solarized result (lower-middle image of six) – a result that is not possible in the darkroom.

value represents black; the brightest value represents white; and intermediate pixel values are evenly distributed throughout the greyscale. Using this command, the original image in the block of six (top, left) was converted to a silhouette image (bottom, right).

pencil drawing

The Find edges Filter (Filter > Stylize > Find Edges) is a personal favourite that may be used to convert an image into a fine, delicate pencil drawing that is particularly suitable when used with fine-art nude images. Choose images with bold outlines for the best effect.

equalizing

The Equalize command, though not strictly a filter, can sometimes deliver creative effects. The brightness values in the image are adjusted so that the darkest

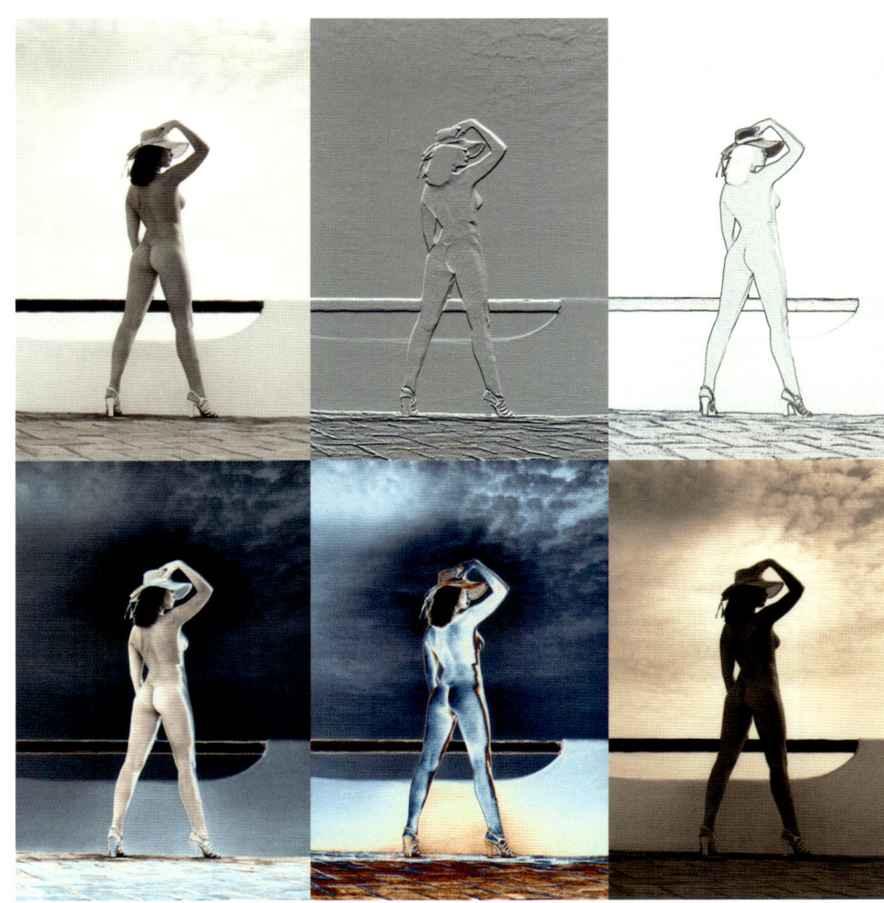

Distortion and blur filters

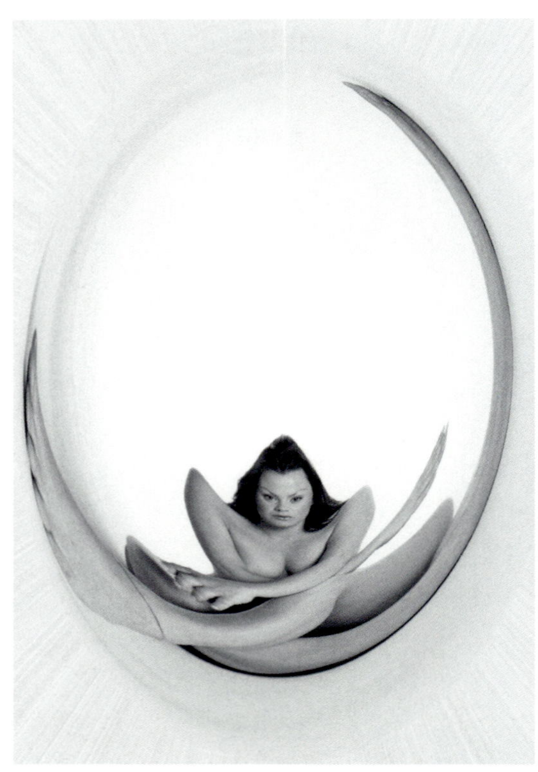

ABOVE: **Spherical distortion.** Application of the Spherical coordinates filter to an image distorts the outer areas more than the centre. In this picture of a model sitting cross-legged on the floor, the result is a strange spherical elongation of her legs and arms.

IMAGE SIZE

The size of the image will have a significant bearing on the induced effect, so it is best to try the filters on the full-sized image rather than a smaller test image. The exact effect seen on the smaller image will not be the same as that created on the larger image. Many of the distortion filters use complex mathematical algorithms to generate the effects and can therefore be very memory-intensive, especially if the image being manipulated is large, so be prepared to wait for quite some time for the computer to complete the transformation if your PC has low RAM.

Distortion and blur filters are a source of quirky and original nude images and can be used to bend, twist and manipulate images in a variety of ways.

distortion filters Contorted images similar to those seen in a hall of mirrors, where the glass is misshapen, can be created with distortion filters. Options include Glass, Ocean Ripple, Pinch, Polar Coordinates, Ripple, Shear, Spherize, Twirl, Wave and Zigzag. Glass gives the impression of seeing the image through a variety of textured glass surfaces with options for the degree of distortion. Ocean Ripple, Ripple, Zigzag and Wave give a variety of rippled wave effects with options for size and magnitude of the displacement. Spherize and Pinch have similar (but opposite) effects of spherically expanding and contracting an image or image selection. The Polar Coordinates filter converts the image between polar and rectangular coordinates, which turns a normal picture into something bizarre, whereas Shear distorts the image about a predefined line.

blur filters These operate in several different ways. The Blur, Blur More, Gaussian Blur and Smart Blur filters act like soft-focus filters on a camera lens and are used to soften images or image selections by averaging pixels next to edges. They are particularly useful for retouching and smoothing skin blemishes and toning down or diffusing over-busy backgrounds. Radial and Motion Blur filters are used for more creative purposes and can introduce an element of movement or motion into an image. Options include zooming, spinning and directional motion effects. The Wind option in the Stylize menu is also useful for introducing movement into an image.

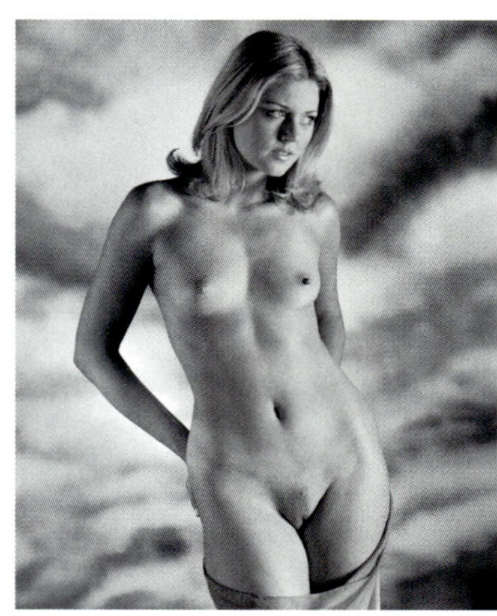

LEFT AND OPPPOSITE: **Sinusoidal distortion.** The distorted, sinusoidal image (opposite) was created using the Shear filter on the original image (left).

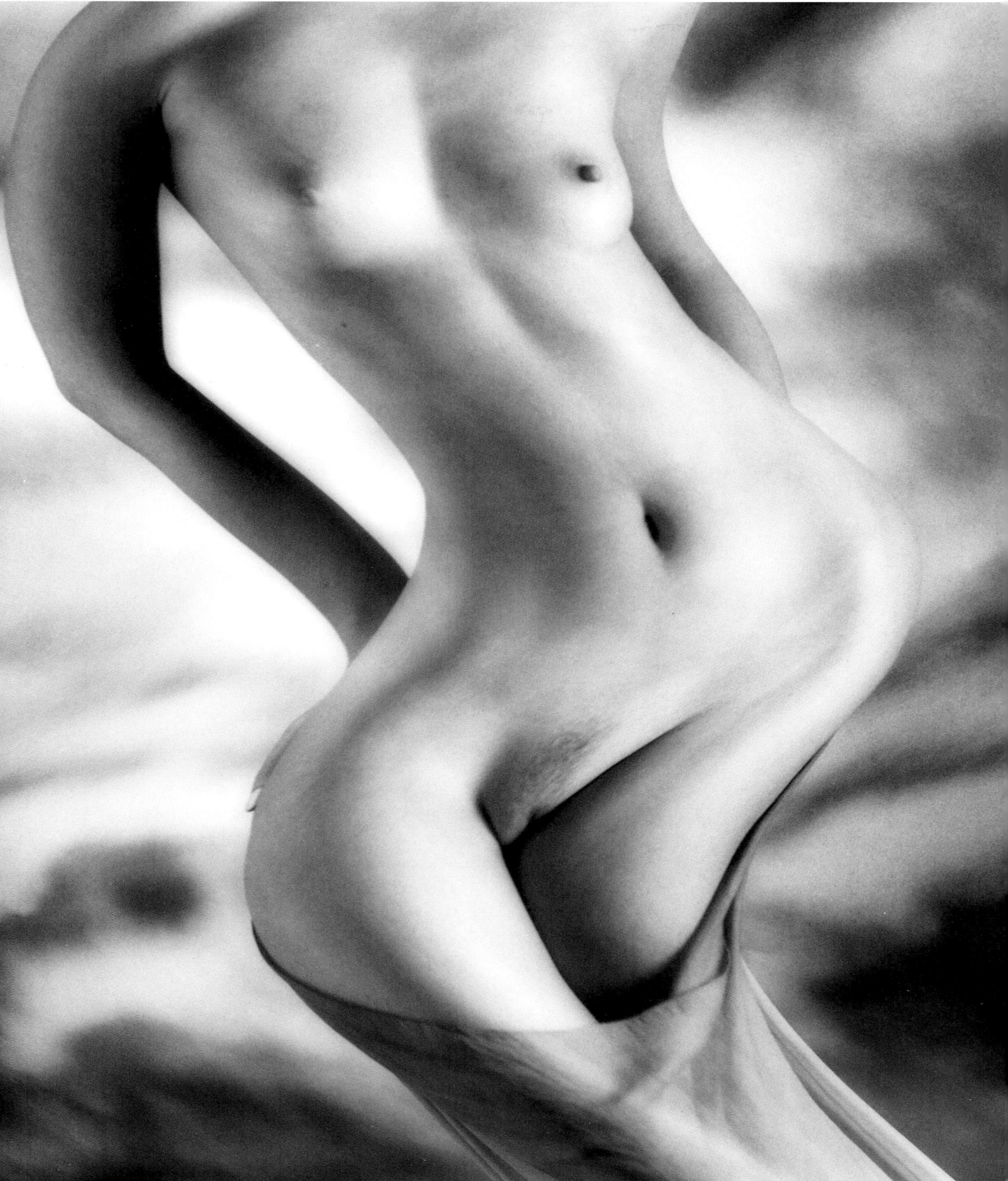

Surfaces

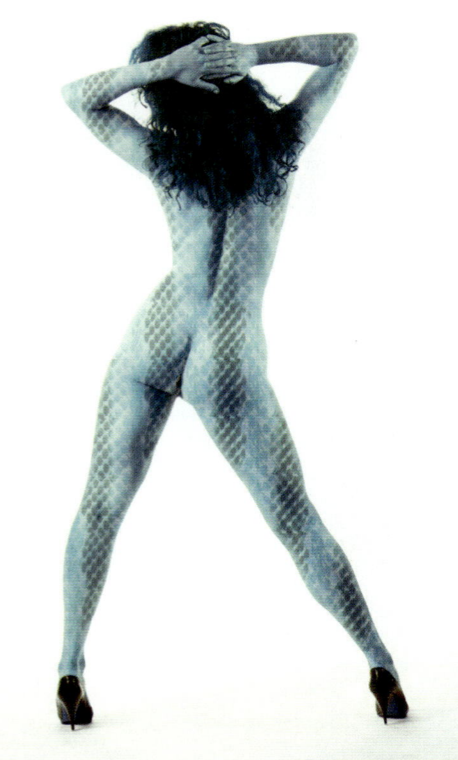

ABOVE: **Body-painting effect.** In this image the model's skin has been transformed into that of a python and the colour changed from flesh tone to blue. The overall effect is reminiscent of body painting.

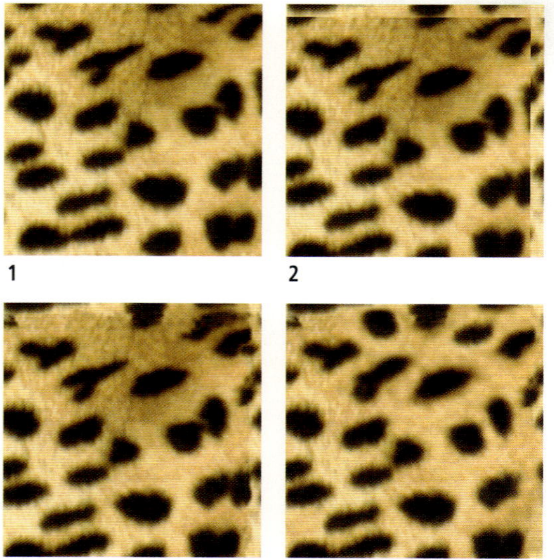

1   2

3   4

LEFT AND OPPOSITE: **Skin effects.** Animal-skin effects, such as the leopard skin in this image, are readily created using the method described in the text.

In the chapter Darkroom know-how (pages 120–37), we explored the ways in which patterns and nude images could be combined, either by projection or making slide sandwiches, to create unusual and creative pieces of artwork. Digital superimposition of patterns and textures onto the surface of a model's skin is another option that has much scope.

patterns on skin Create a patterned tile to cover the desired area of the image. Choose patterns that fit the subject and with elements that make the repetition of the tile less obvious. An example carried out using Photoshop illustrates how this is achieved.

To add the leopard-skin pattern to the nude figure (opposite), a scan of the original sepia-toned black-and-white figure (see page 116) was created, cleaned and optimized for colour and contrast. The figure was then selected, feathered and isolated from the background. A leopard picture was opened and a small section of the animal's fur selected that contained a variety of different types of spot (about 20 spots – fig 1). It was converted into a pattern tile using the Offset filter, choosing 10 pixels in the horizontal field, 10 pixels in the vertical field, and the Wrap Around option. This takes a 10-pixel-wide border from the bottom and wraps it around the top edge and a 10-pixel-wide border from one side and wraps it around the other (fig 2). This ensures that all the edges will match and the tiles fit together seamlessly. The joins where the borders were attached were then retouched using the Rubber Stamp tool, ensuring that the outside edges of the borders were left intact (fig 3). The image was rearranged slightly, using the same tool, to evenly distribute the spots (fig 4). The final image was selected and defined as a pattern using the Define Pattern option in the Edit Menu. The Fill dialogue window was then activated (Shift+Backspace) and the leopard-skin pattern chosen to fill the feathered selection containing the nude figure, using the Multiply mode and 75 per cent opacity options. Slight adjustments were made to the hue, saturation and contrast before obtaining the completed image (opposite).

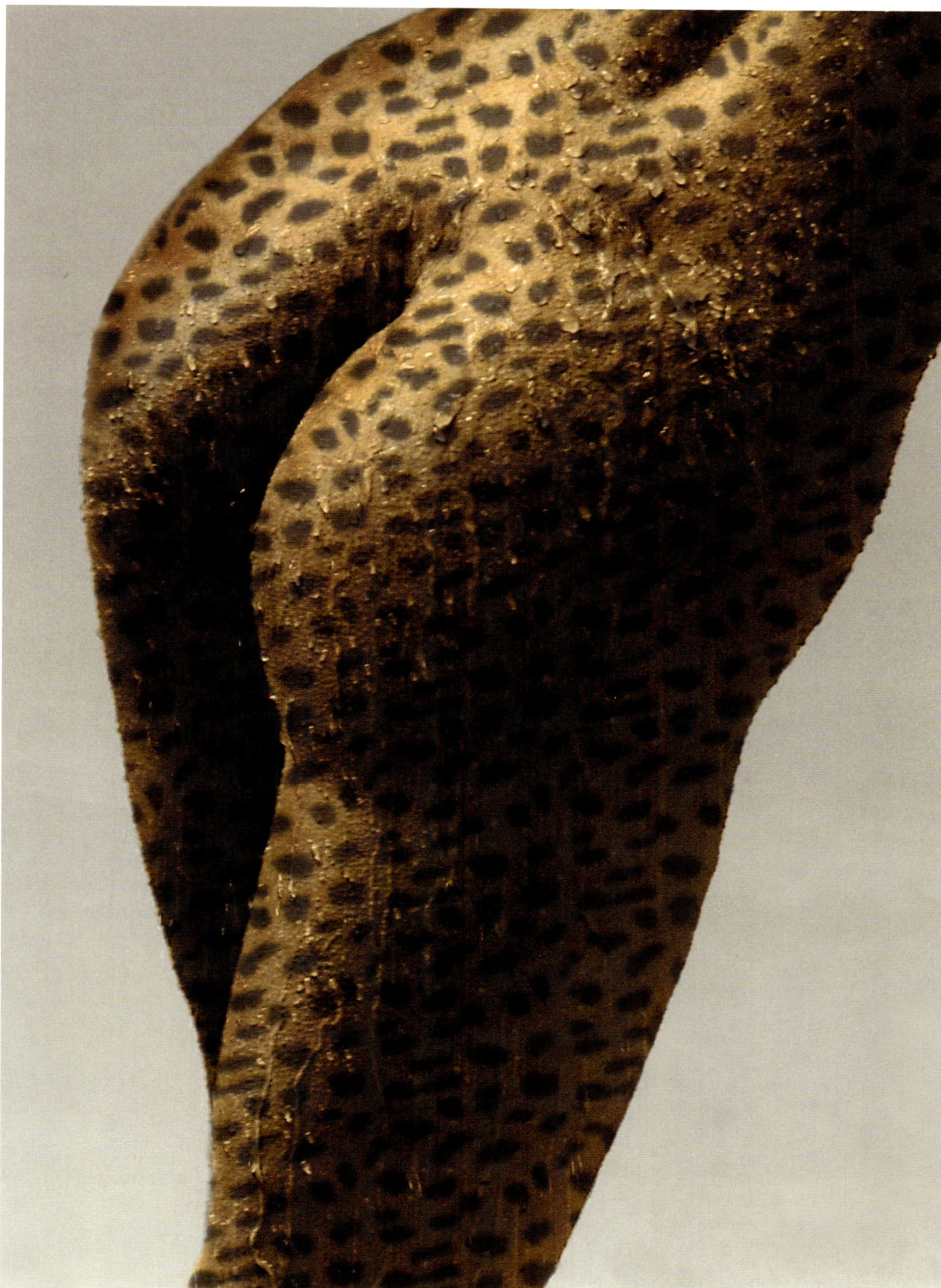

Layers

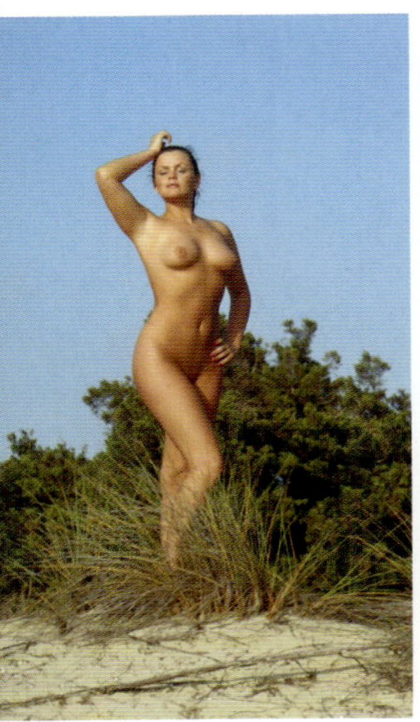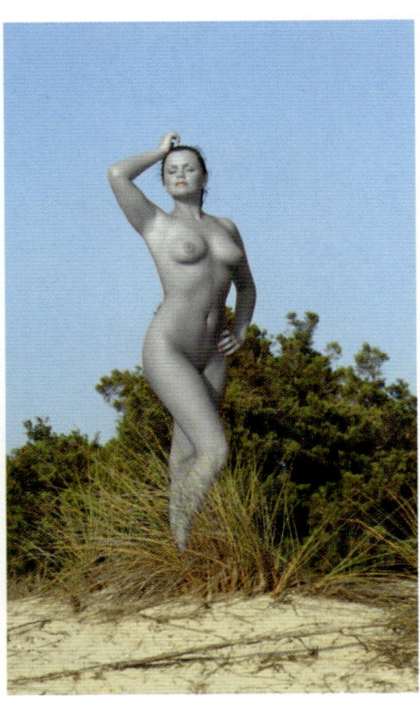

ABOVE: **The metallic look.** A monochrome image of a model juxtaposed against a coloured background (above, right) was created from the original image (above, left) using layers to give the model a metallic look – almost like a metal statue.

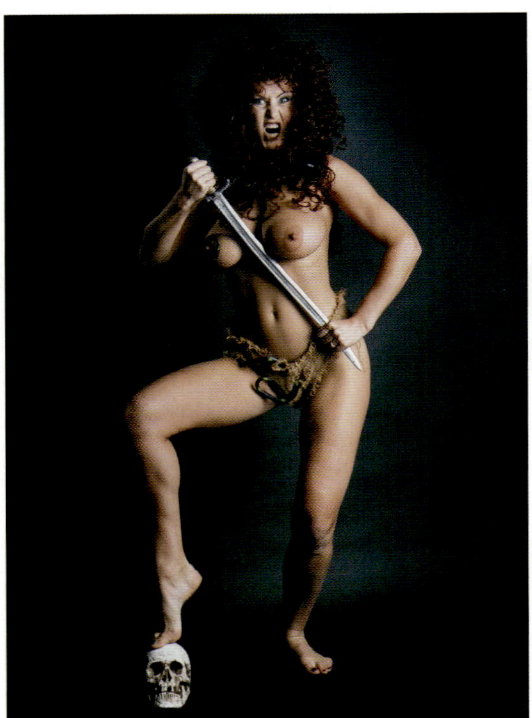

ABOVE AND OPPOSITE: **Combined layers.** Real and false elements are readily combined by the use of layers. In the manipulated image (opposite) only the skin, hair and the halo of light around the model are not as in the original (above).

Layers are a powerful tool when creating digital images and allow sophisticated compositions to be readily constructed.

building up layers

An image initially created in Photoshop consists of a single layer called the background layer, but further layers can be added that can be drawn on, pasted into and manipulated. In simplistic terms this is like having an image with several sheets of transparent paper on top of it, which can be manipulated independently from the base image and later combined to form the final product. Layers can also be interchanged and worked on independently until combined or merged. This allows additional features, such as layer masking, opacity changes and blending modes to be used. Creating images by using layers is illustrated by demonstrating how the two manipulated images shown on these pages were made.

An original image (below left) was scanned, cleaned and optimized for colour and contrast. The background layer was selected, copied and pasted into a new layer to give an identical image above it in perfect registration. The hue of the top layer was then changed through +180 degrees using the Image > Adjust > Hue/Saturation options so that the model's skin was changed to blue. Areas of the top layer (eyes, mouth, sackcloth, skull and sword) were selectively removed using the eraser tool to reveal the lower background layer. A soft brush was used at the pixel level for this operation to ensure that the detail blended in well with the lower image. The two layers were then combined using the Flatten Image command in the Layers palette to give the final image (opposite). The monochrome nude standing against a coloured background (top left) was created in a similar fashion using two layers. In this case the lower layer was decolourized using the Image > Adjust > Desaturate option and the colour image in the top layer removed using the eraser tool to reveal the underlying monochrome figure.

SELECTIVE TONING USING LAYERS

A selectively toned monochrome print, where only a part of the image is toned, can be created easily from a black-and-white print using the two-layer method as described above. The lower layer is turned into a sepia-toned image (see page 145) and selective parts of the upper monochrome image removed to reveal the underlying toned image. When removing part of an upper layer to reveal a different underlying image, it is often easier to see what you are doing if the opacity of the upper layer is reduced to approximately 50 per cent while you are carrying out the process of manipulation.

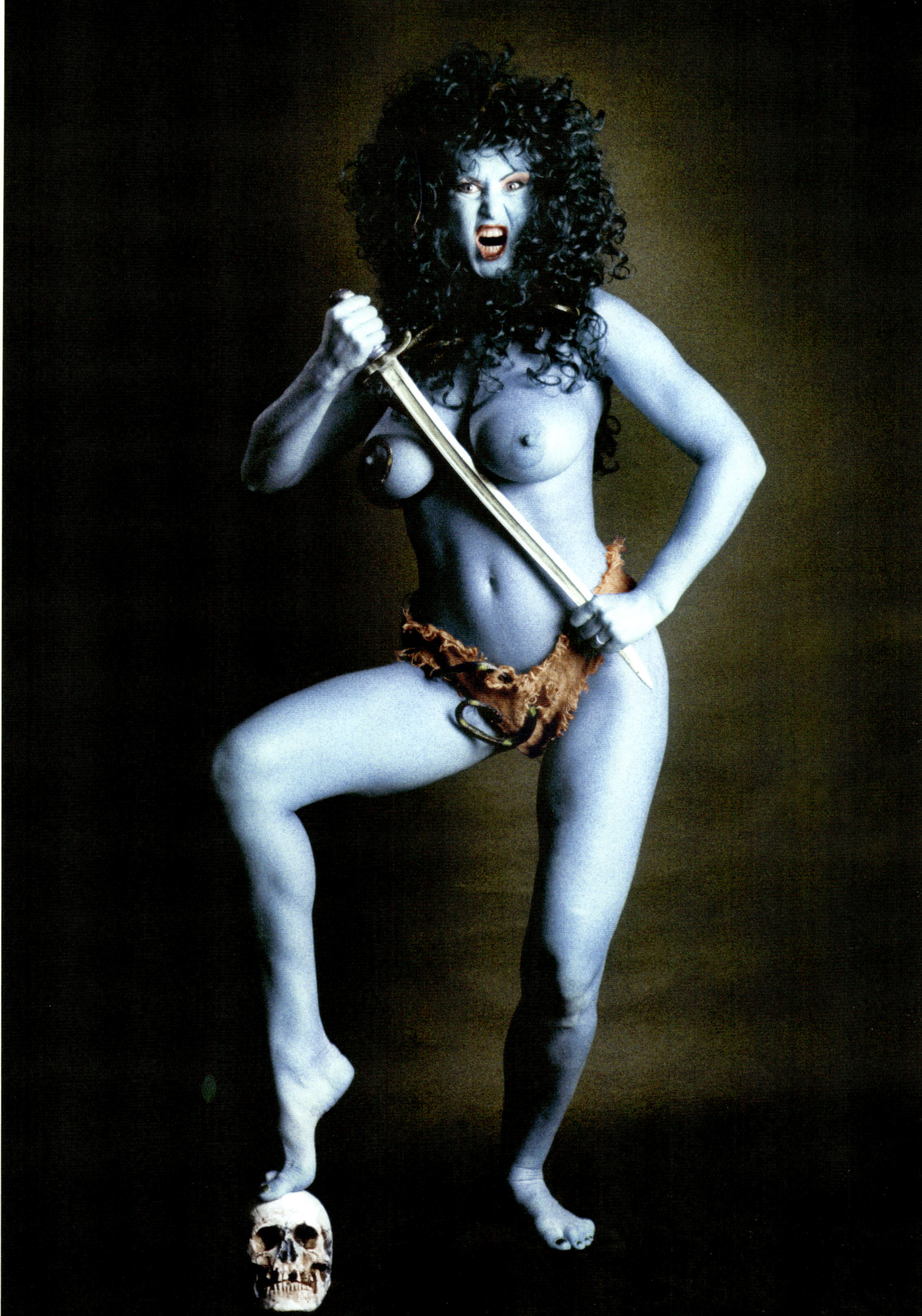

Composite images

By using digital imaging you can combine two, three or more images into one final picture to make a composite image. This is more difficult to do than manipulating a single image, but with the right choice of original images, some skill, a fair amount of patience, and a good deal of creative imagination, the results can be very satisfying – and eyecatching.

personal choice
It is hard to give clear guidelines on the types of images that should be used for this type of work, as everyone will have different opinions on what looks good and may have different ways of combining images. In general, most composite images consist of a single background image, which itself may have several components, with foreground images placed upon it. For the combination to work well, the two should be in harmony and not clash, either in composition or colour. Personally, I prefer plain or relatively uncluttered backgrounds as a foil for the setting, with strong compositional elements in the subject matter. Use the artist's rules of composition when designing images, such as the 'rule of thirds' and 'golden section' to add impact. If you are using the same image several times in one picture, as in the 'angels' picture on pages 138–9 and the 'clay women' picture (left), then use an odd number of figures for the best composition. Mirror images, created using the flip command, are also useful for balancing a composition. Choose one file as the base image and select, copy and paste the component parts into separate layers from other image files (see pages 152–3), working on each layer independently as described earlier. Ensure that the resolution of the component parts is compatible and take care that joins look natural and accurate by using the cloning tool and feathering selections. Use the blending and opacity options in the layers palette to effect realism where necessary. The hue, lightness and saturation of each layer should also be judged and adjusted for compatibility before the image is merged into a single layer.

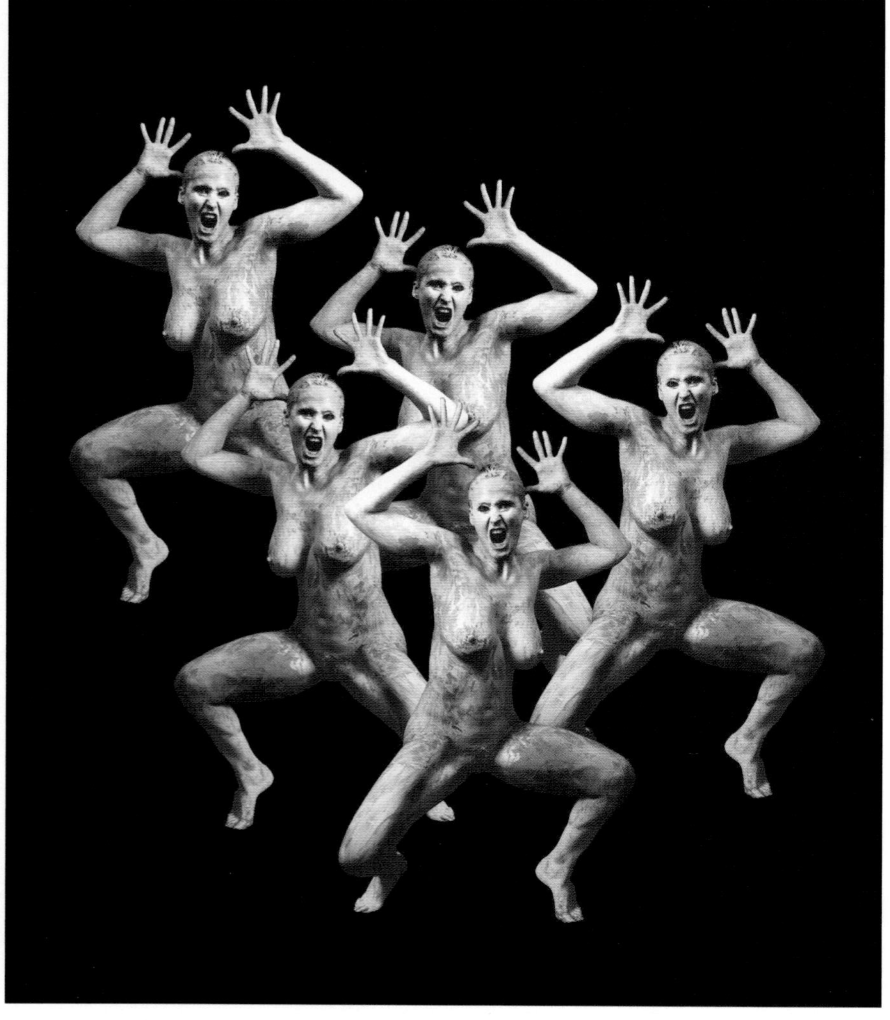

LEFT: **A simple composite.** This fairly straightforward composite was made from one image. The canvas of the original image was expanded to increase the amount of black background and a copy made of the figure. This was isolated by removing the background and copied to give a total of five figures in different layers, which could be moved around and flipped until they formed a good group composition.

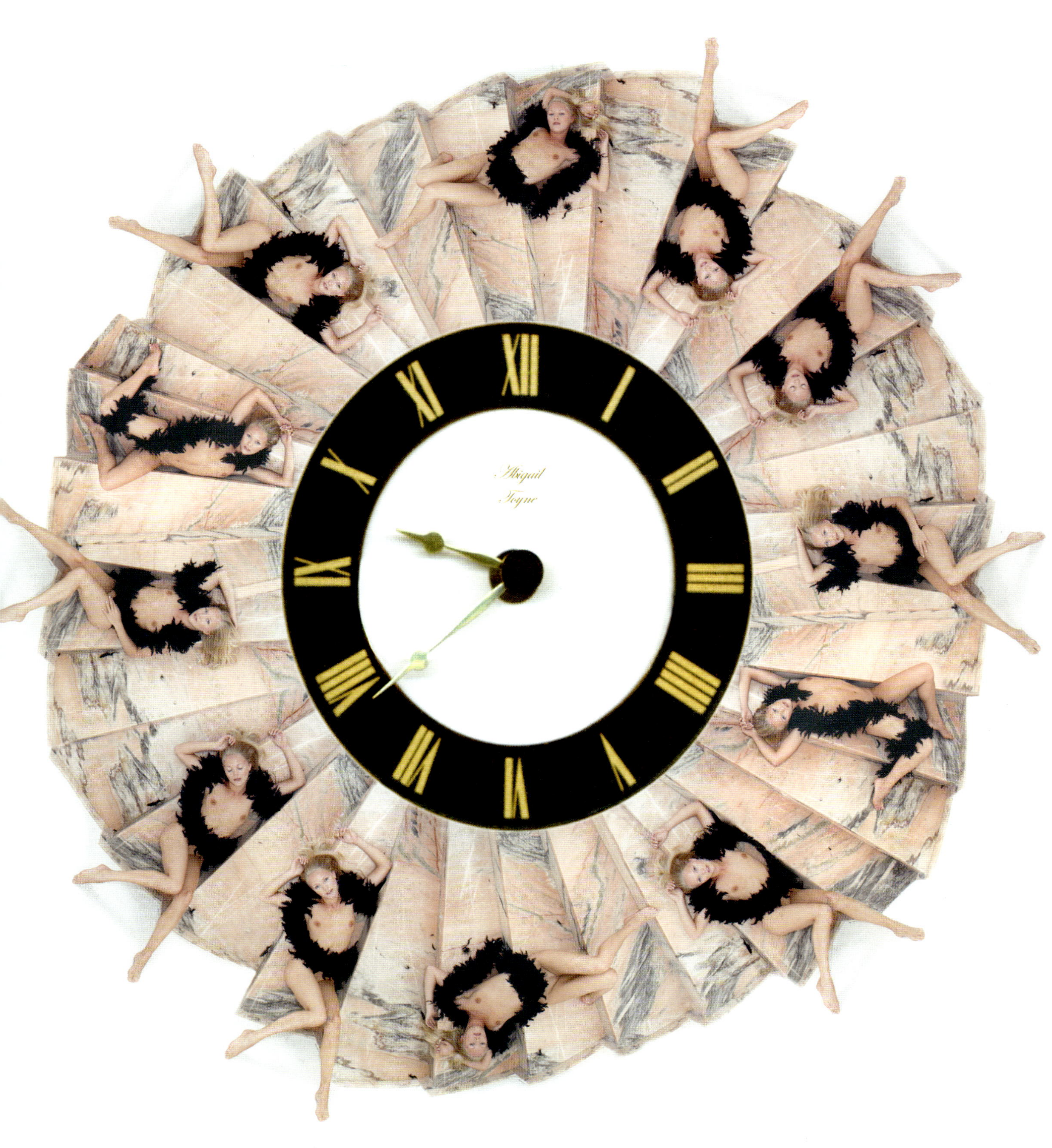

Abigail
Toyne

Model release form

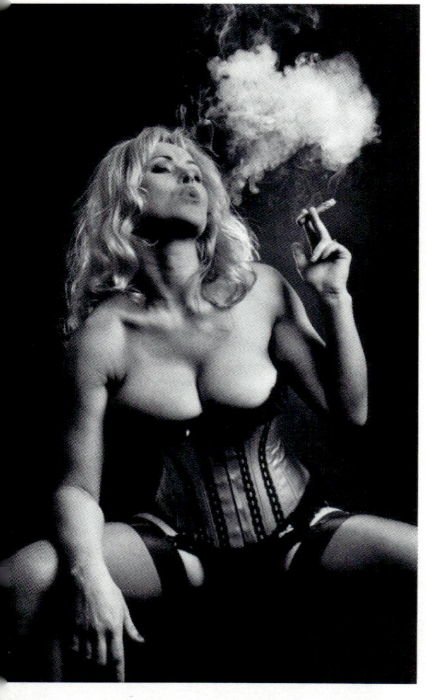

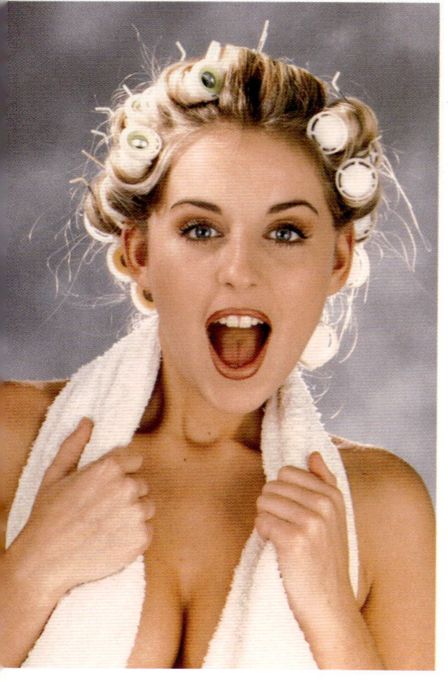

MODEL RELEASE FORM

This release refers to photographs taken of ....

on .... at ....

by (Name of photographer) ....

If job was commissioned, state name of client: ....

State whether photographs are to be used for EDITORIAL or ADVERTISING: ....

If photographs are to be used in advertising a product or services, state brand name of advertising agency concerned:

....

In consideration of having received the sum of £ .... or .... (other gratuity, eg, prints),

I hereby give*: ....

the absolute right and permission to publish in any media[#], the photographs taken of me on the date and at the location referred to above.

Signed (Model's Signature): ....

Name and Address of Model: ....

....

....

Signature of Witness: ....

Name and Address of Witness: ....

* Insert Name of photographer or client   # State where there are any specific exceptions:

....

Toning table

Toning Formulas. As with all chemicals, care should be taken when handling toners and appropriate safety measures should be observed when using them. Rubber gloves and a protective apron are strongly recommended for personal protection and tongs should be used to handle the prints.

Variable Colour Thiocarbamide Sepia Toner Dilute the stock bleach solution A by mixing 1+9 with water and bleach or partially bleach a normally processed black-and-white print. Wash the print well in running water for about 2–5 minutes. Mix toning solution B and alkaline solution C in the proportions indicated in the table for the colour required and make up the solution to one litre with water. Immerse the print in this solution for 1–2 minutes until toning is complete, then wash in running water for 10 minutes (RC) or 30 minutes (FB).

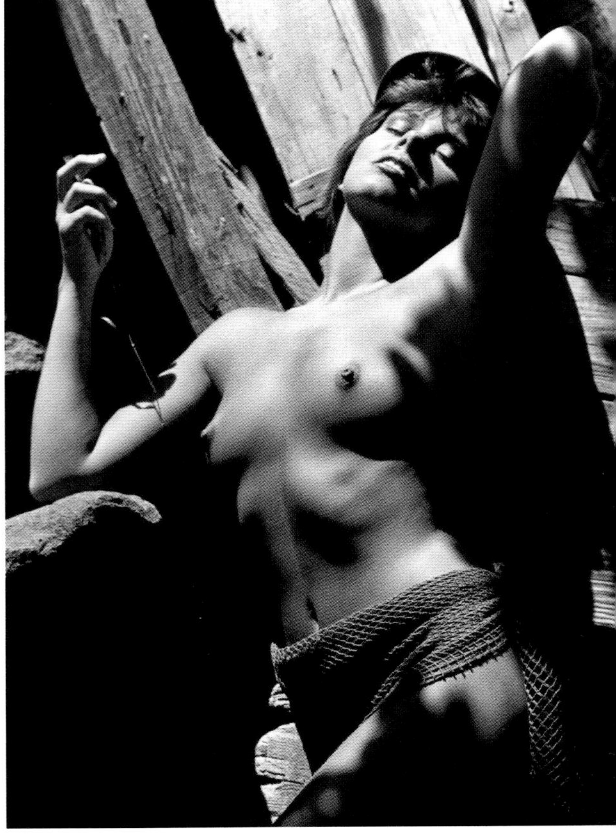

Stock Bleach Solution	A	B	C	Water	Colour
(Dilute 1+9 with water for use)		20ml	100ml	1000ml	purple-brown
		20ml	60ml	1000ml	cold brown
Potassium bromide	50g	20ml	20ml	1000ml	brown
Potassium ferricyanide	50g	60ml	20ml	1000ml	warm brown
Water to make	1000ml	100ml	20ml	1000ml	yellow-brown

Stock Toning Solution B		Stock Alkaline Solution C	
Thiourea	100g	Potassium hydroxide	100g
Water to make	1000ml	Water to make	1000ml

Iron Blue Toner Mix equal parts of stock solutions A and B at time of use. Tone prints until the desired colour is obtained. Prints should be light as toning also intensifies colour. Wash the prints thoroughly in running water for 10 minutes (RC) or 30 minutes (FB). The mixed toner remains fit for use for about one hour.

Stock Solution A		Stock Solution B	
Potassium ferricyanide	1.7g	Ferric ammonium citrate	1.7g
Sulphuric acid, concentrated	3ml	Sulphuric acid, concentrated	3ml
Water to make	1000ml	Water to make	1000ml

Copper Toner Mix equal parts of stock solutions A and B at time of use. Tone prints until the desired colour is obtained (5–30mins). A range of colours can be obtained from purplish-black to brown, red and metallic copper. Prints should be processed normally as there is no effect on density and contrast. Wash the prints thoroughly in running water for 10 minutes (RC) or 30 minutes (FB). The mixed toner remains fit for use for about one hour.

Stock Solution A		Stock Solution B	
Cupric sulphate	7g	Potassium ferricyanide	6g
Trisodium citrate dihydrate	25g	Trisodium citrate dihydrate	25g
Water to make	1000ml	Water to make	1000ml

Index

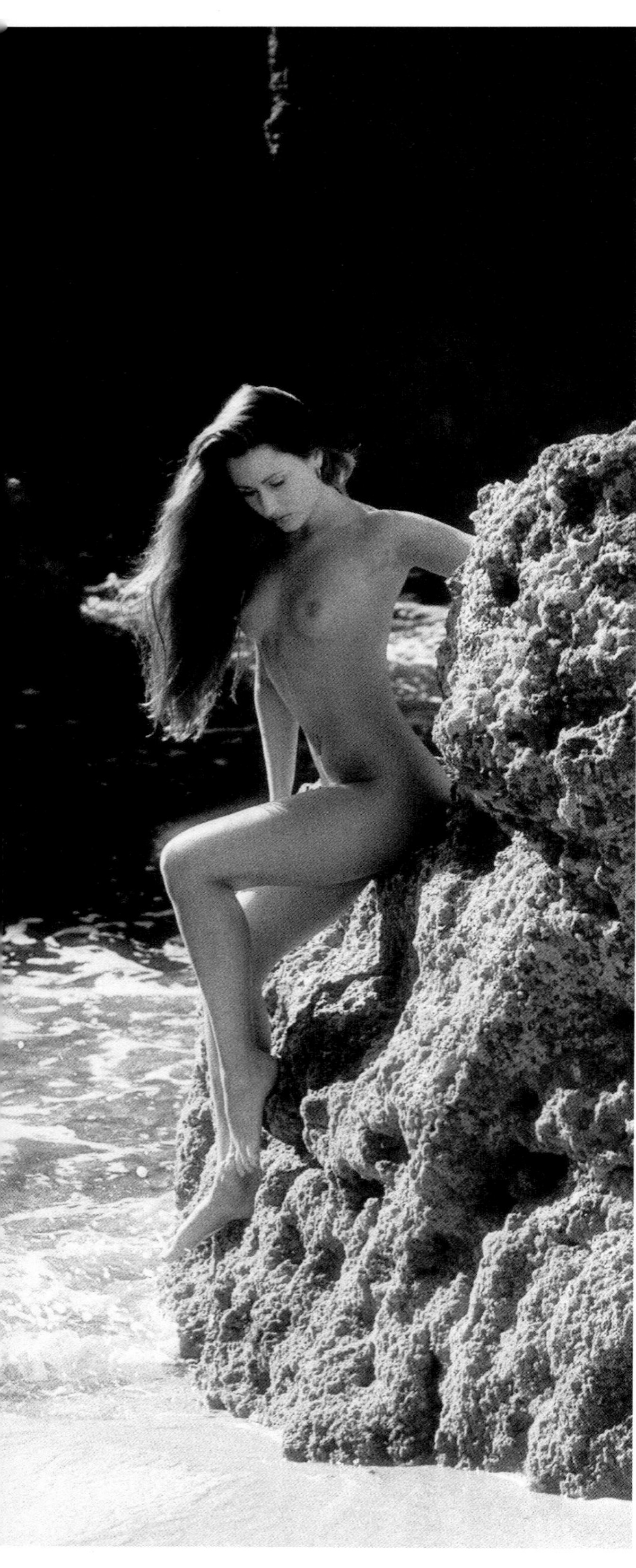

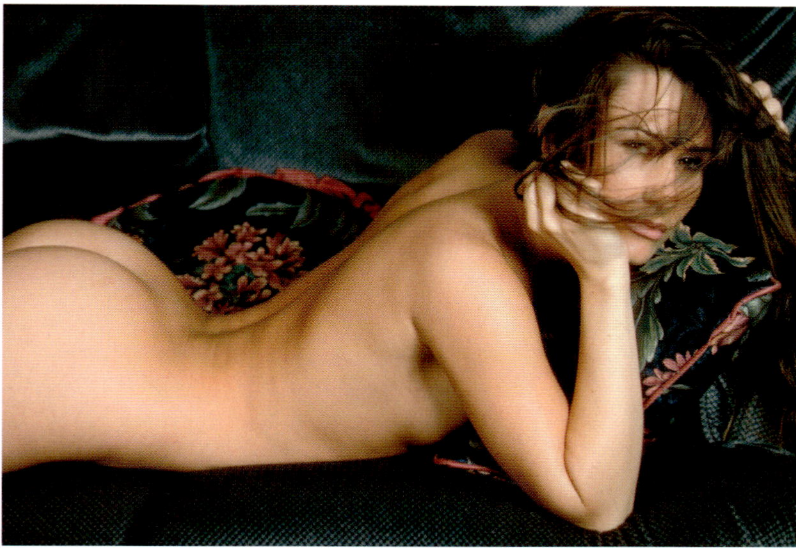

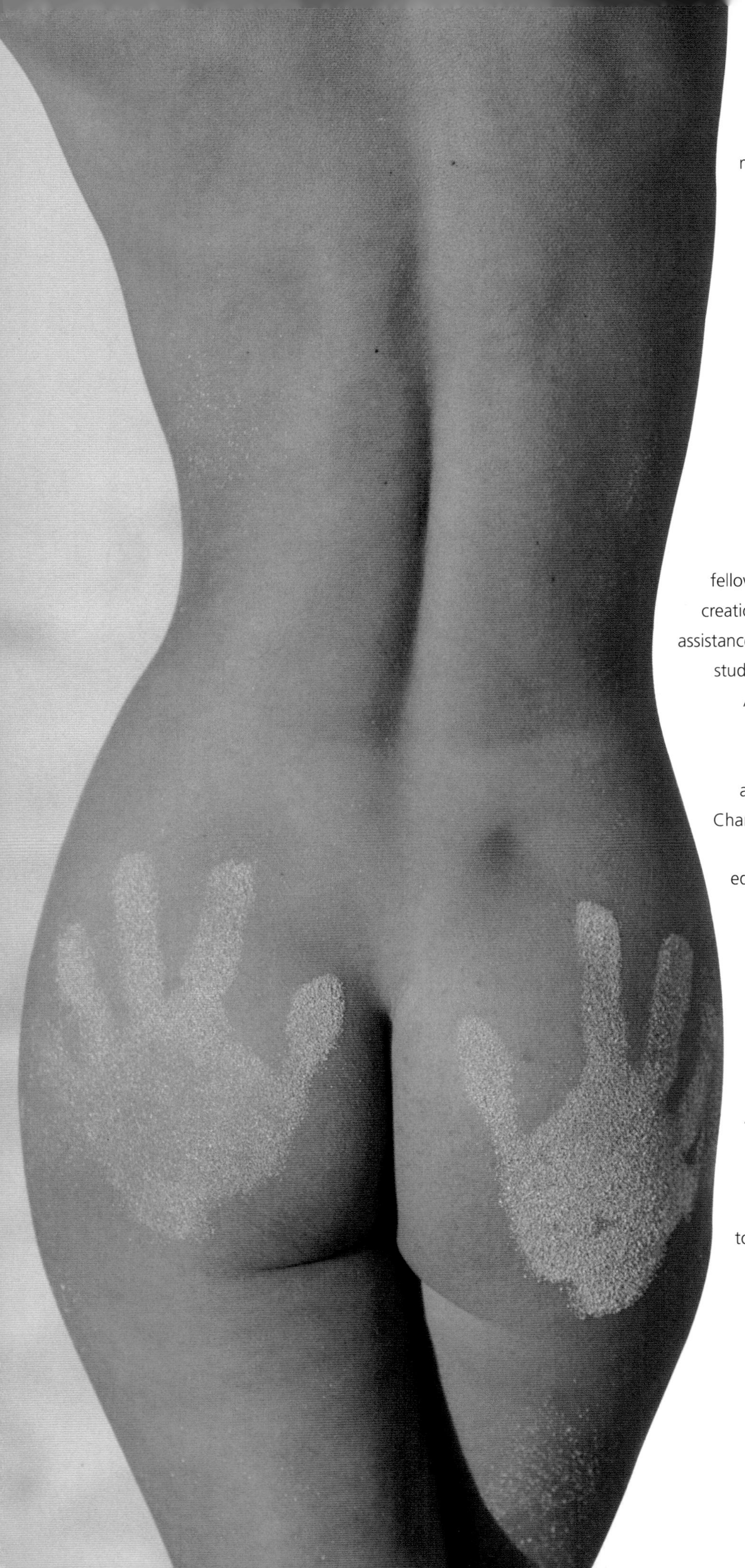

ACKNOWLEDGEMENTS

First of all I would like to thank the following models that appear in this book. You have all left me treasured memories, and this book would have been impossible to produce without you. Many thanks.

Abi, Adele, Ali, Amanda, Andrea, Arlene, Cecile, Cleo, Collette, Danielle, Debbie, Debi, Deborah, Denise, Emma, Fiona, Francine, Jamelah, Janie, Janine-May, Jessica, Jo, Justine, Karen, Kelly, Larissa, Leah, Leila, Lindsay, Lisa C, Lisa S, Mel, Mimi, Natalee, Natasha, Nikki, Samantha-Jane, Samantha, Sarah, Simone, Suzi, Tayla, Tracey C, Tracey E, Verity.

Special thanks go to the following friends and fellow photographers for the parts they played in the creation of certain images in the book, whether it was assistance with lighting set-ups, use of equipment, use of studios or just plain inspiration: Charles Patrick, Clive Austen, David Penprase, Ian Nellist and Jon Gray.

I have been fortunate to have had invaluable advice and assistance given to me by the David & Charles team, Sarah Hoggett (commissioning editor), Sue Cleave (art editor), Freya Dangerfield (senior editor) and Fid Backhouse (copy editor) and I really appreciate all the work they have done in coaching me on the steep learning curve of becoming an author. I am also indebted to William Cheung, Editor of *Practical Photography* magazine, for publishing the article that instigated this project. Without these people the book would probably not have come to fruition. All lighting diagrams in this book were drawn by Ethan Danielson.

Last but by no means least, thanks are also due to Kodak Ltd, and the Kodak Works Photographic Society for the generous use of darkroom and studio facilities.

The author can be contacted via his personal website http://www.photofrenetic.com